MODERN ELOQUENCE
LIBRARY OF
AFTER-DINNER SPEECHES, LECTURES
OCCASIONAL ADDRESSES

REPRODUCTIONS OF MURAL DECORATIONS
FROM THE LIBRARY OF CONGRESS, WASHINGTON

"LABOR"

*Photo-engraving in colors after the original painting by
Charles S. Pearce*

One of a series of Arcadian scenes illustrating the main phases
of an ideal existence.   A companion picture, entitled "Religion,"
is shown in another volume.   "Labor" is represented by two
young men working in the fields.   One is removing the stump of
a tree, and the other is turning over the newly cleared soil to fit
it for planting.

COMMITTEE OF SELECTION

EDWARD EVERETT HALE, Author of "The Man Without a Country."

JOHN B. GORDON, Former United States Senator.

NATHAN HASKELL DOLE, Associate Editor "International Library of Famous Literature."

JAMES B. POND, Manager Lecture Bureau; Author of "Eccentricities of Genius.'

GEORGE MCLEAN HARPER, Professor of English Literature, Princeton University.

LORENZO SEARS, Professor of English Literature, Brown University.

EDWIN M. BACON, Former Editor "Boston Advertiser" and "Boston Post."

J. WALKER MCSPADDEN, Managing Editor "Édition Royale" of Balzac's Works.

F. CUNLIFFE OWEN, Member Editorial Staff "New York Tribune."

TRUMAN A. DEWEESE, Member Editorial Staff "Chicago Times-Herald."

CHAMP CLARK, Member of Congress from Missouri.

MARCUS BENJAMIN, Editor, National Museum, Washington. D. C.

CLARK HOWELL, Editor "Atlanta Constitution."

INTRODUCTIONS AND SPECIAL ARTICLES BY

THOMAS B. REED,	HAMILTON WRIGHT MABIE,
LORENZO SEARS,	JONATHAN P. DOLLIVER,
CHAMP CLARK,	EDWARD EVERETT HALE,
ALBERT ELLERY BERGH.	

NOTE.—A large number of the most distinguished speakers of this country and Great Britain have selected their own best speeches for this Library. These speakers include Whitelaw Reid, William Jennings Bryan, Henry van Dyke, Henry M. Stanley, Newell Dwight Hillis, Joseph Jefferson, Sir Henry Irving, Arthur T. Hadley, John D. Long, David Starr Jordan, and many others of equal note.

CONTENTS

VOLUME VI

ILLUSTRATIONS

VOLUME VI

WENDELL PHILLIPS

THE LOST ARTS

[Lecture by Wendell Phillips, orator (born in Boston, Mass., November 29, 1811, died in Boston, February 2, 1884), delivered first on the lyceum platform in 1838, and thereafter for forty-five years given repeatedly, over two thousand times in all, his biographer states, " to fascinated crowds from Portland to St. Louis, until it netted him $150,-000, the largest sum ever earned by a similar production." It was also delivered gratuitously many times for the benefit of philanthropic, educational, and reform movements.]

LADIES AND GENTLEMEN:—I am to talk to you to-night about " The Lost Arts,"—a lecture which has grown under my hand year after year, and which belongs to that first phase of the lyceum system, before it undertook to meddle with political duties or dangerous and angry questions of ethics; when it was merely an academic institution, trying to win busy men back to books, teaching a little science, or repeating some tale of foreign travel, or painting some great representative character, the symbol of his age. I think I can claim a purpose beyond a moment's amusement in this glance at early civilization.

I, perhaps, might venture to claim that it was a medicine for what is the most objectionable feature of our national character; and that is self-conceit,—an undue appreciation of ourselves, an exaggerated estimate of our achievements, of our inventions, of our contributions to popular comfort, and of our place, in fact, in the great procession of the ages. We seem to imagine that, whether knowledge will die with us, or not, it certainly began with us. We have a pitying estimate, a tender compassion, for the narrowness, ignorance, and darkness of the bygone ages. We seem to ourselves not only to monopolize, but to have begun, the era of light. In other words, we are all running over with a fourth-day-of-July spirit of self-content. I am often reminded of the German whom the English poet Coleridge met at Frankfort. He always took off his hat with profound respect when he ventured to speak of himself. It seems to me, the American people might be painted in the chronic attitude of taking off its hat to itself; and therefore it can be no waste of time, with an audience in such a mood, to take their eyes for a moment from the present civilization, and guide them back to that earliest possible era that history describes for us, if it were only for the purpose of asking whether we boast on the right line. I might despair of curing the habit of boasting, but I might direct it better!

Well, I have been somewhat criticised, year after year, for this endeavor to open up the claims of old times. I have been charged with repeating useless fables with no foundation. Take the subject of glass. This material, Pliny says, was discovered by accident. Some sailors, landing on the eastern coast of Spain, took their cooking utensils and supported them on the sand by the stones that they found in the neighborhood: they kindled their fire, cooked the fish, finished the meal, and removed the apparatus; and glass was found to have resulted from the nitre and sea-sand, vitrified by the heat. Well, I have been a dozen times criticised by a number of wise men, in newspapers, who have said that this was a very idle tale, that there never was sufficient heat in a few bundles of sticks to produce vitrification,—glass-making. I happened, two years ago, to meet, on the prairies of Missouri, Professor Shepherd, of Yale College. I mentioned this criticism to him. "Well," said he, "a little practical life would have freed men from that doubt." He went on: "We stopped last year in Mexico, to cook some venison. We got down from our saddles, and put the cooking apparatus on stones we found there; made our fire with the wood we got there, resembling ebony; and when we removed the apparatus there was pure silver gotten out of the embers by the intense heat of that almost iron wood.—Now," said he, "that heat was greater than any necessary to vitrify the materials of glass." Why not suppose that Pliny's sailors had lighted on some exceedingly hard wood? May it not be as possible as in this case?

So, ladies and gentlemen, with a growing habit of distrust of a large share of this modern and exceedingly scientific criticism of ancient records, I think we have been betraying our own ignorance, and that frequently, when the statement does not look, on the face of it, to be exactly accurate, a little investigation below the surface will show that it rests on a real truth. Take, for instance, the English proverb, which was often quoted in my college days. We used to think how little logic the common people had; and when we wanted to illustrate this in the school-room, —it was what was called a *non sequitur*; the effect did not come from the cause named,—we always quoted the English proverb, "Tenterden steeple is the cause of Goodwin Sands." We said, "How ignorant a population!" But, when we went deeper into the history, we found that the proverb was not meant for logic, but was meant for sarcasm. One of the bishops had £50,000 given to him, to build a breakwater to save the Goodwin Sands from the advancing sea; but the good bishop, instead of building the breakwater to keep out the sea, simply built a steeple; and this proverb was sarcastic, and not logical, that "Tenterden steeple was the cause of the Goodwin Sands." When you contemplate the motive, there was the closest and best-welded logic in the proverb. So I think a large share of our criticism of old legends and old statements will be found in the end to be the ignorance that overleaps its own saddle, and falls on the other side.

Before I proceed to talk of these lost arts, I ought in fairness to make an exception. Over a very large section of literature, there is a singular contradiction to this swelling conceit. There are certain lines in which the moderns are ill satisfied with themselves, and contented to acknowledge that they ought fairly to sit down at the feet of their predecessors. Take poetry, painting, sculpture, architecture, the drama, and almost everything in works of any form that relates to beauty,—with regard to that whole sweep, the modern world gilds it with its admiration. Take the very phrases that we use. The artist says he wishes to go to Rome. "For what?" "To study the masters." Well, all the masters have been in their graves several hundred years. We are all pupils. You tell the poet, " Sir, that line of yours would remind one of Homer," and he is delighted. Stand in front of a painting, in the hearing of the artist, and compare its coloring to that of Titian or Raphael, and he remembers you forever. I recollect once standing in front of a bit of marble carved by Powers, a Vermonter, who had a matchless, instinctive love of art and perception of beauty. I said to an Italian standing with me, " Well, now, that seems to me to be perfection." The answer was, " To be perfection,"— shrugging his shoulders,—" why, sir, that reminds you of Phidias ! " as if to remind you of that Greek was a greater compliment than to be perfection.

Well, now, the very choice of phrases betrays a confession of inferiority; and you see it again crops out in the amount we borrow. Take the whole range of imaginative literature, and we are all wholesale borrowers. In every matter that relates to invention, to use, or beauty, or form, we are borrowers.

You may glance around the furniture of the palaces in Europe, and you may gather all these utensils of art or use ; and, when you have fixed the shape and forms in your mind, I will take you into the museum of Naples, which holds the remains of the domestic life of the Romans, and you shall not find a single one of these modern forms of art or beauty or use, that was not anticipated there. We have hardly added one single line of beauty to the antique.

Take the stories of Shakespeare, who has, perhaps, written his forty-odd plays. Some are historical. The rest, two-thirds of them, he did not stop to invent, but he found them. These he clutched, ready-made to his hand, from the Italian novelists, who had taken them before from the East. Cinderella and her slipper is older than all history, like half a dozen other baby legends. The annals of the world do not go back far enough to tell us their origin.

All the boys' plays, like everything that amuses the child in the open air, are Asiatic. Rawlinson will show you that they came somewhere from the banks of the Ganges or the suburbs of Damascus. Bulwer borrowed the incidents of his Roman stories from legends of a thousand years before. Indeed, Dunlop, who has grouped the history of the novels of all Europe into one essay, says that in the

nations of modern Europe there have been two hundred
and fifty or three hundred distinct stories.   He says at
least two hundred of these may be traced, before Christ-
tianity, to the other side of the Black Sea.   If this were
my topic, I might tell you that even our newspaper jokes
are enjoying a very respectable old age.   Take Maria
Edgeworth's essay on Irish bulls and the laughable mistakes of the Irish.   The tale which either Maria Edgeworth or her father thought the best is that famous story
of a man writing a letter as follows: "My dear friend, I
would write you in detail, more minutely, if there was
not an impudent fellow looking over my shoulder, reading every word."   ("No, you lie; I've not read a word
you have written!")   This is an Irish bull, still it is a very
old one.   It is only two hundred and fifty years older than
the New Testament.   Horace Walpole dissented from
Richard Lovell Edgeworth, and thought the other Irish
bull was the best,—of the man who said, "I would have
been a very handsome man, but they changed me in the
cradle."   That comes from Don Quixote, and is Spanish;
but Cervantes borrowed it from the Greek in the fourth
century, and the Greek stole it from the Egyptian hundreds of years back.

There is one story which it is said Washington has related, of a man who went into an inn, and asked for a glass
of drink from the landlord, who pushed forward a wine-
glass about half the usual size (the teacups also in that day
were not more than half the present size).   The landlord
said, "That glass out of which you are drinking is forty
years old."—"Well," said the thirsty traveler, contempla-
ting its diminutive proportions, "I think it is the smallest
thing of its age I ever saw."   That story as told is given
as a story of Athens three hundred and seventy-five years
before Christ was born.   Why! all these Irish bulls are
Greek,—every one of them.   Take the Irishman who carried around a brick as a specimen of the house he had to
sell; take the Irishman who shut his eyes, and looked into
the glass to see how he would look when he was dead; take
the Irishman that bought a crow, alleging that crows were
reported to live two hundred years, and he meant to set
out and try it; take the Irishman who met a friend who
said to him, "Why, sir, I heard you were dead,"—"Well,"

says the man, " I suppose you see I'm not."—" Oh, no!"
says he, " I would believe the man who told me a good
deal quicker than I would you." Well, those are all
Greek. A score or more of them, of the parallel character, come from Athens.

Our old Boston patriots felt that tarring and feathering
a Tory was a genuine patent Yankee firebrand,—Yankee-
ism. They little imagined that when Richard Cœur de
Lion set out on one of his crusades, among the orders he
issued to his camp of soldiers was, that any one who
robbed a hen-roost should be tarred and feathered. Many
a man who lived in Connecticut has repeated the story of
taking children to the limits of the town, and giving them
a sound thrashing to enforce their memory of the spot.
But the Burgundians in France, in a statute now eleven
hundred years old, attributed valor to the East of France
because it had a law that the children should be taken to
the limits of the district, and there soundly whipped, in
order that they might forever remember the boundary-
line.

So we have very few new things in that line. But I said
I would take the subject of glass. It is the very best
expression of man's self-conceit.

I had heard that nothing had been observed in ancient
times which could be called by the name of glass,—that
there had been merely attempts to imitate it. I thought
they had proved the proposition: they certainly had elaborated it. In Pompeii, a dozen miles south of Naples,
which was covered with ashes by Vesuvius eighteen hundred years ago, they broke into a room full of glass: there
was ground glass, window-glass, cut-glass, and colored
glass of every variety. It was undoubtedly a glassmaker's
factory. So the lie and the refutation came face to face.
It was like a pamphlet printed in London, in 1836, by Dr.
Lardner, which proved that a steamboat could not cross
the ocean; and the book came to this country in the first
steamboat that came across the Atlantic.

The chemistry of the most ancient period had reached
a point which we have never even approached, and which
we in vain struggle to reach to-day. Indeed, the whole
management of the effect of light on glass is still a matter

of profound study. The first two stories which I have to
offer you are simply stories from history.

The first is from the letters of the Catholic priests who
broke into China, which were published in France some
two hundred years ago. They were shown a glass, transparent and colorless, which was filled with a liquor made
by the Chinese, that was shown to the observers, and appeared to be colorless like water. This liquor was poured
into the glass, and then, looking through it, it seemed
to be filled with fishes. They turned this out, and repeated the experiment, and again it was filled with fishes. *examples*
The Chinese confessed that they did not make them; that
they were the plunder of some foreign conquest. This is
not a singular thing in Chinese history; for in some of
their scientific discoveries we have found evidence that
they did not make them, but stole them.

The second story, of half a dozen, relates to the age of
Tiberius, the time of St. Paul; and tells of a Roman who
had been banished, and who returned to Rome, bringing
a wonderful cup. This cup he dashed upon the marble
pavement, and it was crushed, not broken, by the fall. It
was dented some, and with a hammer he easily brought
it into shape again. It was brilliant, transparent, but not
brittle. I once made this statement in New Haven; and
among the audience was Professor Silliman. He was kind
enough to come to the platform when I had ended, and
say that he was familiar with most of my facts, but, speaking of malleable glass, he had this to say,—that it was
nearly a natural impossibility, and that no amount of
evidence which could be brought would make him credit
it. Well, the Romans got their chemistry from the
Arabians; they brought it into Spain eight centuries ago,
and in their books of that age they claim that they got
from the Arabians malleable glass. There is a kind of
glass spoken of there, that, if supported by one end, by its
own weight in twenty hours would dwindle down to a
fine line, and that you could curve around your wrist.
Von Beust, the Chancellor of Austria, has ordered secrecy
in Hungary in regard to a recently discovered process by
which glass can be used exactly like wool, and manufactured into cloth.

These are a few records. When you go to Rome, they

will show you a bit of glass like the solid rim of this
tumbler,—transparent glass, a solid thing, which they lift
up so as to show you that there is nothing concealed;
but in the center of the glass is a drop of colored glass,
perhaps as large as a pea, mottled like a duck, finely
mottled, with the shifting colored hues of the neck, and
which even a miniature pencil could not do more perfectly.   It is manifest that this drop of liquid glass must
have been poured, because there is no joint.   This must
have been done by a greater heat than the annealing
process, because that process shows breaks.

The imitation of gems has deceived not only the lay
people, but the connoisseurs.   Some of these imitations in
later years have been discovered.   The celebrated vase of
the Genoa Cathedral was considered a solid emerald.   The
Roman Catholic legend of it was, that it was one of the
treasures that the Queen of Sheba gave to Solomon, and
that it was the identical cup out of which the Saviour
drank at the Last Supper.   Columbus must have admired
it.   It was venerable in his day; it was death for anybody
to touch it but a Catholic priest.   And when Napoleon
besieged Genoa, the Jews offered to loan the Senate three
million dollars on that single article as security.   Napoleon
took it, and carried it to France, and gave it to the Institute.   Somewhat reluctantly the scholars said, " It is not a
stone : we hardly know what it is."

Cicero said that he had seen the entire Iliad, which
is a poem as large as the New Testament, written on a
skin so thin that it could be rolled up in the compass of a
nut-shell.   Now, this is imperceptible to the ordinary eye.
You have seen the Declaration of Independence in the
compass of a quarter of a dollar, written with glasses.   I
have to-day a paper at home, as long as half my hand,
on which was photographed the whole contents of a London newspaper.   It was put under a dove's wing, and sent
into Paris, where they enlarged it, and read the news.
This copy of the Iliad must have been made by some
such process.

In the Roman theatre,—the Coliseum, which could seat
a hundred thousand people,—the emperor's box, raised to
the highest tier, bore about the same proportion to the
space as this stand does to this hall; and to look down to

the center of a six-acre lot, was to look a considerable distance. ("Considerable," by the way, is not a Yankee word. Lord Chesterfield uses it in his letters to his son, so it has a good English origin.) Pliny says that Nero the tyrant had a ring with a gem in it, which he looked through, and watched the sword-play of the gladiators,— men who killed each other to amuse the people,—more clearly than with the naked eye. So Nero had an opera-glass.

Mauritius the Sicilian stood on the promontory of his island, and could sweep over the entire sea to the coast of Africa with his *nauscopite*, which is a word derived from two Greek words, meaning "to see a ship." Evidently Mauritius, who was a pirate, had a marine telescope.

You may visit Dr. Abbot's museum, where you will see the ring of Cheops. Bunsen puts him five hundred years before Christ. The signet of the ring is about the size of a quarter of a dollar, and the engraving is invisible without the aid of glasses. No man was ever shown into the cabinets of gems in Italy without being furnished with a microscope to look at them. It would be idle for him to look at them without one. He couldn't appreciate the delicate lines and the expression of the faces. If you go to Parma, they will show you a gem once worn on the finger of Michelangelo, of which the engraving is two thousand years old, on which there are the figures of seven women. You must have the aid of a glass in order to distinguish the forms at all. I have a friend who has a ring, perhaps three-quarters of an inch in diameter, and on it is the naked figure of the god Hercules. By the aid of glasses you can distinguish the interlacing muscles, and count every separate hair on the eyebrows. Layard says he would be unable to read the engravings at Nineveh without strong spectacles, they are so extremely small. Rawlinson brought home a stone about twenty inches long and ten wide, containing an entire treatise on mathematics. It would be perfectly illegible without glasses. Now, if we are unable to read it without the aid of glasses, you may suppose the man who engraved it had pretty strong spectacles. So the microscope, instead of dating from our time, finds its brothers in the books of Moses,— and these are infant brothers.

So if you take colors. Color is, we say, an embellishment. We dye our dresses, and ornament our furniture. It is a luxury to gratify the eye. But the Egyptians impressed it into a new service. For them, it was a method of recording history. Some parts of their history were written; but when they wanted to elaborate history they painted it. Their colors are immortal, else we could not know of it. We find upon the stucco of their walls their kings holding court, their armies marching out, their craftsmen in the ship-yard, with the ships floating in the dock; and, in fact, we trace all their rites and customs painted in undying colors. The French who went to Egypt with Napoleon said that all the colors were perfect except the greenish-white, which is the hardest for us. They had no difficulty with the Tyrian purple. The buried city of Pompeii was a city of stucco. All the houses are stucco outside, and it is stained with Tyrian purple,—the royal color of antiquity.

But you cannot rely on the name of a color after a thousand years. So the Tyrian purple is almost a red,— about the color of these curtains. This is a city of all red. It had been buried seventeen hundred years; and if you take a shovel now, and clear away the ashes, this color flames up upon you, a great deal richer than anything we can produce. You can go down into the narrow vault which Nero built as a retreat from the great heat, and you will find the walls painted all over with fanciful designs in arabesque, which have been buried beneath the earth fifteen hundred years; but when the peasants light it up with their torches, the colors flash out before you as fresh as they were in the days of St. Paul. Our fellow-citizen Mr. Page spent twelve years in Venice, studying Titian's method of mixing his colors, and he thinks he has got it. Yet come down from Titian, whose colors are wonderfully and perfectly fresh, to Sir Joshua Reynolds, and although his colors are not yet a hundred years old, they are fading: the colors on his lips are dying out, and the cheeks are losing their tints. He did not know how to mix well. All this mastery of color is as yet unequalled. If you should go with that most delightful of all lecturers, Professor Tyndall, he would show you in the spectrum the vanishing rays of violet, and prove to you that beyond

their limit there are rays still more delicate, and to you
invisible, but which he, by chemical paper, will make visible; and he will tell you that, probably, though you see
three or four inches more than three hundred years ago
your predecessors did, yet three hundred years after our
successors will surpass our limit. The French have a
theory that there is a certain delicate shade of blue that
Europeans cannot see. In one of his lectures to his students, Ruskin opened his Catholic mass-book, and said,
"Gentlemen, we are the best chemists in the world. No
Englishman ever could doubt that. But we cannot make
such a scarlet as that; and even if we could, it would not
last for twenty years. Yet this is five hundred years old!"
The Frenchman says, "I am the best dyer in Europe: nobody can equal me, and nobody can surpass Lyons." Yet
in Cashmere, where the girls make shawls worth thirty
thousand dollars, they will show him three hundred distinct colors, which he not only cannot make, but cannot
even distinguish. When I was in Rome, if a lady wished
to wear a half dozen colors at a masquerade, and have
them all in harmony, she would go to the Jews; for the
Oriental eye is better than even those of France or Italy,
of which we think so highly.

Taking the metals. The Bible in its first chapters
shows that man first conquered metals there in Asia; and
on that spot to-day he can work more wonders with those
metals than we can.

One of the surprises that the European artists received,
when the English plundered the summer palace of the
King of China, was the curiously wrought metal vessels of
every kind, far exceeding all the boasted skill of the workmen of Europe.

Mr. Colton of the Boston "Journal," the first week he
landed in Asia, found that his chronometer was out of
order, from the steel of the works having become rusted.
The London "Medical and Surgical Journal" advises sur-
geons not to venture to carry any lances to Calcutta,—to
have them gilded, because English steel could not bear
the atmosphere of India. Yet the Damascus blades of the
Crusades were not gilded, and they are as perfect as they
were eight centuries ago. There was one at the London
Exhibition, the point of which could be made to touch the

hilt, and which could be put into a scabbard like a cork-
screw, and bent every way without breaking, like an
American politician. Now, the wonder of this is, that perfect steel is a marvel of science. If a London chronometer maker wants the best steel to use in his chronometer,
he does not send to Sheffield, the center of all science, but
to the Punjaub, the empire of the seven rivers, where
there is no science at all. The first needle ever made in
England was made in the time of Henry VIII, and
made by a negro; and when he died, the art died with him.
Some of the first travelers in Africa stated that they found
a tribe in the interior who gave them better razors than
they had; the irrepressible negro coming up in science as
in politics. The best steel is the greatest triumph of metallurgy, and metallurgy is the glory of chemistry.

The poets have celebrated the perfection of the Oriental
steel; and it is recognized as the finest by Moore, Byron,
Scott, Southey, and many others. I have even heard a
young advocate of the lost arts find an argument in
Byron's " Sennacherib," from the fact that the mail of the
warriors in that one short night had rusted before the
trembling Jews stole out in the morning to behold the
terrible work of the Lord. Scott, in his " Tales of the Cru-
saders,"—for Sir Walter was curious in his love of the
lost arts,—describes a meeting between Richard Cœur de
Lion and Saladin. Saladin asks Richard to show him
the wonderful strength for which he is famous, and the
Norman monarch responds by severing a bar of iron which
lies on the floor of his tent. Saladin says, " I cannot do
that "; but he takes an eider-down pillow from the sofa,
and, drawing his keen blade across it, it falls in two pieces.
Richard says, " This is the black art; it is magic; it is the
devil: you cannot cut that which has no resistance "; and
Saladin, to show him that such is not the case, takes a
scarf from his shoulders, which is so light that it almost
floats in the air, and, tossing it up, severs it before it can
descend. George Thompson told me he saw a man in
Calcutta throw a handful of floss-silk into the air, and a
Hindoo sever it into pieces with his sabre. We can produce nothing like this.

Considering their employment of the mechanical forces,
and their movement of large masses from the earth, we

know that the Egyptians had the five, seven, or three mechanical powers; but we cannot account for the multiplication and increase necessary to perform the wonders they accomplished.

In Boston, lately, we have moved the Pelham Hotel, weighing fifty thousand tons, fourteen feet, and are very proud of it; and since then we have moved a whole block of houses twenty-three feet, and I have no doubt we will write a book about it: but there is a book telling how Domenico Fontana of the Sixteenth century set up the Egyptian obelisk at Rome on end, in the Papacy of Sixtus V. Wonderful! Yet the Egyptians quarried that stone, and carried it a hundred and fifty miles, and the Romans brought it seven hundred and fifty miles, and never said a word about it. Mr. Batterson of Hartford, walking with Brunel, the architect of the Thames tunnel, in Egypt, asked him what he thought of the mechanical power of the Egyptians; and he said, "There is Pompey's Pillar: it is a hundred feet high, and the capital weighs two thousand pounds. It is something of a feat to hang two thousand pounds at that height in the air, and the few men that can do it would better discuss Egyptian mechanics."

Take canals. The Suez canal absorbs half its receipts in cleaning out the sand which fills it continually, and it is not yet known whether it is a pecuniary success. The ancients built a canal at right angles to ours; because they knew it would not fill up if built in that direction, and they knew such a one as ours would. There were magnificent canals in the land of the Jews, with perfectly arranged gates and sluices. We have only just begun to understand ventilation properly for our houses; yet late experiments at the Pyramids in Egypt show that those Egyptian tombs were ventilated in the most perfect and scientific manner.

Again, cement is modern, for the ancients dressed and joined their stones so closely, that, in buildings thousands of years old, the thin blade of a penknife cannot be forced between them. The railroad dates back to Egypt. Arago has claimed that they had a knowledge of steam. A painting has been discovered of a ship full of machinery, and a French engineer said that the arrangement of this machinery could only be accounted for by supposing the motive power to have been steam. Bramah acknowledges that he took the idea of his celebrated lock from an ancient Egyptian pattern. De Tocqueville says there was no social question that was not discussed to rags in Egypt.

"Well," say you, "Franklin invented the lightning-rod." I have no doubt he did; but years before his invention, and before muskets were invented, the old soldiers on guard on the towers used Franklin's invention to keep guard with; and if a spark passed between them and the spear-head, they ran and bore the warning of the state and condition of affairs. After that you will admit that Benjamin Franklin was not the only one that knew of the presence of electricity, and the advantages derived from its use. Solomon's Temple, you will find, was situated on an exposed point of the hill: the temple was so lofty that it was often in peril, and was guarded by a system exactly like that of Benjamin Franklin.

Well, I may tell you a little of ancient manufactures. The Duchess of Burgundy took a necklace from the neck of a mummy, and wore it to a ball given at the Tuileries; and everybody said they thought it was the newest thing there. A Hindoo princess came into court; and her father, seeing her, said, "Go home, you are not decently covered,—go home"; and she said, "Father, I have seven suits on;" but the suits were of muslin so thin that the king could see through them. A Roman poet says, "The girl was in the poetic dress of the country." I fancy the French would be rather astonished at this. Four hundred and fifty years ago the first spinning-machine was introduced into Europe. I have evidence to show that it made its appearance two thousand years before.

Why have I groped among these ashes? I have told you these facts to show you that we have not invented everything—that we do not monopolize the encyclopedia. The past had knowledge. But it was the knowledge of the classes, not of the masses. "The beauty that was Greece and the grandeur that was Rome" were exclusive, the possession of the few. The science of Egypt was amazing: but it meant privilege—the privilege of the king and the priest. It separated royalty and priesthood from the people, and was the engine of oppression. When Cambyses came down from Persia and thundered across

Egypt treading out royalty and priesthood, he trampled out at the same time civilization itself.

Four thousand years passed before the people came into existence. To-day learning no longer hides in the convent or slumbers in the palace. No! she comes out into every-day life, joins hands with the multitude and cushions the peasant. Our astronomy looks at but does not dwell in the stars. It serves navigation and helps us run boundaries. Our chemistry is not the secret of the alchemist striving to change base metals into gold. It is Liebig with his hands full of blessings for every farmer, and digging gold out of the earth with the miner's pick-axe. Of all we know I can show you ninety-nine items out of every hundred which the past anticipated and which the world forgot. Our distinction lies in the liberty of intellect and the diffusion of knowledge.

When Gibbon finished his history of Rome, he said: "We have iron and fire: the hand can never go back on the dial of time." He made this boast as he stood, at night, amid the ruins of the Corsani palace, looking out on the churches where the monks were chanting.

But what is to prevent history from repeating itself? Why should our arts not be lost,—our temples of Jupiter not fall,—our Rome not decline? Will our possession of iron and fire preserve them? Before Rome was peopled nations rose and fell with iron in one hand and fire in the other. Any civilization that is exclusive, any arts that are secret and individual must perish.

The distinctive glory of the Nineteenth century is that it distributes knowledge; that it recognizes the divine will, which is that every man has a right to know whatever may be serviceable to himself or to his fellows; that it makes the church, the schoolhouse and the town-hall its symbols, and humanity its care. This democratic spirit will animate our arts with immortality, if God means that they shall last.

TOUSSAINT L'OUVERTURE

[Lecture by Wendell Phillips, delivered first in 1861, and repeated in succeeding years hundreds of times in cities and towns of the Northern States, becoming one of the best-known of American lyceum lectures. Its delivery has been described as "an enchantment; its form often varying in successive presentations, as in the case of 'The Lost Arts.'"]

LADIES AND GENTLEMEN:—I have been requested to offer you a sketch made some years since of one of the most remarkable men of the last generation, Toussaint L'Ouverture, the great St. Domingo chief—an unmixed negro, with no drop of white blood in his veins. My sketch is therefore, as you may readily perceive, at once a biography and an argument—a biography, of course, very brief, of a negro soldier and statesman, and which I offer to you as an argument in behalf of the race from which he sprung. You perceive from the very announcement of my subject, that I am about to compare and weigh races; indeed, I am engaged to-night in what you will think the absurd effort to convince you that the negro race, instead of being that object of pity or contempt which we usually consider it, is entitled, judged by the facts of history, to a place close by the side of the Saxon. Now races love to be judged in two ways—by the great men they produce and by the average merit of the mass of the races. We Saxons are proud of Bacon, Shakespeare, Hampden, Hancock, Washington, Franklin,—the stars we have lent to the galaxy of history; and then we turn with equal pride to the average merit of Saxon blood, since it streamed from its German home. So, again, there are three tests by which races love to be tried. The first, the basis of all, is courage—the element which says, "This continent is mine from the Lakes to the Gulf—let him beware who seeks to divide it." [Cheers.] And the second is the recognition that force is doubled by purpose; liberty regulated by law is the secret of Saxon progress. And the third element is persistency, endurance; first, a purpose, then death or success. Of these three elements is made that

WENDELL PHILLIPS
Photogravure after a photograph from life

Saxon pluck which has placed our race in the van of modern civilization.

In the hour you lend me to-night I am to attempt the Quixotic effort to convince you that the negro blood, instead of standing at the bottom of the list, is entitled if judged either by its great men or its masses, either by its courage, its purpose, or its endurance, to a place as near ours as any other blood known in history. And for the purpose of my argument, I take an island, St. Domingo, about the size of South Carolina, the third spot in America upon which Columbus placed his foot. Charmed by the magnificence of its scenery and fertility of its soil, he gave it the fondest of all names, Hispaniola, Little Spain. His successor, more pious, rebaptized it from St. Dominic, St. Domingo; and when the blacks in 1803 drove out white blood from its surface, they drove our names with us, and began the year 1804 under the old name, Hayti, the land of mountains. It was originally tenanted by the filibusters, French and Spanish, of the early commercial epochs, the pirates of that day as of ours. The Spanish took the eastern two-thirds, the French the western third of the island, and they gradually settled into colonies. The French, to whom my story belongs, became the pet colony of the mother land. Guarded by peculiar privileges, enriched by the scions of wealthy houses, aided by the unmatched fertility of the soil, it soon was the richest gem in the Bourbon crown; and at the period to which I call your attention, about the era of our Constitution, 1789, its wealth was almost incredible. The effeminacy of the white race rivaled that of the Sybarite of antiquity, while the splendor of their private life outshone Versailles, and their luxury found no mate but in the mad prodigality of the Cæsars. At this time the island held about thirty thousand whites, twenty thousand or thirty thousand mulattoes, and five hundred thousand slaves. The slave-trade was active. About twenty-five thousand slaves were imported annually; this only sufficed to fill the gap which the murderous culture of sugar annually produced. The mulattoes, as with us, were children of the slave-holders, but unlike us, the French slave-holder never forgot his child by a bond-woman. He gave him everything but his name—wealth,

rich plantations, gangs of slaves; sent him to Paris for his
education, summoned the best culture of France for the
instruction of his daughters, so that in 1790 the mulatto
race held one-third of the real estate, and one-quarter of
the personal estate of the island. But though educated
and rich, he bowed under the same yoke as with us. Subjected to special taxes, he could hold no public office, and
if convicted of any crime, was punished with double severity. His son might not sit on the same seat at school
with a white boy; he might not enter a church where a
white man was worshipping; if he reached a town on horseback he must dismount and lead his horse by the bridle;
and when he died, even his dust could not rest in the same
soil with a white body. Such was the white race and the
mulatto—a thin film of a civilization beneath which surged
the dark mass of five hundred thousand slaves.

It was over such a population the white man melted in
sensuality; the mulatto feeling all the more keenly his
degradation from the very wealth and culture he enjoyed;
the slave sullen and indifferent, heeding not the quarrels
or the changes of the upper air;—it was over this population that there burst in 1789 the thunderstorm of the
French Revolution. The first words which reached the
island were the motto of the Jacobin Club—"Liberty,
Equality." The white man heard them aghast. He had
read of the streets of Paris running blood. The slave heard
them with indifference; it was a quarrel in the upper air,
between other races, which did not concern him. The
mulatto heard them with a welcome which no dread of
other classes could quell. Hastily gathered into conventions, they sent to Paris a committee of the whole body,
laid at the feet of the National Convention the free gift of
six millions of francs, pledged one-fifth of their annual
rental toward the payment of the national debt, and only
asked in return that this yoke of civil and social contempt
should be lifted from their shoulders.

You may easily imagine the temper in which Mirabeau
and Lafayette welcomed this munificent gift of the free
mulattoes of the West Indies, and in which the petition
for equal civil rights was received by a body which had
just resolved that all men were equal. The Convention
hastened to express its gratitude and issued a decree which

commences thus: "All freeborn Frenchmen are equal before the law." Ogé was selected—the friend of Lafayette, a lieutenant-colonel in the Dutch service, the son of a wealthy mulatto woman, educated in Paris, the comrade of all the leading French Republicans,—to carry the decree and the message of French Democracy to the island. He landed. The decree of the National Convention was laid on the table of the General Assembly of the island. One old planter seized it, tore it in fragments, trampled it under his feet, swearing by all the saints in the calendar that the island might sink before they would share their rights with bastards. They took an old mulatto, worth a million, who had simply asked for his rights under that decree, and hung him. A white lawyer of seventy who drafted the petition, they hung at his side. They took Ogé, broke him on the wheel, ordered him to be drawn and quartered, and one-quarter of his body to be hung up in each of the four principal cities of the island; and then they adjourned.

You can conceive better than I can describe the mood in which Mirabeau and Danton received the news that their decree had been torn in pieces and trampled under foot by the petty legislature of an island colony, and their comrade drawn and quartered by the orders of its governor. Robespierre rushed to the tribune, and shouted: "Perish the colonies rather than sacrifice one iota of our principles!" The Convention reaffirmed their decree and sent it out a second time to be executed.

But it was not then as now, when steam has married the continents. It took months to communicate; and while this news of the death of Ogé and the defiance of the National Convention was going to France and the answer returning, great events had transpired in the island itself. The Spanish or the eastern section, perceiving these divisions, invaded the towns of the western, and conquered many of its cities. One-half of the slave-holders were Republicans, in love with the new constellation which had just gone up in our Northern sky, seeking to be admitted a State in this Republic, plotting for annexation. The other half were loyalists, anxious, deserted, as they supposed themselves, by the Bourbons, to make alliance with George III. They sent to Jamaica, and entreated its gov-

ernor to assist them in their intrigue. At first he sent
them only a few hundred soldiers. Sometime later, General Howe and Admiral Parker were sent with several
thousand men, and finally, the English government entering more seriously into the plot, General Maitland landed
with four thousand Englishmen on the north side of the
island, and gained many successes. The mulattoes were
in the mountains, awaiting events. They distrusted the
government, which a few years before they had assisted
to put down an insurrection of the whites, and which had
forfeited its promise to grant them civil privileges. Deserted by both sections, Blanchelande, the governor, had
left the capital and fled for refuge to a neighboring city.

In this state of affairs the second decree reached the
island. The whites forgot their quarrel, sought out
Blanchelande, and obliged him to promise that he would
never publish the decree. Affrighted, the governor consented to that course, and they left him. He then began
to reflect that in reality he was deposed, that the Bourbons
had lost the sceptre of the island. He remembered his
successful appeal to the mulattoes five years before, to put
down an insurrection. Deserted now by the whites, and
by the mulattoes, only one force was left him in the island
—that was the blacks. They had always remembered with
gratitude the *code noir*, the black code of Louis XIV, the
first interference of any power in their behalf. To the
blacks Blanchelande appealed. He sent a deputation to
the slaves. He was aided by the agents of the Count
d'Artois, afterward Charles X, who was seeking to do in
St. Domingo what Charles II did in Virginia (whence
its name of Old Dominion), institute a reaction against
the rebellion at home. The two joined forces and sent
first to Toussaint. Nature made him a Metternich, a diplomatist. He probably wished to avail himself of this offer, foreseeing the advantage to his race, but to avail himself of it so cautiously as to provide against failure, risking
as little as possible until the intentions of the other party
had been tested, and so managing as to be able to go on
or withdraw as the best interest of his race demanded.
He had practised well the Greek rule, "Know thyself,"
and thoroughly studied his own part. Later in life, when
criticising his great mulatto rival, Rigaud, he showed how

well he knew himself. "I know Rigaud," he said; "he drops the bridle when he gallops, he shows his arm when he strikes. For me, I gallop also, but know where to stop; when I strike I am felt, not seen. Rigaud works only by blood and massacre, I know how to put the people in movement; but when I appear all must be calm."

He therefore said to the envoys: "Where are your credentials?" "We have none." "I will have nothing to do with you." They then sought François and Biassou, two other slaves of strong passions, considerable intellect, and great influence over their fellow-slaves, and said: "Arm, assist the government, put down the English on the one hand, and the Spanish on the other"; and on August 21, 1791, fifteen thousand blacks led by François and Biassou, supplied with arms from the arsenal of the government, appeared in the midst of the colony. It is believed that Toussaint, unwilling himself to head the movement, was still desirous that it should go forward, trusting, as proved the case, that it would result in benefit to his race. He is supposed to have advised François in his course—saving himself for a more momentous hour.

This is what Edward Everett calls the Insurrection of St. Domingo. It bore for its motto on one side of its banner: "Long live the King," and on the other, "We Claim the Old Laws." Singular mottoes for a rebellion! In fact, it was the posse comitatus; it was the only French army on the island; it was the only force that had a right to bear arms; and what it undertook, it achieved. It put Blanchelande in his seat; it put the island beneath his rule. When it was done, the blacks said to the governor they had created, " Now grant us one day in seven; give us one day's labor; we will buy another and with the two buy a third "—the favorite method of emancipation at that time. Like the Blanchelande of five years before, he refused. He said: " Disarm! disperse! " and the blacks answered, " The right hand that has saved you—the right hand that has saved the island for the Bourbons may, perchance, clutch some of our own rights," and they stood still. [Cheering.] This is the first insurrection, if any such there were in St. Domingo,—the first determined purpose on the part of the negro, having saved the government, to save himself.

Now, let me stop a moment, and remind you of one thing. I am about to open to you a chapter of bloody history,—no doubt of it. Who set the example? Who dug up from its grave of a hundred years, the hideous punishment of the wheel, and broke Ogé, every bone, a living man? Who flared in the face of indignant and astonished Europe the forgotten barbarity of quartering the yet palpitating body? Our race. And if the black man learned the lesson but too well, it does not lie in our lips to complain. During this whole struggle, the record is, mark you, by the white man—the whole picture from the pencil of the white race—that for one life the negro took in battle, in hot and bloody fight, the white race took, in the cool malignity of revenge, three to answer for it. Notice also that up to this moment the slave had taken no part in the struggle except at the bidding of the government; and even then not for himself, but only to sustain the laws.

At this moment then, the island stands thus: The Spaniard is on the east, triumphant; the Englishman is on the northwest intrenched; the mulattoes are in the mountains waiting; the blacks are in the valleys victorious; one-half the French slave-holding element is republican, the other half royalist; the white race against the mulatto and the black; the black against both; the Frenchman against the English and Spaniard; the Spaniard against both. It is a war of races and a war of nations. At such a moment L'Ouverture appeared.

He had been born a slave on a plantation in the north of the island—an unmixed negro, his father stolen from Africa. If anything, therefore, that I say of him to-night, moves your admiration, remember the black race claims it all—we have no part nor lot in it. He was fifty years old at this time. An old negro had taught him to read. His favorite books were Epictetus, Raynal, Military Memoirs, Plutarch. In the woods he learned some of the qualities of herbs, and was village doctor. On the estate the highest place he ever reached was that of coachman. At fifty he joined the army as a physician. Before he went he placed his master and mistress on shipboard, freighted the vessel with a cargo of sugar and coffee, and sent them to Baltimore, and never afterward did he forget to send them year by year ample means of support. And I might add that of all the leading negro generals, each one saved the man under whose roof he was born, and protected his family. [Cheering.]

Let me add another thing. If I stood here to-night to tell the story of Napoleon, I should take it from the lips of Frenchmen, who find no language rich enough to paint the great captain of the Nineteenth century. If I were to tell you the story of Washington, I should take it from your hearts,—you, who think no marble white enough in which to carve the name of the Father of his Country. [Applause.] I am about to tell you the story of a negro who has left hardly one written line. I am to glean it from the reluctant testimony of Britons, Frenchmen, Spaniards,—men who despised him as a negro and a slave, and hated him because he had beaten them in many a battle. All the materials for his biography are from the lips of his enemies.

The second story told of him is this: About the time he reached the camp, the army had been subjected to two insults. First, their Commissioners summoned to meet the French Committee were ignominiously and insultingly dismissed; and when, afterward, François, their general, was summoned to a second conference, and went to it on horseback, accompanied by two officers, a young lieutenant, who had known him as a slave, angered at seeing him in the uniform of an officer, raised his riding-whip and struck him over the shoulders. If he had been the savage which the negro is painted to us, he had only to breathe the insult to his twenty-five thousand soldiers and they would have trodden out the Frenchman in blood. But the indignant chief rode back in silence to his tent, and it was twenty-four hours before his troops heard of this insult to their general. Then the word went forth: "Death to every white man!" They had fifteen hundred prisoners. Ranged in front of the camp, they were about to be shot. Toussaint, who had a vein of religious fanaticism like most great leaders,—like Mahommed, like Napoleon, like Cromwell, like John Brown [cheers]—he could preach as well as fight,—mounting a hillock and getting the ear of the crowd, exclaimed: "Brothers, this blood will not wipe out the insult offered to our chief, only the blood in yonder

French camp can wipe it out; to shed that is courage, to shed this is cowardice and cruelty beside"; and he saved fifteen hundred lives. [Applause.]

I cannot stop to give in detail everyone of his efforts. This was in 1793. Leap with me over seven years; come to 1800; what has he achieved? He has driven the Spaniard back into his own cities; conquered him there, and put the French banner over every Spanish town; and for the first time, and almost the last, the island obeys one law. He has put the mulatto under his feet. He has attacked Maitland, defeated him in pitched battles, and permitted him to retreat to Jamaica; and when the French army rose upon Laveaux, their general, and put him in chains, Toussaint defeated them, took Laveaux out of prison, and put him at the head of his own troops. The grateful French in return named him General-in-Chief. *Cet homme fait l'ouverture partout*, said one. "This man makes an opening everywhere"—hence his soldiers named him L'Ouverture, the opening.

This was the work of seven years. Let us pause a moment and find something to measure him by. You remember that Macaulay says, comparing Cromwell with Napoleon, that Cromwell showed the greater military genius, if we consider that he never saw an army till he was forty; while Napoleon was educated from a boy in the best military schools of Europe; Cromwell manufactured his own army; Napoleon at the age of twenty-seven was placed at the head of the best troops Europe ever saw. They were both successful; but, says Macaulay, with such disadvantages the Englishman showed the greater genius. Whether you allow the inference or not, you will at least allow that it is a fair mode of measurement. Apply it to Toussaint. Cromwell never saw an army till he was forty; this man never saw a soldier till he was fifty. Cromwell manufactured his own army—out of what? Englishmen— the best blood in Europe. Out of the middle-class among Englishmen—the best blood of the island. And with it he conquered what? Englishmen—their equals. This man manufactured his army out of what? Out of what you call the despicable race of negroes, debased, demoralized by two hundred years of slavery, one hundred thousand of them imported into the island within four years, unable to speak a dialect intelligible even to each other. Yet out of this mixed and as you say, despicable mass, he forged a thunderbolt and hurled it at what? At the proudest blood in Europe, the Spaniard, and sent him home conquered [cheers]; at the most warlike blood in Europe, the French, and put them under his feet; at the pluckiest blood in Europe, the English, and they skulked home to Jamaica. [Applause.] Now if Cromwell was a general, at least this man was a soldier. I know it was a small territory; it was not as large as the continent; but it was as large as that Attica which, with Athens for its capital, has filled the earth with its fame for two thousand years. We measure genius by quality, not by quantity.

Further, Cromwell was only a soldier; his fame stops there. Not one line in the statute-book of Britain can be traced to Cromwell; not one step in the social life of England finds its motive power in his brain. The State he founded went down with him to his grave. But this man no sooner found himself at the helm of state than the ship steadied with an upright keel, and he began to evince a statesmanship as marvelous as his military genius. History says that the most statesmanlike act of Napoleon was his proclamation of 1802, at the peace of Amiens, when believing that the indelible loyalty of a native-born heart is always a sufficient basis on which to found an empire, he said: "Frenchmen, come home. I pardon the crimes of the last twelve years; I blot out its parties; I found my throne on the hearts of all Frenchmen," and twelve years of unclouded success showed how wisely he judged. Now that was in 1802. In 1800 this negro made a proclamation; it runs thus: "Sons of St. Domingo, come home. We never meant to take your houses or your lands. The negro only asked that liberty which God gave him. Your houses wait for you, your lands are ready; come and cultivate them;"—and from Madrid and Paris, from Baltimore and New Orleans, the emigrant planters crowded home to enjoy their estates, under the pledged word that was never broken, of a victorious slave.

Again, Carlyle has said: "The natural king is one who melts all wills into his own." At this moment he turned to his armies, poor, ill-clad, and half-starved—and said to them: "Go back and work on these estates you have conquered; for an empire can be founded only on order and industry and you can learn these virtues only there." And they went. The French admiral who witnessed the scene, said that in a week his army melted back into peasants.

It was 1800. The world waited fifty years before, in 1846, Robert Peel dared to venture, as a matter of practical statesmanship, the theory of free trade. Adam Smith theorized, the French statesmen dreamed, but no man at the head of affairs had ever dared to risk it as a practical measure. Europe waited till 1846 before the most practical intellect in the world, the English, adopted the great economic formula of unfettered trade. But in 1800 this black, with the instinct of statesmanship, said to the committee who were drafting for him a Constitution: "Put at the head of the chapter of commerce that the ports of St. Domingo are open to the trade of the world." [Cheers.]

With lofty indifference to race, superior to all envy or prejudice, Toussaint had formed this committee of eight white proprietors, and one mulatto—not a soldier nor a negro on the list, although Haytian history proves that with the exception of Rigaud, the rarest genius has always been shown by pure negroes.

Again it was 1800, at a time when England was poisoned on every page of her statute-book with religious intolerance, when a man could not enter the House of Commons without taking an Episcopal communion, when every State in the Union, except Rhode Island, was full of the intensest religious bigotry. This man was a negro. You say that is a superstitious blood. He was uneducated. You say that makes a man narrow-minded. He was a Catholic. Many say that is but another name for intolerance. And yet—negro, Catholic, slave,—he took his place by the side of Roger Williams, and said to his Committee: "Make it the first line of my Constitution that I know no difference between religious beliefs." [Applause.]

Now, blue-eyed Saxon, proud of your race, go back with me to the commencement of the century and select what statesman you please. Let him be either American or European, let him have a brain the result of six generations of culture; let him have the richest training of university routine, let him add to it the better education of practical life; crown his temples with the silver of seventy years; and show me the man of Saxon lineage for whom his most sanguine admirer will wreathe a laurel rich as embittered foes have placed on the brow of this negro—rare military skill, profound knowledge of human nature, content to blot out all party distinctions, and trust a state to the blood of its sons, anticipating Sir Robert Peel fifty years, and taking his station by the side of Roger Williams, before an Englishman or American had won the right—and yet this is the record which the history of rival states makes up for this inspired black of St. Domingo. [Cheers.]

It was 1801. The Frenchmen who lingered on the island described its prosperity and order as almost incredible. You might trust a child with a bag of gold to go from Samana to Port-au-Prince without risk. Peace was in every household; the valleys laughed with fertility; culture climbed the mountains; the commerce of the world was represented in its harbors. At this time Europe concluded the peace of Amiens, and Napoleon took his seat on the throne of France. He glanced his eyes across the Atlantic, and with a single stroke of his pen reduced Cayenne and Martinique back into chains. He then said to his Council: "What shall I do with St. Domingo?" The slave-holder said: "Give it to us." Napoleon turned to the Abbe Gregoire. "What is your opinion?" "I think those men would change their opinions if they changed their skins." Colonel Vincent, who had been private secretary to Toussaint, wrote a letter to Napoleon in which he said: "Sire, leave it alone; it is the happiest spot in your dominions; God raised this man to govern; races melt under his hand. He has saved you this island, for I know of my own knowledge that when the Republic could not have lifted a finger to prevent it, George III offered him any title and revenue if he would hold the island under the British crown. He refused and saved it for France." Napoleon turned away from his Council, and is said to have remarked: "I have sixty thousand idle troops; I must find them something to do." He meant to say: "I am about to seize the crown; I dare not do it in the face of sixty thousand Republican soldiers; I must give them work at a distance to do." The gossip of Paris gives another reason for his expedition against St. Domingo. It is said that the satirists of Paris had christened Toussaint the Black Napoleon; and Bonaparte hated his black shadow. Toussaint had unfortunately once addressed him a letter: "The first of the black to the first of the whites." He did not like the comparison. You would think it too slight a motive. But let me remind you of the present Napoleon, that when the epigrammatists of Paris christened his wasteful and tasteless expense at Versailles Soulouquerie, from the name of Soulouque, the Black Emperor, he deigned to issue a specific order forbidding the use of the word. The Napoleon blood is very sensitive. So Napoleon resolved to crush Toussaint from one motive or another, from the prompting of ambition, or dislike of this resemblance, which was very close. If either imitated the other it must have been the white, since the negro preceded him several years. They were very much alike and they were very French. French even in vanity, common to both. You remember Bonaparte's vain-glorious words to his soldiers at the Pyramids: "Forty centuries look down upon us." In the same mood Toussaint said to the French captain who urged him to go to France in his frigate: "Sir, your ship is not large enough to carry me." Napoleon you know, could never bear the military uniform. He hated the restraint of his rank; he loved to put on the gray coat of the Little Corporal, and wander in the camp. Toussaint also never could bear a uniform. He wore a plain coat, and often the yellow Madras handkerchief of the slaves. A French lieutenant once called him a maggot in a yellow handkerchief. Toussaint took him prisoner next day, and sent him home to his mother. Like Napoleon, he could fast many days; could dictate to three secretaries at once; could wear out four or five horses. Like Napoleon, no man ever divined his purpose or penetrated his plan. He was only a negro and so in him they called it hypocrisy. In Bonaparte we style it diplomacy. For instance, three attempts made to assassinate him all failed, from not firing at the right spot. If they thought he was in the north in a carriage, he would be in the south on horseback; if they thought he was in the city in a house, he would be in the field in a tent. They once riddled his carriage with bullets; he was on

horseback on the other side. The seven Frenchmen who
did it were arrested. They expected to be shot. The next
day was some saint's day; he ordered them to be placed before the high altar, and when the priest reached the prayer
for forgiveness, Toussaint came down from his high seat,
repeated it with him and permitted them to go unpunished.
[Cheers.] He had a wit common to all great command-
ers, which makes its way in a camp. His soldiers getting
disheartened, he filled a large vase with powder, and scat-
tering six grains of rice in it, shook them up, and said:
" See, there is the white—there is the black—what are you
afraid of?" So when people came to him in great numbers for office, as it is reported they do sometimes even
in Washington, he learned the first words of a Catholic
prayer in Latin, and repeating it, would say: " Do you
understand that?" "No, sir." "What! want an office,
and not know Latin? Go home and learn it."

Then again, like Napoleon, he had confidence in his
power to rule men. You remember when Bonaparte returned from Elba, and Louis XVIII sent an army against
him, Bonaparte descended from his carriage, opened his
coat, offering his breast to their muskets, and saying:
" Frenchmen, it is the Emperor!" and they ranged themselves behind him, his soldiers shouting: " *Vive l'Emper-
eur!*" That was in 1815. Twelve years before, Toussaint
finding that four of his regiments had deserted and gone
to Leclerc, drew sword, flung it away, went across the
field to them, folded his arms and said: " Children, can
you point a bayonet at me?" The blacks fell on their knees
praying his pardon. His bitterest enemies watched him
and none of them charged him with love of money, sensuality or cruel use of power. The only instance in which
his sternest critic has charged him with severity is this.
During a tumult, a few white proprietors, who had returned, trusting his proclamation, were killed. His
nephew, General Moise, was accused of indecision in quell-
ing the riot. He assembled a court-martial, and on its ver-
dict ordered his own nephew to be shot, sternly Roman
in thus keeping his promise of protection to the whites.
Above the lust of gold, pure in private life, generous in
the use of his power, it was against such a man that Napoleon sent his army, giving to General Leclerc, the hus-

band of his beautiful sister, Pauline, thirty thousand of his best troops, with orders to reintroduce slavery. Among these soldiers came all of Toussaint's old mulatto rivals and foes.

Holland lent sixty ships. England promised by special message to be neutral; and you know neutrality means sneering at freedom and sending arms to tyrants. [Loud and long continued applause.] England promised neutrality, and the black looked out on the whole civilized world, marshaled against him. America, full of slaves, of course, was hostile. Only the Yankees sold him poor muskets at a very high price. [Laughter.] Mounting his horse, and riding to the eastern end of the island, Samana, he looked out on a sight such as no native had ever seen before. Sixty ships of the line, crowded by the best soldiers of Europe, rounded the point. They were soldiers who never yet had met an equal, whose tread like Cæsar's, had shaken Europe, soldiers who had scaled the Pyramids, and planted the French banners on the walls of Rome. He looked a moment, counted the flotilla, let the reins fall on the neck of his horse, and, turning to Christophe, said: " All France is come to Hayti; they can only come to make us slaves; all is lost! " He then recognized the only mistake of his life—his confidence in Bonaparte, which had led him to disband his army.

Returning to the hills, he issued the only proclamation which bears his name and breathes vengeance: " My children, France comes to make us slaves. God gave us liberty; France has no right to take it away. Burn the cities, destroy the harvests, tear up the roads with cannon, poison the wells, show the white man the hell he comes to make "; and he was obeyed. [Applause.] When the great William of Orange saw Louis XIV cover Holland with troops, he said: " Break down the dykes! give Holland back to ocean "; and Europe said: " Sublime! " When Alexander saw the armies of France descend upon Russia, he said: " Burn Moscow! starve back the invaders! " and Europe answered " Sublime! " This black saw all Europe marshaled to crush him, and gave to his people the same heroic example of defiance.

It is true the scene grows bloodier as we proceed. But remember the white man fitly accompanied his infamous attempt to reduce freemen to slavery with every bloody and cruel device that bitter and shameless hate could invent. Aristocracy is always cruel. The black man met the attempt, as every such attempt should be met, with war to the hilt. In his first struggle to gain his freedom, he had been generous and merciful, saved lives and pardoned enemies, as the people in every age and clime have always done when rising against aristocrats. Now, to save his liberty the negro exhausted every means, seized every weapon and turned back the hateful invaders with the vengeance as terrible as their own, though even now he refused to be cruel.

Leclerc sent word to Christophe that he was about to land at Cape City. Christophe said: "Toussaint is governor of the island. I will send to him for permission. If without it a French soldier sets foot on shore, I will burn the town and fight over its ashes."

Leclerc landed. Christophe took two thousand white men, women and children and carried them to the mountains in safety, and then with his own hands set fire to the splendid palace which French architects had just finished for him, and in forty hours the place was in ashes. The battle was fought in its streets, and the French driven back to their boats. [Cheers.] Wherever they went they were met with fire and sword. Once, resisting an attack, the blacks, Frenchmen born, shouted the Marseilles hymn, and the French soldiers stood still; they could not fight the Marseillaise. And it was not till their officers sabred them on, that they advanced, and then they were beaten. Beaten in the field, the French then took to lies. They issued proclamations saying:—"We do not come to make you slaves; this man Toussaint tells you lies. Join us, and you shall have the rights you claim." They cheated every one of his officers except Christophe and Dessalines, and his own brother Pierre, and finally these also deserted him, and he was left alone. He then sent word to Leclerc: "I will submit; I could continue the struggle for years—could prevent a single Frenchman from safely quitting your camp. But I hate bloodshed. I have fought only for the liberty of my race. Guarantee that. I will submit and come in."

He took the oath to be a faithful citizen; and on the

same crucifix Leclerc swore that he should be faithfully
protected and that the island should be free. As the
French general glanced along the line of his splendidly-
equipped troops, and saw opposite Toussaint's ill-armed
followers, he said to him: " L'Ouverture, had you continued the war, where could you have got arms?" " I
would have taken yours," was the Spartan reply. [Cheers.]
He went down to his house in peace; it was summer. Leclerc remembered that the fever months were coming
when his army would be in hospitals, and when one motion
of that royal hand would sweep his troops into the sea.
He was too dangerous to be left at large. So they summoned him to attend a council; and here is the only charge
made against him—the only charge. They say he was
fool enough to go. Grant it; what is the record? The
white man lies shrewdly to cheat the negro. Knight er-
rantry was truth. The foulest insult you can offer to a
man since the Crusades is, you lie. Of Toussaint, Her-
mona, the Spanish general, who knew him well, said:
" He was the purest soul God ever put into a body."
Of him history bears witness: " He never broke
his word."   Maitland was traveling in the depths of
the woods to meet Toussaint, when he was met by a
messenger, and told that he was betrayed.   He went
on; and met Toussaint, who showed him two letters, one
from the French general, offering him any rank if he
would put Maitland in his power and the other his reply.
It was: " Sir, I have promised the Englishman that he
shall go back." [Cheers.] Let it stand, therefore, that the
negro, truthful as a knight of old, was cheated by his lying
foe. Which race has reason to be proud of such a record?

But he was not cheated. He was under espionage. Suppose he had refused; the government would have doubted
him—would have found some cause to arrest him. He
probably reasoned thus: " If I go willingly, I shall be
treated accordingly; " and he went. The moment he entered the room the officers drew their swords, and told
him he was a prisoner; and one young lieutenant who was
present says: " He was not at all surprised, but seemed
very sad." They put him on shipboard, and weighed
anchor for France. As the island faded from his sight, he
turned to the captain and said: " You think you have

rooted up the tree of liberty, but I am only a branch; I have planted the tree so deep that all France can never root it up." [Cheers.] Arrived in Paris, he was flung into jail, and Napoleon sent his secretary, Caffarelli, to him, supposing he had buried large treasures. He listened a while, then replied: "Young man, it is true I have lost treasures but they are not such as you come to seek." He was then sent to the Castle of St. Joux, to a dungeon twelve feet by twenty, built wholly of stone, with a narrow window, high upon the side, looking out on the snows of Switzerland. In winter, ice covers the floor; in summer it is damp and wet. In this living tomb, the child of the sunny tropic was left to die. From this dungeon he wrote two letters to Napoleon. One of them runs thus:—

"Sire, I am a French citizen. I never broke a law. By the grace of God I have saved for you the best island of your realm. Sire, of your mercy grant me justice."

Napoleon never answered the letters. The commandant allowed him five francs a day for food and fuel. Napoleon heard of it and reduced the sum to three. The luxurious usurper, who complained that the English government was stingy because it allowed him only six thousand dollars a month, stooped from his throne to cut down a dollar to a half, and still Toussaint did not die quick enough.

This dungeon was a tomb. The story is told that in Josephine's time, a young French marquis was placed in it and the girl to whom he was betrothed went to the Empress and prayed for his release. Said Josephine to her: "Have a model of it made and bring it to me." Josephine placed it near Napoleon. He said: "Take it away; it is horrible!" She put it on his footstool and he kicked it from him. She held it to him the third time, and said: "Sire, in this horrible dungeon you have put a man to die." "Take him out," said Napoleon, and the girl saved her lover. In this tomb Toussaint was buried, but he did not die fast enough. Finally the commandant was told to go into Switzerland, to carry the keys of the dungeon with him and to stay four days; when he returned Toussaint was found starved to death. That imperial assassin was taken twelve years after to his prison at St. Helena planned for a tomb as he had planned that of Toussaint, and there he whined away his dying hours in pitiful complaints of curtains and titles, of dishes and rides. God grant that when some future Plutarch shall weigh the great men of our epoch, the whites against the blacks, he do not put that whining child at St. Helena into one scale and into the other the negro meeting death like a Roman without a murmur in the solitude of his icy dungeon!

From the moment he was betrayed the negroes began to doubt the French and rushed to arms. Soon every negro but Maurepas deserted the French. Leclerc summoned Maurepas to his side. He came, loyally bringing with him five hundred soldiers. Leclerc spiked his epaulettes to his shoulders, shot him and flung him into the sea. He took his five hundred soldiers on shore, shot them on the edge of a pit, and tumbled them in. Dessalines from the mountains saw it, and selecting five hundred French officers from his prisons hung them on separate trees in sight of Leclerc's fleet; and born as I was not far from Bunker Hill, I have yet found no reason to think he did wrong. [Cheers.]

They murdered Pierre Toussaint's wife at his own door, and after such treatment that it was mercy when they killed her. The maddened husband who had but a year before saved the lives of twelve hundred white men carried his next thousand prisoners and sacrificed them on her grave.

The French exhausted every form of torture. Negroes were bound together and thrown into the sea; any one who floated was shot; others sunk with cannon-balls tied to their feet; some smothered with sulphur fumes, others strangled, scourged to death, gibbeted; sixteen of Toussaint's officers were chained to rocks in desert islands—others in marshes and left to be devoured by poisonous reptiles and insects. Rochambeau sent to Cuba for bloodhounds. When they arrived young girls went down to the wharf, decked the hounds with ribbons and flowers, kissed their necks, and seated in the amphitheatre, the women clapped their hands to see the negroes thrown to these dogs, previously starved to rage. But the negroes besieged this very city so closely that these same girls in their misery ate the very hounds they had welcomed.

Then flashed forth that defying courage and sublime endurance which show how alike all races are when tried in the same furnace. The Roman wife whose husband faltered when Nero ordered him to kill himself, seized a dagger and mortally wounding her own body, cried: " Poetus, it is not hard to die." The world regards it with proud tears. Just in the same spirit when a negro colonel was ordered to execution and trembled, his wife seized his sword and giving herself a death-wound said " Husband, death is sweet when liberty is gone."

The war went on. Napoleon sent over thirty thousand more soldiers, but disaster still followed his efforts. What the sword did not devour the fever ate up. Leclerc died. Pauline carried his body back to France. Napoleon met her at Bordeaux, saying: " Sister, I gave you an army; you bring me back ashes." Rochambeau—the Rochambeau of our history—left in command of eight thousand troops, sent word to Dessalines: " When I take you I will not shoot you like a soldier, or hang you like a white man; I will whip you to death like a slave." Dessalines chased him from battlefield to battlefield, from fort to fort, and finally shut him up in Samana. Heating cannon-balls to destroy his fleet, Dessalines learned that Rochambeau had begged of the English admiral permission to cover his troops with the English flag, and the generous negro suffered the boaster to embark undisturbed.

Some doubt the courage of the negro. Go to Hayti and stand on those fifty thousand graves of the best soldiers France ever had, and ask them what they think of the negro's sword. And if that does not satisfy you, go to France, to the splendid mausoleum of the Counts of Rochambeau, and to the eight thousand graves of Frenchmen who skulked home under the English flag, and ask them. And if that does not satisfy you, come home, and if it had been October, 1859, you might have come by way of quaking Virginia, and asked her what she thought of negro courage.

And you may also remember this—that we Saxons were slaves about four hundred years, sold with the land, and our fathers never raised a finger to end that slavery. They waited till Christianity and civilization, till commerce and the discovery of America melted away their chains. Spartacus in Italy led the slaves of Rome against the Empress of the world. She murdered him and crucified them. There never was a slave rebellion successful but one and that was in St. Domingo. Every race has been some time or other in chains. But there never was a race that, weakened and degraded by such chattel slavery, unaided tore off its own fetters, forged them into swords and won its liberty on the battlefield, but one, and that was the black race of St. Domingo. God grant that the wise vigor of our government may avert that necessity from our land—may raise into peaceful liberty the four million committed to our care and show under democratic institutions a statesmanship as far-sighted as that of England, as brave as the negro of Hayti!

So much for the courage of the negro. Now look at his endurance. In 1805 he said to the white men, "This island is ours; not a white foot shall touch it." Side by side with him stood the South American republics planted by the best blood of the country of Lope da Vega and Cervantes. They topple over so often that you could no more daguerreotype their crumbling fragments than you could the waves of the ocean. And yet at their side the negro has kept his island sacredly to himself. It is said that at first with rare patriotism the Haytien government ordered the destruction of all the sugar plantations remaining and discouraged its culture, deeming that the temptation which lured the French back again to attempt their enslavement. Burn over New York to-night, fill up her canals, sink every ship, destroy her railroads, blot out every remnant of education from her sons, let her be ignorant and penniless, with nothing but her hands to begin the world over again—how much could she do in sixty years? And Europe, too, would lend you money, but she would not lend Hayti a dollar. Hayti from the ruins of her colonial dependence, is become a civilized state, the seventh nation in the catalogue of commerce with this country, inferior in morals and education to none of the West Indian isles. Foreign merchants trust her goods as willingly as they do our own. Thus far she has foiled the ambition of Spain, the greed of England and the malicious statesmanship of Calhoun. Toussaint made her what she is. In this work there have been grouped around him a score of men mostly of pure negro blood who ably seconded his efforts. They were able in war and skilful in civil affairs, but not like him remarkable for that rare mingling of high qualities which alone makes true greatness and ensures a man leadership among those otherwise almost his equals. Toussaint was indisputably their chief. Courage, purpose, endurance—these are the tests. He did plant a state so deep that all the world has not been able to root it up.

I would call him Napoleon, but Napoleon made his way to empire over broken oaths and through a sea of blood. This man never broke his word. " No retaliation," was his great motto and the rule of his life; and the last words uttered to his son in France were these: " My boy, you will some day go back to St. Domingo; forget that France murdered your father."

I would call him Cromwell, but Cromwell was only a soldier, and the State he founded went down with him into his grave. I would call him Washington, but the great Virginian held slaves. This man risked his empire rather than permit the slave-trade in the humblest village of his dominions.

You think me a fanatic to-night for you read history not with your eyes, but with your prejudices. But fifty years hence, when truth gets a hearing, the Muse of History will put Phocion for the Greek, and Brutus for the Roman, Hampden for England, Fayette for France, choose Washington as the bright, consummate flower of our earlier civilization, and John Brown the ripe fruit of our noonday [thunders of applause], then, dipping her pen in the sunlight, will write in the clear blue, above them all, the name of the soldier, the statesman, the martyr, Toussaint L'Ouverture. [Long continued applause.]

EDGAR ALLAN POE

THE POETIC PRINCIPLE

[Lecture by Edgar Allan Poe, poet and prose writer (born in
Boston, Mass., January 19, 1809; died in Baltimore, Md., October 7,
1849), delivered in the later years of his life, in Boston and at various
other places, "partly," as stated in Stedman and Woodberry's edition
of Poe's works, "as an elocutionary performance." The skilful
blending of criticism with concrete illustration renders this a felicitous
example of Poe's manner in analytic discussion, as it is also a striking
presentation of his view of poetic theory and practice.]

In speaking of the Poetic Principle, I have no design to
be either thorough or profound. While discussing very
much at random the essentiality of what we call Poetry,
my principal purpose will be to cite for consideration some
few of those minor English or American poems which
best suit my own taste, or which, upon my own fancy,
have left the most definite impression. By "minor
poems" I mean, of course, poems of little length. And
here, in the beginning, permit me to say a few words in
regard to a somewhat peculiar principle, which, whether
rightfully or wrongfully, has always had its influence in
my own critical estimate of the poem. I hold that a long
poem does not exist. I maintain that the phrase, "a long
poem," is simply a flat contradiction in terms.

I need scarcely observe that a poem deserves its title
only inasmuch as it excites by elevating the soul. The
value of the poem is in the ratio of this elevating excitement. But all excitements are, through a psychal necessity, transient. That degree of excitement which would
entitle a poem to be so called at all, cannot be sustained
throughout a composition of any length. After the lapse
of half an hour, at the very utmost, it flags—fails—a re-

vulsion ensues—and then the poem is, in effect, and in fact, no longer such.

There are no doubt, many who have found difficulty in reconciling the critical dictum that the "Paradise Lost" is to be devoutly admired throughout, with the absolute impossibility of maintaining for it, during perusal, the amount of enthusiasm which that critical dictum would demand.   This great work, in fact, is to be regarded as poetical only when, losing sight of that vital requisite in all works of Art, Unity, we view it merely as a series of minor poems.   If, to preserve its unity—its totality of effect or impression—we read it (as would be necessary) at a single sitting, the result is but a constant alternation of excitement and depression.   After a passage of what we feel to be true poetry, there follows, inevitably, a passage of platitude which no critical pre-judgment can force us to admire; but if, upon completing the work, we read it again, omitting the first book—that is to say, commencing with the second—we shall be surprised at now finding that admirable which we before condemned—that damnable which we had previously so much admired.   It follows from all this that the ultimate, aggregate, or absolute effect of even the best epic under the sun, is a nullity—and this is precisely the fact.

In regard to the Iliad we have, if not positive proof, at least very good reason for believing it intended as a series of lyrics; but granting the epic intention, I can say only that the work is based on an imperfect sense of Art.   The modern epic is, of the supposititious ancient model, but an inconsiderate and blindfolded imitation.   But the day of these artistic anomalies is over.   If, at any time, any very long poem were popular in reality—which I doubt—it is at least clear that no very long poem will ever be popular again.   That the extent of a poetical work is, *ceteris paribus*, the measure of its merit, seems undoubtedly, when we thus state it, a proposition sufficiently absurd—yet we are indebted for it to the Quarterly Reviews.   Surely there can be nothing in mere size, abstractly considered,— there can be nothing in mere bulk, so far as a volume is concerned, which has so continuously elicited admiration from these saturnine pamphlets!   A mountain, to be sure, by the mere sentiment of physical magnitude, which it conveys, does impress us with a sense of the sublime—but no man is impressed after this fashion by the material grandeur of even "The Columbiad."

Even the Quarterlies have not instructed us to be so impressed by it. As yet, they have not insisted on our estimating Lamartine by the cubic foot or Pollock by the pound—but what else are we to infer from their continual prating about "sustained effort"? If, by "sustained effort" any little gentleman has accomplished an epic, let us frankly commend him, for the effort—if this indeed be a thing commendable—but let us forbear praising the epic on the effort's account. It is to be hoped that common sense, in the time to come, will prefer deciding upon a work of Art rather by the impression it makes—by the effect it produces—than by the time it took to impress the effect, or by the amount of "sustained effort" which had been found necessary in effecting the impression. The fact is, that perseverance is one thing and genius quite another—nor can all the Quarterlies in Christendom confound them. By and by, this proposition, with many which I have been just urging, will be received as self-evident. In the meantime, by being generally condemned as falsities, they will not be essentially damaged as truths.

On the other hand, it is clear that a poem may be improperly brief. Undue brevity degenerates into mere epigrammatism. A very short poem, while now and then producing a brilliant or vivid, never produces a profound or enduring effect. There must be the steady pressing down of the stamp upon the wax. De Beranger has wrought innumerable things, pungent and spirit-stirring, but in general they have been too imponderous to stamp themselves deeply into the public attention, and thus, as so many feathers of fancy, have been blown aloft only to be whistled down the wind.

A remarkable instance of the effect of undue brevity in depressing a poem, in keeping it out of the popular view, is afforded by the following exquisite little Serenade:—

> I arise from dreams of thee,
> In the first sweet sleep of night,
> When the winds are breathing low,
> And the stars are shining bright;

I arise from dreams of thee,
  And a spirit in my feet
Has led me—who knows how?—
  To thy chamber-window, sweet!

The wandering airs they faint
  On the dark, the silent stream—
The champak odors fail
  Like sweet thoughts in a dream;
The nightingale's complaint
  It dies upon her heart,
As I must die on thine,
  O beloved, as thou art!

Oh, lift me from the grass!
  I die, I faint, I fail!
Let thy love in kisses rain
  On my lips and eyelids pale.
My cheek is cold and white, alas!
  My heart beats loud and fast:
Oh! press it close to thine again,
  Where it will break at last!

Very few perhaps are familiar with these lines, yet no less a poet than Shelley is their author. Their warm, yet delicate and ethereal imagination will be appreciated by all, but by none so thoroughly as by him who has himself arisen from sweet dreams of one beloved to bathe in the aromatic air of a southern midsummer night.

One of the finest poems by Willis, the very best in my opinion which he has ever written, has, no doubt, through this same defect of undue brevity, been kept back from its proper position, not less in the critical than in the popular view.

The shadows lay along Broadway,
  'Twas near the twilight-tide,
And slowly there a lady fair
  Was walking in her pride.
Alone walked she; but viewlessly
  Walk'd spirits at her side.

Peace charm'd the street beneath her feet,
  And Honor charm'd the air;
And all astir looked kind on her
  And called her good as fair—

For all God ever gave to her
   She kept with chary care.

She kept with care her beauties rare
   From lovers warm and true;
For her heart was cold to all but gold,
   And the rich came not to woo—
But honor'd well are charms to sell
   If priests the selling do.

Now walking there was one more fair—
   A slight girl, lily-pale;
And she had unseen company
   To make the spirit quail—
'Twixt Want and Scorn she walked forlorn,
   And nothing could avail.

No mercy now can clear her brow
   From this world's peace to pray,
For as love's wild prayer dissolv'd in air,
   Her woman's heart gave way!
But the sin forgiven by Christ in Heaven
   By man is curs'd alway!

In this composition we find it difficult to recognize the
Willis who has written so many mere " verses of society."
The lines are not only richly ideal, but full of energy,
while they breathe an earnestness, an evident sincerity of
sentiment, for which we look in vain throughout all the
other works of this author.

While the epic mania, while the idea that to merit in
poetry prolixity is indispensable, has for some years past
been gradually dying out of the public mind, by mere
dint of its own absurdity, we find it succeeded by a heresy
too palpably false to be long tolerated, but one which, in
the brief period it has already endured, may be said to
have accomplished more in the corruption of our Poetical
Literature than all its other enemies combined.   I allude
to the heresy of " The Didactic."   It has been assumed,
tacitly and avowedly, directly and indirectly, that the ultimate object of all Poetry is Truth.   Every poem, it is
said, should inculcate a moral, and by this moral is the
poetical merit of the work to be adjudged.   We Americans
especially have patronized this happy idea, and we Bostonians very especially have developed it in full.   We have

taken it into our heads that to write a poem simply for
the poem's sake, and to acknowledge such to have been
our design, would be to confess ourselves radically wanting in the true Poetic dignity and force :—but the simple
fact is, that would we but permit ourselves to look into
our own souls we should immediately there discover that
under the sun there neither exists nor can exist any work
more thoroughly dignified, more supremely noble, than
this very poem, this poem *per se*, this poem which is a
poem and nothing more, this poem written solely for the
poem's sake.

With as deep a reverence for the True as ever inspired
the bosom of man, I would nevertheless limit in some
measure its modes of inculcation.   I would limit to enforce them.   I would not enfeeble them by dissipation.
The demands of Truth are severe.   She has no sympathy
with the myrtles.   All that which is so indispensable in
Song is precisely all that with which she has nothing
whatever to do.   It is but making her a flaunting paradox
to wreathe her in gems and flowers.   In enforcing a truth
we need severity rather than efflorescence of language.
We must be simple, precise, terse.   We must be cool,
calm, unimpassioned.   In a word, we must be in that mood
which, as nearly as possible, is the exact converse of the
poetical.   He must be blind indeed who does not perceive
the radical and chasmal difference between the truthful and
the poetical modes of inculcation.   He must be theory-
mad beyond redemption who, in spite of these differences,
shall still persist in attempting to reconcile the obstinate
oils and waters of Poetry and Truth.

Dividing the world of mind into its three most immediately obvious distinctions, we have the Pure Intellect,
Taste, and the Moral Sense.   I place Taste in the middle,
because it is just this position which in the mind it occu-
pies.   It holds intimate relations with either extreme;
but from the Moral Sense it is separated by so faint a
difference that Aristotle has not hesitated to place some
of its operations among the virtues themselves.   Nevertheless we find the offices of the trio marked with a sufficient distinction.   Just as the Intellect concerns itself
with Truth, so Taste informs us of the Beautiful, while
the Moral Sense is regardful of Duty.   Of this latter,

while conscience teaches the obligation and Reason the expediency, Taste contents herself with displaying the charms, waging war upon Vice solely on the ground of her deformity, her disproportion, her animosity to the fitting, to the appropriate, to the harmonious, in a word, to Beauty.

An immortal instinct deep within the spirit of man is thus plainly a sense of the Beautiful. This it is which administers to his delight in the manifold forms, and sounds, and odors, and sentiments, amid which he exists. And just as the lily is repeated in the lake, or the eyes of Amaryllis in the mirror, so is the mere oral or written repetition of these forms, and sounds, and colors, and odors, and sentiments, a duplicate source of delight. But this mere repetition is not poetry. He who shall simply sing with however glowing enthusiasm, or with however vivid a truth of description of the sights, and sound, and odors, and colors, and sentiments, which greet him in common with all mankind—he, I say, has yet failed to prove his divine title. There is still a something in the distance which he has been unable to attain. We have still a thirst unquenchable, to allay which he has not shown us the crystal springs. This thirst belongs to the immortality of man. It is at once a consequence and an indication of his perennial existence. It is the desire of the moth for the star. It is no mere appreciation of the Beauty before us, but a wild effort to reach the Beauty above. Inspired by an ecstatic prescience of the glories beyond the grave, we struggle by multiform combinations among the things and thoughts of Time to attain a portion of that Loveliness whose very elements perhaps appertain to eternity alone. And thus when by Poetry, or when by Music, the most entrancing of the Poetic moods, we find ourselves melted into tears, we weep then, not as the Abbate Gravina supposes, through excess of pleasure, but through a certain petulant, impatient sorrow at our inability to grasp now, wholly, here on earth, at once and forever, those divine and rapturous joys of which through the poem, or through the music, we attain to but brief and indeterminate glimpses. The struggle to apprehend the supernal Loveliness—this struggle, on the part of souls fittingly constituted—has given to the world all that which it (the world) has ever been enabled at once to understand and to feel as poetic.

The Poetic Sentiment, of course, may develop itself in various modes,—in Painting, in Sculpture, in Architecture, in the Dance,—very especially in Music—and very peculiarly and with a wide field, in the composition of the Landscape Garden. Our present theme however, has regard only to its manifestation in words. And here let me speak briefly on the topic of rhythm. Contenting myself with the certainty that Music, in its various modes of metre, rhythm, and rhyme, is of so vast a moment in Poetry as never to be wisely rejected—is so vitally important an adjunct, that he is simply silly who declines its assistance, I will not now pause to maintain its absolute essentiality. It is in Music perhaps that the soul most nearly attains the great end for which, when inspired by the Poetic Sentiment, it struggles—the creation of supernal Beauty. It may be, indeed, that here this sublime end is, now and then, attained in fact. We are often made to feel, with a shivering delight, that from an earthly harp are stricken notes which cannot have been unfamiliar to the angels. And thus there can be little doubt that in the union of Poetry with Music in its popular sense, we shall find the widest field for the Poetic development. The old Bards and Minnesingers had advantages which we do not possess—and Thomas Moore, singing his own songs, was, in the most legitimate manner, perfecting them as poems.

To recapitulate then:—I would define, in brief, the Poetry of words as the Rhythmical Creation of Beauty! Its sole arbiter is Taste. With the Intellect, or with the Conscience, it has only collateral relations. Unless incidentally, it has no concern whatever either with Duty or with Truth.

A few words, however, in explanation. That pleasure which is at once the most pure, the most elevating and the most intense, is derived, I maintain, from the contemplation of the Beautiful. In the contemplation of Beauty we alone find it possible to attain that pleasurable elevation, or excitement of the soul, which we recognize as the Poetic Sentiment, and which is so easily distinguished from Truth, which is the satisfaction of the Reason, or from Passion, which is the excitement of the Heart.

I make Beauty, therefore—using the word as inclusive of the sublime—I make Beauty the province of the poem, simply because it is an obvious rule of Art that effects should be made to spring as directly as possible from their causes:—no one as yet having been weak enough to deny that the peculiar elevation in question is at least most readily attainable in the poem. It by no means follows, however, that the incitements of Passion, or the precepts of Duty, or even the lessons of Truth, may not be introduced into a poem, and with advantage; for they may subserve incidentally, in various ways, the general purposes of the work:—but the true artist will always contrive to tone them down in proper subjection to that Beauty which is the atmosphere and the real essence of the poem.

I cannot better introduce the few poems which I shall present for your consideration than by the citation of the Poem to Mr. Longfellow's "Waif":—

> The day is done, and the darkness
>   Falls from the wings of Night,
> As a feather is wafted downward
>   From an eagle in his flight.
>
> I see the lights of the village
>   Gleam through the rain and the mist,
> And a feeling of sadness comes o'er me
>   That my soul cannot resist;
>
> A feeling of sadness and longing,
>   That is not akin to pain,
> And resembles sorrow only
>   As the mist resembles the rain.
>
> Come, read to me some poem,
>   Some simple and heartfelt lay,
> That shall soothe this restless feeling,
>   And banish the thoughts of day.
>
> Not from the grand old masters,
>   Not from the bards sublime,
> Whose distant footsteps echo
>   Through the corridors of Time.
>
> For, like strains of martial music,
>   Their mighty thoughts suggest
> Life's endless toil and endeavor;
>   And to-night I long for rest.

Read from some humbler poet,
   Whose songs gushed from his heart
As showers from the clouds of summer,
   Or tears from the eyelids start;

Who through long days of labor
   And nights devoid of ease,
Still heard in his soul the music
   Of wonderful melodies.

Such songs have power to quiet
   The restless pulse of care,
And come like the benediction
   That follows after prayer.

Then read from the treasured volume
   The poem of thy choice,
And lend to the rhyme of the poet
   The beauty of thy voice.

And the night shall be filled with music,
   And the cares that infest the day
Shall fold their tents like the Arabs,
   And as silently steal away.

With no great range of imagination, these lines have been justly admired for their delicacy of expression. Some of the images are very effective. Nothing can be better than—

————The bards sublime,
Whose distant footsteps echo
Through the corridors of Time.

The idea of the last quatrain is also very effective. The poem on the whole, however, is chiefly to be admired for the graceful insouciance of its metre, so well in accordance with the character of the sentiments, and especially for the ease of the general manner. This " ease," or naturalness, in a literary style, it has long been the fashion to regard as ease in appearance alone—as a point of really difficult attainment. But not so:—a natural manner is difficult only to him who should never meddle with it—to the unnatural. It is but the result of writing with the understanding, or with the instinct, that the tone in composition, should always be that which the mass of mankind would adopt—and must perpetually vary, of course, with the occasion. The author who, after the fashion of the "North American Review," should be upon all occasions, merely "quiet," must necessarily upon many occasions, be simply silly or stupid, and has no more right to be considered "easy" or "natural" than a Cockney exquisite, or than the Sleeping Beauty in the waxworks.

Among the minor poems of Bryant, none has so much impressed me as the one which he entitles "June." I quote only a portion of it:—

> There, through the long, long summer hours,
>   The golden light should lie,
> And thick young herbs and groups of flowers
>   Stand in their beauty by.
> The oriole should build and tell
> His love-tale, close beside my cell;
>   The idle butterfly
> Should rest him there, and there be heard
> The housewife-bee and humming-bird.
>
> And what, if cheerful shouts at noon,
>   Come, from the village sent,
> Or songs of maids, beneath the moon,
>   With fairy laughter blent?
> And what if, in the evening light,
> Betrothed lovers walk in sight
>   Of my low monument?
> I would the lovely scene around
> Might know no sadder sight nor sound.
>
> I know, I know I should not see
>   The season's glorious show,
> Nor would its brightness shine for me,
>   Nor its wild music flow;
> But if, around my place of sleep,
> The friends I love should come to weep,
>   They might not haste to go.
> Soft airs, and song, and light and bloom
> Should keep them lingering by my tomb.
>
> These to their soften'd hearts should bear
>   The thought of what has been,
> And speak of one who cannot share
>   The gladness of the scene;

Whose part in all the pomp that fills
The circuit of the summer hills,
        Is—that his grave is green;
And deeply would their hearts rejoice
To hear again his living voice.

The rhythmical flow here is even voluptuous—nothing could be more melodious. The poem has always affected me in a remarkable manner. The intense melancholy which seems to well up, perforce, to the surface of all the poet's cheerful sayings about his grave, we find thrilling us to the soul—while there is the truest poetic elevation in the thrill. The impression left is one of a pleasurable sadness. And if, in the remaining compositions which I shall introduce to you, there be more or less of a similar tone always apparent, let me remind you that (how or why we know not) this certain taint of sadness is inseparably connected with all the higher manifestations of true Beauty. It it, nevertheless,—

A feeling of sadness and longing
    That is not akin to pain,
And resembles sorrow only
    As the mist resembles the rain.

The taint of which I speak is clearly perceptible even in a poem so full of brilliancy and spirit as the " Health " of Edward Coate Pinkney :—

I fill this cup to one made up
    Of loveliness alone;
A woman, of her gentle sex
    The seeming paragon;
To whom the better elements
    And kindly stars have given
A form so fair, that like the air,
    'Tis less of earth than heaven.

Her every tone is music's own,
    Like those of morning birds,
And something more than melody
    Dwells ever in her words;
The coinage of her heart are they,
    And from her lips each flows
As one may see the burden'd bee
    Forth issue from the rose.

Affections are as thoughts to her,
    The measures of her hours;
Her feelings have the fragrancy,
    The freshness of young flowers;
And lovely passions, changing oft,
    So fill her, she appears
The image of themselves by turns—
    The idol of past years!

Of her bright face one glance will trace
    A picture on the brain,
And of her voice in echoing hearts
    A sound must long remain;
But memory, such as mine of her,
    So very much endears,
When death is nigh my latest sigh
    Will not be life's, but hers.

I fill'd this cup to one made up
    Of loveliness alone,
A woman, of her gentle sex
    The seeming paragon—
Her health! and would on earth there stood,
    Some more of such a frame,
That life might be all poetry,
    And weariness a name.

It was the misfortune of Mr. Pinkney to have been born too far South. Had he been a New Englander it is probable that he would have been ranked as the first of American lyrists, by that magnanimous cabal which has so long controlled the destinies of American Letters, in conducting the thing called the "North American Review." The poem just cited is especially beautiful; but the poetic elevation which it induces we must refer chiefly to our sympathy in the poet's enthusiasm. We pardon his hyperboles for the evident earnestness with which they are uttered.

It was by no means my design, however, to expatiate upon the merits of what I should read you. These will necessarily speak for themselves. Boccalini, in his "Advertisements from Parnassus," tells us that Zoilus once presented Apollo a very caustic criticism upon a very admirable book;—whereupon the god thanked him for the beauties of the work. He replied that he only busied

himself about the errors.   On hearing this, Apollo, hand-
ing him a sack of unwinnowed wheat, bade him pick out
all the chaff for his reward.

Now this fable answers very well as a hit at the critics
—but I am by no means sure that the god was in the right.
I am by no means certain that the true limits of the critical
duty are not grossly misunderstood.   Excellence, in a
poem especially, may be considered in the light of an
axiom, which need only be properly put to become self-
evident.   It is not excellence if it requires to be demon-
strated as such:—and thus to point out too particularly
the merits of a work of Art, is to admit that they are not
merits alogether.

Among the " Melodies " of Thomas Moore is one whose
distinguished character, as a poem proper, seems to have
been singularly left out of view.   I allude to his lines
beginning, "Come, rest in this bosom."   The intense
energy of their expression is not surpassed by anything
in Byron.   There are two of the lines in which a sentiment
is conveyed that embodies the all in all of the divine
passion of Love—a sentiment which, perhaps, has found its
echo in more, and in more passionate, human hearts than
any other single sentiment ever embodied in words :—

> Come, rest in this bosom, my own stricken deer,
> Though the herd have fled from thee, thy home is still here;
> Here still is the smile that no cloud can o'ercast,
> And a heart and a hand all thy own to the last.
>
> Oh! what was love made for, if 'tis not the same
> Through joy and through torment, through glory and shame?
> I know not, I ask not, if guilt's in that heart,
> I but know that I love thee, whatever thou art.
>
> Thou hast called me thy Angel in moments of bliss
> And thy Angel I'll be 'mid the horrors of this—
> Through the furnace, unshrinking, thy steps to pursue,
> And shield thee, and save thee—or perish there too!

It has been the fashion of the late days to deny Moore
Imagination while granting him Fancy—a distinction
originating with Coleridge, than whom no man more fully
comprehended the great powers of Moore.   The fact is,
that the fancy of this poet so far predominates over all his

other faculties, and over the fancy of all other men, as to have induced, very naturally, the idea that he is fanciful only. But never was there a greater mistake. Never was a grosser wrong done the fame of a true poet. In the compass of the English language I can call to mind no poem more profoundly, more weirdly imaginative in the best sense, than the lines commencing, "I would I were by that dim lake"—which are the composition of Thomas Moore. I regret that I am unable to remember them.

One of the noblest—and, speaking of Fancy, one of the most singularly fanciful of modern poets, was Thomas Hood. His "Fair Ines" had always for me an inexpressible charm :—

> Oh, saw ye not fair Ines?
>   She's gone into the West,
> To dazzle when the sun is down,
>   And rob the world of rest:
> She took our daylight with her,
>   The smiles that we love best,
> With morning blushes on her cheek
>   And pearls upon her breast.
>
> Oh, turn again, fair Ines,
>   Before the fall of night,
> For fear the moon should shine alone
>   And stars unrival'd bright;
> And blessed will the lover be
>   That walks beneath their light,
> And breathes the love against thy cheek
>   I dare not even write!
>
> Would I had been, fair Ines,
>   That gallant cavalier
> Who rode so gaily by thy side
>   And whisper'd thee so near!
> Were there no bonny dames at home,
>   Or no true lovers here,
> That he should cross the seas to win
>   The dearest of the dear?
>
> I saw thee, lovely Ines,
>   Descend along the shore,
> With bands of noble gentlemen,
>   And banners wav'd before;

And gentle youth and maidens gay,
   And snowy plumes they wore;
It would have been a beauteous dream,
   If it had been no more!

Alas, alas, fair Ines,
   She went away with song;
With Music waiting on her steps,
   And shoutings of the throng.
But some were sad and felt no mirth,
   But only Music's wrong,
In sounds that sang Farewell, Farewell,
   To her you've loved so long.

Farewell, farewell, fair Ines!
   That vessel never bore
So fair a lady on its deck,
   Nor danced so light before—
Alas for pleasure on the sea,
   And sorrow on the shore!
That smile that blest one lover's heart
   Has broken many more!

"The Haunted House," by the same author, is one of the truest poems ever written, one of the truest, one of the most unexceptionable, one of the most thoroughly artistic, both in its theme and in its execution. It is moreover, powerfully ideal—imaginative. I regret that its length renders it unsuitable for the purposes of this lecture. In place of it permit me to offer the universally appreciated "Bridge of Sighs":—

One more Unfortunate,
Weary of breath,
Rashly importunate
Gone to her death!

Take her up tenderly,
Lift her with care;
Fashion'd so slenderly,
Young and so fair!

Look at her garments
Clinging like cerements;
Whilst the wave constantly
Drips from her clothing:

Take her up instantly,
Loving, not loathing.

Touch her not scornfully;
Think of her mournfully,
Gently and humanly;
Not of the stains of her;
All that remains of her
Now is pure womanly.

Make no deep scrutiny
Into her mutiny,
Rash and undutiful;
Past all dishonor,
Death has left on her
Only the beautiful.

Still, for all slips of hers,
One of Eve's family—
Wipe those poor lips of hers
Oozing so clammily,
Loop up her tresses
Escaped from the comb,—
Her fair auburn tresses;
While wonderment guesses
Where was her home?

Who was her father?
Who was her mother?
Had she a sister?
Had she a brother?
Or was there a dearer one
Still, and a nearer one
Yet, than all other?

Alas! for the rarity
Of Christian charity
Under the sun!
Oh! it was pitiful!
Near a whole city full,
Home she had none.

Sisterly, brotherly,
Fatherly, motherly,
Feelings had changed:
Love, by harsh evidence,
Thrown from its eminence—
Even God's providence
Seeming estranged.

Where the lamps quiver
So far in the river,
With many a light
From window and casement
From garret to basement,
She stood, with amazement,
Houseless by night.

The bleak wind of March
Made her tremble and shiver;
But not the dark arch,
Or the black flowing river:
Mad from life's history,
Glad to death's mystery,
Swift to be hurl'd
Anywhere, anywhere,
Out of the world!

In she plunged boldly,
No matter how coldly
The rough river ran—
Over the brink of it:
Picture it—think of it,
Dissolute Man!
Lave in it, drink of it,
Then, if you can!

Take her up tenderly,
Lift her with care;
Fashion'd so slenderly,
Young and so fair!

'Ere her limbs frigidly
Stiffen too rigidly,—
Decently, kindly,
Smooth and compose them;
And her eyes, close them,
Staring so blindly!

Dreadfully staring
Through muddy impurity,
As when with the daring
Last look of despairing
Fixed on futurity.

Perishing gloomily,
Spurred by contumely,

Cold inhumanity,
Burning insanity,
Into her rest—
Cross her hands humbly,
As if praying dumbly,
Over her breast!

Owning her weakness,
Her evil behavior,
And leaving, with meekness,
Her sins to her Saviour!

The vigor of this poem is no less remarkable than its
pathos. The versification, although carrying the fanciful
to the very verge of the fantastic, is nevertheless admirably adapted to the wild insanity which is its thesis.

Among the minor poems of Lord Byron is one which
has never received from the critics the praise which it undoubtedly deserves:—

Though the day of my destiny's over,
  And the star of my fate hath declined,
Thy soft heart refused to discover
  The faults which so many could find;
Though thy soul with my grief was acquainted,
  It shrunk not to share it with me,
And the love which my spirit hath painted
  It never hath found but in thee.

Then when nature around me is smiling,
  The last smile which answers to mine,
I do not believe it beguiling,
  Because it reminds me of thine;
And when winds are at war with the ocean,
  As the breasts I believed in with me,
If their billow excite an emotion,
  It is that they bear me from thee.

Though the rock of my last hope is shivered,
  And its fragments are sunk in the wave,
Though I feel that my soul is delivered
  To pain—it shall not be its slave.
There is many a pang to pursue me:
  They may crush, but they shall not contemn—
They may torture, but shall not subdue me—
  'Tis of thee that I think—not of them.

Though human, thou didst not deceive me,
  Though woman, thou didst not forsake,
Though loved, thou forborest to grieve me,
  Though slandered, thou never couldst shake—
Though trusted, thou didst not disclaim me,
  Though parted, it was not to fly,
Though watchful, 'twas not to defame me,
  Nor mute that the world might belie.

Yet I blame not the world, nor despise it,
  Nor the war of the many with one—
If my soul was not fitted to prize it,
  'Twas folly not sooner to shun:
And if dearly that error hath cost me,
  And more than I once could foresee,
I have found that whatever it lost me,
  It could not deprive me of thee.

From the wreck of the past, which hath perished,
  Thus much I at least may recall,
It hath taught me that which I most cherished
  Deserved to be dearest of all;
In the desert a fountain is springing,
  In the wide waste there still is a tree,
And a bird in the solitude singing,
  Which speaks to my spirit of thee.

Although the rhythm here is one of the most difficult, the versification could scarcely be improved. No nobler theme ever engaged the pen of poet. It is the soul-elevating idea that no man can consider himself entitled to complain of Fate while in his adversity he still retains the unwavering love of woman.

From Alfred Tennyson, although in perfect sincerity I regard him as the noblest poet that ever lived, I have myself time to cite only a very brief specimen. I call him, and think him, the noblest of poets, not because the impressions he produces are at all times the most profound— not because the poetical excitement which he induces is at all times the most intense—but because it is at all times the most ethereal—in other words, the most elevating and most pure. No poet is so little of the earth, earthy. What I am about to read is from his last long poem, " The Princess ":—

Tears, idle tears, I know not what they mean,
Tears from the depth of some divine despair
Rise in the heart, and gather to the eyes,
In looking on the happy Autumn fields,
And thinking of the days that are no more.

Fresh as the first beam glittering on a sail,
That brings our friends up from the underworld,
Sad as the last which reddens over one
That sinks with all we love below the verge;
So sad, so fresh, the days that are no more.

Ah, sad and strange as in dark summer dawns
The earliest pipe of half-awaken'd birds
To dying ears, when unto dying eyes
The casement slowly grows a glimmering square;
So sad, so strange, the days that are no more.

Dear as remember'd kisses after death
And sweet as those by hopeless fancy feign'd
On lips that are for others; deep as love,
Deep as first love, and wild with all regret;
O Death in Life, the days that are no more.

Thus, although in a very cursory and imperfect manner, I have endeavored to convey to you my conception of the Poetic Principle. It has been my purpose to suggest that, while this principle itself is strictly and simply the Human Aspiration for Supernal Beauty, the manifestation of the Principle is always found in an elevating excitement of the soul, quite independent of that passion which is the intoxication of the Heart, or of that truth which is the satisfaction of the Reason. For in regard to passion, alas! its tendency is to degrade rather than to elevate the soul. Love, on the contrary,—Love, the truth, the divine Eros—the Uranian as distinguished from the Dionæan Venus—is unquestionably the purest and truest of all poetical themes. And in regard to Truth, if, to be sure, through the attainment of a truth we are led to perceive a harmony where none was apparent before, we experience at once the true poetical effect, but this effect is referable to the harmony alone, and not in the least degree to the truth which merely served to render the harmony manifest.

We shall reach, however, more immediately a distinct

conception of what the true Poetry is, by mere reference to a few of the simple elements which induce in the Poet himself the true poetical effect.   He recognizes the ambrosia which nourishes his soul in the bright orbs that shine in heaven, in the volutes of the flower, in the clustering of low shrubberies, in the waving of the grain-fields, in the slanting of tall eastern trees, in the blue distance of mountains, in the grouping of clouds, in the twinkling of half-hidden brooks, in the gleaming of silver rivers, in the repose of sequestered lakes, in the star-mirroring depth of lonely wells.   He perceives it in the songs of birds, in the harp of Æolus, in the sighing of the night-wind, in the repining voice of the forest, in the surf that complains to the shore, in the fresh breath of the woods, in the scent of the violet, in the voluptuous perfume of the hyacinth, in the suggestive odor that comes to him at eventide from far distant undiscovered islands, over dim oceans, illimitable and unexplored.   He owns it in all noble thoughts, in all unworldly motives, in all holy impulses, in all chivalrous, generous, and self-sacrificing deeds.   He feels it in the beauty of woman, in the grace of her step, in the lustre of her eye, in the melody of her voice, in her soft laughter, in her sigh, in the harmony of the rustling of her robes. He deeply feels it in her winning endearments, in her burning enthusiasms, in her gentle charities, in her meek and devotional endurances, but above all, ah, far above all, he kneels to it, he worships it in the faith, in the purity, in the strength, in the altogether divine majesty of her love.

Let me conclude by the recitation of yet another brief poem, one very different in character from any that I have before quoted.   It is by Motherwell, and is called "The Song of the Cavalier."   With our modern and altogether rational ideas of the absurdity and impiety of warfare, we are not precisely in that frame of mind best adapted to sympathize with the sentiments, and thus to appreciate the real excellence of the poem.   To do this fully we must identify ourselves in fancy with the soul of the old cavalier:—

> A steed! a steed! of matchless speede!
> A sword of metal keene!
> Al else to noble heartes is drosse—
> Al else on earth is meane

The neighynge of the war-horse prowde,
  The rowleing of the drum,
The clangour of the trumpet lowde—
  Be soundes from heaven that come.
And oh! the thundering press of knightes
  When as their war-cryes welle,
May tole from heaven an angel bright,
  And rowse a fiend from hell.

Then mounte! then mounte, brave gallants, all,
  And don your helmes amaine;
Deathe's couriers, Fame and Honour, call
  Us to the fielde againe.
No shrewish tears shall fill your eye
  When the sword-hilt's in our hand—
Heart-whole we'll part, and no whit sighe
  For the fayrest of the land;
Let piping swaine, and craven wight,
  Thus weepe and puling crye,
Our business is like men to fight,
  And hero-like to die!

JAMES BURTON POND

MEMORIES OF THE LYCEUM

[Lecture by Major J. B. Pond, lecture manager (born in Cuba, Allegany County, N. Y., June 11, 1838; ———), delivered originally in New York City in 1895, and subsequently repeated in various cities.]

LADIES AND GENTLEMEN:—My friends often ask how I got into the lyceum business. I drifted into it, the same as most people do who have to find some place for which they are fitted. It was my fortune to be raised on the frontier. My father was one of the pioneers of Wisconsin. He was an abolitionist. The Bible and the New York "Trybune," not "Tribune," were almost synonymous in our family, and about the only library we had. Wisconsin was a sort of refuge for the fugitive slave, and my father kept an underground station. Many a night I have slept out on the prairie with some runaway slaves, with father and the neighbors protecting them against the United States Marshal. I found myself, when eighteen years of age, carrying a Sharp's rifle in 1856 with John Brown, in Kansas.

In 1873, after the war and emancipation of the slaves, I found myself associated with the first Gentile paper in Utah—"The Salt Lake Tribune." About that time the railroad had reached Zion, and there was a tremendous influx of Gentiles. We had territorial officers who could not be used by the Mormons, and there was considerable excitement. President Brigham Young and several Mormon leaders were put under arrest. There were so many Gentiles that they could not possibly find accommodations at the hotels, and Brigham Young proclaimed to his people that they could open their houses and receive them

as boarders, and that a fair price for their board—not ex-
orbitant, but a fair price—should be charged. He thought
three dollars a week a good price for board.

It happened that a Methodist minister (the Rev. C. C.
Stratton) and his wife obtained board with Ann Eliza
Young, then Brigham Young's last and nineteenth wife,
who was keeping house by herself in a small cottage. Ann
Eliza was born in Mormonism and reared in Utah by her
mother, who was an educated woman and one of the first
converts of Joseph Smith, living in Nauvoo, Ill., for several years before they migrated to Utah. Ann Eliza was a
very intelligent woman, but her whole life was circum-
scribed by Mormonism. She had never attended any
other church, and never read any other literature than
Mormon books. She was a conscientious woman. It
was through this Methodist minister and his wife that she
apostatized.

One evening it was arranged that Ann Eliza should tell
her story to the guests of the hotel (the Walker House),
where she had taken refuge under the protection of the
officials of the territory—Governor Woods and Chief Justice McKean, who lived there. I was there also and had
something to do with making the arrangements. She did
give her story—the most interesting and thrilling story
that anybody ever heard. That speech was telegraphed
to the Associated Press, and the next day came telegrams
from theatrical managers, showmen, and speculators from
all parts of the country. One was from P. T. Barnum
and another from James Redpath, the owner of the
Lyceum Bureau, in Boston, whom I had met and known
in Kansas in 1856. It asked her to lecture.

Our people decided that if Ann Eliza could tell that
story in Washington, we would get some attention and
legislation. Up to that time we had been able to get little attention and no legislation. I happened to be available and went to Washington with her. I made a proposition that if she would go on a lecture tour I would man-
age it. She accepted it. That's where I first became a
manager.

Although she was to speak first in Washington, they
were determined to hear her in Laramie and Denver en
route. I got the school-room in Laramie, charged $1.50

and sold 400 tickets, and took in $600 that evening. Next in Denver, she spoke in the New Baptist Church, the largest auditorium in the city at that time.

Armed with letters of introduction to Speaker James G. Blaine, President U. S. Grant, and many members of Congress, we reached Washington, where we got into the Speaker's room and she sent her card to Speaker Blaine. He was in the Speaker's chair. He came out and shook hands with her. He discovered at once that she was a lady, a woman with a cause, and an earnest one, and in a moment his attention was riveted. In a few minutes somebody else came into the Speaker's room, and soon that room was packed with members of Congress. She held an ovation for two hours. Everybody wanted to see and hear her. Two days after that she did tell her story in Washington. Forty-eight hours later the Poland bill for the relief of the oppressed in Utah was a law.

I took a desk in Mr. Redpath's office in Boston, and booked Mrs. Young's time in New England and the Eastern States, while with an Eastern lady as chaperone, she traveled and lectured nightly to as large audiences as were being drawn by the most popular lecturers of that period. At the end of the season she had earned over $20,000. She was able in two years to leave Utah with her children and her relations, and she never returned.

I shall now tell of some of the famous men and women who have been lyceum favorites that I have known since I began the conduct of a lyceum bureau in 1875, and most of whom it has been my pleasure to call my friends.

The great triumvirate of lecture kings consisted of Gough, Beecher, and Wendell Phillips. Other men for a season, and sometimes for a few years, were as popular as any of them, but it was a calcium-light popularity, whereas the popularity of the "Big Three" endured for their entire lives.

Phillips held his place the longest, beginning lyceum work about 1845, and continuing it to his death, nearly forty years later. Gough was the most supremely popular —not the greatest of the three intellectually, but most level to the largest number of the plain people. Beecher came parallel with him and had a higher influence. Beecher touched the hearts of men; Gough held by the

fear of the effects of wrong-doing; Phillips, through the
intellect, reached the conscience of his generation.

John B. Gough never faced an audience that he did not
capture and captivate; and not in the United States only,
not in the North only, where his popularity never wavered,
but in the South, where Yankees were not in favor, and in
the Canadian Provinces, where they were disliked, and
in every part of England, Scotland, and Ireland as well.
He delighted all kinds and conditions of men. He was at
his best before an educated audience in an evangelical
community. But when he addressed a " mission " audience
in North street, Boston, or in the Five Points, in New
York, he charmed the gamin and the poorest classes who
gathered there as much as he charmed the cultivated as-
semblages in Music Hall, Boston, then admitted to be the
finest audiences that Boston and its suburbs could turn out.

Mr. Gough never asked a fee in his life. He left his
remuneration to the public who employed him. It rose
year after year, beginning with less than a dollar at times,
until, when the bureau did his business for him, it reached
from $200, the lowest fee, to $500 a night. In the last
years of his life his income exceeded $30,000. He prob-
ably delivered more lectures than any man who has lived
in the present age. From a carefully kept record we find
that from 1842 to 1852 he lectured on an average of 300
times a year, making 3,000 lectures. From 1862 to 1870
he averaged 260 times a year, or 2,080 lectures on temperance. Of these, 1,160 were delivered in Great Britain.
After 1870 Mr. Gough lectured on miscellaneous subjects. Each year he prepared a new lecture upon a fresh
topic. From 1861 to the time of his death, February 11,
1886, he delivered 3,526 lectures, making in all 9,600 addresses before 9,000,000 hearers. It was my privilege, in
1879, to see in Mr. Gough's library four large books containing the names of over 140,000 men, women, and children who, by his own personal efforts had been induced
to sign the pledge.

It was the habit of John B. Gough, for forty years, to
carry two overcoats on his lecture tours. After his lectures he put both of them on—the first, a light one, which
he buttoned up tight, and the second, a very heavy one, a
sort of combination of heavy ulster and the regulation

overcoat. His two-hour lecture was an unbroken succession of contortions and antics that left him dripping with perspiration. It required all this clothing to protect his body from the air before he changed his wet clothing for dry. On his return to his hotel, Mrs. Gough was always in waiting with fresh clothing. A valet at once set to work rubbing him down, exactly as is the custom of grooming a racehorse at the end of the heat. After this process he appeared apparently as fresh as ever. He would eat a bowl of bread and milk, and always an old-fashioned bowl. Mrs. Gough was his constant companion, but did not attend the lectures. During the last twelve years of their travel together she did not hear him once. Gough was a man of the people, the son of a workingman, and himself a workingman, self-educated but not what is technically called a scholar.

Wendell Phillips was the most polished and graceful orator our country ever produced. He spoke as quietly as if he were talking in his own parlor and almost entirely without gestures, yet he had as great a power over all kinds of audiences as any American of whom we have any record. Often called before howling mobs, who had come to the lecture-room to prevent him from being heard, and who would shout and sing to drown his voice, he never failed to subdue them in a short time. One illustration of his power and tact occurred in Boston. The majority of the audience was hostile. They yelled and sang and completely drowned his voice. The reporters were seated in a row just under the platform, in the place where the orchestra plays in an ordinary theatre. Phillips made no attempt to address the noisy crowd, but bent over and seemed to be speaking in a low tone to the reporters. By and by the curiosity of the audience was excited; they ceased to clamor and tried to hear what he was saying to the reporters. Phillips looked at them and said quietly:—

"Go on, gentlemen, go on. I do not need your ears. Through these pencils I speak to thirty millions of people."

Not a voice was raised again. The mob had found its master and stayed whipped until he sat down.

Eloquent as he was as a lecturer, he was far more effective as a debater. Debate was for him the flint and steel which brought out all his fire. His memory was something wonderful. He would listen to an elaborate speech for hours, and, without a single note of what had been said, in writing, reply to every part of it as fully and completely as if the speech were written out before him. Those who heard him only on the platform, and when not confronted by an opponent, have a very limited comprehension of his wonderful resources as a speaker. He never hesitated for a word, or failed to employ the word best fitted to express his thought on the point under discussion. Mr. Phillips was decidedly old-fashioned in many of his ways. When at home, for example, he did his own marketing, and he knew how to buy. His chief purchases, however, were always in the dainties for his invalid wife. His own table habits were of the simplest. He was quite apt to answer his own door-bell.

William Lloyd Garrison was the equal of Phillips in one respect only—in moral courage and unselfish devotion to the slave.

There never was a more benevolent face than William Lloyd Garrison's. He had a kindly eye, a winning smile, a gentleness of way, a crisp, straightforward style of talking, and a merciless movement in straight lines of thought. He visited England after the war was over and the emancipation of the slaves was accomplished, and received unusual courtesies. At a dinner given him by the British Anti-Slavery Society, he was presented with a gold watch. As he took it in his hand he said: "Well, gentlemen, if this had been a rotten egg, I should have known what to do with it, but as it is a gold watch, I have nothing to say."

Charles Sumner was an aristocrat. He was my father's ideal. After I had got back from Kansas and visited my father's home in Wisconsin, father said to me: "James, the Honorable Charles Sumner is going to speak at R——. We must hear him."

So we arranged to go. We walked nine miles to hear him speak. My father never spoke of him without giving him his title. He had enjoyed that speech intensely. I do not know whether I did or not. Father occupied a front seat with the intention of rushing up to the platform and greeting him by the hand when he was finished, but the Honorable Charles was too quick for him. He disappeared, got to his hotel, and nobody saw him.

Father said: "James, the Honorable Charles Sumner is going to Milwaukee to-morrow morning, and we can ride with him a part of the way." We were on the train early the next morning, and so was the Honorable Charles Sumner. He was sitting reading in the drawing-room car. Father stepped up and said: "The Honorable Charles Sumner? I have read all of your speeches. I feel that it is the duty of every American to take you by the hand. This is my son. He has just returned from the Kansas conflict."

Honorable Charles Sumner did not see father nor his son, but he saw the porter, and said: "Can you get me a place where I will be undisturbed?"

Colonel Robert G. Ingersoll was without doubt one of the greatest popular orators of the age. He never received the full credit due to his great success as an orator during his lifetime, as his vehement assaults on the Christian religion aroused so many and such powerful enmities. But without regarding his creed, judging him solely by his power as an orator, no nation can to-day produce his equal. There was poetry, wit, humor, sarcasm, and tenderest pathos in nearly every lecture he delivered, whether on religion or politics.

When coming from New England one day with Mr. Beecher, Colonel Ingersoll was in the same car. After a pleasant salutation between the two, the Colonel went to his seat. In his mischievous way, Mr. Beecher said: "I have written that man's epitaph." He showed me written on the margin of a newspaper, with his pencil, two words: "Robert Burns."

Henry Ward Beecher was my nearest and dearest friend for eleven years. Excepting only Arizona and New Mexico, there was not a State or Territory in the Union in which we had not traveled together. I was near him in the days of 1875-77, at the time of his deepest sorrow, when he was reviled and spit upon; I saw the majestic courage with which he passed through gaping crowds at railroad stations, and at the entrances of hotels and public halls—a courage which I had not conceived mere human-

ity could possess. I have looked upon him when I felt
that I would give my poor life a thousand times could that
sacrifice alleviate the sufferings that I knew he was under-
going.

It was on January 23, 1877, that I had arranged with
W. T. Powell, of Richmond, Va., for Mr. Beecher to lecture in that city. Mr. Powell was manager of the Richmond Theatre, and was to pay $400 for the lecture. It
was to be on Tuesday evening, and as Mr. Beecher lectured Monday evening in Baltimore, we had arranged to
take the sleeper immediately after the Baltimore lecture
and be in Richmond early the following morning.

As we went aboard the sleeper at Baltimore a telegram
was put into my hands, which read as follows: "No use
coming. Beecher will not be allowed to speak in Richmond. No tickets sold."

I at once replied: "Have started. Mr. Beecher will be
on hand to keep his contract." I did not mention the incident to Mr. Beecher.

Just before our arrival in Richmond the following morning, Mr. Powell came to me on the train and told me that
the feeling against Mr. Beecher was so bitter that it would
not do for him to attempt to speak; that not a ticket had
been sold, and he dared not advertise. Mr. Beecher and
I went direct to the Exchange Hotel, and as we registered
our names I saw at once that there was a general disposition, from the hotel-clerk down to the negro porter and
the bell-boy, to guy us. We went down to breakfast,
and the waiter and head-waiter who seated us were dis-
gustingly uncivil. Mr. Beecher made no remarks. We
ate our breakfast, and as we passed out of the dining-room
into a long hall we met a pretty little golden-haired child.
Mr. Beecher, in his characteristic manner, stopped and
began talking to and caressing the child, taking some
candy from his pocket (he never was without bait for children), offered it, and was just getting into the little,
girl's favor, when the mother came along and snatched
her away, as though she were rescuing her from a fierce
beast of prey.

Mr. Beecher walked quietly to his room. I left instructions at the hotel office that no one was to knock
at his door. Mr. Powell called and assured me that it

would be all Mr. Beecher's life was worth to attempt to speak in Richmond. I told him that I would let him off that night from his contract if he would rent me the theatre. He consented, and I at once got out some bills and dodgers and advertised Mr. Beecher to speak that evening. The Legislature was in session and passed an informal vote that none of them would go near the theatre. The Tobacco Board did the same.

Evening arrived and I could get no one to attend the door, so I did it myself. Mr. Powell applied for an extra force of a dozen police, which was of no account, as they were wholly in sympathy with the crowd. The Rev. Dr. Grey, the principal Presbyterian minister, and the head of a leading institution of learning in Richmond, wrote the chief of police that though he distinctly wished it to be understood that he did not endorse or favor Mr. Beecher's speaking in Richmond, he sincerely hoped that the threat to egg Mr. Beecher would not be carried into effect. As each member of the Legislature and the Tobacco Board knew that none of the other members would attend the lecture, each embraced the opportunity to go; and there, to their surprise, they all met. It was a crowd of men who made the best of the joke they had played upon themselves. They were hilarious and disrespectful.

The time came for me to go after Mr. Beecher. I had no door-tender, but the theatre was full of men, and my pockets were stuffed with dollars, so I left the door to take care of itself. I found him ready. While in the carriage on our way from the hotel to the theatre not a word passed between us, and during the day neither of us had spoken of the situation. When we arrived at the stage door of the theatre the dozen policemen were keeping the crowd back. As we alighted from the carriage at the door a general yell went up. We met Mr. Powell on the stage. He called me to one side and said:—

"Don't you introduce Mr. Beecher. The gallery is full of eggs. You will have trouble."

I stepped into the waiting-room. Mr. Beecher said: "Go ahead; I am ready." I walked on the stage and he followed. As we sat down I saw the theatre full of men only. The crowd was disposed to be uncivil; canes began to rake the baluster of the balcony railing and feet to

pound the floor, and in less than a minute a yell fairly
shook the theatre.   Mr. Beecher signaled me to proceed.

I stood a moment for them to get quiet, and then introduced him to his first Virginian audience.

Mr. Beecher was to speak on "Hard Times," but had
decided to change the subject to the "Ministry of
Wealth."   As he rose and stepped toward the footlights,
another yell went up.   He stood unmoved, and waited for
some time; finally a lull came, and he began.   He said
that there was a natural law that brains and capital controlled the commercial world, and it could not be changed
even by the Virginia Legislature, which opened with
prayer and closed with the benediction. The Legislature
were all there, and the public, like any other public, were
ready to accept any good-natured drive at the Legislature.   It was not many minutes before the audience was
in full sympathy with the speaker, and for two and a half
hours Mr. Beecher addressed that crowd, swaying them
with his mighty eloquence, and telling them such truths
as they never before had listened to.   His peroration was a
tribute to the Commonwealth of Virginia, the Mother of
Presidents, her history and her people, and closed with a
brief retrospect: how she had prospered when she set her
mark high and bred her sons for Presidents, and position,
but how changed when she came to breed men for the
market; how manfully and nobly her worthy sons had
kissed the sod, and how sad had been her lot.   But in all
her prosperity and adversity, God had not forsaken her.
Industry brought prosperity, and soon, very soon, Virginia was to be one of the brightest stars in the constellation of States.

Such applause and cheers as he got during that address
I have never before or since heard.   He stepped off the
stage and into the carriage, and we were in our rooms
at the hotel before half the audience could get out of the
theatre.   After getting to his room Mr. Beecher threw
himself back in a large chair in front of a blazing wood
fire and laughingly said: "Don't you think we have captured Richmond?"

He had no more than spoken when the door opened
and a crowd of men came rushing in.   My first impression
was that it was a mob, as it did not seem that there had

been time for them to come from the theatre; but I was mistaken.

The foremost was a tall man with a slouch hat. (They were all in slouch hats.) He said: " Mr. Beecher, this is our ' Leftenant '-Governor. We have come to thank you for that great speech. This is our member for So-and-so, and this is Judge Harris," and so on, introducing a score or more of prominent Virginians. " Mr. Beecher, we want you to stay and speak for us to-morrow evening. We want our women to hear you," etc.

Mr. Beecher was in his most happy humor. He shook the Virginians warmly by the hand. He told them that he was announced for Washington the following evening, and his time was all booked for the season. They offered to raise $500 if he would remain over. The following morning at seven o'clock many Virginians were at the station to see him off. All the morning papers contained extensive synopses of the lecture and favorable notices.

After that first appearance Mr. Beecher spoke twice in Richmond to the choicest audiences that the old capital could turn out. I consider this the greatest lecture I ever knew Mr. Beecher to give.

In 1863 Mr. Beecher made a single speech in Great Britain, as Oliver Wendell Holmes wrote, but it was delivered in piecemeal in different places. Its exordium was on October 9, in Manchester—its peroration was pronounced on the 20th of the same month in Exeter Hall, London. The public is more or less familiar with the result of that mission.

After a few months' absence he returned to America, having finished a more remarkable embassy than any envoy who has represented us in Europe since Franklin pleaded the cause of the young Republic at the Court of Versailles. He had no official existence; but through the heart of the people he reached nobles, ministers, courtiers, and the throne itself. He whom " The Times " attacked, he whom " Punch " caricatured, was a power in the land. The change of the ruling classes in England, who were strong for the South, was at once manifest. As Mr. Scott, who introduced him in Exeter Hall, told me years later: " You should have been here to witness the effect of that speech as he swayed his enthusiastic audience hither and thither by his convincing arguments and appeal."

After my first experience as a manager with Ann Eliza Young and my joining the Redpath Lyceum Bureau, the field enlarged quite as rapidly as was desirable. Women speakers were notably in demand, quite in contrast with the public requirements of later years. The suffrage agitation held place in the North with anti-slavery discussions and correlative topics. It was the twin sister of the temperance movement which Gough so graphically and eloquently presented, and there were strong personalities among the women lecturers. Their cause commanded, in days of public scorn and denial, the splendid service of orators like Wendell Phillips, Frederick Douglass, and George William Curtis, as well as scholars and speakers like Higginson, Hale, and others whose names come to me in crowding memories.

But their most efficient arguments for mental, civic, and industrial equality were always best illustrated in the person and speech of their own brilliant agitators: Lucy Stone, the incomparable Susan B. Anthony, Elizabeth Cady Stanton, and a score and more of others.

Susan B. Anthony is one of the best-known women of our times, and one of our ablest women orators. She will occupy in the history of the Women's Rights movement the same position that William Lloyd Garrison held in the history of the anti-slavery movement—the position of a sincere pioneer whose fidelity to principle and tenacity of purpose never faltered or failed. She deserves a place in the foremost ranks of the champions of her sex, for she has given her whole life and her whole heart to the work. It seems probable that these veteran women may live to see the triumph of their cause.

Julia Ward Howe comes from a long line of Puritan ancestry. She was an ardent worker in the anti-slavery cause. In 1856-57 she and her husband, Dr. Howe, edited an anti-slavery paper, the Boston "Commonwealth," and were leaders with Garrison, Sumner, Phillips, Higginson, and Theodore Parker. It was Dr. and Mrs. Howe who brought about meetings in Boston for the discussion of the problems of the Abolitionists on one side and pro-slavery advocates on the other. Robert Toombs of

Georgia, and Colonel Sam Houston of Texas, took part. "I remember," said Mrs. Howe, "we had lively times."

All through the Kansas Free-State struggle and the startling raid at Harper's Ferry, in which the Doctor's name was closely connected with that of "Old John Brown," Mrs. Howe was the unflinching helpmate of the brave philanthropist and scholar with whose name her own is interwoven. In 1861 Mrs. Howe wrote the "Battle-Hymn of the Republic."

She has spoken to French scholars and wits in their own tongue and chief city. In Florence and Rome she has spoken to Italian audiences, having in Rome, during her last visit, also read two sermons to liberal congregations. She is a person of great wit, as well as learning, being as a speaker essentially and intellectually womanly; but she can startle her audience even now by some unexpected and spirited outburst of opinion that justifies her high reputation as a poet and her noble record as a brave, clear thinker. She could always have more engagements than she desired.

Mrs. Livermore is the most successful woman on the platform I have known. She was one of the first American women to fill a pulpit or occupy an editorial position. She had given her public "testimony" against chattel slavery before her marriage, upon her return home from Virginia, where, in the early forties, she had been occupied as a governess. I first saw her among the reporters in the Wigwam in Chicago in 1860, when Abraham Lincoln was first nominated for President.

At that time she was the busiest woman in the Northwest, editing her husband's paper, carrying on a regular correspondence for other journals, writing books and magazine articles, managing hospitals and homes, while advancing an extended temperance agitation. Withal her home was always attended to.

The Civil War found the largest of places for this great-brained woman. At the request of President Henry W. Bellows of the United States Sanitary Commission, she and her friend, Miss Jane O. Hoge of Chicago, became associates in the Northwest and co-operated in all the vast labors of both sanitary and Christian commissions. Soon after being placed in charge of the North-western branch, she, with a few other women, went to Washington to talk with President Lincoln.

"Can no woman go to the front?" Mrs. Livermore asked.

"No civilian, either man or woman, is permitted by law," said Mr. Lincoln. But the great heart of the greatest man in America was superior to the law, and he placed not a straw in their way.

Mrs. Livermore's first broad experience of the war was after the battle of Fort Donelson. There were no hospitals for the men, and the wounded were hauled to the steamers in rough Tennessee wagons, most of them dying before they reached St. Louis. Some poor fellows were chopped out of the frozen mud where they had been lying from Saturday morning until Sunday evening.

She asked a blue-eyed lad of nineteen, with both legs and arms shattered:—

"How did it happen that you were left so long?"

"Why, you see they could not stop to bother with us. They had to take the fort."

Petroleum V. Nasby was the *nom de plume* of David R. Locke of Ohio. At the beginning of the Civil War he was a young and obscure man, editing a little country paper in the interior of Ohio. It occurred to him that it would be a good idea to write a series of letters, one a week, exposing and ridiculing the Democratic party. These letters pretended to be written in earnest by a Confederate war office-seeker. They succeeded in deceiving even the county Democrats for a time.

One meeting of "the faithful" framed a resolution commending the fidelity to Democratic principles shown in the Nasby letters, but urging Mr. Nasby, for the sake of policy, not to be so outspoken. The sarcasm was so broad, that it is difficult if one reads them to-day for the first time, to understand how the most illiterate partisans could mistake them. But at a time when men's passions were red-hot, and their prejudices volcanic, they were universally applauded by the upholders of the Union. The circulation of Locke's paper rose rapidly, and he became one of the most famous men in America in less than a year. He soon bought an interest in the Toledo "Blade," which he made one of the most popular journals of the continent.

From being a poor country editor, Locke had become one of the wealthiest men in the West, and died a millionaire.

Of course, as soon as he had won a national reputation, he was invited to lecture. He used to boast that he made, during his first lecture season, the longest and most lucrative lecture tour recorded in the annals of the lyceum. He lectured every secular night for nine or ten months, and made over $30,000 by the tour. His lectures until some time after the war were very popular; but he had none of the graces of the orator, and as the war fever abated, he gradually lost his hold, and retired from the field.

Josh Billings was a popular humorous lecturer for several years. There is hardly a village of five thousand people and over within a radius of five hundred miles of New York where he has not given his lecture on " Milk," the only lecture which he ever had. He insisted that a tumbler of milk should always be on the table in front of him, to which he never alluded in any way whatever. He always sat down while he lectured. " I lecture for nothing, with $100 thrown in," he said. He was a delightful man to know personally—kind, gentle, sincere, and very sympathetic, with an intense fondness for children. A child riding in the same car with him could hardly escape his patronage and attention, and what was specially peculiar about him, as with Mr. Beecher, he always attracted children to him.

" Mark Twain " became a lecturer in California in 1869, after he had returned to San Francisco from the Sandwich Islands. He had written from there a series of picturesque and humorous letters for the Sacramento " Union," a California journal, and was asked to lecture about the Islands. He tells of his first experience with great glee. He had written the lecture and committed it to memory, and was satisfied with it. Still, he dreaded a failure on the first night, as he had had no experience in addressing audiences. Accordingly, he made an arrangement with a woman friend, whose family was to occupy one of the boxes, to start the applause if he should give her the sign

by looking in her direction and stroking his mustache.
He thought that if he failed to " strike " the audience he
would be encouraged by a round of applause, if any one
would start it after he had made a good point.

Instead of failure his lecture was a boundless success.
The audience rapturously applauded every point, and
" Mark " forgot all about his instructions to the lady.
Finally, as he was thinking of some new point that occurred to him as he was talking, without a thought of the
lady at all, he unconsciously put his hand up to his
mustache, and happened to turn in the direction of the
box. He had said nothing just then to cause even his ap-
preciative audience to applaud; but the lady took his action for the signal, and nearly broke her fan in striking
it against the edge of the box. The whole house joined
her applause.

This unexpected and malapropos applause almost
knocked " Mark " off his pins; but he soon recovered himself, and became at once one of the favorites of the platform. He lectured a year or two in the West, and then,
by Petroleum V. Nasby's advice, in 1872-73 James Redpath invited him to come East, and he made his first appearance in Boston, in the Redpath Lyceum Music Hall.
His success was instantaneous, and he has ever since remained the universal platform favorite to this date, not
only in America, in Australia, in India, in the Cape Colonies, and throughout Great Britain; but in Austria and in
Germany, where large crowds pay higher prices to see
and to hear " Mark Twain " than any other private citizen
that has ever lived.

" Mark Twain " eats only when he is hungry. I have
known him to go days without eating a particle of food;
at the same time he would be smoking constantly when
he was not sleeping. He insisted that the stomach would
call when in need, and it did. I have known him to sit
for hours in a smoking-car on a cold day, smoking his pipe
and reading his German book with the window wide open.
I once said: " Mark, do you know it's a cold day and you
are exposing yourself before that open window, and you
are booked to lecture to-night? "

" I do—know—all—about it. I am letting some of
God's fresh air into my lungs for that purpose. My stom-

ach is all right and under these conditions I am not afraid of taking cold."

"But," said I, "the car is cold, and you are making the passengers uncomfortable by insisting on that window being wide open."

"They deserve to be uncomfortable for not knowing how to live and take care of themselves." He closed the window, however.

"Mark" seldom had a cold, and with the exception of carbuncles was never ill.

Business relations and traveling bring out the nature of a man. After my close relations with "Mark Twain" for sixteen years, I can say that he is not only what the world knows him to be, a humorist, a philosopher, and a genius, but a sympathetic, honest, brave gentleman.

Bill Nye was an editor when I first met him, and as I had been a printer, of course I felt akin to him. His first lecture under my auspices was given in Bridgeport, Conn.

Mr. Nye, like every human who attempts to make a whole evening of fun, found lecturing irksome. The audience would fairly bubble over with laughter until every fun-liking muscle of their faces relaxed and left one sombre wet-blanket expression all over the assemblage; and there they had to sit, and the humorist had to proceed to the end of the programme without a response. It was the same with "Mark Twain" until he took a running-mate and interspersed pathos by introducing George W. Cable, and by means of a varied programme achieved the greatest success ever known in the way of a platform entertainment.

James Whitcomb Riley's recitals of his own pathetic and humorous dialect poems have touched the tender chords in the hearts of the people, and they have vibrated in sympathy with the joys of his creations. His name is one of the best-loved household words in our cultivated American homes.

After he had acquired fame as a very successful reader of his poems, Mr. Nye thought that by combining with him they might be as successful as some others. So Riley was approached and the result was a combination of humor and pathos for the season of 1888-89.

The Nye-Riley combination started in Newark, N. J.,

November 13, 1888. It was our trial venture. I was ill
and unable to be present. The receipts were light, for
both men were of Western fame, and had yet to acquire
reputations in the East. They found some fault because
I was not present, so I got out of bed and went the following evening to Orange, N. J., where we found a very
small audience, so small that Nye refused to go on, and
wished to end the business then and there. It was not
until after much persuasion that he consented to appear.
The show was a great success "artistically," but the box-
office receipts were only fifty-four dollars.

It was not a pleasant day for the manager, that followed. The Actors' Fund had an entertainment in one
of the theatres, and I had contributed these "Twins of
Genius" as my share of the numerous attractions. They
were the success of the occasion, and the newspapers so
declared the next day. From that time, applications began to come in from all over the country, East, West,
North, and South. I ran the show myself in Boston, se-
curing Tremont Temple for the occasion.

"Mark Twain" had come to Boston on purpose to attend the entertainment, as he had never heard these
"Twins of Genius." I caught him in the lobby of the
Parker House, and told him that he must introduce them.
He replied that he believed I was his mortal enemy, and
determined that he should never have an evening's enjoyment in my presence. He consented, however, and
conducted his brother humorist and the Hoosier poet to
the platform. Mark's presence was a surprise to the audience, and when they recognized him the demonstration
was tremendous. The audience rose in a body, and men
and women shouted at the very top of their voices. Hand-
kerchiefs waved, the organist even opened every forte key
and pedal in the great organ, and the noise went on un-
abated for minutes. It took some time for the crowd to
get down to listening, but when they did subside, as Mark
stepped to the front, the silence was as impressive as the
noise had been, as Mark said afterward. At that supreme
moment nothing was heard but—silence! I had engaged
a stenographer to take down the speech, and this is what
"Mark" said:—

"I am very glad indeed to introduce these young people

to you and at the same time get acquainted with them myself. I have seen them more than once for a moment, but have not had the privilege of knowing them personally as intimately as I wanted to. I saw them first, a great many years ago, when Mr. Barnum had them, and they were just fresh from Siam. The ligature was their best hold then, but literature became their best hold later, when one of them committed an indiscretion, and they had to cut the old bond to accommodate the sheriff. In that old former time this one was Chang, that one was Eng. The sympathy existing between the two was most extraordinary; it was so fine, so strong, so subtle, that what the one ate the other digested, when one slept the other snored, if one sold a thing the other scooped the usufruct. This independent and yet dependent action was observable in all the details of their daily life—I mean this quaint and arbitrary distribution of originating cause and resulting effect between the two: between, I may say, this dynamo and this motor. Not that I mean that the one was always dynamo, and the other always motor—or, in other words, that the one was always the creating force, the other always the utilizing force,—no, no, for while it is true that within certain well-defined zones of activity, the one was always dynamo and the other always motor, within certain other well-defined zones these positions became exactly reversed. For instance, in moral matters Mr. Chang Riley was always dynamo, Mr. Eng Nye was always motor; for while Mr. Chang Riley had a high, in fact an abnormally high and fine, moral sense, he had no machinery to work it withal; whereas Mr. Eng Nye, who hadn't any moral sense at all, and hasn't yet, was equipped with all the necessary plant for putting a noble deed through, if he could only get the inspiration, on reasonable terms, outside. In intellectual matters, on the other hand, Mr. Eng Nye was always dynamo, Mr. Chang Riley was always motor; Mr. Eng Nye had a stately intellect, but couldn't make it go; Mr. Chang Riley hadn't, but could. That is to say, that while Mr. Chang Riley couldn't think things himself, he had a marvelous natural grace in setting them down and weaving them together when his pal furnished the raw material. Thus, working together, they made a strong team; laboring together, they could do

miracles; but break the circuit and both were impotent.
It has remained so to this day; they must travel together,
conspire together, beguile together, hoe, and plant, and
plow, and reap, and sell their public together, or there's
no result. I have made this explanation, this analysis, this
vivisection, so to speak, in order that you may enjoy these
delightful adventurers understandingly. When Mr. Eng
Nye's deep and broad and limpid philosophies flow by in
front of you, refreshing all the regions round about, with
their gracious floods, you will remember that it isn't his
water; it's the other man's, and he is only working the
pump. And when Mr. Chang Riley enchants your ear,
and soothes your spirit, and touches your heart with the
sweet and genuine music of his poetry—as sweet and
as genuine as any that his friends, the birds and the bees,
make about his other friends, the woods and the flowers,—
you will remember, while placing justice where justice is
due, that it isn't his music, but the other man's—he's only
turning the crank.

" I beseech for these visitors a fair field, a single-minded,
one-eyed umpire, and a score-bulletin barren of goose-
eggs if they earn it—and I judge they will and hope they
will. Mr. James Whitcomb Chang Riley will now go to
the bat."

It was a carnival of fun in every sense of the word.
Bostonians will not have another such treat in this generation. It was Mark's last appearance in Boston.

James Whitcomb Riley and Nye were a peculiar pair.
They were everlastingly playing practical jokes.

I remember when we were riding together, in the smoking compartment, between Columbus and Cincinnati.
Mr. Nye was a great smoker and Mr. Riley did not dislike
tobacco. An old farmer came over to Mr. Nye and said:—

" Are you Mr. Riley? I heard you was on the train."

" No, I am not Mr. Riley. He is over there."

" I knew his father and I would like to speak with him."

" Oh, speak with him, yes. But he is deaf, and you want
to speak loud."

So the farmer went over to him and said in a loud voice:
" Is this Mr. Riley? "

" Er, what? "

" Is this Mr. Riley? "

"What did you say?"

"Is this Mr. Riley?"

"Riley, oh! yes."

"I knew your father."

"No bother."

"I knew your father."

"What?"

"I knew your father!"

"Oh, so did I."

And in a few moments the farmer heard Nye and Riley talking in ordinary tones of voice. Imagine his chagrin!

Henry M. Stanley under my management, delivered one hundred lectures in America, after his discovery of Emin Pasha. They were very successful. He received $100,000 for the hundred lectures. The first was delivered in Carnegie Hall, New York, November 11, 1890. It was a remarkable event. He was introduced by Chauncey M. Depew. The gross receipts were $17,800. Such a jam never was known before, and the carriage crush about the building was almost beyond police control. The lecture originally announced was "The Relief of Emin Pasha." At Mr. Stanley's suggestion, "Through the Great Forest" was chosen, which brought in the story of the pigmies and other remarkable discoveries made.

The tour that followed this entrée was like the march of a triumphal hero. From the start to the finish, one hundred and ten lectures, Stanley showed signs of steady improvement. He was good at the start, but shortly became a fine speaker and then a better speaker, and before he had finished he was the best descriptive speaker I ever heard. He had overcome difficulties that would discourage any other man; as Casati wrote of him (Casati, ten years with Emin Pasha in Africa): "Jealous of his own authority, Stanley will not tolerate interference, neither will he take the advice of any one. Difficulties do not discourage him, neither does failure frighten him, as with extraordinary celerity of perception he finds his way out of every embarrassment."

Stanley is one of the best-read men I have ever met. He is familiar with the histories of all civilized and uncivilized peoples. As a journalist he is appreciated by reporters and interviewers more highly than any man I

ever knew except Mr. Beecher. Never did he refuse to see
a representative of the press who sent up his card. If
busy, he would say: "Please make my compliments to
the gentleman and say that as soon as I am disengaged
I will be pleased to see him."

Altogether, I have never parted with a client with
greater regret, or found one holding me in bonds of friendship and respect to so great a degree.

Matthew Arnold came to this country and gave one hundred lectures. Nobody ever heard any of them, not even
those sitting in the front row. At his first appearance in
Chickering Hall every seat was sold at a high price.
Chauncey M. Depew introduced the speaker. I was looking after the business in the front of the house. There was
not a seat to be had excepting a few that were held by
speculators on the sidewalk. As Mr. Depew and Matthew
Arnold appeared before the audience somebody told me
that General and Mrs. Grant had just arrived and had
seats in the gallery, but some other people were occupying
them. I immediately got a policeman and working
through the standing crowd, found that they were the last
two seats on the aisle in the gallery. We had no difficulty
in getting the occupants to vacate as soon as they discovered who held the tickets. We had just heard the last few
sentences of Mr. Depew's introduction when Matthew
Arnold stepped forward, opened out his manuscript, laid it
on the desk, and his lips began to move. There was not
the slightest sound audible from where I stood. After a
few minutes General Grant said to Mrs. Grant, "Well,
wife, we have paid to see the British lion; we cannot hear
him roar, so we had better go home." They left the hall.
A few minutes later there was a stream of people leaving
the place. All those standing went away very early.
Later on, the others who could not endure the silence
moved away as quietly as they could.

Henry Watterson I have known for twenty-five years.
A Democratic leader and editor of the most influential
paper in the South, he has counted such men as Greeley,
Raymond, James, Whitelaw Reid, Dana, McGill, and John
Swinton among his nearest friends and advisers. He was
looked upon by his political opponents as one of the safest
of their advisers. I think he has had the entrée to the

White House during every administration since Grant's, excepting Hayes', although I hardly think he and President Cleveland were over fond of each other.

There are conditions under which a close friend of the Colonel can learn all about him—his remarkable social experiences, especially among the men and women of the lyric and dramatic stage. At one time he knew every great actor, actress, singer, and manager in the English-speaking world, and they were all his friends.

Colonel Watterson has been a successful lecturer during the last two decades and has covered as much territory as any other man. He is equally popular in New England and in the South; is a favorite in Texas, California, Arkansas, Kansas, Iowa, and all the Western States. He has given his lecture on " Abraham Lincoln " before crowded houses in Southern cities where, when he was a rebel captain, he would joyfully have directed the Federal President's execution.

George Kennan was introduced to me by Mr. Roswell Smith, president of the Century Company. His letters on Siberia were appearing in " The Century Magazine " and creating a great deal of interest. I asked him if he would lecture, and got a favorable reply. I also sent out " feelers " to my customers, and to my surprise applications came pouring in from all parts of the country. I saw that success was almost certain and proposed to Mr. Kennan a certain sum of money for two hundred lectures. I offered him $100 a lecture—$20,000 for two hundred lectures—and to pay all of his expenses, which he accepted.

It was the season of 1889 and 1890. Mr. Kennan was in wretched health during the entire tour, devoting his nights to writing letters and sending his earnings to the poor Siberian exiles whom he had known in that country. He was loaded down, and was almost broken down, with sympathy for the poor people, whose cause he was so ably championing in this country. But notwithstanding all of his other work, he traveled and lectured two hundred consecutive secular nights, traveling almost every day. Not an audience was disappointed nor a railroad connection missed. Mr. Kennan cleared $20,000 that season from his lectures.

Robert E. Peary, Civil Engineer, U. S. Navy, returned

in the autumn of 1892 from his second Arctic exploration,
bringing with him a number of dogs, the sledges on which
he made his journeys, and a collection of Esquimau sou-
venirs, such as sledges, dog-harness, clothing, tents, spears,
fishing-tackle, cooking utensils, and furniture, and gave
an exhibition in the Academy of Music, Philadelphia,
under the auspices of the Academy of Science, which I
attended. It was an interesting exhibit. Mr. Peary gave
a delightful lecture, illustrated with some of the finest
stereoscopic views of Arctic scenery I had every seen presented, views which he had himself taken while on the
expedition. I tried my best to secure him for some lectures in various cities, but being an officer of the Government and under orders, it was impossible to make the arrangement. Later on, however, he obtained leave of absence with permission to fit out a second expedition, and
he was allowed to lecture from January to April, so I
arranged for what proved to be one of the most vigorous
lecture campaigns that I had ever managed up to that
time.

We began in the Academy of Music, Brooklyn, and up
to the first of April (one hundred and three days), Mr.
Peary gave one hundred and sixty-five lectures. The five
dogs were as much a drawing feature as Peary himself,
and were a great advertising card, especially where there
was sleighing, as Henson, Mr. Peary's colored servant,
who had accompanied him on the expedition, hitched them
up and drove them about the cities wherever they went,
attracting the attention and wonder of the entire communities. They seemed to take as much interest in the
show as they probably had shown in their great overland
journeys across the Greenland Ice Cap with their master.
The dogs were very fond of being petted, and liked ladies
and children. After the lecture they were brought on
the stage and the children in the audience were allowed
to rush forward and meet them. There was never an instance of the dogs showing the slightest ill-temper or of
objecting to be caressed or fed by the auditors. One remarkable thing about the dogs was that they would insist
upon their rights and their share of the entertainment.
They would wait very patiently until the time for Mr.
Peary to finish, but if he happened to speak a little longer

than the ususal time, the dogs would set up a howl so that he would have to stop. They never became uneasy until their own time arrived.

Of all the tours I ever had the pleasure of managing none met with greater success on a short notice than this one. The profits for those few weeks were about $18,000. Yet Mr. Peary was disappointed, for he was fitting out a second Arctic expedition and needed something like $80,000 for his scheme, and he was obliged to resort to other means to raise the funds that he needed. However, he never once complained, I never heard him speak an unkind word either to the employees or to his dogs.

He is a great worker. His stenographer and typewriter accompanied him, and he carried on an immense correspondence, together with his other work, perfecting all his plans for his expedition.

In closing, ladies and gentlemen, permit me to say that the lyceum platform stands for ability, genius, education, reform and entertainment. On it the greatest readers, orators and thinkers have stood. On it reform has found her noblest advocates, literature her finest expression, progress her bravest pleaders, and humor its happiest translations. Some of the most gifted, most highly-educated, and warmest-hearted men and women of the English-speaking race have in the last fifty years given their best efforts to the lyceum, and by their noble utterances have made its platform not only historic, but symbolic of talent, education, genius, and reform.

JOHN RUSKIN

WORK

[Lecture by John Ruskin, critic (born in London, England, February 8, 1819; died in Coniston, Lancaster county, England, January 20, 1900), delivered before the Camberwell Working Men's Institute, January 24, 1865. This lecture is the first of the group published under the title of " The Crown of Wild Olive," which, with " Sesame and Lilies," is perhaps the most widely read of Mr. Ruskin's works.]

MY FRIENDS:—I have not come among you to-night to endeavor to give you an entertaining lecture; but to tell you a few plain facts, and ask you a few plain questions. I have seen and known too much of the struggle for life among our laboring population, to feel at ease, under any circumstances, in inviting them to dwell on the trivialities of my own studies; but, much more, as I meet to-night, for the first time, the members of a working Institute established in the district in which I have passed the greater part of my life, I am desirous that we should at once understand each other, on graver matters. I would fain tell you, with what feelings, and with what hope, I regard this Institute, as one of many such, now happily established throughout England, as well as in other countries; and preparing the way for a great change in all the circumstances of industrial life; but of which the success must wholly depend upon our clearly understanding the conditions, and above all, the necessary *limits* of this change. No teacher can truly promote the cause of education, until he knows the mode of life for which that education is to prepare his pupil. And the fact that he is called upon to address you, nominally, as a " Working Class," must compel him, if he is in any wise earnest or thoughtful, to in-

quire in the outset, on what you yourselves suppose this
class distinction has been founded in the past, and must
be founded in the future. The manner of the amusement,
and the matter of the teaching, which any of us can offer
you, must depend wholly on our first understanding from
you, whether you think the distinction heretofore drawn
between working men and others is truly or falsely
founded. Do you accept it as it stands? do you wish it to
be modified? or do you think the object of education is to
efface it, and make us forget it forever?

Let me make myself more distinctly understood. We
call this—you and I—a "Working Men's" Institute, and
our college in London, a "Working Men's" College.
Now, how do you consider that these several institutes
differ, or ought to differ, from "idle men's" institutes and
"idle men's" colleges? Or by what other word than
"idle" shall I distinguish those whom the happiest and
wisest of working men do not object to call the "Upper
Classes"? Are there necessarily upper classes? necessarily lower? How much should those always be elevated,
how much these always depressed? And I pray those
among my audience who chance to occupy, at present,
the higher position, to forgive me what offence there may
be in what I am going to say. It is not I who wish to say
it. Bitter voices say it; voices of battle and of famine
through all the world, which must be heard some day,
whoever keeps silence. Neither, as you well know, is it to
you specially that I say it. I am sure that most now present know their duties of kindness, and fulfil them, better
perhaps than I do mine. But I speak to you as representing your whole class, which errs, I know, chiefly by
thoughtlessness, but not therefore the less terribly. Wilful error is limited by the will, but what limit is there to
that of which we are unconscious?

Bear with me, therefore, while I turn to these workmen, and ask them what they think the "upper classes"
are, and ought to be, in relation to them. Answer, you
workmen who are here, as you would among yourselves,
frankly; and tell me how you would have me call your
employers. Am I to call them—would *you* think me
right in calling them—the idle classes? I think you would
feel somewhat uneasy, and as if I were not treating my

subject honestly, or speaking from my heart, if I proceeded in my lecture under the supposition that all rich people were idle. You would be both unjust and unwise if you allowed me to say that;—not less unjust than the rich people who say that all the poor are idle, and will never work if they can help it, or more than they can help.

For indeed the fact is, that there are idle poor and idle rich; and there are busy poor and busy rich. Many a beggar is as lazy as if he had ten thousand a year; and many a man of large fortune is busier than his errand-boy, and never would think of stopping in the street to play marbles. So that, in a large view, the distinction between workers and idlers, as between knaves and honest men, runs through the very heart and innermost nature of men of all ranks and in all positions. There is a working class—strong and happy,—among both rich and poor; there is an idle class—weak, wicked, and miserable,—among both rich and poor. And the worst of the misunderstandings arising between the two orders come of the unlucky fact that the wise of one class (how little wise in this!) habitually contemplate the foolish of the *other*. If the busy rich people watched and rebuked the idle rich people, all would be right among *them*: and if the busy poor people watched and rebuked the idle poor people, all would be right among *them*. But each looks for the faults of the other. A hardworking man of property is particularly offended by an idle beggar; and an orderly, but poor, workman is naturally intolerant of the licentious luxury of the rich. And what is severe judgment in the minds of the just men of either class becomes fierce enmity in the unjust—but among the unjust *only*. None but the dissolute among the poor look upon the rich as their natural enemies, or desire to pillage their houses and divide their property. None but the dissolute among the rick speak in opprobrious terms of the vices and follies of the poor.

There is, then, no worldly distinction between idle and industrious people; and I am going to-night to speak only of the industrious. The idle people we will put out of our thoughts at once—they are mere nuisances—what ought to be done with *them*, we'll talk of at another time. But there are class distinctions among the industrious

themselves;—tremendous distinctions, which rise and fall
to every degree in the infinite thermometer of human
pain and of human power,—distinctions of high and low,
of lost and won, to the whole reach of man's soul and
body.

These separations we will study, and the laws of them,
among energetic men only, who, whether they work or
whether they play, put their strength into the work, and
their strength into the game; being in the full sense of
the word "industrious," one way or another,—with purpose, or without.   And these distinctions are mainly
four:—

I. Between those who work, and those who play.

II. Between those who produce the means of life, and
those who consume them.

III. Between those who work with the head, and those
who work with the hand.

IV. Between those who work wisely, and those who
work foolishly.

For easier memory, let us say we are going to oppose,
in our examination,—

    I. Work to play;
    II. Production to consumption;
    III. Head to hand; and,
    IV. Sense to nonsense.

I.   First, then, of the distinction between the classes who
work and the classes who play.   Of course we must agree
upon a definition of these terms,—work and play,—before
going farther.   Now, roughly, not with vain subtlety of
definition, but for plain use of the words, " play " is an
exertion of body or mind, made to please ourselves, and
with no determined end; and work is a thing done because
it ought to be done, and with a determined end.   You
play, as you call it, at cricket, for instance.   That is as
hard work as anything else; but it amuses you, and it has
no result but the amusement.   If it were done as an ordered form of exercise, for health's sake, it would become
work directly.   So, in like manner, whatever we do to
please ourselves, and only for the sake of the pleasure,
not for an ultimate object, is " play," the " pleasing thing,"

not the useful thing. Play may be useful in a secondary
sense (nothing is indeed more useful or necessary); but
the use of it depends on its being spontaneous.

Let us, then, inquire together what sort of games the
playing class in England spend their lives in playing at.

The first of all English games is making money. That
is an all-absorbing game; and we knock each other down
oftener in playing at that than at football, or any other
roughest sport; and it is absolutely without purpose; no
one who engages heartily in that game ever knows why.
Ask a great money-maker what he wants to do with his
money—he never knows. He doesn't make it to do anything with it. He gets it only that he *may* get it. "What
will you make of what you have got ?" you ask. "Well,
I'll get more," he says. Just as, at cricket, you get more
runs. There's no use in the runs, but to get more of them
than other people is the game. And there's no use in the
money, but to have more of it than other people is the
game. So all that great foul city of London there,—
rattling, growling, smoking, stinking,—a ghastly heap of
fermenting brickwork, pouring out poison at every pore,
—you fancy it is a city of work ? Not a street of it ! It is
a great city of play; very nasty play, and very hard play,
but still play. It is only Lord's cricket ground without
the turf,—a huge billiard table without the cloth, and
with pockets as deep as the bottomless pit; but mainly
a billiard table, after all.

Well, the first great English game is this playing at
counters. If differs from the rest in that it appears
always to be producing money, while every other game
is expensive. But it does not always produce money.
There's a great difference between " winning " money and
" making " it; a great difference between getting it out of
another man's pocket into ours, or filling both.

Our next great English games, however, hunting and
shooting, are costly altogether; and how much we are
fined for them annually in land, horses, gamekeepers, and
game laws, and the resultant demoralization of ourselves,
our children, and our retainers, and all else that accom-
panies these beautiful and special English games, I will
not endeavor to count now: but note only that, except for
exercise, they are not merely useless games, but deadly

ones, to all connected with them. For through horse-racing you get every form of what the higher classes everywhere call " Play," in distinction from all other plays: that is, gambling; and through game-preserving, you get also some curious laying out of ground; that beautiful arrangement of dwelling-house for man and beast, by which we have grouse and black-cock—so many brace to the acre, and men and women—so many brace to the garret. I often wonder what the angelic builders and surveyors— the angelic builders who build the "many mansions" up above there; and the angelic surveyors, who measured that four-square city with their measuring reeds—I wonder what they think, or are supposed to think, of the laying out of ground by this nation.

Then, next to the gentlemen's game of hunting, we must put the ladies' game of dressing. It is not the cheapest of games. And I wish I could tell you what this "play" costs, altogether, in England, France, and Russia annually. But it is a pretty game, and on certain terms I like it; nay, I don't see it played quite as much as I would fain have it. You ladies like to lead the fashion:—by all means lead it—lead it thoroughly,—lead it far enough. Dress yourselves nicely, and dress everybody else nicely. Lead the *fashions for the poor* first; make *them* look well, and you yourselves will look, in ways of which you have now no conception, all the better. The fashions you have set for some time among your peasantry are not pretty ones; their doublets are too irregularly slashed, or as Chaucer calls it "all to-slittered," though not for "queintise," and the wind blows too frankly through them.

Then there are other games, wild enough, as I could show you if I had time.

There's playing at literature, and playing at art;—very different, both, from working at literature, or working at art, but I've no time to speak of these. I pass to the greatest of all—the play of plays, the great gentlemen's game, which ladies like them best to play at,—the game of War. It is entrancingly pleasant to the imagination; we dress for it, however, more finely than for any other sport; and go out to it, not merely in scarlet, as to hunt, but in scarlet and gold, and all manner of fine colors; of course we could fight better in gray, and without feathers; but all nations have agreed that it is good to be well dressed at this play. Then the bats and balls are very costly; our English and French bats, with the balls and wickets, even those which we don't make any use of, costing, I suppose, now, about fifteen millions of money annually to each nation; all which you know is paid for by hard laborer's work in the furrow and furnace. A costly game!—not to speak of its consequences; I will say at present nothing of these. The mere immediate cost of all these plays is what I want you to consider; they are all paid for in deadly work somewhere, as many of us know too well. The jewel-cutter, whose sight fails over the diamonds; the weaver, whose arm fails over the web; the iron-forger, whose breath fails before the furnace—*they* know what work is—they, who have all the work, and none of the play, except a kind they have named for themselves down in the black north country, where "play" means being laid up by sickness. It is a pretty example for philologists, of varying dialect, this change in the sense of the word, as used in the black country of Birmingham, and the red and black country of Baden Baden. Yes, gentlemen, and gentlewomen, of England, who think "one moment unamused a misery, not made for feeble man," this is what you have brought the word "play" to mean, in the heart of merry England! You may have your fluting and piping; but there are sad children sitting in the market-place, who indeed cannot say to you, "We have piped unto you, and ye have not danced": but eternally shall say to you, "We have mourned unto you, and ye have not lamented."

This, then, is the first distinction between the "upper and lower" classes. And this is one which is by no means necessary; which indeed must, in process of good time, be by all honest men's consent abolished. Men will be taught that an existence of play, sustained by the blood of other creatures, is a good existence for gnats and jellyfish; but not for men: that neither days, nor lives, can be made holy or noble by doing nothing in them: that the best prayer at the beginning of a day is that we may not lose its moments; and the best grace before meat, the consciousness that we have justly earned our dinner. And when we have this much of plain Christianity preached to us again, and cease to translate the strict words, " Son, go work to-day in my vineyard," into the dainty ones: " Baby, go play to-day in my vineyard," we shall all be workers, in one way or another; and this much at least of the distinction between " upper " and " lower " forgotten.

II. I pass then to our second distinction; between the rich and poor, between Dives and Lazarus,—distinction which exists more sternly, I suppose, in this day, than ever in the world, Pagan or Christian, till now.   Consider, for instance, what the general tenor of such a paper as the " Morning Post " implies of delicate luxury among the rich; and then read this chance extract from it:—

" Yesterday morning, at eight o'clock, a woman, passing a dung-heap in the stone-yard near the recently erected almshouses in Shadwell Gap, High street, Shadwell, called the attention of a Thames police-constable to a man in a sitting position on the dung-heap, and said she was afraid he was dead.   Her fears proved to be true.   The wretched creature appeared to have been dead several hours.   He had perished of cold and wet, and the rain had been beating down on him all night.   The deceased was a bone-picker.   He was in the lowest stage of poverty, poorly clad, and half-starved.   The police had frequently driven him away from the stone-yard, between sunset and sunrise, and told him to go home.   He selected a most desolate spot for his wretched death.   A penny and some bones were found in his pockets.   The deceased was between fifty and sixty years of age.   Inspector Roberts, of the K division, has given directions for inquiries to be made at the lodging-houses respecting the deceased, to ascertain his identity if possible."—" Morning Post," Nov. 25, 1864.

Compare the statement of the finding bones in his pocket with the following, from the " Telegraph " of January 16 of this year:—

"Again, the dietary scale for adult and juvenile paupers was drawn up by the most conspicuous political economists in England.   It is low in quantity, but it is sufficient to support nature; yet within ten years of the passing of the Poor Law Act, we heard of the paupers in the Andover Union gnawing the scraps of putrid flesh and suck-

ing the marrow from the bones of horses which they were
employed to crush."

You see my reason for thinking that our Lazarus of
Christianity has some advantage over the Jewish one.
Jewish Lazarus expected, or at least prayed, to be fed
with crumbs from the rich man's table; but *our* Lazarus is
fed with crumbs from the dog's table.

Now this distinction between rich and poor rests on
two bases. Within its proper limits, on a basis which
is lawful and everlastingly necessary; beyond them, on a
basis unlawful, and everlastingly corrupting the framework of society. The lawful basis of wealth is, that a
man who works should be paid the fair value of his work;
and that if he does not choose to spend it to-day, he should
have free leave to keep it, and spend it to-morrow. Thus,
an industrious man working daily, and laying by daily,
attains at last the possession of an accumulated sum of
wealth, to which he has absolute right. The idle person
who will not work, and the wasteful person who lays nothing by, at the end of the same time will be doubly poor—
poor in possession, and dissolute in moral habit; and he
will then naturally covet the money which the other has
saved. And if he is then allowed to attack the other, and
rob him of his well-earned wealth, there is no more any
motive for saving, or any reward for good conduct; and
all society is thereupon dissolved, or exists only in systems
of rapine. Therefore the first necessity of social life is the
clearness of national conscience in enforcing the law—that
he should keep who has JUSTLY EARNED.

That law, I say, is the proper basis of distinction between rich and poor. But there is also a false basis of distinction; namely, the power held over those who are earning wealth by those who already possess it, and only use it
to gain more. There will be always a number of men who
would fain set themselves to the accumulation of wealth
as the sole object of their lives. Necessarily, that class of
men is an uneducated class, inferior in intellect, and more
or less cowardly. It is physically impossible for a well-
educated, intellectual, or brave man to make money the
chief object of his thoughts; just as it is for him to make
his dinner the principal object of them. All healthy people
like their dinners, but their dinner is not the main object

of their lives. So all healthily-minded people like making
money—ought to like it, and to enjoy the sensation of
winning it; but the main object of their life is not money;
it is something better than money. A good soldier, for
instance, mainly wishes to do his fighting well. He is
glad of his pay—very properly so, and justly grumbles
when you keep him ten years without it—still, his main
notion of life is to win battles, not to be paid for winning
them. So of clergymen. They like pew-rents, and baptismal fees, of course; but yet, if they are brave and well-
educated, the pew-rent is not the sole object of their lives,
and the baptismal fee is not the sole purpose of the baptism; the clergyman's object is essentially to baptize and
preach, not to be paid for preaching. So of doctors.
They like fees no doubt,—ought to like them; yet if they
are brave and well-educated, the entire object of their
lives is not fees. They, on the whole, desire to cure the
sick; and,—if they are good doctors, and the choice were
fairly put to them,—would rather cure their patient and
lose their fee, than kill him, and get it. And so with all
other brave and rightly-trained men; their work is first,
their fee second—very important always, but still *second*.
But in every nation, as I said, there are a vast class who
are ill-educated, cowardly, and more or less stupid. And
with these people, just as certainly the fee is first, and the
work second, as with brave people the work is first and the
fee second. And this is no small distinction. It is between
life and death *in* a man, between heaven and hell *for* him.
You cannot serve two masters;—you *must* serve one or
other. If your work is first with you, and your fee second, work is your master, and the lord of work, who is
God. But if your fee is first with you, and your work
second, fee is your master, and the lord of fee, who is the
Devil; and not only the Devil, but the lowest of devils—
the "least erected fiend that fell." So there you have it
in brief terms; Work first—you are God's servants; Fee
first—you are the Fiend's. And it makes a difference,
now and ever, believe me, whether you serve Him who
has on His vesture and thigh written, "King of Kings,"
and whose service is perfect freedom; or him on whose
vesture and thigh the name is written, "Slave of Slaves,"
and whose service is perfect slavery.

However, in every nation there are, and must always be, a certain number of these Fiend's servants, who have it principally for the object of their lives to make money. They are always, as I said, more or less stupid, and cannot conceive of anything else so nice as money. Stupidity is always the basis of the Judas bargain. We do great injustice to Iscariot, in thinking him wicked above all common wickedness. He was only a common money-lover, and, like all money-lovers, did not understand Christ;— could not make out the worth of Him, or meaning of Him. He never thought He would be killed. He was horror-struck when he found that Christ would be killed; threw his money away instantly, and hanged himself. How many of our present money-seekers, think you, would have the grace to hang themselves, whoever was killed? But Judas was a common, selfish, muddle-headed, pilfering fellow; his hand always in the bag of the poor, not caring for them. Helpless to understand Christ, yet believed in Him, much more than most of us do; had seen Him do miracles, thought He was quite strong enough to shift for Himself, and he, Judas, might as well make his own little bye-perquisites out of the affair. Christ would come out of it well enough, and he have his thirty pieces. Now, that is the money-seeker's idea, all over the world. He doesn't hate Christ, but can't understand Him— doesn't care for Him—sees no good in that benevolent business; makes his own little job out of it at all events, come what will. And thus, out of every mass of men, you have a certain number of bagmen—your " fee-first " men, whose main object is to make money. And they do make it—make it in all sorts of unfair ways, chiefly by the weight and force of money itself, or what is called the power of capital; that is to say, the power which money, once obtained, has over the labor of the poor, so that the capitalist can take all its produce to himself, except the laborer's food. That is the modern Judas's way of " carrying the bag," and "bearing what is put therein."

Nay, but (it is asked) how is that an unfair advantage? Has not the man who has worked for the money a right to use it as he best can? No, in this respect, money is now exactly what mountain promontories over public roads were in old times. The barons fought for them fairly:—

the strongest and cunningest got them; then fortified
them, and made everyone who passed below pay toll.
Well, capital now is exactly what crags were then. Men
fight fairly (we will, at least, grant so much, though it is
more than we ought) for their money; but, once having
got it, the fortified millionaire can make everybody who
passes below pay toll to his million, and build another
tower of his money castle. And I can tell you, the poor
vagrants by the roadside suffer now quite as much from
the bag-baron, as ever they did from the crag-baron.
Bags and crags have just the same result on rags. I have
not time, however, to-night to show you in how many
ways the power of capital is unjust; but remember this one
great principle—you will find it unfailing—that whenever
money is the principal object of life with either man or
nation, it is both got ill, and spent ill; and does harm
both in the getting and spending; but when it is not the
principal object, it and all other things will be well got
and well spent. And here is the test, with every man, of
whether money is the principal object with him, or not.
If in mid-life he could pause and say, "Now I have
enough to live upon, I'll live upon it; and having well
earned it, I will also well spend it, and go out of the world
poor, as I came into it," then money is not principal with
him; but if, having enough to live upon in the manner
befitting his character and rank, he still wants to make
more, and to *die* rich, then money is the principal object
with him, and it becomes a curse to himself, and generally
to those who spend it after him. For you know it *must*
be spent some day; the only question is whether the man
who makes it shall spend it, or some one else, and generally it is better for the maker to spend it, for he will
know best its value and use. And if a man does not choose
thus to spend his money, he must either hoard it or lend
it, and the worst thing he can generally do is to lend it;
for borrowers are nearly always ill-spenders, and it is with
lent money that all evil is mainly done, and all unjust war
protracted.

For observe what the real fact is, respecting loans to
foreign military governments, and how strange it is. If
your little boy came to you to ask for money to spend in
squibs and crackers, you would think twice before you

gave it him, and you would have some idea that it was wasted, when you saw it fly off in fireworks, even though he did no mischief with it. But the Russian children and Austrian children come to you, borrowing money, not to spend in innocent squibs, but in cartridges and bayonets to attack you in India with, and to keep down all noble life in Italy with, and to murder Polish women and children with; and *that* you will give at once, because they pay you interest for it. Now, in order to pay you that interest, they must tax every working peasant in their dominions; and on that work you live. You therefore at once rob the Austrian peasant, assassinate or banish the Polish peasant, and you live on the produce of the theft, and the bribe for the assassination! That is the broad fact—that is the practical meaning of your foreign loans, and of most large interest of money; and then you quarrel with Bishop Colenso, forsooth, as if *he* denied the Bible, and you believed it! though, every deliberate act of your lives is a new defiance of its primary orders.

III. I must pass, however, now to our third condition of separation, between the men who work with the hand and those who work with the head.

And here we have at last an inevitable distinction. There *must* be work done by the arms, or none of us could live. There *must* be work done by the brains, or the life we get would not be worth having. And the same men cannot do both. There is rough work to be done, and rough men must do it; there is gentle work to be done, and gentlemen must do it; and it is physically impossible that one class should do, or divide, the work of the other. And it is of no use to try to conceal this sorrowful fact by fine words, and to talk to the workman about the honorableness of manual labor, and the dignity of humanity. Rough work, honorable or not, takes the life out of us; and the man who has been heaving clay out of a ditch all day, or driving an express train against the north wind all night, or holding a collier's helm in a gale on a lee-shore, or whirling white-hot iron at a furnace mouth, is not the same man at the end of his day, or night, as one who has been sitting in a quiet room, with everything comfortable about him, reading books, or classing butterflies, or painting pictures. If it is any comfort to you to be told that the rough work is the more honorable of the two, I should be sorry to take that much of consolation from you; and in some sense I need not.   The rough work is at all events real, honest, and, generally, though not always, useful; while the fine work is, a great deal of it, foolish and false as well as fine, and therefore dishonorable; but when both kinds are equally well and worthily done, the head's is the noble work, and the hand's the ignoble.   Therefore, of all hand work whatsoever, necessary for the maintenance of life, those old words, " In the sweat of thy face thou shalt eat bread," indicate that the inherent nature of it is one of calamity: and that the ground, cursed for our sake, casts also some shadow of degradation into our contest with its thorn and its thistle; so that all nations have held their days honorable, or " holy," and constituted them " holy-days " or " holidays," by making them days of rest; and the promise, which, among all our distant hopes, seems to cast the chief brightness over death, is that blessing of the dead who die in the Lord, that " they rest from their la-bors, and their works do follow them."

And thus the perpetual question and contest must arise, who is to do this rough work? and how is the worker of it to be comforted, redeemed, and rewarded? and what kind of play should he have, and what rest, in this world, some-times, as well as in the next?   Well, my good laborious friends, these questions will take a little time to answer yet.   They *must* be answered: all good men are occupied with them, and all honest thinkers.   There's grand head work doing about them; but much must be discovered, and much attempted in vain, before anything decisive can be told you.   Only note these few particulars, which are already sure.

As to the distribution of the hard work.   None of us, or very few of us, do either hard or soft work because we think we ought; but because we have chanced to fall into the way of it, and cannot help ourselves.   Now, nobody does anything well that they cannot help doing: work is only done well when it is done with a will; and no man has a thoroughly sound will unless he knows he is doing what he should, and is in his place.   And, depend upon it, all work must be done at last, not in a disorderly, scrambling, doggish way, but in an ordered, soldierly,

human way—a lawful or "loyal" way. Men are enlisted
for the labor that kills—the labor of war: they are
counted, trained, fed, dressed, and praised for that. Let
them be enlisted also for the labor that feeds: let them be
counted, trained, fed, dressed, praised for that. Teach
the plough exercise as carefully as you do the sword
exercise, and let the officers of troops of life be held as
much gentlemen as the officers of troops of death; and
all is done: but neither this, nor any other right thing, can
be accomplished—you can't even see your way to it—
unless, first of all, both servant and master are resolved
that, come what will of it, they will do each other justice.

People are perpetually squabbling about what will be
best to do, or easiest to do, or advisablest to do, or profit-
ablest to do; but they never, so far as I hear them talk,
ever ask what it is *just* to do. And it is the law of heaven
that you shall not be able to judge what is wise or easy,
unless you are first resolved to judge what is just, and to
do it. That is the one thing constantly reiterated by our
Master—the order of all others that is given oftenest—
"Do justice and judgment." That's your Bible order;
that's the "Service of God,"—not praying nor psalm-singing. You are told, indeed, to sing psalms when you are
merry, and to pray when you need anything; and, by the
perverseness of the Evil Spirit, we get to think that praying and psalm-singing are "service." If a child finds itself
in want of anything, it runs in and asks its father for it—
does it call that doing its father a service? If it begs for
a toy or a piece of cake—does it call that serving its
father? That, with God, is prayer, and He likes to hear it:
He likes you to ask Him for cake when you want it; but
He doesn't call that "serving Him." Begging is not serving: God likes mere beggars as little as you do—He likes
honest servants, not beggars. So when a child loves its
father very much, and is very happy, it may sing little
songs about him; but it doesn't call that serving its father;
neither is singing songs about God, serving God. It is
enjoying ourselves, if it's anything; most probably it is
nothing; but if it's anything, it is serving ourselves, not
God. And yet we are impudent enough to call our
beggings and chantings "Divine service": we say
"Divine service will be 'performed'" (that's our word—

the form of it gone through) "at so-and-so o'clock."
Alas! unless we perform Divine service in every willing
act of life, we never perform it at all.   The one Divine
work—the one ordered sacrifice—is to do justice; and it is
the last we are ever inclined to do.   Anything rather than
that!   As much charity as you choose, but no justice.
"Nay," you will say, "charity is greater than justice."
Yes, it is greater; it is the summit of justice—it is the
temple of which justice is the foundation.   But you can't
have the top without the bottom; you cannot build upon
charity.   You must build upon justice, for this main reason, that you have not, at first, charity to build with.   It
is the last reward of good work.   Do justice to your
brother (you can do that, whether you love him or not),
and you will come to love him.   But do injustice to him,
because you don't love him; and you will come to hate
him.

   It is all very fine to think you can build upon charity
to begin with; but you will find all you will have got to
begin with, begins at home, and is essentially love of yourself.   You well-to-do people, for instance, who are here
to-night, will go to "Divine service" next Sunday, all
nice and tidy, and your little children will have their tight
little Sunday boots on, and lovely little Sunday feathers
in their hats; and you'll think, complacently and piously,
how lovely they look going to church in their best!   So
they do: and you love them heartily, and you like sticking
feathers in their hats.   That's all right: that *is* charity;
but it is charity beginning at home.   Then you will come
to the poor little crossing-sweeper, got up also,—it, in its
Sunday dress,—the dirtiest rags it has,—that it may beg
the better: you will give it a penny, and think how good
you are, and how good God is to prefer your child to the
crossing-sweeper and bestow on it a divine hat, feathers,
and boots, and the pleasure of giving pence instead of
begging for them.   That's charity going abroad.   But
what does Justice say, walking and watching near us?
Christian Justice has been strangely mute, and seemingly
blind; and, if not blind, decrepit, this many a day: she
keeps her accounts still, however—quite steadily—doing
them at nights, carefully, with her bandage off, and
through acutest spectacles (the only modern scientific in-

vention she cares about). You must put your ear down ever so close to her lips to hear her speak; and then you will start at what she first whispers, for it will certainly be, " Why shouldn't that little crossing-sweeper have a feather on its head, as well as your own child?" Then you may ask Justice, in an amazed manner, " How she can possibly be so foolish as to think children could sweep crossings with feathers on their heads?" Then you stoop again, and Justice says—still in her dull, stupid way— " Then, why don't you, every other Sunday, leave your child to sweep the crossing, and take the little sweeper to church in a hat and feather?" Mercy on us (you think), what will she say next? And you answer, of course, that " you don't, because everybody ought to remain content in the position in which Providence has placed them." Ah, my friends, that's the gist of the whole question. *Did* Providence put them in that position, or did *you*? You knock a man into a ditch, and then you tell him to remain content in the " position in which Providence has placed him." That's modern Christianity. You say—" *We* did not knock him into the ditch." We shall never know what you have done or left undone, until the question with us every morning, is not how to do the gainful thing, but how to do the just thing during the day; nor until we are at least so far on the way to being Christian, as to acknowledge that maxim of the poor half-way Mahometan, " One hour in the execution of justice is worth seventy years of prayer."

Supposing, then, we have it determined with appropriate justice, *who* is to do the hand work, the next questions must be how the hand-workers are to be paid, and how they are to be refreshed, and what play they are to have. Now, the possible quantity of play depends on the possible quantity of pay; and the quantity of pay is not a matter for consideration to hand-workers only, but to all workers. Generally, good, useful work, whether of the hand or head, is either ill-paid, or not paid at all. I don't say it should be so, but it always is so. People, as a rule. only pay for being amused or being cheated, not for being served. Five thousand a year to your talker, and a shilling a day to your fighter, digger, and thinker, is the rule. None of the best head work in art, literature, or science, is

ever paid for. How much do you think Homer got for his
Iliad? or Dante for his Paradise? only bitter bread and
salt, and going up and down other people's stairs.   In
science, the man who discovered the telescope, and first
saw heaven, was paid with a dungeon; the man who invented the microscope, and first saw earth, died of starvation, driven from his home.   It is indeed very clear that
God means all thoroughly good work and talk to be done
for nothing.   Baruch, the scribe, did not get a penny a
line for writing Jeremiah's second roll for him, I fancy;
and St. Stephen did not get bishop's pay for that long sermon of his to the Pharisees; nothing but stones.   For,
indeed, that is the world-father's proper payment.   So
surely as any of the world's children work for the world's
good, honestly, with head and heart; and come to it,
saying, "Give us a little bread, just to keep the life in
us," the world-father answers them, "No, my children,
not bread; a stone, if you like, or as many as you need,
to keep you quiet and tell to future ages, how unpleasant
you made yourself to the one you lived in."

But the hand-workers are not so ill off as all this comes
to.   The worst that can happen to *you* is to break stones;
not be broken by them.   And for you there will come a
time for better payment; we shall pay people not quite so
much for talking in Parliament and doing nothing, as for
holding their tongues out of it and doing something;
we shall pay our ploughman a little more, and our lawyer
a little less, and so on: but, at least, we may even now
take care that whatever work is done shall be fully paid
for; and the man who does it paid for it, not somebody
else; and that it shall be done in an orderly, soldierly,
well-guided, wholesome way, under good captains and
lieutenants of labor; and that it shall have its appointed
times of rest, and enough of them; and that in those times
the play shall be wholesome play, not in theatrical gardens, with tin flowers and gas sunshine, and girls dancing
because of their misery; but in true gardens, with real
flowers, and real sunshine, and children dancing because
of their gladness; so that truly the streets shall be full
(the "streets," mind you, not the gutters) of children,
playing in the midst thereof.   We may take care that
workingmen shall have at least as good books to read

as anybody else, when they've time to read them; and as comfortable firesides to sit at as anybody else, when they've time to sit at them. This, I think, can be managed for you, my laborious friends, in the good time.

IV. I must go on, however, to our last head, concerning ourselves all, as workers. What is wise work, and what is foolish work? What the difference between sense and nonsense, in daily occupations?

There are three tests of wise work:—that it must be honest, useful, and cheerful.

I. It is HONEST. I hardly know anything more strange than that you recognize honesty in play, and you do not in work. In your lightest games, you have always some one to see what you call "fair-play." In boxing, you must hit fair; in racing, start fair. Your English watchword is "fair-*play*," your English hatred, "foul-*play*." Did it never strike you that you wanted another watchword also, "fair-*work*," and another and bitterer hatred— "foul-*work*"? Your prize-fighter has some honor in him yet; and so have the men in the ring round him: they will judge him to lose the match, by foul hitting. But your prize-merchant gains his match by foul selling, and no one cries out against that. You drive a gambler out of the gambling-room who loads dice, but you leave a tradesman in flourishing business who loads scales! For observe, all dishonest dealing *is* loading scales. What difference does it make whether I get short weight, adulterate substance, or dishonest fabric?— unless that flaw in the substance or fabric is the worse evil of the two. Give me short measure of food, and I only lose by you; but give me adulterate food, and I die by you. Here, then, is your chief duty, you workmen and tradesmen—to be true to yourselves, and to us who would help you. We can do nothing for you, nor you for yourselves, without honesty. Get that, you get all; without that, your suffrages, your reforms, your free trade measures, your institutions of science, are all in vain. It is useless to put your heads together, if you can't put your hearts together. Shoulder to shoulder, right hand to right hand, among yourselves, and no wrong hand to anybody else, and you'll win the world yet.

II. Then, secondly, wise work is USEFUL. No man

minds, or ought to mind, its being hard, if only it comes
to something; but when it is hard, and comes to nothing;
when all our bees' business turns to spiders'; and for
honeycomb we have only resultant cobweb, blown away
by the next breeze—that is the cruel thing for the worker.
Yet do we ever ask ourselves, personally, or even nation-
ally, whether our work is coming to anything or not?   We
don't care to keep what has been nobly done; still less do
we care to do nobly what others would keep; and, least
of all, to make the work itself useful instead of deadly
to the doer, so as to exert his life indeed, but not to waste
it.   Of all wastes, the greatest waste that you can commit
is the waste of labor.   If you went down in the morning
into your dairy, and found that your youngest child had
got down before you, and that he and the cat were at play
together, and that he had poured out all the cream on the
floor for the cat to lap up, you would scold the child, and
be sorry the cream was wasted.   But if, instead of wooden
bowls with milk in them, there are golden bowls with
human life in them, and instead of the cat to play with—
the devil to play with; and you yourself the player; and
instead of leaving that golden bowl to be broken by God
at the fountain, you break it in the dust yourself, and pour
the human life out on the ground for the Fiend to lick up
—that is no waste!

What! you perhaps think, "to waste the labor of men
is not to kill them."   Is it not?   I should like to know
how you could kill them more utterly—kill them with second deaths, seventh deaths, hundredfold deaths?   It is the
slightest way of killing to stop a man's breath.   Nay, the
hunger, and the cold, and the whistling bullets—our love-
messengers between nation and nation—have brought
pleasant messages to many a man before now; orders of
sweet release, and leave at last to go where he will be
most welcome and most happy.   At the worst you do but
shorten his life, you do not corrupt his life.   But if you
put him to base labor, if you bind his thoughts, if you
blind his eyes, if you blunt his hopes, if you steal his joys,
if you stunt his body, and blast his soul, and at last leave
him not so much as strength to reap the poor fruit of his
degradation, but gather that for yourself, and dismiss him
to the grave, when you have done with him, having, so

far as in you lay, made the walls of that grave everlasting; (though, indeed, I fancy the goodly bricks of some of our family vaults will hold closer in the resurrection day than the sod over the laborer's head), this you think is no waste and no sin!

III. Then, lastly, wise work is CHEERFUL, as a child's work is. And now I want you to take one thought home with you, and let it stay with you.

Everybody in this room has been taught to pray daily, "Thy kingdom come." Now, if we hear a man swear in the streets, we think it very wrong, and say he "takes God's name in vain." But there's a twenty times worse way of taking His name in vain, than that. It is to *ask God for what we don't want.* He doesn't like that sort of prayer. If you don't want a thing, don't ask for it: such asking is the worst mockery of your King you can insult Him with; the soldiers striking Him on the head with the reed was nothing to that. If you do not wish for His kingdom, don't pray for it. But if you do, you must do more than pray for it; you must work for it. And, to work for it, you must know what it is: we have all prayed for it many a day without thinking. Observe, it is a kingdom that is to come to us; we are not to go to it. Also, it is not to be a kingdom of the dead, but of the living. Also, it is not to come all at once, but quietly; nobody knows how. "The kingdom of God cometh not with observation." Also, it is not to come outside of us, but in our hearts: "the kingdom of God is within you." And, being within us, it is not a thing to be seen, but to be felt; and though it brings all substance of good with it, it does not consist in that: "the kingdom of God is not meat and drink, but righteousness, peace, and joy in the Holy Ghost:" joy, that is to say, in the holy, healthful and helpful Spirit. Now, if we want to work for this kingdom, and to bring it, and enter into it, there's one curious condition to be first accepted. You must enter it as children, or not at all; "Whosoever will not receive it as a little child shall not enter therein." And again, "Suffer little children to come unto me, and forbid them not, *for of such is the kingdom of heaven.*"

Of such, observe. Not of children themselves, but of such as children. I believe most mothers who read that text think that all heaven or the earth—when it gets to be like heaven—is to be full of babies. But that's not so. "Length of days, and long life and peace," that is the blessing, not to die, still less to live, in babyhood. It is the *character* of children we want, and must gain at our peril; let us see, briefly, in what it consists.

The first character of right childhood is that it is Modest. A well-bred child does not think it can teach its parents, or that it knows everything. It may think its father and mother know everything,—perhaps that all grown-up people know everything; very certainly it is sure that *it* does not. And it is always asking questions, and wanting to know more. Well, that is the first character of a good and wise man at his work. To know that he knows very little;—to perceive that there are many above him wiser than he; and to be always asking questions, wanting to learn, not to teach. No one ever teaches well who wants to teach, or governs well who wants to govern; it is an old saying (Plato's, but I know not if his, first), and as wise as old.

Then, the second character of right childhood is to be Faithful. Perceiving that its father knows best what is good for it, and having found always, when it has tried its own way against his, that he was right and it was wrong, a noble child trusts him at last wholly, gives him its hand, and will walk blindfold with him, if he bids it. And that is the true character of all good men also, as obedient workers, or soldiers under captains. They must trust their captains;—they are bound for their lives to choose none but those whom they *can* trust. Then, they are not always to be thinking that what seems strange to them, or wrong in what they are desired to do, *is* strange or wrong. They know their captain: where he leads they must follow,—what he bids, they must do; and without this trust and faith, without this captainship and soldiership, no great deed, no great salvation, is possible to man.

Then the third character of right childhood is to be Loving. Give a little love to a child, and you get a great deal back. It loves everything near it, when it is a right kind of child; would hurt nothing, would give the best it has away, always, if you need it; does not lay plans for getting everything in the house for itself, and delights in helping people; you cannot please it so much as by giving it a chance of being useful, in ever so humble a way.

And because of all these characters, lastly, it is Cheerful. Putting its trust in its father, it is careful for nothing—being full of love to every creature, it is happy always, whether in its play or in its duty. Well, that's the great worker's character also. Taking no thought for the morrow; taking thought only for the duty of the day; trusting somebody else to take care of to-morrow; knowing indeed what labor is, but not what sorrow is; and always ready for play—beautiful play. For lovely human play is like the play of the Sun. There's a worker for you. He, steady to his time, is set as a strong man to run his course, but also, he *rejoiceth* as a strong man to run his course. See how he plays in the morning, with the mists below, and the clouds above, with a ray here and a flash there, and a shower of jewels everywhere;—that's the Sun's play; and great human play is like his—all various—all full of light and life, and tender, as the dew of the morning.

So then, you have the child's character in these four things—Humility, Faith, Charity, and Cheerfulness. That's what you have got to be converted to. "Except ye be converted and become as little children."—You hear much of conversion nowadays; but people always seem to think they have got to be made wretched by conversion, —to be converted to long faces. No, friends, you have got to be converted to short ones; you have to repent into childhood, to repent into delight, and delightsomeness. You can't go into a conventicle but you'll hear plenty of talk of backsliding. Backsliding, indeed! I can tell you, on the ways most of us go, the faster we slide back the better. Slide back into the cradle, if going on is into the grave:—back, I tell you: back—out of your long faces, and into your long clothes. It is among children only, and as children only, that you will find medicine for your healing and true wisdom for your teaching. There is poison in the counsels of the *men* of this world; the words they speak are all bitterness, "the poison of asps is under their lips," but, "the sucking child shall play by the hole of the asp." There is death in the looks of men. "Their eyes are privily set against the poor"; they

are as the uncharmable serpent, the cockatrice, which slew
by seeing. .But " the weaned child shall lay his hand on
the cockatrice den." There is death in the steps of men:
" their feet are swift to shed blood; they have compassed
us in our steps like the lion that is greedy of his prey, and
the young lion lurking in secret places "; but, in that kingdom, the wolf shall lie down with the lamb, and the fatling
with the lion, and " a little child shall lead them." There
is death in the thoughts of men: the world is one wide
riddle to them, darker and darker as it draws to a close;
but the secret of it is known to the child, and the Lord of
heaven and earth is most to be thanked in that " He has
hidden these things from the wise and prudent, and has
revealed them unto babes." Yes, and there is death—
infinitude of death in the principalities and powers of men.
As far as the east is from the west, so far our sins are—*not*
set from us, but multiplied around us: the Sun himself,
think you he *now* " rejoices " to run his course, when he
plunges westward to the horizon, so widely red, not with
clouds, but blood? And it will be red more widely yet.
Whatever drought of the early and latter rain may be,
there will be none of that red rain. You fortify yourselves, you arm yourselves against it in vain; the enemy
and avenger will be upon you also, unless you learn that
it is not out of the mouths of the knitted gun, or the
smoothed rifle, but " out of the mouths of babes and suck-
lings " that the strength is ordained, which shall " still the
enemy and avenger."

MINOT JUDSON SAVAGE

AMERICAN WIT AND HUMOR

[Lecture by Minot J. Savage, clergyman and author, associate pastor of the Church of the Messiah, New York City, since 1896, previously for twenty-two years pastor of the Church of the Unity, Boston (born in Norridgewock, Maine, June 10, 1841; ———), delivered first in Washington, D. C., December 7, 1891, and repeated in many places during succeeding seasons.]

LADIES AND GENTLEMEN:—" Why we Laugh " is the title of a book by the Hon. S. S. Cox. It is packed full of reminiscences of wit and humor; but I have looked through it in vain to find any adequate reason for its title. A great many " whys " are asked in this world, but very few of them are ever answered. We laugh when we feel like it and because we feel like it. Can any research go deeper than that? Certain words, expressions, scenes, situations, happenings make us feel like it; but who can tell why? Writers have analyzed wit and humor in the effort to discover their secret. Some have done it very wisely, like John Weiss in " Wit, Humor, and Shakespeare." They tell us, in general, that it is the element of surprise or incongruity that makes us laugh. But not all surprises and incongruities are laughable; some of them are inexpressibly sad. To say that we laugh at the funny surprises and incongruities, but not at the others, is only a truism; it is only to say that we laugh when we feel like it, and not when we feel like doing something else. So it brings us back to where we began.

To press the matter a little further, can anyone tell us why tears should be the expression of sorrow and laughter of joy? Or, since tears are the expression of sorrow, why

does violent laughter frequently end in tears—as when we
" laugh till we cry "—while in this case the tears do not
mean sorrow at all?

Of course the anatomist can explain that such and such
emotions do produce such and such effects through brain
and nerve and muscle; but when he is done, the mystery of
the *why* is as deep as ever.

> " Let dogs delight to bark and bite,
>   For 'tis their nature to,"

Sings old Dr. Watts.

> Let men and women cry and laugh,
>   For 'tis their nature to.

Can we get beyond " 'tis their nature to"? I think we
shall have to be content with that.   And, since tears are
common, we will be glad and grateful that laughter also
is common and natural.

But if evolution is true, ought we not to expect to find
at least some traces of this tendency among our " poor relations," the animals? Kittens play, but they show no
sign of either smiles or tears. When the dog is gambolling
about his master there is sometimes a slight movement of
the lips that might be taken for an incipient smile. But
except in the case of Mother Hubbard's dog, the one that
" laughed to see such sport," in Mother Goose, there is
no authentic case of anything more than that. John Weiss
quotes from Lady Barker's book, " Station Life in New
Zealand," the story of a pet cockatoo that used to amuse
himself by frightening the turkeys and hens by pretending
to be a hawk. He would circle in the air over their heads,
imitating the cry of the hawk, until they had fled to shelter
in the bushes and other places of safety; then he would
burst out into a wild peal of laughter. At last, alighting
on a hen-coop filled with trembling chickens, he would
call out, in a suffocated voice, " You'll be the death of
me ! "

There are too many such stories to allow us to regard
them as mere coincidences. What do you think, for example, of this one? An Indian paroquet that had lived in
the soldier's barracks and picked up much that was not

entirely adapted to the drawing-room, at last became the property of an English lady. One day a visitor called who had a most decided squint; whereupon the parrot cried out: "Twig her eye! What a beauty!" I have myself known a parrot that would chirrup and whistle till it had started up a horse left standing at the door, and then burst out laughing as though it appreciated the joke. And some of the higher apes have reached certain facial expressions that closely resemble the clown's, and certain cachinatory sounds not far removed from laughter.

But a perception of the delicate relations and contrasts in which lie hidden the secrets of wit requires a high order of mental development such as we should not expect to find below the human. Not only this, but it is in the highest ranges of the human that we find the highest manifestations of wit and humor and the keenest appreciation of them. A lack of this faculty generally indicates a low grade of intellect. Barbarians are commonly very grave and solemn, and the idiot is the perfection of solemnity. Now and then we find ponderously sensible people who do not condescend to smile; but when one never sees anything to smile at, it is because there is a serious defect of mental vision.

Before I come to the special matter of American wit and humor I wish to take my turn at analyzing wit and humor in general.

Wit may take many forms, but it resides essentially in the thought or the imagination. In its highest forms it does not deal in things but with ideas. It is the shock of pleased surprise which results from the perception of unexpected likeness between things that differ or of an unexpected difference between things that are alike. Or it is where utterly incongruous things are apparently combined in the expression of one idea. Wit may be bitter or kindly or entirely neutral so far as the feelings are concerned. When extremes of feeling, one way or the other, are concerned, then it takes on other names which will be considered by themselves.

But not to stop any longer with definition, it is almost pure wit when some one said of an endless talker that he had "occasional brilliant flashes of silence." So of the saying of Mr. Henry Clapp. You know it is said of Shake-

speare, " He is not for a day, but for all time." Speaking
of the bore who calls when you are busy and never goes,
Mr. Clapp said, " He is not for a time, but for all day."
And what could be more deliciously perfect than the following: Senator Beck of Kentucky was an everlasting
talker. One day a friend remarked to Senator Hoar, " I
should think Beck would wear his brain all out talking so
much." Whereupon Mr. Hoar replied, " Oh, that doesn't
affect him any: he rests his mind when he is talking." This
has, indeed, a touch of sarcasm; but it is as near the pure
gold of wit as you often get. Or, take this. There being
two houses both of which are insisted on as the real birthplace of the great philosopher and statesman, Mark Twain
gravely informs us that " Franklin was twins, having been
born simultaneously in two different houses in Boston."

One of the finest specimens of clear-cut wit is the saying
of the Hon. Carroll D. Wright. Referring to the common
saying, he once keenly remarked: " I know it is said that
figures won't lie, but, unfortunately, liars will figure."

In contradistinction from wit, humor deals with incidents, characters, situations. True humor is altogether
kindly; for, while it points out and pictures the weaknesses
and foibles of humanity, it feels no contempt and leaves no
sting. It has its root in sympathy and blossoms out in
toleration.

It would take too long at this point in my lecture to
quote complete specimens of humor; for that would mean
spreading out before you detailed scenes or full descriptions. But fortunately it is not necessary. Cervantes,
Shakespeare, Charles Lamb, Dickens and a host of others
will readily occur to you. But what could do better of its
kind than this? General Joe Johnston was one day riding
leisurely behind his army on the march. Food had been
scarce and rations limited. He spied a straggler in the
brush beside the road. He called out sharply, " What are
you doing here?" Being caught out of the ranks was a
serious offense, but the soldier was equal to the emergency.
So to the General's question he replied, "Pickin' 'simmons."
The persimmon, as you know, has the quality of puckering
the mouth, as a certain kind of wild cherry used to mine
when I was a boy. "What are you picking 'simmons for?"
sharply rejoined the General. Then came the humorous

reply that disarmed all of the officer's anger and appealed to his sympathy, while it hinted all "the boys" were suffering for the cause. "Well, the fact of it is, General, I'm trying to shrink up my stomach to the size of my rations, so I won't starve to death."

The attempt has been made by some to establish a sort of aristocracy of wit that should leave certain so-called plebeian forms of it out of the best intellectual society. But I confess that, in this matter, I am a democrat. So long as I can claim such good company as Charles Lamb, I propose to stick to my love for even the pun and the conundrum. It is true, the pun is only a play upon words, and, in its simplest form, is easy and may be cheap. But if it is bad enough—i. e., difficult and complicated enough—it is very good indeed. Whether it be called plebeian or not, its pedigree is of the most ancient. Some of the old Sanscrit writings are as full of puns as a Christmas pudding of plums. The classic writers have not disdained them. They have found place even in the Bible. In that famous passage in the New Testament where Jesus says "Thou art Peter, and on this rock I will build my church," the Greek original has it, "Thou art Petros, and on this petra I will build," etc., petros and petra in each case meaning a stone. What could be finer of its kind than representing the great Lord Napier, on his capturing the city of Scinde in India, as having sent a despatch to England made up of the one Latin word, Peccavi—I have sinned? When Havelock took the city of Lucknow, he is said to have sent home word, "We are in Luck-now." But it is probably carrying the matter a little too far for history to represent Drake, after the flight of the Armada, as having sent Queen Elizabeth a message in the one word Cantharides—"The Spanish fly." That is probably a falsehood strong enough to blister the tongue of its inventor. That was not a bad pun of the doctor who, when a young lady came to him and told him she was about to be married, but was losing her sight and did not know what to do, advised her to go right on, telling her that if anything would open her eyes, marriage would. When Foote was asked if he had ever been in Cork, he said "No, but I've seen a good many drawings of it." One of the best was that of a friend of the poet Campbell. When "Hohenlinden" was very popular, this

friend, on going out after a call on Campbell, fell down-
stairs in the dark. Campbell rushed into the hall on hearing the noise, and called out "What's that?" When, from
the hall below came the reply, "'Tis I, sir, rolling rapidly."

One of the best puns I know is the following, contained
in one of the best of all the nonsense verses I am acquainted with :—

> "A famous American preacher
> Said the hen was a beautiful creature.
> The hen, upon that,
> Laid an egg in his hat,
> And thus did *the Henry Ward Beecher*."

A conundrum is a question the answer to which must
involve a pun. One that is bad enough to be good is this.
Who is the most noted chicken-slayer mentioned by
Shakespeare? The uncle in Hamlet who "did murder
most foul." And here is another, very bad. Why is a
swallow like a smoking chimney? Because it has a
crooked flue. I heard of a man who objected to that, because he said it was not good grammar: crooked flew, he
said, was all nonsense. There is a series of three conundrums connected together, which I think are good—if
conundrums ever are good. The first two are common,
but the third you may not know so well. Here they are:
Why is there no need of people's being hungry in the
desert? Because of the sand which is there. How did the
sandwiches come there? Ham and his descendants were
bred and mustered there. Yes, but besides ham and
bread and mustard, a perfect sandwich needs some butter:
how did they get the butter? Why, when Lot was driven
out of Sodom, his wife was turned into salt, and all the
family butter ran into the desert.

From the depths of the conundrum we will now rise to
higher ground.

Irony is saying in words the opposite of what you really
mean, while you depend on the occasion or a tone of voice
to indicate what you do mean. Antony says, "But
Brutus is an honorable man; so are they all, all honorable
men." But the seeming compliment stabs. Jerrold's wife
was not an attractive woman, not one who would be
sought first as partner in a dance, and he was not on the

best of terms with her. One night they were at a party together. Jerrold himself was playing whist in an adjoining room, when some one said to him, " Jerrold, who is that man dancing with your wife? " He half glanced over his shoulder towards the open door and replied, " Oh, I don't know; some member of the Humane Society, I presume."

Irony may be playful in its ridicule, but sarcasm is bitter. The word is of Greek origin and means to tear flesh, as of dogs that rend. It is a caustic that burns. One of the best specimens I know of is that of Lady Mary Wortley Montagu against her own sex. She said: "The one thing that reconciles me to the fact of being a woman is the reflection that it delivers me from the necessity of being married to one." One nearly as good, and used as a weapon on behalf of a better cause, is that of Montesquieu, against those who opposed the idea that negroes were human. "It wouldn't do to suppose that negroes were men, lest it should turn out that whites were not." And what could bite harder than that of the Rev. Petroleum V. Nasby, when he represented the anti-colored Christians of the country as proposing to revise the New Testament and make a certain famous text read: "Suffer the little (white) children to come unto me?" Or what could be keener than the sarcasm of Lincoln when he remarks on the curious fact that if a man's property were stolen, it still remained his by right, but if he himself were stolen, he lost the title to his own body and soul.

One of the funniest kinds of fun is the bull; for here you not only laugh at the absurdity of the saying, but also at the absurdity of the unconscious mental confusion out of which it comes. A good case occurred in a church close by my own. The minister, out hunting, had carelessly rested the muzzle of his gun on his foot, and by its accidental discharge had shot off one of his toes. The next Sunday, a brother minister occupied his pulpit, and prayed that the pastor might be sanctified through the affliction caused by this "untoward event." We read of such cases now and then but hardly believe them; and yet I know a lady who, on sending home from the seashore a trunk full of clothes for the laundry, locked the key to the trunk inside, and wrote home to say that they would find it there.

The Board of Councilmen in a Mississippi town voted the following resolutions at one of its meetings:—

1st. Resolved, by this Council, that we build a new jail.

2d. Resolved that the new jail be built out of the materials of the old jail.

3d. Resolved that the old jail be used till the new jail is finished.

A famous Irishman, Sir Boyle Roche, suspecting the opposition of some sort of underhand intentions, revealed his acuteness and his purpose to head off the enemy, in the following terms: "I smell a rat; I feel it in the air; and I will nip it in the bud."

Of close kinship with the bull, and belonging to the same species, is the anti-climax. The completest specimen of this that I have ever heard is that of the local orator in Vermont. He was called on to make the opening address at the Agricultural Fair, and closed his peroration thus: "Fellow-citizens, there have been three great days in the history of our country. The first was when the morning stars sang together and all the sons of God shouted for joy. The second was when Columbus sailed on his great voyage for the discovery of a new world. But the third and the greatest of all, fellow-citizens, is to-day, to-day, fellow-citizens, the day of the opening of the Windsor County Fair!"

Some of the wittiest sayings, of the nature of irony or sarcasm, are yet neither, because, while they hit hard, the predominant element in them is good-nature, and they are not intended to leave any bitterness behind them. The victim may feel that he "owes one" to the perpetrator, but no friendship is broken. These are only good-natured railing. One day Beecher was riding up Broadway in a stage, when Park Benjamin got in. "How are you, Park?" "How are you, Ward?" and they settled into friendly chat. At last Beecher said, "Park, why don't you ever come over to hear me preach?" "Well, Ward," replied Benjamin, "I'll tell you if you'll not get mad about it." "Go on," said Beecher. "Well, the fact of it is," said Benjamin, "my mother always brought me up from a child to feel that it was wrong for me to go to places of amusement on Sunday."

One other kind of wit remains to be noted—the reparteé. Sometimes, as retort, it is of the nature of the bitterest sarcasm. But it constitutes a species by itself. For pure reparteé, perhaps no man in this country has ever equalled George D. Prentice of the Louisville (Ky.) "Journal." "Villainy is afoot," says Governor Medary, a rival editor. "Has the editor lost his horse?" innocently inquires Prentice. "Have I changed?" asked another opponent. "That depends on whether you ever were honest," replies the wit. When the editor of another paper called him the most scurrilous editor in the country, Prentice replied that in making so impolite a 'remark he undoubtedly "forgot himself." A not over courteous man, speaking to a woman who claimed that women should have equal rights, sneeringly asked, "What would you do, madam, if you were a gentlemen?" "I am not sure," she replied; "what would you do if you were one?"

Let us borrow now one specimen from abroad. I think it nearly, if not quite, perfect. You remember the famous saying of Sydney Smith that it was impossible to put a joke into a Scotchman's head except by a surgical operation. Two or three years ago, at a dinner in Edinburgh, a large gathering of both English and Scotch professors were present. In an after-dinner speech Professor John Stuart Blackie—I think it was—referred to Sydney Smith's saying, and then added: "That is all right. No Scotchman is inclined to dispute it. But, then, it is to be remembered that he was referring to English jokes."

It is now high time for me to turn to the consideration of what is called peculiarly American Wit and Humor. For while wit and humor are human, they have their national and local features and their special forms of development. But while the American variety is sometimes spoken of as though it were an entirely new thing in the world, it is really, like the American nation itself, only an offshoot of the English which has taken on a new and more vigorous growth in a new soil and is modified by the touch of a new environment. And then it is more nearly universal and cosmopolitan than the English, because almost all races have contributed to make up our people— the Chinese, the Spaniard, the German, the Scandinavian, the Irishman—all these figure in our laughter, as they figure in our multiform life.

But the true Yankee variety is supposed to be chiefly
characterized by a half-boastful and altogether gigantic
exaggeration, as if an attempt were being made to fit it to
the size of the country.   And his idea of the size of the
country is well illustrated by the famous toast,—"The
United States; bounded on the East by the primeval
chaos, on the North by the Aurora Borealis, on the West
by the precession of the Equinoxes, and on the South by
the Day of Judgment!"   It was this kind of Yankee who
when an Englishman asked him what he thought of the
Thames replied, "Why the whole of your little river
hasn't got water enough in it to make a gargle for the
mouth of the Mississippi."   It was a spiritual brother of
this man who, when a Swiss asked him, as he arrived in
the country from Italy, if he had noticed the magnificence
of the Alps, replied, "Waal, now, I come to think of it,
I guess I did pass some risin' ground!"

But this quality of humorous exaggeration, though it
has received a new impulse here, is thoroughly Shakespearean.   And this is natural; for New England was an
English shoot sent out here· at the time of England's
grandest literary and political life, when both letters and
liberty were at their best in the hearts and brains of her
noblest sons.   Take a bit of Shakespearean exaggeration,
from "The Merchant of Venice" :—"Gratiano speaks an
infinite deal of nothing more than any man in all Venice.
His reasons are as two grains of wheat hid in two bushels of
chaff; you shall seek all day ere you find them; and when
you have them, they are not worth the search."   And
Falstaff is fairly Munchausenish in his inflation.   As to the
uniform of his soldiers, he says, "There's but a shirt and
a half in all my company; and the half-shirt is two napkins
pinned together."   There is a ring about this very similar
to the Yankee's description of a man who was "so thin
that it took two of him to cast a shadow."

But even Falstaff is outdone by the Yankee who wrote
to his wife from the gold mines, saying "I have only one
shirt left.   It is in such a condition that the smallest hole
in it is the one I put my head through, and it is in so many
different pieces that I have to have it washed by the
dozen."

But though American humor is first cousin to the English, it has undoubtedly taken on new proportions here and blossomed out into new varieties. Nowhere in the world is there such a popular demand for it, and such popular quickness of appreciation. Not only do the large number of humorous weeklies testify to this, but, as nowhere else in the world, it has become a staple product of all the dailies.

There is one phase of our humorous development that is so characteristic and so striking that it demands a somewhat prolonged attention. I refer to the humorous letter-writing on political and social topics. I do not recall anything in any other country quite like it. The "Junius Letters" were stinging political satires, but they were not humorous. Thackeray's "Yellow Plush Papers," and "Book of Snobs" have a nearer resemblance, and yet they do not fall into the same category. We may claim this perhaps as an indigenous growth, smacking only of our soil. The number of these writers is very large. As to most of them I can only mention their names or recall to your memories certain characteristics. Of one or two I shall wish to take more special notice.

The first of our humorous letter-writers, famous in his day though now largely forgotten, was Mr. Seba Smith, born in Buckfield, Maine, and editor of a Portland paper. He wrote during Jackson's administration over the *nom de plume* of Major Jack Downing.

Then came Lieutenant George H. Derby, who wrote the wondrously witty letters of John Phœnix. An officer in the army and located in California, he more than once risked his place by the comic and comically illustrated reports which he sent to Jefferson Davis, then Secretary of War. One of his achievements—funnier for him than for his friend—was changing the politics of a weekly paper which was left in his hands for two or three months by the editor who had come East.

But the outbreak of the war was the stimulating cause of such a growth of witty, humorous, and satirical literature as was never seen before. It was not merely humorous, but had a purpose behind its mummer's mask; and so it played a large part in directing public opinion. Some of these writers rendered quite as valuable service to the country as did the winners of battles.

Among the names popular at that time may be mentioned K. Q. Philander Doesticks, Orpheus C. Kerr, the then anonymous writer of the "New Gospel of Peace," now known to have been the Shakespearean scholar, Richard Grant White; Dunn Browne, and, king of them all, the Rev. Petroleum V. Nasby. Lowell's incomparable "Biglow Papers" belong to another class, a class by themselves, and are too important to be treated of here.

Other names, not so intimately associated with wartimes, are those of Bill Arp, a Southern wit; the Fat Contributor, the Hawk-eye man, Max Adler, Danbury News Man, Brick Pomeroy, M. Quad, Mrs. Partington, Bill Nye, Hans Breitman, Josh Billings, and a long list, as the papers say, "too numerous to mention."

This lecture has to set limits somewhere; and so I purposely leave out of present account such classic names as those of Irving, Holmes, and Lowell. Nor can I deal with Lincoln.

Two names still remain unspoken,—the names of the two princes of American Wit and Humor, in the popular sense in which we are now using those terms. These two are Artemus Ward and Mark Twain. I shall give you only detached sayings of others; but these two demand more particular attention.

And first, let us consider the latter one of these, Mark Twain. It is fortunate for me that you all know him so well; for, like the old Athenian wag—the joke is as ancient as that—I can only bring specimen bricks as samples of a house. I shall try to select such as I hope are less familiar.

One very unfortunate thing in being noted as a wag is, that it is very difficult to get anybody to take you seriously. They suspect a joke lurking somewhere in the seemingly most solemn utterance. As Jerrold once said, he gets to be looked on as so funny that people begin to laugh about the table if he only asks some one to pass the vinegar-cruet. I say this, because Mark Twain is much more than a humorist. His "Innocents Abroad" is one of the best books of travel I know of, even with the humor left out. While his "Roughing It" and "Life on the Mississippi" are such pictures of phases of early pioneer life in this country as no one else has been able to give us.

Mr. Howells has given us, in " A Boy's Town," a most admirable book about boys for men to read. But " Tom Sawyer " is the best boy's book about a boy that ever was written. And the great English critic, Mr. Andrew Lang, thinks that while we are waiting for somebody to write the great American novel, Mark Twain has already written it, and that its name is " Huckleberry Finn." Purely as a novel, he places it among the highest.

It is only justice to note this; but we are now concerned with his humor.

Knowing his boyhood was spent in Hannibal, Missouri, which is the scene of " Tom Sawyer," I asked him one day if he was born there. With his purely natural but comical drawl, he replied : " No-o, I wasn't born there ; I was born out near Pa-a-ris (Missouri) ; but when I was fifteen months old I went to Hannibal with my father and mother, and liked it so well that I concluded to make that my home."

My first knowledge of him was in California in 1865 and 1866. He had been to the Sandwich Islands, from which he had written letters to a Sacramento paper. The whole Pacific coast was laughing over them. On his return he lectured on the Sandwich Islands. I heard him in Grass Valley. It was a wonderful success. I recall many local hits that it would take too long to explain to an Eastern audience. I remember how he described the horse he rode. He said he had a great many fine points ; and drolly added, " I hung my hat on one of them." He gave a really magnificent description of an eruption of Mauna Loa, and then dropped his audience from the sublime to the ridiculous, by remarking in a tone of the greatest relief,—" I'm glad I've got that mountain off my mind." It was in this lecture that he first told the story of the meanest corporation that he ever heard of. A man was working for this company, drilling holes for blasting rock. He got to work on a place where there was a charge that had not gone off. So, as he sat quietly drilling away, an explosion occurred. He went up and up till he didn't look any bigger than a hat ; and then up and up till he didn't look any bigger than a walnut ; and then up and up till he went out of sight. Then he began to come down and down till he looked as big as a walnut ; and then down and down till he looked as big as a hat ; then down

and down till he sat once more right in the place he had
left, and went on drilling as if nothing had happened. He
was absent just sixteen minutes and forty-two seconds,
and—the company was so mean they docked him for loss
of time.

Soon after my return to the East his first book was published, called "The Celebrated Jumping Frog of Calaveras
County." The dedication of the book is worth quoting:
"To John Smith whom I have often met in my travels
about the world. I believe it is the custom for a person
to whom a book is dedicated to buy a copy. If this custom shall be followed in the present instance, a princely
affluence is about to burst upon the author." After this
came his "Innocents Abroad," and the world recognized
one of the greatest laughter-creators of all time.

I pass by his tears at the grave of Adam, his exquisite
fooling of the guide who would tell him of Christopher
Columbus, his art criticisms, and stop for only one incident
in this book. This I will relate from memory as the book
is not by me as I write. He is resting in his tent in Palestine, and sees a camel devouring his overcoat, which he
had carelessly left in his way. The coat contained a lot of
his papers, among which was his last letter to New York.
First he tells us the camel, after putting his foot on the
coat to keep it in place, tore off the velvet collar with his
teeth, seeming to regard it as a very dainty morsel. Then
he swallowed the sleeves one after the other. Pretty soon
he got to the pockets, and he watched anxiously to see the
result. He swallowed one of his jokes, which, he says,
shook him up like an earthquake. Soon however he
came to something more serious—he tried to swallow one
of his sober statements of fact. But this was too much,
even for a camel. He managed to get it down, but the
effect was fatal. He gave a few convulsive shudders and
fell over "as stiff as a carpenter's workbench." [At this
point the lecturer was accustomed to read some choice
extract from some one of Mark Twain's books, as for example, his after-dinner speech on "The Weather."]

The last good thing I have heard of Mark is of his having gone out one morning for a call on Mrs. Stowe. Now,
he is not over-careful about his dress, and on his return
his horrified wife discovered that he had been without any

necktie. After properly "dressing him down," as a good wife knows how, she got him into an apologetic frame of mind. Whereupon he wrote a humble letter to Mrs. Stowe and enclosed the necktie to complete the call.

I must now pass to Artemus Ward. He is easily the prince of all American wits of his class. His real name was Charles F. Browne, and he was born in Waterford, Oxford county, Maine, in 1834, and died of consumption in England when not quite thirty-three years of age.

Description of what one has himself seen and heard is generally better than hearsay report or book quotation. In the winter of 1862 I heard him lecture in Bangor, Maine, when I was a theological student there.

It is worth noting that the idea of his lecturing at all struck his friends as very funny indeed. But he decided to do it because he found that people on the stage were making capital out of his gold mine, and he concluded that he might as well work it himself. His subject, the night I heard him, was "The Babes in the Wood." As he comes on the platform, let me try to describe him. He was tall, spare, hollow-chested, and consumptive-looking. His hair was light, his nose aquiline, and his face smooth with the exception of a light mustache. He had everything written, for his jokes were carefully elaborated. His manner was quiet, hesitating, and deprecatory. When Ingersoll is going to perpetrate a witticism you can see it rising in his face like the flush that precedes the appearance of a full moon. But Artemus never smiled; and while the audience was in a roar, he would look up with a sort of wistful glance of innocent inquiry, as if he wondered what it was all about. And the most exquisite thing about his fun was the appearance of an artless lack of intention in saying the most incongruous and comical things. It was wit, almost pure wit. His comicalities were composed of almost pure fancy, out of his own head; and not the picturing of droll scenes from the street. So it not infrequently occurred that those of his audience who would have haw-hawed at a clown did not quite catch his flitting fancies that were as delicate and as elusive as the texture and colors of a soap-bubble.

One of the funniest things of the whole evening, to me, was the watching an old man who sat near me. He

would now and then interject a remark or a criticism:—
"The darned fool! He ain't said not a single word o'
sense the whole evening," etc., etc.   It would have done
the soul of Artemus himself good to have heard him.

I have never seen this lecture in print; but I will give
a few specimens as I recall them.   He did not allude to his
subject until the very end, when he remarked that the
babes in the wood were good children, and added: "I like
little boys and little girls;" and, then, as though in the
most casual way it had occurred to him, "and I like big
girls too."

About this time we were getting some remarkably
imaginative descriptions of battles written by correspondents who were not there.   One of the most brilliant of
these, one that was copied and commented on in England, was an account of the battle of Pea Ridge by a newspaper man who was a hundred miles from the field when
the battle took place.   With this in mind, Artemus took
occasion to refer to the transcendent genius, wit, fancy,
and power of Shakespeare.   Then he went on, as though
he had to recognize the fact that even the greatest were
not quite perfect; "but he would never have done at all as
the war correspondent of a modern newspaper; for he
lacked the requisite fancy and imagination."

He had a way of utilizing any matter that was then fresh
in the popular mind.   Almost the first victory of the war
had then been gained in the capture of Fort Donelson.
Of course, the people were wild over it.   Artemus had
been describing the special genius of special men, saying it
was one man's "forte" to do one thing and another man's
forte to do another thing; and so he unsuspectingly led
up to the remark, "General Buckner's forte"—he was the
rebel commander of Donelson—and then he stopped as
though it had just occurred to him and went on: "Oh, by
the way, he hasn't got any fort; he had one, but they took
it away from him."   And the enthusiastic house was in an
uproar of gladness.

He spoke of wealth and its perils, saying: "How often
do sudden fortunes ruin young men!"   Then, with a mus-
ing, far-away look in his face, he added,—"I should like to
be ruined."

So he went through his lecture from beginning to end

as though he were an innocent and artless teacher of trite truisms and commonplaces who only accidentally stumbled on these incongruous things, which surprised him as much as they did anybody else. When one of his witticisms exploded and the audience with it, he appeared to be looking round for the cause, as anxiously as a man who steps on a boy's torpedo and feels it go off under his foot.

He lectured on "The Mormons," on "Two Minutes in Africa," and he had an atrociously funny panorama of a journey across the plains. Pointing to some of his alleged pictures, he would say: "I am not an artist. I never paint myself—if I were a young woman of forty-five summers perhaps I might sometimes paint—myself. When I was quite small, I showed some signs of artistic promise. I drew, even as an infant, the attention of the passers-by— and when a small child I once drew a cart—over a bridge. And people who looked on, said I had a future before me. N. B.—I have noticed that most people's futures are before them." Then, pointing to a group of objects in one corner of the painting, he would go on: "Those objects visible in the lower right-hand corner there are horses. I speak of it particularly because you might mistake them for a pile of rocks. I myself, for the first three months, told my audiences that they were cows. But one day I met the artist and he corrected my mistake; he explained to me that they were horses." And all this with the most serious air of imparting to an inquiring audience the most serious and important information.

There was one form of the practical joke that he sometimes indulged in. It was his special delight to mystify people. Mark Twain tells a story of how Artemus fooled him. He got him to drink a cocktail and then began to talk to him in apparently the most dead-earnest manner. He actually said nothing whatever, did not complete a sentence. But his manner was so innocent that Mark thought he must be serious and that the trouble was that the cocktail had gone to his head.

One day on the cars he spotted a man that he suspected would prove a bore, and so he made up his mind to avoid getting into any talk with him. But soon the bore opened up: "That last move of Lincoln's was a pretty shrewd one, eh?" Artemus looked bland, and said briefly: "Who's Lincoln?" The bore looked at him a minute, and sank back with a breathless stare. But he had the quality of perseverance; so he tried again. "Do you think Chase will make a go of his financial scheme?" "Chase, scheme," mused Artemus, "I never heard of either of them." Then the man began to wonder what planet this fellow had come from. After waiting a while, he thought he'd hit him on a sure thing, so he turned and said: "What do you think of Grant as a general?" "Really, my friend," said Artemus, "you seem to be talking about people that I never heard of." Then the man grew excited; he thought this fellow might be dangerous, an escaped lunatic, or he wondered if he were idiotic. He did not like sitting so near him. So he got up and walked once or twice up and down the aisle of the car, looking him over. Then he thought he would try once more and be a little sarcastic. So he stopped in front of him, and exclaimed: "See here, you, who do you know, anyhow? Did you ever hear of Adam?" Then, with an earnest, wistful look of inquiry, he murmured, "Adam, Adam— what was his other name?" And as the listeners burst into a roar of laughter, the would-be conversationalist thought he would be happier in some other car.

In the smoking-room of the St. Nicholas Hotel late one night Artemus Ward played one of his favorite practical jokes. A number of strangers were reading the papers. Suddenly Ward called out: "George, George!" Two or three of the men whose names were George looked up. "Why did you leave Schenectady?" inquired Ward, without looking at any one in particular.

"If you mean me, sir," said a peppery person, "I never was at Schenectady in my life and I don't know you, sir."

"You were doing well there, George," continued Ward, imperturbably; "why did you leave the place?"

"Confound you, sir," shouted the stranger, "I tell you I never saw Schenectady!" and he threw down his paper and stalked out of the room."

"His conscience troubles him," said Ward; "but I wish he had told me why he left Schenectady."

Then all the strangers shook their heads and muttered that they had always thought there was something strange about that Schenectady man, and Artemus was happy. The way in which he would seriously deal with one of his own jokes is well illustrated by the following instance: At his first lecture the New York audience did not know what to make of him. He seemed so nervous; fidgeted about so; lost his place; never said a word about the advertised subject of his lecture.

"Call me pet names, love; call me a bird," he murmured, "and I called her a boiled owl." Then he waited for the laugh. It came very slow; first a solitary snicker; then two or three chuckles. "When I said that in Chicago," continued Artemus, gravely, "I had to go before a justice of the peace and take my solemn affidavit that a boiled owl was a bird before one of them could catch the point." Then everybody roared. New Yorkers are not going to be duller than Chicagoans.

In the last year of his life he decided to go to London. It was with a good deal of trepidation; for he wondered if the English would take to his kind of fun. But it became the crowning triumph of his life. At his first lecture in Egyptian Hall crowds were turned away. The literary men, the wits, the nobility, all thronged after him. He was a favorite in the clubs; and " Punch " had had no contributor who had attracted so much attention since Thackeray. His posters and even the admission tickets became famous. To one of his lectures, on " The Mormons," the tickets read: "Admit the bearer, and one wife."

One sly dig at " Punch " is worthy of notice. He had perpetrated a witticism, and then added, in parenthesis, as he frequently did,—" This is a goak." Then he stopped, as if he had committed an impropriety, and added, " I do not know that I ought to do this; for I am not sure that comic papers ever have any jokes in them. I have never seen any that had. And yet," he went on, as though advancing a proposition that might admit of argument, " I don't think it would hurt a comic paper to have a joke in it once in a while."

In less than a year after reaching England, crowned with the love of two continents, and mourned by all readers of the English tongue, Artemus Ward died of consumption in Southampton, being a little less than thirty-three years old.

"The love of two continents," I have said. Yes; for
he never made an enemy. He did not care enough, even
for his joke, to wound a friend with it. Even the genial
Charles Lamb could reply to a doting mother when she
asked him how he liked babies: "B-b-boiled, madam":
and the mother did not love him so well afterwards. And
when a gentleman sitting between Madame de Stael and
a very handsome woman, politely said: "How happy I
am to be situated between wit and beauty," the famous
French wit could not resist the stinging reply: "Yes, and
to possess neither of them." And when a plain man said
to Jerrold: "My mother was a most beautiful lady," the
satirist looked at him a moment and said: "Then it was
your father that was"— Artemus never lost a friend
for the sake of a hit, and all who knew him were his
friends.

I cannot leave him without mention of one or two of
his sayings, which are too precious to be omitted. A profound philosophy of life underlies one of his reflections.
How many a time have I seen cases that brought it to
mind! On a certain occasion he had attempted to do a
big thing and had disastrously collapsed. Thinking it
over, he quietly remarks, "The fact is I tried to do too
much—and did it!" On another occasion, a frivolous
young man had made fun of his show, and shown no respect for what he called his "venerable hairs." Then he
turned to him, and said: "Young man, such conduct
will not pass unpunished. Some judgment will surely be-
fall you." Then he goes on, and those who, like him, have
tried to hoe corn among the rocks of a Maine farm, will
appreciate the exquisite drollery: "Sure enough; a year
had not passed by, before this young man's uncle died,
and left him a farm down in Oxford county, Maine."

Gentle, lovable Artemus Ward; he breathed the intellectual air of the truest wit and made the world brighter
for every line he ever wrote.

American wit and humor! How can I leave such a
theme and pass by all the bright sayings of statesmen, of
lawyers, of ministers? Here alone is material for, not a
lecture, but for books. But time is left—if indeed any is
left—only for one phase more of the subject. So universal
is the taste for fun, that almost every paper you pick up

has a department devoted to it. And, if our American life must be such a race and strain as it is, I think it is well that there should come the relief of smiles to its terrible tension. If a man can laugh, he can bear a great deal. There is neither crime nor insanity in laughter. When a man can laugh at his own troubles he is safe. When Goldsmith talks of " the loud laugh that spoke the vacant mind " I cannot help thinking his own mind must have been more vacant than usual. For wit and humor are not only almost exclusively human, but they are characteristic of the highest and most refined development of humanity. We do not think of the English dinner-table as over bright when General Schenck tried one of his jokes with such disastrous results. The name of the host was Mr. Christmas—a not uncommon name in England. General Schenck, when our Minister at the Court of St. James, was entertained by this Mr. Christmas. In the course of the dinner the General said: " By the way, Mr. Christmas, there was an American on the steamer with me when I came over who must have been a relation of yours." " Ah," said Mr. Christmas, with a look of bland inquiry, " and who might he have been? " " Oh," replied the General, " he was a man famous in the West by the name of Ben. Holliday." " Oh, but, General, I don't think I have any relative by the name of Holliday." So the joke died a natural death. But after dinner, an anxious inquirer came up to the General, and said: " But, really, General Schenck, was this Mr. Holliday a relation of Mr. Christmas, don't you know? "

The point I wish a little further to speak of is such a widespread newspaper wit and humor as is not known in any other land. Some of the funniest things in all the world are those intermittent flashes of newspaper wit. Take this: Scene, an art exhibit. Under a tender, soulful little sketch by Jones, hangs a placard that reads " Do not touch the picture with cane or umbrella." Whereupon a preternaturally smart boy inscribes the words—as though nothing else would do justice to the subject— " Take a axe."

Or, here is wit—in three lines: " Talk about it's not being healthy to sleep in feathers! Just look at a spring chicken, and see how tough he is! "

Here is the paragraph which tells of the man who did not cry at his wife's funeral, because "she was not a blood relation."

Here is another clipping: Waiter (looking in on a noisy card-party in hotel bedroom)—"I've been sent to ask you to make less noise, gentlemen. The gentleman in the next room says he can't read." Host of the party—"Tell him he ought to be ashamed of himself. Why I could read when I was five years old."

Another. An orator said: "There is not a man, woman, or child in this house, who has arrived at the age of fifty years, but has felt this truth thundering through their ears for centuries."

The other day a Boston publishing house, which had recently brought out an edition of "The Complete Angler," received a letter addressed to Izaak Walton, Esq. It was from a clipping bureau, informing that gentleman that his book was attracting considerable attention, and requesting to be allowed to send notices from all papers in the United States and Canada!

Here is one that suggests the shrinking modesty of a man. On the fly-leaf of one of his own books was found written—"Presented to John Jones, as a mark of esteem —by himself."

Or how is this? A man has married a second wife. She is not a very young thing. He brings her home and presents her to his children, saying: "Here is your new mamma." Whereupon a small boy squares off, and looking at her with his hands in his pockets, calls out, "Say, pa, you've been sold! She ain't new at all."

And so the refreshing stream of fun runs on. There are Western cities that I have seen located in the desert regions, where water is a luxury—but by sinking artesian wells, or from the far-off hills, a source of supply has been found. And things are so arranged that a shining little stream runs sparkling along next the sidewalks, on either side of all the streets. So the thirsty roots of the trees find drink, and the grasses and flowers flourish and are fair. So from the far-off sources of delicate thought and fancy come these flashing, dancing streams of wit and humor and, through the conduits of the daily and weekly papers, run alongside the dusty pathways of the world's every-day drudgery and toil. They help to keep us young and fresh. The ripples of laughter soothe us, and the blossoms of good-nature brighten our weary way. They are the highest men who have the keenest sense for these things; and so it follows that this sense is close akin to that which is divinest in us. And, as we love to think that the grandest development of the race is to be here in America, so it is wholly appropriate that nowhere else should there be so striking a growth as our own American wit and humor.

GEORGE MARY SEARLE

ARE THE PLANETS HABITABLE?

[Lecture by George M. Searle, clergyman and astronomer (born in London, England, June 27, 1839; ———), delivered before the Catholic University of America, Washington, D. C.]

Having completed our survey of the planetary system in which we live, a question naturally occurs to us, which has occurred to every inquiring mind since the real dimensions of the orbs belonging to it were known. To the great majority of mankind it is, and is rightly, a question of greater interest than any one with which mathematics or physics has to deal; of greater interest, since life is a much higher and nobler thing than machinery, and the spiritual far above the material. This question is, " Are these planets which, like our earth, move in their appointed paths around the sun, and on which there is certainly ample room for a population far greater than what our globe could support, actually inhabited by beings in any way like ourselves?"

Almost every astronomer has probably been asked what his views are on this question, and whether his science has anything to tell us about it. At each successive increase in the size of telescopes, men vaguely hope that with the new optical power it may be possible to discover some signs of sentient, and perhaps even of intelligent, life in the celestial worlds. " How much does this telescope magnify?" is always the interesting question to the popular mind. The professional astronomer perhaps is not looking so much for that. He wants to get more light; to see and to delineate faint nebulæ, to follow a comet as far as he can into the darkness of space, in order to determine its orbit as well as possible; but the world in general has comparatively little sympathy with him in this. The discovery of one intelligent being outside this planet of ours would be more interesting to most men here than all the comets which ever have been or ever will be seen.

Is it then possible that the power of telescopes will at any time be so increased that any discovery of this kind can be made? That is what people would like to know. Let us answer this question in the first place.

The moon is our nearest neighbor. If we can magnify enough to see an object the size of a man on any of the planetary orbs, we must first be able to see such an object on the moon. Is it possible to obtain a magnifying power sufficient for this?

It is possible, we answer, to have such a magnifying power; but the difficulty is to avail ourselves of such a power when we have got it. The great and turbulent sea of atmosphere which lies above us is a seemingly insuperable difficulty. To some extent, of course, we can get free from this by placing our telescope on some high mountain; but there is no mountain high enough to place us altogether out of the atmosphere, and if there were one, we could not live or carry a telescope there. At the highest point at which observations would be possible, which probably would be a good deal below the summit of the Himalayas, enough air still would remain above us to prevent our using a power high enough to discern men like ourselves on the face of our satellite. The tremulousness and waviness produced in the telescopic image by the air, which is, of course, increased the more we magnify, would hopelessly obscure outlines so delicate as those here concerned, and make of such small points a simple invisible blur.

Even for the moon, then, the direct discovery of animal life by increased optical power would seem to be a dream which will never be realized. The difficulty, of course, is immensely increased for any other celestial object. No other planet comes nearer to us than about one hundred times the moon's distance; and, moreover, in examining them, we should have to contend with the confusion of outlines coming from their atmospheres as well as from our own.

We may then as well give up hope of trying to answer the question: " Are the planets inhabited?" as one which never will be solved for us in this world by any natural means; and fall back on another, on which science, certainly, can give us some light—namely, " Are they inhabitable? are the physical conditions such in them, so far as we can ascertain, that the life of man or of any highly organized animal could there subsist?"

Now, I say the " planets "; for it seems to me that we may as well put the great central body of our system, the sun itself, out of the question. I think it is pretty clear that the surface at least of this enormous globe is in such a state as to make it absolutely impossible for us to conceive of any organized life existing there. It is true that we do not know exactly how much complexity of structure is required in matter as a basis of life; but we can hardly consider life in the proper sense as belonging to a chemical molecule, and everything would indicate that on the surface of the sun matter is reduced to its simply chemical or molecular state. Any structures or organisms which we call alive would instantly be destroyed in that intense flame; even inanimate shapes like those of crystals would not survive its action for a moment.

But may there not be a cooler region below the sun's surface, protected in some way from the intense heat of the exterior? Such a theory was entertained in the last century and even in this; but it is pretty safe to say that no one now would hold it. That it should have held its ground so long is due perhaps, in great measure, to the authority of Sir William Herschel. I do not think it was ever satisfactorily explained just how the interior was protected from the immense radiation of its envelope; certainly it is hard for us to see nowadays, knowing as we do the radiating power of the surface (10,000 horse power per square foot, as we find it to be), how such a blaze as this could even be supposed to be cut off from any point within. To suggest a cool place in the interior of the sun is much as if one should advise a person suffering from the heat of a furnace to wrap himself up well and take a seat inside. Moreover, we know from spectroscopic indications now, particularly from those of oxygen in the sun, that the farther in we go, the hotter it gets; and this also would follow from the only theory which can reasonably account for the formation of the sun, and the maintenance of its heat.

We may pretty certainly say, then, that in any common-sense way of using the word, the sun is not habitable. Absolutely speaking, of course, all space is habitable; there is no conclusive reason why an organized being should require nutriment or air, and hence an animal might be conceived as being launched into space as a planet on his own account. But what we mean by a place being habitable is, that it should furnish the requisites and conveniences belonging to a life similar in its principal features to that with which we are acquainted, It is not a thing which can be strictly defined; nevertheless, we know well enough for practical purposes what we are talking about, and we know that such a place as this empty space is not " habitable."

From the consideration of the sun we will pass to that of the next most conspicuous object to us in the planetary system—that is to say, the moon. I have already expressed in a previous lecture the views generally entertained by astronomers about the moon. It is pretty certain that the side of it which we see offers nothing in the way of a convenience of life except mere standing-room. There is hardly a doubt that its surface consists simply of bare rock, unvaried by water, soil, or any kind of vegetation; that if there be any atmosphere upon it, it is so excessively rarefied as to be, for purposes of life, practically equivalent to none.

As to the other side, of course, we can say nothing positively. It may perhaps in some way be different from this. But taking the ordinary and (to say the least) very probable view as to the method of formation of the planetary masses, by cooling from a liquid condition, it is hard to see how there could possibly be any considerable difference of shape or of density between the half of the lunar sphere which is turned toward us and that which is turned away. And unless there be such a difference, the other side must be as destitute of atmosphere as this; and if of atmosphere, of water as well; for the water or other fluid, if existing in any quantity, would form an atmosphere, if none previously existed.

The moon then hardly seems to present the condition required for what we should call a habitable planet; though it fails in a very different way from the sun. The moon is dead; the sun is too much alive. The moon may have been habitable and inhabited once; the sun may be in the future.

So far, our survey has not been very encouraging. But we have not yet considered the planets properly so-called.

In considering them from this point of view, let us proceed in the contrary order to that which we followed in describing them in detail. Let us start at the outer limit, with the great twin planets, as we may call them, on account of their great similarity, widely separated in space as they are—namely, Uranus and Neptune.

These would perhaps generally be imagined as very cheerless habitations for intelligent beings, on account of their distance from the sun, and the comparatively small amount of light and heat which that great central fire sends to them, if that which the earth receives be taken as the standard. Particularly would this impress us in the case of Neptune. Its distance from the sun is about thirty times ours, and, according to the oft-repeated law of the inverse squares of the distances, the light and heat which it gets from the sun is only one nine-hundredth part of that which we receive. But let us not give up the matter as hopeless on this account. One nine-hundredth part of sunlight is not such a faint illumination, after all. It is nearly seven hundred times the light of the full moon, and indeed equal to that given by a large electric arc lamp at a distance of a few feet. There would be no difficulty about reading by means of it; it would be quite sufficient for all the ordinary practical purposes for which sunlight is used here. And then there is another consideration which is of very great weight.

It is this: You know that, as I have said, what astronomers increase the size of telescopes for is to gather more light, rather than to get greater magnifying power. A telescope of two inches diameter, or aperture, as it is technically called, will give four times as much light as one of only one inch; one of ten inches will give twenty-five times as much as the two-inch, or a hundred times as much as the one-inch.   The great Lick telescope, of three feet aperture, makes a star look about thirteen hundred times as bright as a one-inch spy-glass, and enables us to see stars about twenty thousand times fainter than any which can be seen with the naked eye.   And the same rule would hold for the eye itself.   If we should increase the size of the pupil of the eye, we should see fainter objects than we do now; and we indeed actually do this when we go from bright light into a dark room.   We can easily see how the pupil dilates to accommodate itself to reduced light, by simply examining another person's eye in these changed conditions, or our own before a looking-glass.   The eye of a cat changes much more.   If the retina of the cat's eye is as sensitive as our own, she must habitually see stars five or six times fainter than any which we can discern without a glass, and the heavens must present to her a magnificent appearance, if she cares to look at them.   Probably she actually uses this increased light rather to discover mice than stars; but her astronomical opportunities are there all the same, though she may not avail herself of them.

It is true that this increased light is obtained in the eye at some sacrifice of definition, or sharpness of vision in detail; but still an inhabitant of Neptune might have a good deal larger pupil, in proportion to the size of his eye, than ours.   And then, again, there is no reason why the retina itself should not be made much more sensitive to light than ours; and here we have an increase which has no limit, so far as we can tell.   It would be an injury to us to have our optic nerve more sensitive; the strong sunlight to which we are exposed would hurt us.   But there is no reason why the Neptunians should not have what would be a benefit to them.

The whole question, then, of light in the solar system is one of little consequence; eyes could easily in any planet be such as to suit the exigencies of the case.

With regard to heat, the question is a little more difficult, but not very much.   If we should assume that the 500° Fahrenheit by which our temperature here is raised above that of space are simply due to our distance from the sun, and that Neptune could only have one nine-hundredth part of that, of course the temperature there would practically be that of space itself, or 460° below the Fahrenheit zero. But we know that, in fact, the genial warmth of the earth is in a great measure due to its atmospheric garment or blanket; and we cannot be at all sure that an atmosphere may not exist on Neptune which may make the absorption so much greater than the radiation that an equality between the two would not be reached before the planet had accumulated from its scanty solar supply enough to make its temperature equal to ours.

And, besides, there is no certainty that these greater outer planets may not still retain a great deal of their own intrinsic heat; that they may yet be warm enough, even on the surface, to act as a source of heat to their inhabitants. Indeed, the danger here is rather that they are too hot than too cold. Yes, that is the trouble with all the great outer planets, with Jupiter and Saturn, as well as Uranus and Neptune, as we shall shortly see. As far as atmosphere is concerned, the spectroscope would indicate rather a dense one on both Uranus and Neptune, and of the same character on each. Uranus shows belts on its planets. On the whole, we may say that there is quite what we may call a probability that Uranus and Neptune are in a habitable condition; the probability, is, however, as we may say, rather negative than positive; we cannot give any certain reason why they should not be; but there are really no positive indications to show that they are fit to be the abode of life. The arguments against habitability become much stronger in the case of the two giants of the planetary system, Saturn and Jupiter, which come next in order as we proceed toward the sun. The brilliancy of Jupiter's surface, and the rapidity of the changes which we see there, exceeding what the moderate light and heat which it receives from the sun would be likely to produce, seem to be quite strong arguments that it is still in a condition to emit light and heat to a considerable extent on its own account; and, indeed, that its temperature is still sufficient to keep it in a fluid state. If its surface be indeed in the condition of molten metal, it certainly becomes uninhabitable in the common-sense view of the subject; for in melted metal no organism composed of ordinary chemical elements could possibly subsist.

These arguments apply with somewhat diminished force to Saturn. Another, however, which may perhaps be derived from the lightness or small density of all the four great exterior planets of which we have been speaking, is strongest in the case of this one. This lightness may indicate that they have not yet shrunk to their proper dimensions, for it seems reasonable enough to suppose that the chemical constituents throughout the solar system are the same; that all the planets are chips out of the same block; and that when all are reduced to the physical state of the earth they would have about the same density. But this does not seem to amount to much; for though it holds well enough in the cases of Mars and Venus, it notably fails in that of Mercury, if the determinations of the mass of that planet can be considered as trustworthy. The density of Mercury would appear, it will be remembered, to be twice that of the earth; which would prove most undoubtedly that it was made of decidedly heavier materials, unless we maintain that it is very much more solidified than the earth, which would seem to be improbable. When a planet has once become, like the earth, solid on the surface, no further perceptible shrinkage is possible except by a complete breaking up of the crust, which could hardly result except from a collision.

But to return to the great planets of which we have been speaking. I think few, if any, astronomers believe them to be habitable in their present condition; for, though the case is more doubtful for Uranus and Neptune, still they have in their general features, so much resemblance to Jupiter and Saturn, that it is usually presumed that they are in the same state. But no one could pretend to be certain with regard to the matter.

Before we leave this portion of our system, however, we must not omit a part of it which is eminently worth considering with reference to the present question. I mean the numerous satellites, which are such a striking feature in it.

Let us consider specially those of Jupiter, about which we know the most. The four moons of Jupiter are all quite considerable bodies, ranging in size from that of our moon to that of the planet Mars. There is plenty of room on them for a very large population; the surface of the largest does not fall far short of that of the land part of our own globe. There is no reason why they should not be in the same general physical state as the earth is; we have already seen that, as far as light and heat are concerned, they may be considered as amply provided; perhaps, indeed, even better than we; for the great planet itself, round which they circulate, would probably serve as a much better luminary by night than our own moon, and may very probably contribute not a little to keeping them comfortably warm, if it is indeed still in a melted and glowing condition. We may well believe that it is indeed a second sun to them, and if the satellites of Jupiter keep, like our own moon, the same side always turned toward the primary planet, that favored side would enjoy a continual warmth, which might indeed be excessive.

Similar remarks may, of course, be made of all the other satellites which we find in this great region, revolving round Saturn, Uranus, and Neptune. Much has been said of the splendor of the Saturnian sky as seen from the planet itself, with the great ring arching over the heavens and the satellites circling along it. It is far more likely that, if this splendor is seen at all, it is from the satellites, from which, especially from Japetus, the most remote, whose orbit lies outside of the plane of the ring, a most magnificent view of the noble planet, with its rings and the other satellites, could be had. Saturn from Japetus would look as it does to us with a magnifying power of about three hundred and fifty diameters; or, to use another illustration, the ball of the planet would look about three and a half times the diameter of the moon, and the rings nearly nine times that diameter.

We come next, in our inward course, to the planet Mars. Here, for the first time, we begin to see positive signs, instead of mere negative possibilities, of what we have been looking for.

We have noticed, as we passed this planet on our way outward from the sun, the similarity of its surface to that of the earth, the permanent configurations on it of what we have a good right to assume to be land and water.

We have seen its polar ice-caps, its green seas, and red earth; and we know that it has an atmosphere which, though not as dense as our own, is still enough, as it would seem, for life. We know that it has a day almost exactly the same as ours, and not only this, but seasons substantially like our own, as far as the varying angle is concerned at which the sun's rays strike its surface, though it is true that these are a good deal interfered with by the considerable variation in the sun's heat, depending on the eccentricity of its orbit; still this would not amount to so very much. In this latitude, for instance, on the earth, we receive more than three times the heat from the sun in one day in the middle of June than we get in the middle of December, on any given area, say a square mile or a square yard, owing to the combined influence of the greater height of the sun above the horizon and the greater length of the daylight. About the same would be the case in the same latitude on Mars. The effect of the eccentricity would be quite considerable, making the sun's heat once and a half as great at the nearest point as at the farthest; still, if we can sustain the threefold multiplication, a half as much again might be added, without the variation becoming intolerable. Moreover, this great variation would only occur when the summer solstice of one of the hemispheres coincided with the point of nearest approach to the sun. During half the time, the eccentricity would tend to moderate, instead of to accentuate, the seasons, as it does with us here in the northern hemisphere now.

Mars is certainly the most favorable case for those who would believe the planets to be habitable. It really seems that it might be inhabited by men like ourselves. As remarked on a previous occasion, its climate seems, from the small size of the polar ice-caps, to be warmer than that of the earth, in spite of its greater distance from the sun.

As to Venus and Mercury, we can hardly form any decided opinion. They seem to be surrounded by dense, cloudy atmospheres, which may tend, in a great measure, to keep off the intense heat of the sun. A rather singular thing has lately been observed, or at least thought to be observed, by Schiaparelli, with regard to Mercury—that is, that some markings on it seem to indicate that its period of rotation round its axis is the same as that of its revolution round the sun; or, in other words, that it acts as our moon does, keeping always the same face toward the center round which it revolves. This would seem to be borne out by the white spot on the black disk of the planet, which has been reported by various observers as regularly visible at the time of its transits across the sun's face. If this white spot is a real object, it would seem that it is always turned away from the sun. If this can be accepted, it would be, of course, to some extent, an argument against the habitability of Mercury, as its inhabitants would be deprived of the vicissitude of day and night, and the side turned constantly toward the sun would probably, in spite of everything, become uncomfortably warm.

Now that we have—though quite hurriedly—completed our consideration of the planets as to their suitableness for habitation, what answer shall we give to the question with which we started? Before giving it, another reflection must be made, which will brighten the prospect a good deal for those who would fain believe all these magnificent orbs to be the abode of life like ours.

It is this: Will it not suffice to satisfy the minds of those who cannot believe that these great globes, similar in so many respects to ours, can be tenantless, to hold that they are habited for a portion, though not for the whole, of their history? For myself, I do not feel the craving for the plurality of worlds, as it is called, which seems to be general. I must confess that I have never been able, personally, to feel the force of the argument which strikes most minds so powerfully, that these habitations could not have been made by their Creator except to be actually inhabited. The mere size and mass of an object seem to me to amount to little. Jupiter itself, or Saturn, with its beautiful ring and satellite system, simply as a mass of matter or a mechanical construction, is a far less noble creation of God than a single human soul; nor does it seem to me that the mere size of these planets makes them much more remarkable, or requires more reason for their formation, than if they were only a few feet in diameter. The technical study of astronomy, no doubt, has the effect of reducing the impression made by

mere magnitude on the mind; whether this is a delusion
or the removal of a delusion, of course I cannot say.
That the mere size of a body itself does not require inhabitants for it, seems plain from the generally confessed
impossibility of inhabiting the sun, the surface of which
far exceeds that of all the planets put together—that is to
say, that it does not require them at every moment; but it
may be, if you will, that it does require that at some time
or other it should be used for such a purpose.   The general belief is, we may say, an argument for the fact.

And, of course, the argument for the plurality of worlds
is strenghtened if, besides size or standing-room, as we
may say, we see some other conditions indicating conveniences for life, though they be imperfect or incomplete.
If we see a house with only its framework up, we say,
" Nobody lives there now, but it is being built for some
one; " and if we see a house in ruins, we say, " Somebody
lived there once."

Now, this is certainly very plausible; and I think that
the history of our own earth, so far as it can be learned
from science, increases the probability of the opinion that
the planets, and perhaps even the sun itself, were made
to be inhabited at some time or other.   The teaching of
geology is that our own earth was for a long time uninhabitable; that it subsequently became fitted to be the
abode of the inferior and simpler forms of life, and finally
became ready for the reception of man; and we can hardly
shut our eyes, either, to the scientific conclusion that, from
the operation of natural causes alone, it would at some
time in the distant future become uninhabitable again,
though in a different way; that it would become, simply
from the changes which must come from the gradual
progress of cooling necessarily going on in the solar system, no longer a building which its Creator is forming, but
a cold and desolate ruin like the moon.

The history of this earth is probably the history of the
other planets, if they are to be allowed to develop in a
natural way.   Some, like the moon, seem to have passed
farther along the road than our own planet.   This is probably the case with Mars, the most habitable in appearance
of them all.   As a rule, of course, the smaller a planet is,
other things being equal, the more rapidly it will cool

from its originally incandescent state; Mars then should be older—that is, have passed through more of its successive changes—than we. It looks so, besides. The seas seem to be drying up, the air thinning away. On the other hand, the great superior planets, Jupiter, Saturn, Uranus, and Neptune are young, and have the best part of their life before them.

What portion of the total life of a planet is that in which it becomes habitable by beings like ourselves we cannot very well determine. If we accept the estimates of geology, the time that the human race has been here is a very small part of our world's history. But how much longer this earth would naturally remain a possible residence for us we cannot say with accuracy. It would seem probable, however, that the period in which all the necessary conditions of life would simultaneously exist can hardly be a very considerable part of the whole. The inhabitants of a planet in the stage of decadence from its most perfect state could, no doubt, on the principle of the "survival of the fittest," accommodate themselves to their more unfavorable circumstances for a good while; but the time would come when the struggle would have to be abandoned.

If it is true that the period of habitability by the high organisms is a small part of a planet's life, obviously the chance is small for any planet in particular of its being in that period now or at any particular time. We must say that it probably is not, unless we have, as in the case of Mars, some positive indications that it is. So far as we can trust such positive indications, Venus and Mercury are approaching that part of their life that the earth is in at present; the earth seems at one time to have had the very dense and vaporous atmosphere that apparently surrounds them now.

To sum up now, briefly, the results to which our examination has led us: In the first place, our observations should probably be modified by the very plausible theory, now generally adopted, that all the bodies of our system, sun, and planets, have passed and are passing through a series of changes, beginning with a state of great heat and expansion, in which and for a long time no life is possible on their surfaces, and in a great part of which indeed, as in the case of the sun at present, they can hardly be

said to have a surface at all.   As the changes due to the
gradual cooling and contraction proceed, life in its simpler
forms becomes possible, and in course of time a state is
reached like that of this globe at present, in which the conditions for highly organized life are at their best.

Assuming this, the question of fact becomes: Is there
any other planet or satellite in the system in which this
state of maximum habitability, if we may so call it, now
exists?   We can say with great confidence that it does not
on Jupiter and Saturn; that the chances are much against
it on Uranus and Neptune; that Venus and Mercury are
probably still too young for it; but that there is a reasonable probability for it on Mars, though this planet seems
to be passing into the decline, the steps of which we do
not clearly understand, but of which we see perhaps the
final result in the torn, scarred, and desolate surface of
our own satellite.   With regard to the satellites of the
great planets, we have absolutely to suspend judgment.
As the period of habitability is probably less than that of
development, though of this we are far from certain, the
chances are perhaps against any particular one of them
being in that state just now; but as they number at least
seventeen altogether, the probability that some one of
them may be habitable is not so inconsiderable.   As to the
satellites of Mars, and the swarm of asteroids, they seem
to be too small to retain an atmosphere sufficient for the
support of beings like ourselves.   If they had a course
to run, it has probably been concluded long ago.

In speaking of the natural life and development of the
planets, we are, of course, looking at the matter merely
from a scientific point of view.   Of course, most Christians believe that long before the natural life of this earth
is concluded, it will suffer a final catastrophe which will
at least close the history of the human race on it as it
exists now.   Such catastrophes may, of course, occur to
any planet by natural as well as supernatural causes; by
collision with some other body, for instance; or to the
whole planetary system, by some large body striking on
the sun.   One thing which we may perhaps look forward
to is a time when, after the death or destruction of all the
planets, the sun itself ceasing to be a luminary and furnace
for bodies circulating around it, may itself become the

great seat and home of life. In theorizing on this point we have no past experience or history to guide us. We shall see as we go on to discuss the stellar systems that we have at least one case, perhaps more than one, of a body sunlike in dimensions, which has either ceased to give light, or never gave it. It is only in exceptional cases that we have any means of recognizing the existence of such bodies; they may be very numerous. Neither can we tell whether the other innumerable brilliant suns scattered through space have attendant planets like our own. But it would be strange if they had not. If any considerable proportion of them have, evidently the chance that there are other habitable worlds in the universe becomes very great.

GARRETT PUTNAM SERVISS

Photogravure after a photograph from life

GARRETT PUTNAM SERVISS

NAPOLEON BONAPARTE

[Lecture by Garrett P. Serviss, journalist, author, lecturer in astronomy (born in Sharon Springs, N. Y., March 24, 1851; ———), delivered in many places during the season of 1898 and '99.]

LADIES AND GENTLEMEN:—Whenever the pendulum that ticks centuries swings back to the starting point men always begin to talk of what occurred a hundred years ago. Standing to-day at the meeting of two centuries we can actually observe this law in operation. But no political event marking the close of the Nineteenth century will make so deep a notch in history as did one that came about at the end of the Eighteenth. Community of interests makes every king the brother of every other king, and at the close of the Eighteenth century the kings had all Europe under their thumbs.

Then came the French Revolution, and a king of France lost his head, as a king of England had lost his a hundred and forty-four years earlier. The result, in one respect, was, in both cases, similar. When the English revolutionists beheaded their king, France, to say the least of it, encouraged his successor. When the French revolutionists indulged in regicide, England repaid the debt with interest bigger than the principal.

But the uprising in France had been against a more terrible oppression, and the pent-up forces released by it were more dreadful in their explosive violence. The consequence was that the beheading of the Bourbon caused greater consternation among the royalists than had that of the Stuart. When the head of Louis XVI fell into the basket, every king in Europe felt the shock in his ver-

tebræ. They all knew that it meant for them a struggle
to the death; they must shoot down this mad dog of
revolution! They must grind under an iron heel this
scorpion of "liberty and equality."

At this instant, when France, made wild by the quick
removal of long-borne burdens, and crazed by the sudden
enjoyment of new-found privileges, was facing her myriad
of foes with the reckless daring and superhuman strength
of a maniac crossed—and Europe, black with the thunder-
clouds and ablaze with the lightnings of war, was bearing
down to annihilate her—suddenly there strode upon the
scene the most commanding figure that the world had
beheld since the days of Cæsar. Napoleon Bonaparte
came—to rule the storm!

Born in the little island of Corsica, which was too small
to be an independent nation and too proud willingly to
submit to foreign rule, Napoleon, to begin with, was virtually a man without a country. But, the island being
under French control, he naturally looked to France in
the search for avenues of advancement, and having a
strong inclination to mathematics he made good progress
in the military school at Brienne, and, later, in that at
Paris.

His favorite books—and this is always an important
point to consider in such cases—were Plutarch's Lives
the Roman histories of Tacitus, and the poems called
Ossian's. The great astronomer Laplace was one of his
examiners when he had completed his course, and then he
became a second-lieutenant in the artillery.

While his person was slight and his stature considerably
below the average, he was very handsome. The earliest
authentic portrait of him is said to have been painted upon
the order of Madame Columbier of Valence, where his
regiment was first stationed. It is a picture remarkable
for beauty. Everybody has heard the story of how Madame Columbier's daughter used to prefer young Bonaparte for her companion when the young people went into
the garden to eat cherries. It was all quite in the order
of nature, of course, and yet one can hardly help smiling
at the thought of this man, who was so soon to become
the master of Europe, and the mightiest personality on
the earth, eating cherries with a pretty girl, and taking

dancing lessons to increase his social popularity! [Applause.]

Napoleon struggled desperately with poverty at the beginning of his career, and was driven to many shifts in order to get along, and these, it seems to me, have been very unfairly represented by one of his recent biographers, who conveys the impression that they denoted extraordinary moral obliquity in the young man. But his opportunity came at last, as it had to come to one of his capacity. The English were assisting the counter-revolution at Toulon in Southern France, and had sent a fleet to garrison and defend the city. The Convention government in Paris—for by this time the king and queen had been beheaded and the revolutionists were in full control—was conducting a siege of Toulon in the regular old-fashioned way. At length, Lieutenant Napoleon Bonaparte was sent to command the artillery operating against the town. Not very much was thought of him at that time, but he saw at a glance what ought to be done. The harbor of Toulon is shut off from the Mediterranean Sea by a rocky promontory, and the English fleet lay inside the harbor.

"Don't waste time besieging the city," said Bonaparte, "take that promontory!"

The proposition seems a very clear one, yet the Convention generals apparently did not appreciate it. Luckily the young artillery officer was allowed to have his way. He got the promontory, and the English got—out. That was not merely the end of the siege of Toulon, it was the beginning of a revolution in the art of war!

When you are in Paris one of the things to see is the old church of Saint Roch, for it denotes the second stride taken by Napoleon from poverty to empire. Less than two years after the fall of Toulon, the Convention government was threatened with overthrow by an uprising of insurrectionary sections. Fortunately Bonaparte had been appointed to command the troops defending the government, and he put a ring of steel around the Convention so quickly that the members themselves did not know what had been done.

This is the famous scene that was dramatized by Carlyle in his prose poem on the French Revolution. On come the insurgents and seize the church. But Bonaparte had foreseen the importance of the position and planted his guns on the spot. With yells and cheers the insurgents advance upon the troops:—

"Steady!"—so runs Carlyle's depiction—"The artillery officer is steady as bronze; can, if need were, be quick as lightning."

The mob bursts into a wild onslaught.

"Whereupon, thou bronze artillery officer? 'Fire!' say the bronze lips, and blaze and thunder go his great guns," and blaze and thunder again until "the French revolution is blown into space!"

At this moment, when the star of Napoleon has just begun to sparkle on the horizon, Josephine appears upon the scene, treasuring in her memory the words of an old negro sorceress, pronounced while she was yet a child in far-off, palm-shaded San Domingo, and predicting that she should one day be greater than a queen. Well, whatever else may be thought of Josephine, at any rate she brought good fortune to Napoleon. Through her acquaintance with leading men he was placed close to the head of affairs as soon as their marriage had been solemnized.

All this while, remember, the kings are making war upon France. England, Austria, the German Empire, Sardinia and Naples, are all in the coalition against her. A new general is needed to command the French army in Italy, and Napoleon, largely through Josephine's influence, gets the place. It is from the balmy shores of the Riviera that the modern Cæsar makes his third stride, and this time dazzles the world! Here begins that terrible striking-at-the-center which so dumfounded all of the older generals, and successively dashed into pieces the mightiest armies that Europe could assemble!

Napoleon found the French army in Italy clothed in rags, scattered and disorganized along the Riviera. Behind it on the sea was the English fleet; confronting it on the mountains, in overwhelming force, were the Austrians and Sardinians. Within a week he had concentrated his little army and was over the mountains, pointing his soldiers to the rich plain of Lombardy!

The old Austrian general Beaulieu was in command of

the enemy. Beaulieu had been informed that a young French general was coming against him, but he was a veteran, and the news did not disturb him. But within less than a fortnight, he and his Sardinian lieutenant had fought five pitched battles with the young general, with such breathless rapidity of repetition and such crushing succession of hopeless defeat, that, before they comprehended what had struck them, the Austrians were fleeing down the Po, the Sardinians were annihilated in the mountains, and Napoleon was thundering at the gates of Turin!

The king of Sardinia already had enough. He saved his capital from capture by promptly accepting the terms which the young conqueror dictated, and withdrew from the war. As Mr. Bret Harte would have put it, "the subsequent proceedings interested him no more." [Applause.]

In the meantime Beaulieu with his Austrians got behind the river Po. They thought they were out of the whirlwind—but it had only just begun to blow!

Napoleon induced the enemy to believe that he was about to cross the Po at Valenza. That was exactly the spot where Beaulieu, who made war according to rule, would have crossed if he had been in the French general's place. But Bonaparte, who always made his own rules, hurried his army fifty miles down the river and had it ferried across, and when the Austrians woke up the whirlwind was in their rear.

They ran—to get behind another river, the Adda. This time Beaulieu carefully looked out for all the ferries, but now Napoleon seemed to be thinking only of the bridges. There was one at Lodi. Behind it was the Austrian army and a huge park of artillery which could sweep the bridge from end to end. Napoleon brought up his artillery at his end of the bridge and began a furious cannonade.

"Ah, yes," the old Austrian general said to himself, "I knew it! the boy is after the bridge,"—and then he forgot the fords! [Applause.]

When the proper moment had arrived, Napoleon sent his cavalry round to one of the neglected fords, and after it had crossed and fallen upon the rear of the enemy, the

"Little Corporal"—for it was at this famous fight that
his admiring soldiers dubbed him with that immortal name
—seized a standard, and, followed by Lannes and one or
two other officers, led a charge, in the face of the grape-
shot, across the bridge! The Austrians were bayonetted
at their guns, and Beaulieu lost no time in getting behind
a third river, the Mincio.

Beaulieu being now out of his way Napoleon entered
the royal city of Milan in triumph and gave his tired army
a few days' rest, while he levied upon the opulent town
for money and supplies and sent off some of its choicest
artistic treasures to Paris. In the meanwhile an uprising
against the invaders occurred in Lombardy, and the city
of Pavia, whose ancient bridge and beautiful cathedral
are admired by all modern travelers in Italy, was wrenched
from the possession of the French. Napoleon advanced
upon Pavia, blew open its gates and put down the insurrection with a savage severity which henceforth made his
name feared as much as it was admired. Thus every new
undertaking developed some unexpected side of his character.

Then he took Beaulieu in hand once more. A little
rapid maneuvering compelled the Austrian to shut himself
up in the strongly fortified town of Mantua, which was
called "the citadel of Italy." Mantua, lying in a marshy
plain, could be approached only by means of five cause-
ways. Napoleon immediately seized four of these, but
the fifth was too strong to be stormed, and so he began a
siege.

Meanwhile the Austrian government, finding that
Beaulieu was no match for the young French general,
sent another famous soldier, General Wurmser, with
30,000 fresh men to drive the invader out of Italy. The
Austrian forces altogether numbered 80,000, the French
only 30,000. But Napoleon, who could always make
one man count for three or four through the rapidity of
his combinations, beat the enemy here, crushed him there,
and finally sent him flying for refuge to the mountains
of the Tyrol.

Then Wurmser advanced again to the attack with
30,000 fresh troops, but was beaten worse than before,

and only succeeded in getting in out of the storm by shutting himself up in Mantua.

Next the Austrian government sent a third tried soldier, Marshal Alvinzi, with another army into Italy.   But
the marshal had no better success than his predecessors,
and Napoleon, still keeping his grip upon Mantua, annihilated the fourth army that had been hurled against
him.   A fifth Austrian army, also commanded by Alvinzi,
advanced to the attack.   This was routed in the tremendous battle of Rivoli, among the mountains, where Napoleon added immensely to his influence over his troops
by his personal daring, having three horses shot under
him in the course of the battle.

A few days after Rivoli, Wurmser surrendered Mantua.

The Archduke Charles, the most celebrated general in
Europe, was now matched against Napoleon with a sixth
Austrian army, but Charles suffered the fate of all the
others, and then, at last, Austria sued for peace, while
Napoleon whirled on his heel and advanced against
Venice, which had declared war and attacked him in the
rear while he was busy with the Austrians.

"You have treacherously shed French blood," he said
to the Doge, who begged for peace when he learned that
the terrible victor was actually marching upon Venice,
"you have treacherously shed French blood and the lion
of St. Mark must lick the dust!"

The Venetians, not daring to fight, threw down their
arms.   Napoleon put an end to the rule of the Doges,
set up a new republic in Venice, and sent the famous
bronze horses of San Marco and other priceless treasures
of art to Paris.

Thus ended the Italian campaigns, the greatest marvel
in military history.

"From that time," said Napoleon at St. Helena, "I
saw what I might become.   I already beheld the world
beneath me, as if I were being carried through the air!"
[Applause.]

Our next scene is in Egypt, and on the banks of the
Nile we shall behold the development of another phase
in the character of this amazing man.

The Egyptian expedition has always been for historians

a hard nut to crack. "Why was it ever undertaken?" they ask. Well, it seems to me that at least a partial answer may be found in the enormous development of the imagination in Napoleon. He was the Shakespeare of war—a tremendous realist and a superb romanticist in one and the same person, and subject to no rules whatever. Did you ever hear of an army organized on the plan of Napoleon's army for the invasion of Egypt? One of its most carefully selected divisions consisted of a band of learned men—men of science, men of letters—intended to open up the marvels of the ancient Nile land to the modern world.

"Napoleon was only a soldier," sneer some of his enemies. But they forget his Egyptian army when they say that. No man who was "only a soldier" would have chosen a staff consisting of artists, architects, astronomers, historians, civil engineers, linguists, archæologists—or would have established in the land he conquered an institute through which to distribute rewards, not to the shedders of blood but to the decipherers of inscriptions and the discoverers of forgotten memories of former ages. [Applause.]

When King Cambyses invaded Egypt and laid siege to the town of Pelusium, which was situated not far from the place where Napoleon landed, finding that the walls resisted all his engines he bethought him that among the Egyptians cats were sacred animals. Immediately he filled a bag with them, and, commanding his followers to do the same, galloped around the city throwing cats at the enemy. As the sacred animals dropped gyrating and squalling from the air, the Egyptians fell upon their knees and Cambyses took the town.

That is one of the most Napoleonic feats recorded in ancient times. Napoleon would probably have done the same thing if he had lived in the same time. But living in a different time he did the same thing in a different manner. He paralyzed the Egyptians by throwing cats at them symbolically—that is to say, by flattering them. He adopted their customs, he learned to ride camels, he read the Koran, he commanded the soldiers never to interfere with their religious observances. Lord Rosebery seems to think that Napoleon actually became at heart a Mohammedan. But, in this instance, his lordship fails to understand the man. Napoleon became so much interested in the East that even its prevailing religion remained a prominent object in his thoughts to the end of his days, but it is absurd to suppose that he really believed in Mohammed—except as a conqueror. [Applause.]

At this time the Mamelukes, originally imported slaves of the Egyptians, had turned the tables upon their masters and become the rulers of the country, and Napoleon, pursuing his invariable policy of first dividing the enemy when he could, began by separating the Egyptians from their Mameluke oppressors. After that he had only the Mamelukes to fight.

When the French army, advancing up the Nile, came in sight of the Pyramids, they beheld the great host of the Mamelukes encamped in the vast plain—their splendid cavalry ready for a charge, their dazzling banners and pennons enlivening the landscape, and their camp strongly fortified with artillery. The hearts of the Western soldiers sank at the formidable spectacle, but Napoleon's eagle eye detected at a glance what nobody else had noted —that there was a fatal defect in the enemy's plan of defence; their cannon had no carriages, consequently they could fire in only one direction!

"Soldiers! Forty centuries are watching you from yonder pyramids! Forward, by the right flank!"

The situation cleared in an instant. By simply swerving a little to one side he had rendered the cannon of the Mamelukes useless, and before they could realign them, their army was ground to powder.

Then an Oriental dream opened before the eyes of this Homeric conqueror, whose birth sheet had been a tapestry representing scenes from the Iliad. While his soldiers were wondering at the strange faces and costumes and customs, and tasting the delight of a life as strange to their occidental experience as if they had been transported to another planet, and while his army of savants, under his direction and encouragement, was investigating pyramids, Sphinxes, and temples, ransacking tombs, delving in labyrinths, measuring and picturing strange gigantic statues, and causing the buried wonders of ancient Egypt to rise before the astonished eyes of mankind, Napoleon

himself was dreaming of other conquests, and rehearsing
in his memory as from an eminence he gazed upon Cairo,
the Queen of the Nile, the deeds of Alexander and the
conquering march of Mahomet!

When the musical cry of the muezzin fell from the
minarets and stirred the ærial chords of Egypt's golden
atmosphere, *he* could see, through and beyond the spires
of Cairo, the magical gleam of distant Bagdad and even
the towers of Bombay reflected in the dark blue mirror
of the Indian ocean.   Everything that he had reached for
thus far, he had attained!   Cæsar at fifty years of age had
not climbed higher than he now stood at thirty.   Did not
the Sphinx itself, brooding upon the world with its un-
guessed secret, silently command *him* to march toward
the *rising* sun?   It was to men who left such monuments
as these and who, when they marched to conquest, swept
empires whose domains extended from noon to sunset—
not petty States crowded among European mountains,
such as he had already trampled under foot, with scarce
an effort—it was to men of that stamp and of these boundless opportunities that he felt *himself* akin, and by their
deeds he measured his own!   [Applause.]

There is no doubt that Napoleon found a strange inspiration in Egypt.   Its very architecture carries the mind
into vast spaces and summons visions of enchantment.
Its ancient glories were always before his eyes and in his
thoughts.   Its antique rulers, disturbed by the rude hand
of science, rose from their sarcophagi, as if to greet him
their brother of a later age!   He made his engineers restore the canals which had been closed and forgotten for
centuries, and thus caused the waters of the Nile to enrich
the land as they had not done since the days of the
Pharaohs.   He revived the agriculture of Egypt; he
nearly lost his life in exploring the Red Sea where Moses
was said to have crossed; he visited the Mount Sinai peninsula, and he had surveys made which in our day have
resulted in the Suez Canal.

His dream of Oriental conquest led him next into the
Holy Land.   He put the Turks to flight at El Arish and
took the ancient city of Joppa or Jaffa, on the seacoast of
Palestine, by storm.   The prisoners who had been paroled
at El Arish, but who were found again in arms at Jaffa,

were led out on the sandhills and shot, and their bones were afterward piled into a pyramid. Napoleon was as pitiless as a glacier. "He would shorten a straight line to come at his object," says Emerson, and yet, as Emerson also remarks, he was not cruel, although merciless, and besides, he had a kind of courage which most men lack. When the plague broke out among his soldiers in the hospital at Jaffa, he went among them and rebuked the cowardice of the attendants, who had fled at the very name of so dreaded a disease, by himself, with his own hands, dressing their ulcers. Some of the men believed there was healing in his touch. He may almost have believed it himself, for he certainly possessed that supreme confidence in his star of destiny which has marked every man of his stamp, and which shines forth in the familiar story of Cæsar's words to the frightened boatman who was rowing him across a stormy water, "Have no fear—thou carriest Cæsar and his fortunes!" [Applause.]

But in one thing fortune did not favor him. From the day of his arrival in Palestine the old fortified town of Acre, famous since the Crusades for its desperate sieges, held out against him. He had left the larger part of his army in Egypt, he had no siege artillery and he had not force enough with him to carry the place by storm. Yet he would not desist. While he beleaguered the town, a great army of Mussulmans was assembling in the interior and a Turkish fleet was hastening to re-enforce the heroic garrison, which included a large number of English soldiers under Sir Sidney Smith. Junot, sent to disperse the Mussulmans, came near being overwhelmed at Nazareth, but Napoleon, flying to the rescue, saved him. Within a week he scattered the enemy again in the field, but still Acre held out, and at length it became necessary to retreat into Egypt.

"It was the turning-point in my career," said Napoleon long years afterward. "Acre sent me back to Europe."

There is no other man in history in whose life we can find so many points where we are tempted to believe that we see the hand of a higher power interposed!

On arriving in Egypt, the young general returned to Cairo and resumed his schemes for the reorganization of the country. But a great rising of the Mamelukes soon

called him in haste to Alexandria and he destroyed the
enemy in the battle of Aboukir.   This was his last feat of
arms beyond the borders of Egypt.   In France things
had been going from bad to worse.   A new coalition,
comprising England, Austria, Naples, Turkey and for the
first time, Russia, had been formed against her, and the
celebrated Russian general Suvarof had driven the French
out of Italy.   This crisis made clear another point in Napoleon's character—no scruples ever obscured, in his
mind, the main chance.   His intuition told him that his
best opportunity lay at home—and home he went, hand-
ing the army in Egypt over to Marshal Kleber.

When he originally sailed for Egypt the famous English admiral Nelson was watching to intercept him, but
while Nelson sailed up and down the Mediterranean in
the search, Napoleon went straight to Alexandria and
landed his army, and too late, while the French were conquering Egypt, Nelson at last found their fleet and destroyed it.

Now Napoleon had only two frigates left.   With these
he unhesitatingly embarked for home.   That he succeeded in safely traversing nearly the entire length of the
Mediterranean, which swarmed with English ships, is one
of the apparent miracles of history.   While the officers
and sailors worried about the enemy, the general passed
the time reading the Bible, the Iliad, and the Koran by
day and watching the stars by night.   When he approached the French coast he found an English fleet
guarding it, but sailing unnoticed at midnight through the
midst of the enemy, he landed at the old town of Frejus,
celebrated for its remains of ancient Roman days, on the
morning of October 9, 1799.

He had been absent about seventeen months.   His
would-be rivals at home had watched his departure with
joy, believing that in Egypt he would be lost to the eyes
of the world.   Now they saw their mistake; he came back
a greater figure than he was before.   There was the magic
of the Orient about him now.

I do not intend to enter into the details of the political
events which followed Napoleon's return to France.   The
existing government was weak and unpopular and he
overthrew it.   You may read volumes on the subject, but

that is the whole gist of fact that you will get. As Mr.
John C. Ropes says in his excellent book on Napoleon,
if it was an arbitrary government that he set up, it was no
less an arbitrary government that he overthrew, and he
was better fitted to govern than were the men he turned
out. It was either Napoleon or the Bourbons, and
France had had enough of the Bourbons.

The event occurred in the palace of St. Cloud in the
environs of Paris. The palace was destroyed during the
siege in 1871, but the splendid grounds and fountains remain. Beside the so-called Council of Ancients there
was a more numerous branch of the Legislature, the Council of Five Hundred, and it was in this body that Napoleon
encountered the greatest opposition. When he undertook to dismiss the assembly by force some of the legislators rushed upon him with daggers. But his soldiers were
watching through doors and windows, and when they
saw their beloved general in peril they came to the rescue.

The upshot was that the hall was cleared at the point
of the bayonet, although nobody was hurt, the old government was overthrown and Napoleon set up a new government in its stead, making himself its head as First Consul.

This done he began to think of restoring the prestige of
France on European battlefields, where it had been seriously compromised during his absence in Egypt.

The curtain now rises on the great Napoleonic drama of
the Alps.

It is probable that no man in all history, not even Alexander, ever passed before the eyes of mankind, from one
dramatic situation to another, each rising in vividness of
interest and power of climax as Napoleon did! First we
have the dazzling Italian campaigns; then the invasion of
Egypt which captivates the imagination like an Arabian
tale, and now the famous passage of the Alps, in the representation of which so many artists have competed,—to be
followed by a victory which shook Europe like an earthquake.

And, I suppose, too, that there can be no doubt that
however or wherever Napoleon might have chosen to
strike his enemies at this time he would have been certain
of overwhelming victory. Other generals had not yet
learned his new methods and his name alone had already

become more powerful on the battlefield than the presence
of an army corps. But having the actor's perception of
the value of striking situations, he felt that his course
must still be crescendo. A victory, however complete,
would not now answer his purpose. It was the manner
rather than the matter, the method rather than the result,
that would count this time—and so he resolved to lead an
army over the snowy Alps, and, descending into the valley
of the Po, in the rear of his old enemy the Austrians, to
annihilate them with one blow.

He chose for the purpose the grand St. Bernard pass
leading out of the valley of the Rhone in Switzerland.
Many of you have been over it and you know what a
splendid trip it now is on the magnificent road that has
taken the place of the mule-path up which Napoleon
dragged his artillery. In these days of telegraphs it would
be impossible to do what he then did without the enemy
knowing all about it. But even in the year 1800 there
was perhaps no other man living who could have accomplished the feat, because no other had the necessary
promptness of decision and incredible rapidity of execution. "They do not know the value of time!" was his
constant criticism of the generals whom he whipped.

Just before the summit of the pass is reached there are
immense precipices fronting the old road, and I once stood
on the spot for a long time, trying to reconstruct the scene
when Napoleon sent his cannon up that way. Nothing
was impossible to that man—at that time! The guns
were dismounted and placed in grooves hollowed in the
trunks of trees; a hundred soldiers were hitched to each
log—and up they went!

Beyond the little lake at the summit you look down into
Italy, and the same gray peaks that saw the conqueror
pass are frowning there now. But Napoleon lost no time
in admiring the scenery. Quick he had come up the Swiss
side; quicker he must go down the Italian side. He must
surround the Austrians before they knew he had left
Paris. The difficulties were still enormous, and the men
were worn with exertion. But as the weary column
halted for a moment, one *look* from the general set it in
motion again. If nature interposed apparently insuperable obstacles—"Sound the charge!" cried Napoleon, and

instantly the drums beat, the trumpets blared, the icy
peaks responded to the unwonted sounds of war and,
dreaming of Lodi, Rivoli, and Egypt, the soldiers were up
and over! [Applause.]

At last, descending into the valley of Aosta, they left
the desolation behind and arrived once more in the world
of grass, trees, and flowers. For four days they had
crossed the mighty barrier of the Alps!

The Austrians were as completely surprised as Napoleon had anticipated. He first closed every avenue of
escape and then nipped them at Marengo! In one month
the war was ended. The sentiment with which the world
beheld the career of the Little Corsican was now no longer
mere wonder and admiration—it had become fascina-
tion!

Two years of peace followed, and for more than four
years Napoleon did not take the field in person. And
now we see him in a new light. This time was devoted
to the reorganization of France. The world has gradually
come to the conviction that Napoleon was as wonderful a
statesman and administrator as he was a general. His
favorite place of abode during this interval was at the
château of Malmaison. Here he perfected his celebrated
reconciliation with the church, known as the concordat.
He had no sympathy with the atheists who had tried to
overthrow all religion during the Revolution. Walking
in the garden of the château one evening, conversing with
an opponent of the concordat, he suddenly pointed up at
the starry sky and exclaimed:—

"Who made all that? Last Sunday evening I was
walking here alone when the church bells of the village
of Ruel rang at sunset. I was strongly moved, so vividly
did the image of early days come back to me with that
sound. If it be thus with me, how must it be with others?
In re-establishing the church I consult the wishes of the
vast majority of the people."

During this time, too, he labored on his great legal
work, the Code Napoleon, which still forms the structure
of French law and of the law of some of the neighboring
countries. His industry was prodigious; he worked night
and day, tiring out his secretaries and sending them to bed
one after another, and yet the only stimulant he took was

—lemonade. The secretaries, perhaps, took something stronger.

But again the scene changes and a new spectacle opens. On the 2d of December, 1804, in the great church of Notre Dame, in Paris, Napoleon and Josephine were crowned emperor and empress. France chose him by a virtually unanimous vote; there is no getting behind that. Pope Pius VII came from Rome to consecrate the diadems and bless the imperial couple, but Napoleon crowned himself, not suffering the Pope to perform that ceremony, and then, in turn, crowned Josephine. In David's great painting of the coronation scene one of the most interesting sights is Napoleon's mother sitting in the center of the gallery and watching her son.

In the meantime England, Russia, and Sweden were making war on Napoleon. When his old enemy Austria joined the coalition in 1805, Napoleon once more took the field. Suddenly breaking up the great military camp he had formed at Boulogne to threaten England, he marched into the center of Germany, surrounded the Austrian General Mack and captured his entire army. This stroke opened the way to the gates of Vienna, and Napoleon entered the imperial city on the Danube in November, 1805, and took up his residence in the celebrated palace of Schoenbrum.

The Emperor Francis Joseph had abandoned his capital, and with his army was hastening to effect a junction with the Czar of Russia, who had advanced to a point about seventy-five miles north of Vienna. Napoleon, although his situation was perilous, in the heart of a hostile country, and outnumbered, boldly followed the enemy, intending to strike one of his dazing blows.

He struck it on the 2d of December, the first anniversary of his coronation as emperor, at Austerlitz. On the night before the battle his soldiers made a great illumination with improvised torches in his honor. Francis Joseph and the Czar, with their united armies, were dreaming of victory. They had not even yet learned that there was no hope of beating Napoleon, on the old lines. They played into his hands in a pitifully helpless manner, and when the right moment came he struck three successive blows with the rapidity of lightning. One smashed their center and they saw their army cut in two; the second demolished their right wing; the third annihilated the left wing, and that was the end of it.

A characteristic incident, which reveals by a flash the source of the terror that Napoleon's name inspired in Europe, occurred at the close of this battle. Broken battalions of the enemy were escaping across the ice covering a small lake. The French were firing at them, yet letting them get away. The Emperor, who meant that this victory should be so crushing as not to call for a second, galloped to the front, his eyes ablaze:—

"You are losing time, firing at men!" he exclaimed, "cannonade the ice!"

They broke the ice with cannon balls, and, according to some accounts, twenty thousand Russians and Austrians were engulfed!

Then the haughty Emperor of Austria was compelled to meet his conqueror at the headquarters of the French.

"Look what kind of a palace you have compelled me to occupy," said Napoleon, pointing to his army tent.

"You have made such good use of it," replied Francis Joseph, "that you ought not to complain of the accommodation."

It was while the conqueror was rearranging the German states after Austerlitz that Prussia rose against him. —Prussia, a name still formidable on account of her victories under her great king, Frederick II. All Europe held its breath when it saw the veterans of Marengo and Austerlitz marching to meet the army that Frederick the Great had trained to victory. It was the old story of the Macedonian phalanx against the Roman legion; which would win? Napoleon had no doubt on that subject. For him it was simply the new against the old, and he was the creator of the new.

By his customary rapid maneuvering he cooped the enemy up, and then in a single night on the heights above Jena, where nobody had dreamed that such a thing could be done, he planted a battery of artillery that commanded the next day's battlefield.

The battle of Jena was simply a repetition of its predecessors. It meant virtual annihilation for the Prussian army. Horace Vernet, in his great painting of the battle

of Jena, has embodied a significant anecdote. He has
represented the scene at the moment when, as Napoleon
rides along the front of a waiting column, one of the soldiers in line, impatient at delay, throws up his cap, and
cries: "Forward!"

"What is that?" exclaims the general, reining his
horse. "Does some beardless boy think he knows what
I ought to do? Let him wait until he has commanded in
thirty battles, before he presumes to give me advice!"

We shall see the consequences of the moral change in
Napoleon that had made that exclamation possible. He
never would have dreamed of saying such a thing in Italy
or in Egypt.

After the victory of Jena occurred the conqueror's famous visit to the tomb of Frederick at Potsdam. He paid
all due honor to the memory of the Prussian hero, but he
sent the dead king's sword to Paris. Yet in this he was
only following ancient ideals, as he followed them all his
life. It was what Sylla had done after the capture of Athens, Alexander after the battle of Issus, and Scipio after
the conquest of Carthage.

Prussia now lay prostrate, Austria, too, was humbled
in the dust; but Russia, although beaten, was unsubdued.
Napoleon advanced to Warsaw and put his army in winter
quarters while he laid his plans for the subjugation of
Russia. No man, in those days, understood the power
of Russia as he did. He knew that he must have it on his
side, through victory or through alliance. He began his
campaign against the Russians early in February and he
found them the most determined fighters he had yet encountered. In the awful battle of Eylau they nearly defeated him. But finally in June, 1807, he got them well
in hand and put an end to the war by the bloody victory
of Friedland.

Then occurred the celebrated meeting with the Czar
Alexander on the raft at Tilsit, a meeting resulting in the
treaty of peace bearing the name of that place. But there
was some one else concerned in these negotiations whose
presence lent to them a romantic charm not ordinarily
associated with stern deliberations of that kind—the beautiful queen, Louisa of Prussia. The King of Prussia,
hoping that the Czar would assist him, was striving to

save his kingdom from annihilation. One of the principal points in dispute was the possession of the fortified town of Magdeburg. Queen Louisa had gone to Tilsit with the avowed determination of coaxing or cajoling Napoleon into allowing her to keep Magdeburg. It was a battle with wit and beauty for weapons, in which he came as near defeat as he was at Eylau. One day at the dinner-table, when the queen was still harping on Magdeburg, the Emperor, in order to turn the conversation, began to praise a rose which she wore at her bosom. Louisa instantly snatched it off and extended it toward Napoleon: "Will your Majesty accept this rose in exchange for Magdeburg?"

But he was not to be caught. "The beauty of the rose," he said, "so befits the hand that bears it that I cannot be guilty of dividing them."

The throne of Napoleon at Fontainebleau had now come to represent a mightier imperial power than Europe had ever known. Only that of Charlemagne could be compared with it, and even that was not erected upon such a series of astounding victories and such a succession of overthrows of the old order of things. He had made himself an emperor; he had made all of his brothers and sisters kings and queens. And yet he could almost number with his fingers the years that had elapsed since he and all of them were haunted with poverty, and so low in the social scale that the lackey of the pettiest duke or count in Europe would have scorned them.

It was after the peace of Tilsit that occurred the conquest of Spain, the beginning, perhaps, of his decline; his first great mistake, to be followed by another tremendous campaign into the center of Europe, culminating in the victory of Wagram and the humiliation of Austria once more.

The next step introduces us to a domestic scene, partaking of the character of tragedy—the divorce from Josephine. It is a curious fact, which those who believe that such things are governed only by fate and destiny have not failed to point out, that whereas up to the time of this divorce Napoleon's star had continually risen, thereafter it no less continuously declined, and there are

Josephine he divorced himself from Fortune also. But
the rational explanation of the undoubted fact is that there
had been a change in the man, in his hopes and ambition,
and this unfortunate divorce was the first notable expression of that change.

Napoleon now turned to his old enemy Francis Joseph,
a monarch whom he had again and again trodden under
foot, and demanded the hand of his daughter, Maria
Louisa, in marriage. The conqueror of Austerlitz and
Wagram never had to ask twice for what he wanted. The
divorce from Josephine occurred in December, 1809; the
marriage with the Austrian princess in April, 1810.

Napoleon's son, born in April, 1811, bore the baptismal
name of Francis Charles Joseph. Under the name of
Duke of Reichstadt, he lived to the age of twenty-one
years, dying in 1832, eleven years after the death of his
father. He possessed something of his father's classic
beauty, but there is no evidence that he would ever have
developed a spark of his father's genius. Some philosopher has declared that only boys who resemble their
mothers become great men!

And now comes the beginning of the end, one of the
greatest tragedies of history, the invasion of Russia, Napoleon's second great mistake. His first mistake produced victory for the time being; his second brought him
down, like a man who steps unprepared on smooth ice.

On the morning of September 14, 1812, having forced
his way by some of the bloodiest victories he ever won,
Napoleon standing on the "Hill of Salvation," beheld
spread at his feet "Mother Moscow," the ancient and
sacred capital of the Czars. The French soldiers were in
ecstasy at the sight. Here again they beheld the barbaric
splendor of the Orient, now strangely mingled with the
gloomier and more mysterious magnificence of the North.
The emperor himself was moved at the sight. "Behold,
at last, that celebrated capital!" he exclaimed. The towers of the Kremlin gleamed across the snowy landscapes,
and the French soldiers believed that in this great city of
palaces a long and triumphant rest from their labors
awaited them. The memory of the vast ocean-like ex-
panse which they had crossed, in the face of strange and
fierce foes, wading breast high in blood-stained snow,—

all this was but a dream now that the capital of their enemies was in their grasp.

To the ever active imagination of Napoleon this was the
Egypt of the North, and it awoke appropriate schemes of
conquest. If he could not repeat the marches and triumphs of Sesostris, the still mightier theatre on which
Genghis Khan had acted was before him; perhaps he could
reverse the march of the Tartars, and from the West
sweep the East as they from the East had swept the West.
The only power on the continent of Europe that had
proved itself capable of facing him now lay prostrate with
his foot on its neck!

But now, for the first time in his career, Napoleon was
met with a truly Napoleonic stroke. If the Russians
could not stand against him in the battlefield they could do
something more effective; they could burn their sacred
city about his ears, and they did it. Here was an enemy
he could not fight. The flames of the burning houses,
towers, and churches, gleamed upon miles and miles of
snow, but to the utmost verge of the wintry horizon not
an enemy was in sight. The Russians had vanished in
the immensity of Muscovite space. An empire was not
to be won battling with snowflakes. From a capital in
ashes no terms could be dictated! So there was nothing
for it but to retreat.

Then, like magic, countless as the snowflakes and fierce
and swift as the wintry blasts they rode upon, came the
enemy, the terrible Cossacks, a cavalry more dreadful
than the Mamelukes of the desert, and smote the retreating columns struggling in the snow-choked roads and the
ice-gorged rivers, smote and fled, but to return and smite
and flee again, and that most awful form of warfare that
dogs wage upon a wounded stag fast in a drift. [Ap-
plause.]

You have all read the story of the passage of the river
Beresina during that retreat. Not many years ago there
was living in the city of Brooklyn a man who was a soldier
in that army of Napoleon, and who passed through those
scenes and lived to fight for his emperor again at Waterloo. The stories that that old man told of the horrors
of the Beresina would have sent a shudder through the
Sphinx.

It was Napoleon's first flight. There is no disguising
it, it was flight. Not inspired by terror, however, inspired
by necessity. He must get back to France; he must raise
another army. They could not crush the conqueror and
master of Europe with one reverse. He got back to
France, he raised another army, though few of his old
veterans were in it; three hundred thousand of them were
asleep forever in the snows of Russia.

Yet he marched back into the heart of Europe. The
master painter Meissonier has shown us how he looked.
Well might the nations tremble at the sight of that grim
countenance; there rode embodied Marengo! Austerlitz!
Jena! Friedland! It was Napoleon against the world,
and the world had cause to doubt the issue. Victory
perched once more on his banners—how could she desert
him? But the spell was broken—forever lost amid Northern snows. His victories no longer produced the effect
of magic, for his enemies had seen him down and knew
now that he was mortal. Yet he never fought better. At
Dresden, where he saved the day by himself leading a
charge, a German writer, Hoffmann, saw him in the midst
of his men: "Then for the first time," wrote Hoffmann,
"I saw his face. He came on with the eye of a tyrant
and the voice of a lion, urging on his breathless soldiers!"
But all Europe was in the tiger hunt now, and at Leipsic
they overwhelmed him with numbers. Then the allies
actually entered France. He beat them back in seven
pitched battles!

But he could not be everywhere, and while he was driving the enemies like whipped dogs in one part of the field,
from another direction they descended upon Paris. When
he heard of the danger of his beloved capital he flew to
the rescue. In his impatience he rode on ahead of his
little army. He would not believe the allies were in
Paris, no one could persuade him that he was too late,
until he began to meet the broken and retreating battalions. Then his good sense told him all was lost. "This
comes of trusting to traitors and cowards!" he exclaimed,
and hurrying to Fontainebleau, he threw himself into a
chair to consider one of the most momentous problems
ever presented to the mind of a man—fight or yield?

There was no one in all this broad earth who could help

him to solve that question. On the eminence to which he had climbed he was far above the dense atmosphere of advice.

He resolved to abdicate. In his abdication he made no provision whatever for himself. The Czar Alexander, surprised and touched by this, exclaimed: "I have been his friend, I will now be his advocate. I propose that he retain his imperial title and be given the government of some island, such as Elba." The representatives of the other allied powers agreed to this arrangement, England alone spitefully refusing to recognize his imperial title. The allies placed a puppet on the throne of France in the person of Louis XVIII.

Napoleon went to Elba at the end of April, 1814; on the first of March, 1815, he landed at Cannes in Southern France. He had no army, but he knew how and where to get one. He had been watching events in Europe and he knew that Louis XVIII was as unpopular as he was incapable. Napoleon was going back to his empire and, with that sublime self-confidence which had all but won the whole earth for him, he counted on regaining his soldiers with a mere glance of his eye.

And in this he was not mistaken. At Grenoble he won the most remarkable of all victories. On one side, unarmed, Napoleon. On the other side the troops of the king. The emperor advances alone. The troops receive him, not with bullets, but with shouts and tears of joy. One of the old grenadiers was asked if he could have been persuaded to fire upon his emperor. He laughed as he made his ramrod ring in his empty musket. "They are all like that!" he exclaimed. But they loaded them when they fell in behind Napoleon!

On the 19th of March he was at the deserted palace of Fontainebleau. Louis XVIII had fled, leaving Paris to the keeping of Marshal Macdonald with a large army; but the next day, when Napoleon advanced to Melun, the marshal fled to join his master, and soldiers and officers went over to the emperor.

At Vienna, in the meantime, a congress of the allied powers had been in session. Like a bombshell in their midst fell the astounding news that Napoleon had landed in France and reconquered the country without firing a

shot. Of course, they outlawed him. Then they raised
an army of a million men to put him down. To prevent
the junction of their hosts Napoleon hurried into the Neth-
erlands, where the English and the Prussians were assembling. At Ligny he defeated Blucher, the Prussian general, and drove him eastward. A day or two later Ney
fought Wellington to a stand-still at Quatre Bras, and
Wellington retreated to Waterloo. Sending Marshal
Grouchy to keep Blucher on the run, Napoleon in person
advanced against the English position. All would have
been plain sailing if Grouchy had done what was expected
of him. But he stuck fast at Gambloux—whether
through treachery or incapacity is a question that has
never been settled—and the wily Blucher, finding the pressure released, immediately swung round westward and
hastened to join Wellington. Even then the catastrophe
might have been averted if Napoleon had been his old self.
Lord Rosebery has shown how a strange apathy had come
upon that marvelous mind, once as quick and resistless as
lightning. This apathy acted like a spell upon him at
Waterloo. Everything he did on that fatal Sunday was
done too late.

Every visitor to the field of Waterloo is impressed by
the battered château of Hougomont, and its garden walls,
the key to the position of the allies. With Hougomont
taken Napoleon knew that he would have the battle won.
But although he hurled column after column against it
the seven thousand British soldiers within held their
ground.

Meanwhile the Prussians arrived on the field, and from
that moment the emperor had to begin a new battle while
still continuing the old one. Only an irresistible blow
crushing the center of the English line could now save the
day for him. He rode out on his white horse, bared his
head, and the Old Guard sprang forward as though
launched from his outstretched hand. It would have required repeated blows of that character to accomplish
his purpose, and he had the means for delivering but one.
The needed men were in another part of the field trying to
hold back the Prussians. The Old Guard, unsupported,
broke and retreated.

The end had come; the tiger hunters had got the great

beast down at last! For one moment it had seemed that Napoleon was about to put himself at the head of his men to retrieve the day, but his fatal lethargy prevailed. His army, once broken, melted like snow in the south wind, and the emperor rode off the field as if dazed. He stopped in a peasant's hut to rest, and the descendants of the humble family which, with mingled awe and pity, saw the great conqueror sitting by their little fireside, boast of that scene to-day. There was the master of the world swept by the tempest of fate into the shelter of their door, and bowed like a stricken eagle at their humble hearth!

He retired to Malmaison, where in the plenitude of his power he had heard those church bells ringing that reminded him of his youth and where, a year before, Josephine had died of a broken heart, murmuring "My Achilles is fallen." When the approach of the enemy drove him away he went to the seacoast and surrendered himself to the captain of the English frigate "Bellerophon." He chose his bitterest enemies for his custodians.

And in that act once more he recalled antique ideals, and proved himself to be, at the end of his career, what Paoli had pronounced him at the beginning, "one of Plutarch's men." But, unfortunately for him, he was the only representative of that race of mortals left on the earth! The English government sent him to the lone volcanic rock of St. Helena, and all the world breathed more freely when it heard the news.

"Europe," exclaims Lord Rosebery, "buckled itself to the unprecedented task of gagging and paralyzing an intelligence and force which were too gigantic for the welfare and security of the world. That is the strange, unique, hideous problem which makes the records of St. Helena so profoundly painful and fascinating."

At St. Helena Napoleon lived, guarded as no other prisoner ever was, or will be, from the middle of October, 1815, until the opening days of May, 1821, a period of nearly six years. Unhappy that he had not perished at the height of his power, he meditated on the greatness of his fall. Among the thoughts that the world will longest

treasure are those that were caught by eager secretaries
and listeners from the lips of Napoleon at St. Helena.

The story of the wild storm that whipped the South
Atlantic ocean on the night between the 5th and 6th of
May, 1821, has often been told.   At its height, in the dark
night, when the rocky shores of St. Helena were booming to the rushing sea and the roar of the hurricane shook
the island to its center, the Man of Marengo passed the
walls of his prison!

In 1840 France asked England to give back her emperor.   Elizabeth Barrett Browning has told the story in
six poetic lines:—

> " France cried—' Behold thou, England.   I would have
> The dead, whereof thou wottest, from that grave!'
> And England answered, in the courtesy
> Which ancient foes, turned lovers, may befit,
> ' Take back thy dead, and when thou buryest it
> Throw in all former strifes 'twixt thee and me.' "

Transported to Paris, the body of Napoleon was placed
in the most imposing mausoleum on the face of the earth.
The artistic genius of the Latin race, the power to suggest
and produce dramatic effect, was never more triumphantly
exhibited than at the tomb of Napoleon.

In the little gallery at Brussels where are exhibited the
works of that most eccentric painter Antoine Joseph
Wiertz, there is to be seen over the doorway a large picture called " The Lion of Waterloo."   It represents the
famous field as viewed from the French side at night.   In
the background, towering against the half-illuminated
sky, is the great pyramid of the Belgian lion, but the pedestal on its top is empty.   Overhead the sky is filled with
driving storm wrack, and huge winged things are flitting
through the gloom.   Right down in front, almost in contact with the spectator, is the lion.   Mane erect, eyes blazing, huge and terrible, he is in the act of rending an immense black eagle.   The ground around them swims with
blood and behind the lion, dimly marking his track, are
red blotches glowing like embers on the ground, yet plainly not fire, but blood!   The idea suggested seems to be
that on dark, stormy nights the lion descends from his
pedestal and, rushing across the field where the last

charges were made, re-enacts the awful scenes of the battle.

And this, I fear, must stand as a true representation of the Napoleonic era, for these are the thoughts and these the scenes which his name conjures up. Let not the bitterest enemy of Napoleon deny to him the name and fame of the greatest maker of war and the greatest winner of victories that the world has ever known! Greater than Cæsar, greater than Hannibal, greater than Alexander. Let him have all the glory; let him be the bright particular star-of-war, the great representative figure in the Valhalla of Mars. and then, let us rejoice that he belongs to our time, for thus he predicts the daybreak! There is no hour so dark as that which precedes the dawn. We may well believe that history will never frame a second Napoleon. She has done her best in that line, and now she turns to nobler things. Let the century that knew him wrap the tattered flags of war about it and lie down to dreams of slaughter, but let us look forward across that new century, whose sunrise now brightens the hills of coming time, believing that it will usher in the thousand years, the ten thousand years, ah! the endless era of peace universal. [Applause.]

HENRY WHEELER SHAW

("JOSH BILLINGS")

MILK

[Lecture by Henry W. Shaw—" Josh Billings "—humorist and satirist (born in Lanesborough, Mass., April 21, 1818; died in Monterey,
Cal., October 14, 1885), delivered on many platforms during his career
as a lecturer, which began in 1863. It was his custom to read his lecture, in the dialect which he employed, while seated at a reading-
desk, and he had a habit of peering over his glasses at his audience
when an especially good point was made, or a bit of homely wisdom
thrown out.]

LADIES AND GENTLEMEN:—I hope you are all well.
Thare is lots ov folks who eat well and drink well, and yet
are sick all the time. Theze are the folks who alwuz
" enjoy poor health." Then I kno lots ov people whoze
only reckomendashun iz, that they are helthy—so iz an
onion. [Laughter.]

The subject of my lecture is Milk—plain M-i-l-k.

The best thing I've ever seen on milk is cream.
[Laughter.] That's right [joining]. " People of good
sense" are thoze whoze opinyuns agree with ours. [Re-
newed laughter.] People who agree with you never bore
you. The shortest way to a woman's harte iz to praze her
baby and her bonnet, and to a man's harte to praze hiz
watch, hiz horse and hiz lectur. Eliar Perkins sez a man
iz a bore when he talks so much about hisself that you
kant talk about yourself. [Laughter.]

Still I shall go on talking.

Comik lekturing iz an unkommon pesky thing to do.
It iz more unsarting than the rat ketching bizzness az a

From " Kings of Platform and Pulpit," edited by " Eli Perkins " and published by the
Saalfield Publishing Co., Akron, Ohio.

1011

means ov grace, or az a means ov livelyhood. Most enny boddy thinks they kan do it, and this iz jist what makes it so bothersum tew do. When it iz did jist enuff, it iz a terifick success, but when it iz overdid, it iz like a burnt slapjack, very impertinent. [Applause.]

Thare aint but phew good judges ov humor, and they all differ about it. If a lekturer trys tew be phunny, he is like a hoss trying to trot backwards, pretty apt tew trod on himself. [Laughter.] Humor must fall out ov a man's mouth, like musik out ov a bobalink, or like a yung bird out ov its nest, when it iz feathered enuff to fly.

Whenever a man haz made up hiz mind that he iz a wit, then he iz mistaken without remedy, but whenever the publick haz made up their mind that he haz got the disease, then he haz got it sure. Individuals never git this thing right, the publik never git it wrong.

Humor iz wit with a rooster's tail feathers stuck in its cap, and wit iz wisdom in tight harness.

If a man is a genuine humorist, he iz superior to the bulk ov hiz audience, and will often hev tew take hiz pay for hiz services in thinking so. Altho fun iz designed for the millyun, and ethiks for the few, it iz az true az molasses that most all aujiences hav their bell wethers, people who show the others the crack whare the joke cums laffing in. Where are they to-night? [Laughter.] I hav known popular aujences deprived ov all plezzure during the recital ov a comik lektur, just bekauze the right man, or the right woman, want thare tew point out the mellow places.

The man who iz anxious tew git before an aujience, with what he calls a comik lektur, ought tew be put immediately in the stocks, so that he kant do it, for he iz a dangerous person tew git loose, and will do sum damage. It iz a very pleasant bizzness tew make people laff, but thare iz much odds whether they laff *at you*, or laff at *what yu say*. When a man laffs at *yu*, he duz it because it makes him feel superior to you, but when yu pleaze him with what yu have uttered, he admits that yu are superior tew him. [Applause.] The only reazon whi a monkey alwus kreates a sensashun whareever he goes, is simply bekause —he is a monkey.

Everyboddy feels az tho they had a right tew criticize a comik lectur, and most ov them do it jist az a mule criti-

cizes things, by shutting up both eyes and letting drive
with hiz two behind leggs. [Laughter.] One ov the meanest things in the comik lektring employment that a man
haz to do iz tew try and make that large class of his aujience laff whom the Lord never intended should laff. Thare
iz sum who laff as eazy and az natral az the birds do, but
most ov mankind laff like a hand organ—if yu expect tew
git a lively tune out ov it yu hav got tew grind for it.
[Laughter and applause.] In delivering a comik lektur
it iz a good general rule to stop sudden, some time before
yu git through.

This brings me to Long branch.

Long branch iz a work ov natur, and iz a good job.
It iz a summer spot for men, wimmin and children, espeshily the latter. Children are az plenty here, and az
sweet az flowers, in an out door gardin. I put up at the
Oshun Hotel the last time i was there, and I put up more
than I ought to. [Laughter.] Mi wife puts up a good
deal with me at the same hotel, it iz an old-fashioned way
we have ov doing things. She allways goes with me, to
fashionable resorts, whare young widows are enny ways
plenty, to put me on mi guard, for i am one ov the easyest
creatures on reckord to be impozed upon, espeshily bi
yung widders. She is an ornament to her sex, mi wife iz.
I would like to see a young widder, or even an old one, git
the start ov me, when mi wife iz around. [Laughter.] If
I just step out sudden, to get a weak lemonade, to cool mi
akeing brow, mi wife goes to the end ov the verandy with
me, and waits for me, and if i go down onto the beach to
astronomize just a little, all alone, bi moonlite, she stands
on the bluff, like a beakon lite, to warn me ov the breakers.
[Applause and laughter.]

The biggest thing they hav got at Long branch, for
the present, iz the pool ov water, in front ov the hotels.
[Laughter.] This pool iz sed bi good judges to be 3,000
miles in length, and in sum places five miles thick. Into
this pool, every day at ten o'klock, the folks all retire,
males, females, and widders, promiskuss. The scenery
here iz grand, especially the pool, and the air iz az bracing
az a milk puntch. Drinks are reasonable here, espeshily
out ov the pool, and the last touch ov civilizashun haz
reached here also, sum enterprising mishionary haz just

opened a klub house, where all kinds ov gambling is taught.

Long branch iz a healthy place. Men and women here, if they ain't too lazy, liv sumtimes till they are eighty, and destroy the time a good deal as follows: The fust thirty years they spend in throwing stuns at a mark, the seckond thirty they spend in examining the mark tew see whare the stuns hit, and the remainder is divided in cussing the stun-throwing bizziness, and nussing the rumatizz. [Laughter.]

A man never gits to be a fust klass phool until he haz reached seventy years, and falls in luv with a bar maid of nineteen, and marrys her, and then—

[At this point the lecturer took out his Waterbury watch, and with the remark, "You kant do two things to wonst," stopped to wind it up. Then he proceeded.]

I luv a Rooster for two things. One iz the crow that iz in him, and the other iz, the spurs that are on him, to bak up the crow with.

The man or mule who can't do any hurt in this world kan't do any good. [Laughter.]

This brings me to the Mule—the pashunt mule. The mule is pashunt because he is ashamed of hisself. [Laughter.] The mule is haf hoss and haf jackass, and then kums to a full stop, natur diskovering her mistake. Tha weigh more accordin tu their heft than enny other creeter, except a crowbar. [Laughter.] Tha kant heer enny quicker nor further than the hoss, yet their ears are big enuff fur snowshoes. You kan trust them with enny one whose life aint worth more than the mule's. The only way tu keep them into a paster is tu turn them into a medder jineing and let them jump out. [Laughter.] Tha are reddy for use jest as soon as tha will do tu abuse. Tha aint got enny friends, and will live on huckleberry bush, with an akasional chance at Kanada thissels. Tha are a modern invention. Tha sell fur more money than enny other domestic animal. You kant tell their age by looking into their mouth enny more than you could a Mexican cannon. Tha never have no disease that a good club won't heal. If tha ever die tha must come right to life agin, fur I never herd nobody say "ded mule." I never owned one, nor never mean to, unless there is a

United States law passed requiring it. I have seen educated mules in a sircuss. Tha could kick and bite tre-
menjis. Enny man who is willing to drive a mule ought
to be exempt by law from running for the legislatur.
Tha are the strongest creeters on arth, and heaviest according tu their size. I herd of one who fell oph from
the tow-path of the Eri canawl, and sunk as soon as he
touched bottom, but he kept on towing the boat tu the
next stashun, breathing through his ears, which was out
of the water about two feet six inches. I didn't see this
did, but Bill Harding told me of it, and I never knew Bill
Harding tu lie unless he could make something out of it.
[Laughter.]

There is but one other animal that kan do more kicking
than a mule, and that is a Quire Singer. [Laughter.] A
quire singer giggles during the sermon and kicks the rest
of the week. My advice to quire singers is as follows:—

Put your hair in cirl papers every Friday nite soze to
have it in good shape Sunday morning. If your daddy
is rich you can buy some store hair. If he is very rich
buy some more and build it up high onto your head; then
get a high-priced bunnit that runs up very high at the high
part of it, and get the milliner to plant some high-grown
artificials onto the highest part of it. This will help you
sing high, as soprano is the highest part. [Applause.]

When the tune is giv out, don't pay attention to it, and
then giggle. Giggle a good eel. [Laughter.]

Whisper to the girl next you that Em Jones, which sets
on the 2d seet from the front on the left-hand side, has
her bunnit with the same color exact she had last year, and
then put your book to your face and giggle.

Object to every tune unless there is a solow into it for
the soprano. Coff and hem a good eel before you begin
to sing. [Laughter.]

When you sing a solow shake the artificials off your
bunnit, and when you come to a high tone brace yourself
back a little, twist your head to one side and open your
mouth the widest on that side, shet the eyes on the same
side jest a triphle, and then put in for dear life. [Laugh-
ter.]

When the preacher gets under hed way with his preach-
in, write a note on the blank leaf into the fourth part of

your note book. That's what the blank leaf was made
for. Git sumbody to pass the note to sumbody else, and
you watch them while they read it, and then giggle.
[Laughter.]

If anybody talks or laffs in the congregashun, and the
preacher takes notis of it, that's a good chants for you to
giggle, and you ought to giggle a great eel. The preacher
darsent say any thing to you bekaus you are in the quire,
·and he can't run the meetin' house at both ends without
the quire. If you had a bow before you went into the
quire, give him the mitten—you ought to have somebody
better now.

Don't forget to giggle.

The quire singer suggests the bumble-bee.

The bumble-bee iz more artistic than the mule and as
busy as a quire singer. The bumble-bee iz a kind ov big
fly who goes muttering and swearing around the lots during the summer looking after little boys to sting them, and
stealing hunny out ov the dandylions and thissells. Like
the mule, he iz mad all the time about sumthing, and don't
seem to kare a kuss what people think ov him. [Laugh-
ter.]

A skool boy will studdy harder enny time to find a
bumble-bee's nest than he will to get hiz lesson in arith-
metik, and when he haz found it, and got the hunny out
ov it, and got badly stung into the bargin, he finds thare
aint mutch margin in it. Next to poor molassis, bumble-
bee hunny iz the poorest kind ov sweetmeats in market.
Bumble-bees have allwuss been in fashion, and probably
allwuss will be, but where the fun or proffit lays in them,
i never could cypher out. The proffit don't seem to be in
the hunny, nor in the bumble-bee neither. They bild their
nest in the ground, or enny whare else they take a noshun
too, and ain't afrade to fite a whole distrikt skool, if they
meddle with them. I don't blame the bumble-bee, nor
enny other fellow, for defending hiz sugar: it iz the fust,
and last law of natur, and i hope the law won't never run
out. The smartest thing about the bumble-bee iz their
stinger. [Laughter.]

Speaking of smart things brings me to the hornet.

The hornet is an inflamibel buzzer, sudden in hiz im-
preshuns and hasty in his conclusion, or end. [Laughter.]

Hiz natral disposishen iz a warm cross between red pepper in the pod and fusil oil, and hiz moral biaz iz, "git out ov mi way." They have a long, black boddy, divided in the middle by a waist spot, but their phisikal importance lays at the terminus of their subburb, in the shape ov a javelin. This javelin iz alwuz loaded, and stands reddy to unload at a minuit's warning, and enters a man az still az thought, az spry az litening, and az full ov melankolly as the tooth-ake. [Laughter.] Hornets never argy a case; they settle awl ov their differences ov opinyon by letting their javelin fly, and are az certain to hit az a mule iz.

This testy kritter lives in congregations numbering about 100 souls, but whether they are mail or female, or conservative, or matched in bonds ov wedlock, or whether they are Mormons, and a good many ov them kling together and keep one husband to save expense, I don't kno nor don't kare. [Laughter.] I never have examined their habits much, I never konsidered it healthy. [Laughter.] Hornets build their nests wherever they take a noshun to, and seldom are disturbed, for what would it profit a man tew kill ninety-nine hornets and hav the one hundredth one hit him with hiz javelin? They bild their nests ov paper, without enny windows to them or back doors. They have but one place ov admission, and the nest iz the shape ov an overgrown pineapple, and is cut up into just as many bedrooms as there iz hornets. It iz very simple to make a hornet's nest if yu kan, but i will wager enny man three hundred dollars he kant bild one that he could sell to a hornet for half price. [Laughter.]

Hornets are as bizzy as their second couzins, the bee, but what they are about the Lord only knows; they don't lay up enny honey, nor enny money; they seem to be bizzy only jist for the sake ov working all the time; they are alwus in as mutch ov a hurry as tho they waz going for a dokter. I suppose this uneasy world would grind around on its axle-tree onst in twenty-four hours, even ef thare want enny hornets, but hornets must be good for sumthing, but I kant think now what it iz. Thare haint been a bug made yet in vain, nor one that want a good job; there is ever lots of human men loafing around blacksmith shops, and cider mills, all over the country, that don't

seem to be necessary for anything but to beg plug tobacco
and swear, and steal water melons, but yu let the cholera
break out once, and then yu will see the wisdom of having
just sich men laying around; they help count. [Laugh-
ter.]

Next tew the cockroach, who stands tew the head, the
hornet haz got the most waste stummuk, in reference tew
the rest of hiz boddy, than any of the insek populashun,
and here iz another mystery; what on 'arth duz a hornet
want so much reserved corps for?   I hav jist thought—
tew carry his javelin in; thus yu see, the more we diskover
about things the more we are apt to know.   It iz always
a good purchase tew pay out our last surviving dollar for
wisdum, and wisdum iz like the misterious hen's egg; it
ain't laid in yure hand, but iz laid away under the barn,
and yu have got to sarch for it.   [Applause.]

The hornet iz an unsoshall kuss, he iz more haughty
than he is proud, he is a thorough-bred bug, but his breeding and refinement has made him like sum other folks I
know ov, dissatisfied with himself and every boddy else;
too much good breeding ackts this way sometimes.

Hornets are long-lived—I kant state jist how long their
lives are, but I know from instinkt and observashen that
enny krittur, be he bug or be he devil, who iz mad all the
time, and stings every good chance he kan git, generally
outlives all his nabers.   [Laughter.]   The only good way
tew git at the exact fiteing weight of the hornet is tew
tutch him, let him hit you once with his javelin, and you
will be willing to testify in court that somebody run a one-
tined pitchfork into yer; and as for grit, i will state for the
informashun of thoze who haven't had a chance tew lay in
their vermin wisdum az freely az I hav, that one single
hornet, who feels well, will brake up a large camp-meet-
ing.   [Laughter.]

What the hornets do for amuzement is another question
i kant answer, but sum ov the best read and heavyest
thinkers among the naturalists say they have target ex-
cursions, and heave their javelins at a mark; but I don't
imbide this assershun raw, for i never knu enny body so
bitter at heart as the hornets are, to waste a blow.

Thare iz one thing that a hornet duz that i will give him
credit for on my books—he alwuz attends tew his own

bizziness, and won't allow any boddy else tew attend tew it, and what he duz iz alwuz a good job; you never see them altering enny thing; if they make enny mistakes, it is after dark, and aint seen. If the hornets made half az menny blunders az the men do, even with their javelins, every boddy would laff at them.

Hornets are clear in another way, they hav found out, by trieing it, that all they can git in this world, and brag on, is their vittles and clothes, and yu never see one standing on the corner ov a street, with a twenty-six-inch face on, bekause sum bank had run oph and took their money with him.

In ending oph this essa, I will cum tew a stop by concluding, that if hornets was a little more pensive, and not so darned peremptory with their javelins, they might be guilty of less wisdum, but more charity. [Laughter.]

This brings me to Flirts.

Flirts are like hornets, only men like to be stung by them. Some old bachelors git after a flirt, and don't travel as fast as she doz, and then concludes awl the female group are hard to ketch, and good for nothing when they are ketched.

A flirt is a rough thing to overhaul unless the right dog gets after her, and then they make the very best of wives.

When a flirt really is in love, she is as powerless as a mown daisy. [Laughter.] Her impudence then changes into modesty, her cunning into fears, her spurs into a halter, and her pruning-hook into a cradle.

The best way to ketch a flirt is tew travel the other way from which she is going, or sit down on the ground and whistle some lively tune till the flirt comes round. [Laughter.]

Old bachelors make the flirts and then the flirts get more than even, by making the old bachelors.

A majority of flirts get married finally, for they hev a great quantity of the most dainty tidbits of woman's nature, and alwus have shrewdness to back up their sweetness. Flirts don't deal in po'try and water grewel; they have got to hev brains, or else somebody would trade them out of their capital at the first sweep.

Disappointed luv must uv course be oll on one side;

this ain't any more excuse fur being an old bachelor than it iz fur a man to quit all kinds of manual labor, jist out uv spite, and jine a poor-house bekase he kant lift a tun at one pop. [Applause and laughter.]

An old bachelor will brag about his freedom to you, his relief from anxiety, hiz indipendence. This iz a dead beat, past resurrection, for everybody knows there ain't a more anxious dupe than he iz. All his dreams are charcoal sketches of boarding-school misses; he dresses, greases hiz hair, paints his grizzly mustache, cultivates bunyons and corns, to please his captains, the wimmen, and only gets laffed at fur hiz pains. I tried being an old bachelor till I wuz about twenty years old, and came very near dieing a dozen times. I had more sharp pain in one year than I hev had since, put it all in a heap. I was in a lively fever all the time.

I have preached to you about flirts (phemale), and now I will tell you about Dandies.

The first dandy was made by Dame Nature, out of the refuse matter left from making Adam and Eve. He was concocted with a bouquet in one hand and a looking-glass in the other. His heart was dissected in the thirteenth century, and found to be a pincushion full of butterflies and sawdust. He never falls in love, for to love requires both brains and a soul, and the dandy has neither. He is a long-lived bird; he has no courage, never marries, has no virtues, and is never guilty of first-class vices.

What about Marriage? They say love iz blind, but a good many fellows see more in their sweethearts than I can. Marriage is a fair transaction on the face ov it. But thare iz quite too often put-up jobs in it. It is an old institushun—older than the Pyramids, and az phull ov hyrogliphics that nobody can parse. History holds its tongue who the pair waz who fust put on the silken harness, and promised to work kind in it, thru thick and thin, up hill and down, and on the level, rain or shine, survive or perish, sink or swim, drown or flote. But whoever they waz, they must hev made a good thing out of it, or so menny' ov their posterity would not hev harnessed up since and drove out. Thare iz a grate moral grip to marriage; it iz the mortar that holds the sooshul bricks together.

But thare ain't but darn few pholks who put their money in matrimony who could set down and give a good written opinyun whi on airth they come to did it.   This iz a grate proof that it iz one ov them natral kind ov acksidents that must happen, jist az birds fly out ov the nest, when they hev featherz enuff, without being able tew tell why.

Sum marry for buty, and never diskover their mistake: this is lucky.   Sum marry for money, and don't see it. Sum marry for pedigree, and feel big for six months; and then very sensibly cum tew the conclusion that pedigree ain't no better than skim-milk.   Sum marry bekawze they hev been highsted sum whare else; this iz a cross match, a bay and a sorrel: pride may make it endurable.   Sum marry for luv, without a cent in their pockets, nor a friend in the world, nor a drop ov pedigree.   This looks desperate, but it iz the strength of the game. [Applause.]

If marrying for luv aint a success, then matrimony is a ded beet.

Sum marry because they think wimmen will be scarce next year, and live tew wonder how the crop holdz out. Sum marry tew get rid ov themselves, and discover that the game waz one that two could play at, and neither win. Sum marry the second time tew get even, and find it a gambling game—the more they put down the less they take up.   Sum marry, tew be happy, and, not finding it, wonder where all the happiness goes to when it dies. Sum marry, they can't tell why, and live they can't tell how.   Sum marry in haste, and then sit down and think it carefully over.   Sum think it over careful fust, and then set down and marry.   Both ways are right, if they hit the mark.   [Applause.]   Sum marry rakes tew convert them. This iz a little risky, and takes a smart missionary to do it. Sum marry coquetts.   This iz like buying a poor farm heavily mortgaged, and working the balance of your days to clear oph the mortgages.   [Applause.]

Married life haz its chances, and this iz just what gives it its flavor.   Every boddy luvs tew phool with the chances, bekawze every boddy expekts tew win.   But I am authorized tew state that every boddy don't win. [Applause and laughter.]   But, after all, married life iz full az certain az the dry goods bizness.   Kno man kan

tell jist what calico haz made up its mind tew do next.
Calico don't kno even herself. Dry goods ov all kinds
iz the child ov circumstansis.

The man who stands on the banks shivering, and
dassent, iz more apt tew ketch cold than him who pitches
head fust into the river.

Thare iz but few who never marry bekawse they *won't*
—they all hanker, and most ov them starve with bread
before them (spread on both sides), jist for the lack ov
grit.

Marry young! iz mi motto. I hev tried it, and I know
what I am talking about. If enny boddy asks you whi you
got married (if it needs be), tell him *" yu don't recollekt."*

Marriage iz a safe way to gamble—if yu win, yu win a
pile, and if yu loze, yu don't loze enny thing, only the
privilege of living dismally alone and soaking your own
feet. [Laughter.]

I repeat it, in italics, *marry young!* Thare iz but one
good excuse for a marriage late in life, and that is—*a
second marriage.*

When you are married, don't swap with your mother-
in-law, unless yu kin afford to give her the big end of the
trade. [Applause.] Say "how are you" to every boddy.
Kultivate modesty, but mind and keep a good stock of
impudence on hand. Be charitable—three-cent pieces
were made on purpose. It costs more to borry than it
does to buy. Ef a man flatters yu, yu can kalkerlate he is
a roge, or yu are a fule. Be more anxus about the pedigree yur going to leave than yu are about the wun somebody's going to leave you. [Applause.] Sin is like
weeds—self-soan and sure to cum. Two lovers, like two
armies, generally get along quietly until they are
engaged.

I will now give young men my advice about getting
married.

Find a girl that iz nineteen years old last May, about
the right hight, with a blue eye, and dark-brown hair and
white teeth. Let the girl be good to look at, not too
phond of musik, a firm disbeleaver in ghosts, and one ov
six children in the same family. Look well tew the
karakter ov her father; see that he is not the member ov
enny klub, don't bet on elekshuns, and gits shaved at least

three times a week. [Laughter.] Find out all about her
mother, see if she haz got a heap ov good common sense,
studdy well her likes and dislikes, eat sum ov her hum-
made bread and apple dumplins [laughter], notiss whether
she abuzes all ov her nabors, and don't fail tew observe
whether her dresses are last year's ones fixt over.
[Laughter.] If you are satisfied that the mother would
make the right kind ov a mother-in-law, yu kan safely
konklude that the dauter would make the right kind of a
wife. [Applause.]

What about courtin' ?

Courting is a luxury, it is sallad, it is ise water, it is a
beveridge, it is the pla spell ov the soul. The man who
has never courted haz lived in vain [applause]; he haz bin
a blind man amung landskapes and waterskapes; he has
bin a deff man in the land ov hand orgins, and by the side
ov murmuring canals. [Laughter.] Courting iz like two
little springs ov soft water that steal out from under a
rock at the fut ov a mountain and run down the hill side
by side singing and dansing and spatering each uther,
eddying and frothing and kaskading, now hiding under
bank, now full ov sun and now full of shadder, till bime
by tha jine and then tha go slow. [Laughter.]

I am in favor ov long courting; it gives the parties a
chance to find out each uther's trump kards; it iz good
exercise, and it jist as innersent as two merino lambs.
Courting iz like strawberries and cream, wants tew be did
slow, then yu git the flavor.

Az a ginral thing i wouldn't brag on uther gals mutch
when i was courting, it mite look az tho yu knu tew mutch.

If yu will court three years in this wa, awl the time on
the square, if yu don't sa it iz a leettle the slikest time in
yure life, yu kan git measured for a hat at my expense,
and pa for it. [Laughter and applause.]

Don't court for munny, nor buty, nor relashuns, theze
things are jist about az onsartin as the kerosene ile refining
bissness, libel tew git out ov repair and bust at enny
minnit. [Applause.] Court a gal for fun, for the luv yu
bear her, for the vartue and bissness thare is in her; court
her for a wife and for a mother; court her as yu wud court
a farm—for the strength ov the sile and the parfeckshun
ov the title; court her as tho' she want a fule, and yu a

nuther; court her in the kitchen, in the parlor, over the wash tub, and at the pianner; court this wa, yung man, and if yu don't git a good wife and she don't git a good hustband, the falt won't be in the courting. [Applause.]

Yung man, yu kan rely upon Josh Billings, and if yu kant make these rules wurk, jist send for him, and he will sho yu how the thing is did, and it shant kost you a cent.

I will now give the following Advice to Lecture Committees outside of this town:

1. Don't hire enny man tew lectur for yu (never mind how moral he iz) unless yu kan make munny on him.

2. Selekt ten ov yure best lookin and most talking members tew meet the lekturer at the depot.

3. Don't fail tew tell the lekturer at least fourteen times on yure way from the depot tew the hotel that yu hav got the smartest town in kreashun, and sevral men in it that are wuth over a millyun. [Applause.]

4. When yu reach the hotel introduce the lekturer imejiately to at least twenty-five ov yure fust-klass citizens, if you hav tew send out for them.

5. When the lekturer's room iz reddy go with him in masse to hiz room and remind him four or five more times that yu had over three thousand people in yure city at the last censuss, and are a talking about having an opera house.

6. Don't leave the lekturer alone in his room over fifteen minits at once; he might take a drink out ov his flask on the sli if yu did.

7. When yu introjuce the lekturer tew the aujience don't fail tew make a speech ten or twelve feet long, occupying a haff an hour, and if yu kan ring in sumthing about the growth ov yure butiful sitty, so mutch the better. [Laughter.]

8. Always seat nine or ten ov the kommity on the stage, and then if it iz a kommik lektur, and the kommity don't laff a good deal, the aujience will konklude that the lektur iz a failure; and if they do laff a good deal, the aujience will konklude they are stool-pigeons. [Laughter.]

9. Jist az soon az the lectur is thru bring seventy-five or eighty ov the richest ov yure populashun up onto the stage and let them squeeze the hand and exchange talk with the lekturer.

10. Go with the lekturer from the hall tew hiz room in a bunch, and remind him once or twice more on the way that yure sitty iz a growing very rapidly, and ask him if he don't think so.

11. If the lekturer should inquire how the comik lekturers had succeeded who had preceded him, don't forget tew tell him that they were all failures. This will enable him tew guess what they will say about him just az soon az he gits out ov town. [Laughter.]

12. If the lekturer's fee should be a hundred dollars or more, don't hesitate tew pay him next morning, about five minnits before the train leaves, in old, lop-eared one-dollar bills, with a liberal sandwiching ov tobbakko-stained shinplasters. [Laughter.]

13. I forgot tew say that the fust thing yu should tell a lekturer, after yu had sufficiently informed him ov the immense growth ov yure citty, iz that yure people are not edukated up tew lekturs yet, but are grate on nigger-minstrels. [Applause.]

14. Never fail tew ask the lekturer whare he finds the most apprechiatev audiences, and he won't fail tew tell you (if he iz an honest man) that thare ain't no State in the Union that begins tew compare with yures. [Laughter.]

15. Let fifteen or twenty ov yure kommity go with the lekturer, next morning, tew the kars, and az each one shakes hands with him with a kind ov deth grip, don't forget tew state that yure citty iz growing very mutch in people.

16. If the night iz wet, and the inkum ov the house won't pay expenses, don't hesitate tew make it pay by taking a chunk out ov the lekturer's fee. The lekturers all like this, but they are too modest, as a klass, tew say so. [Laughter.]

17. I know ov several other good rules tew follow, but the abuv will do tew begin with.

Your Schoolmaster will tell you the rest.

Thare iz one man in this world to whom i alwus take oph mi hat, and remain uncovered untill he gits safely by, and that iz the distrikt skoolmaster. When I meet him, I look upon him az a martyr just returning from the stake, or on hiz way thare tew be cooked. He leads a more

lonesum and single life than an old bachelor, and a more
anxious one than an old maid.   He iz remembered jist
about az long and affektionately az a gide board iz by a
traveling pack pedler.   If he undertakes tew make his
skollars luv him, the chances are he will neglekt their
larning; and if he don't lick them now and then pretty
often, they will soon lick him.   [Laughter.]   The distrikt skoolmaster hain't got a friend on the flat side ov
earth.   The boys snowball him during recess; the girls put
water in hiz hair die; and the skool committee make him
work for haff the money a bartender gits, and board him
around the naberhood, whare they giv him rhy coffee,
sweetened with mollasis, tew drink, and kodfish bawls
three times a day for vittles.   [Laughter.]

And, with all this abuse, I never heard ov a distrikt
skoolmaster swareing enny thing louder than—*Condem it.*

Don't talk tew me about the pashunce ov anshunt Job.
Job had pretty plenty ov biles all over him, no doubt, but
they were all ov one breed.   Every yung one in a distrikt
skool iz a bile ov a different breed, and each one needs a
different kind ov poultiss tew git a good head on them.
[Laughter.]

A distrikt skoolmaster, who duz a square job and takes
hiz codfish bawls reverently, iz a better man to-day tew
hav lieing around loose than Solomon would be arrayed
in all ov hiz glory.   Solomon waz better at writing proverbs and manageing a large family, than he would be tew
navigate a distrikt skool hous.

Enny man who haz kept a distrikt skool for ten years,
and boarded around the naberhood, ought tew be made a
mager gineral, and hav a penshun for the rest ov his natral
days, and a hoss and waggin tew do hiz going around in.
But, az a genral consequence, a distrikt skoolmaster hain't
got any more warm friends than an old blind fox houn
haz.   He iz jist about az welkum az a tax gatherer iz.   He
iz respekted a good deal az a man iz whom we owe a debt
ov fifty dollars to and don't mean tew pay.   [Applause.]
He goes through life on a back road, az poor az a wood
sled, and finally iz missed—but what ever bekums ov hiz
remains, i kant tell.   Fortunately he iz not often a sensitive man; if he waz, he couldn't enny more keep a distrikt
skool than he could file a kross kut saw.   [Laughter.]

Whi iz it that theze men and wimmen, who pashuntly and with crazed brain teach our remorseless brats the tejus meaning ov the alphabet, who take the fust welding heat on their destinys, who lay the stepping stones and enkurrage them tew mount upwards, who hav dun more hard and mean work than enny klass on the futstool, who have prayed over the reprobate, strengthened the timid, restrained the outrageous, and flattered the imbecile, who hav lived on kodfish and vile coffee, and hain't been heard to sware—whi is it that they are treated like a vagrant fiddler, danced to for a night, paid oph in the morning, and eagerly forgotten?

I had rather burn a coal pit, or keep the flys out ov a butcher's shop in the month ov August, than meddle with the distrikt skool bizzness. [Applause.]

I propose now to close by making Twelve Square Remarks, to-wit:—

1. A broken reputashun iz like a broken vase; it may be mended, but allways shows where the krak was. [Applause.]

2. If you kant trust a man for the full amount, let him skip. This trying to git an average on honesty has allways bin a failure. [Applause.]

3. Thare iz no treachery in silence; silence is a hard argument to beat.

4. Don't mistake habits for karacter. The men ov the most karacter hav the fewest habits. [Applause.]

5. Thare iz cheats in all things; even pizen is adulterated.

6. The man who iz thoroughly polite iz two-thirds ov a Christian, enny how. [Applause.]

7. Kindness iz an instinkt, politeness only an art. [Applause.]

8. Thare iz a great deal of learning in this world which iz nothing more than trying to prove what we don't understand.

9. Mi dear boy, thare are but few who kan kommence at the middle ov the ladder and reach the top; and probably you and I don't belong to that number. [Applause.]

10. One ov the biggest mistakes made yet iz made by the man who thinks he iz temperate, just becauze he puts

more water in his whiskey than his nabor does.   [Applause.]

11. The best medicine I know ov for the rumatism iz to thank the Lord—that it aint the gout.   [Laughter.]

12. Remember the poor.   It costs nothing.   [Laughter and applause.]

SIR HENRY MORTON STANLEY
Photogravure after a photograph from life

SIR HENRY MORTON STANLEY

THROUGH THE GREAT FOREST

[Lecture by Henry M. Stanley, journalist and African explorer (born John Rowlands, near Denbigh, Wales, January 28, 1841; subsequently taking his present name from a merchant of New Orleans, La., for whom he sometime worked, and who adopted him as a son), delivered in the Metropolitan Opera-House, New York City, November 11, 1890. This was during Mr. Stanley's second lecture tour in the United States, in the season of 1890-91, after his return from the successful "Emin Pasha Relief Expedition." He was introduced to the large and distinguished audience by Chauncey M. Depew in the following words: "LADIES AND GENTLEMEN:—Three years ago a distinguished American traveler and explorer was delighting his friends in New York at a famous dinner given in his honor with an account of his adventures. He was jubilant over the promising pleasures and profits of a lecture tour just begun when a cable was handed to him from King Leopold of Belgium, summoning him to Europe. With characteristic promptness and energy he sailed the next morning, and we heard of him soon after leading an expedition into the wilds of Africa for the relief of Emin Pasha. For nearly three years no tidings came of him, and he was mourned as lost, but to-night Mr. Stanley reappears to take up where he dropped it at the call of duty the suspended lecture course of 1887. We are preparing to celebrate fitly the four hundredth anniversary of the discovery of America. We strain our vision to pierce through the vista of the centuries and view the personality of Columbus. But in greeting Stanley we are repeating, in our republican way, the pageant of the reception at the court of Ferdinand and Isabella, and will more accurately present for the quadricentennial ceremonies of the populous, prosperous, and cultured nations of Africa the character and contemporaneous appreciation of their benefactor. Many cities proudly claimed to be the birthplace of Homer, and already envious localities in the old world are prolific in parish registers which identify Mr. Stanley with them. But no matter under what sun he first saw the light, his great discoveries and won-

derful achievements have been made and performed by him as an
American citizen. His motto has always been, "A man might as well
march to meet his fate as wait to find it," and the results have been
safety and immortality. [Applause.] It is a career intensely American
and dramatic. A merchant's education fits him for business, a soldier's and a sailor's life for travel and adventure, the dangers and opportunities of a war correspondent inure him to hardship, and they
all together cultivate fertility of resource in perils of savage, perils of
flood, and perils of the wilderness.

" The distinctive events which have given to civilization a knowledge
of our planet and pushed progress around the earth are the conquests
of Alexander the Great, the travels of Marco Polo, the discoveries of
Columbus, and the explorations of Stanley. The Macedonian hero,
who sat sighing by the Ganges because he had no more worlds to con-
quer, was simply a soldier seeking glory, mad with the excitement
of war and indifferent to its results or its miseries. The Venetian
merchant whose wondrous narrative has been the amusing fiction of
six centuries, and the reality of ours, and who has made travelers'
tales and bouncing lying synonymous terms, was bent only upon commerce and trade. Columbus was hazarding everything upon the possi-
bility of finding the fabled El Dorado and revelling in gold. But the
advancing ages have tended upward, and we are capable in these so-
called practical and prosaic times of unequaled effort and supreme
courage for a sentiment and for humanity. The daring and gentle missionary whose revelation of the possibilities of Africa has interested
all nations in his work and in himself, had been given up as one more
martyr in the service of mankind, and Stanley's first effort was not
commerce or conquest, but to find and relieve Livingstone. A free
state founded as a breakwater against that sum of all infamies—the
slave trade—the continent crossed, the mysteries of its lakes and
streams reduced to a geographical certainty, the problem of the ages,
the sources of the Nile, successfully solved, would seem to entitle the
explorer to rest and peace. But a governor, his army, and his province were situated somewhere in the dark unknown, and beleaguered
by fanatical and blood-thirsty foes. The anthem of universal applause
rises from all peoples when Stanley reappears, bringing back to safety
and home Emin Pasha and his followers. [Applause.] The Paladins
of Charlemagne were the ideals of one century, and Chevalier Bayard
has been of many others. The one represented resistless force and the
other knightly courtesy upon the field of battle. The Christianity and
humanity of our day impel to grander deeds than those which made
immortal these warriors and knights, and with results which render
their achievements utterly insignificant. The great Powers of Europe have taken the territories brought to light by the discoveries of
Stanley and divided them among themselves for the relief of their
overcrowded populations and the building of greater Germanys and

Englands upon the fertile plateaus and along the rich valleys of the Dark Continent. The dangers which threatened civilization itself are indefinitely postponed by the opening of these new fields for settlement and enterprise, the savage nations of Africa will be redeemed and the earth enriched and heaven recruited. [Applause.] This summer, when the expedition of Stanley and the partition of Africa were the first topics of discussion in court and camp, in society and the slums, a man of the highest position and power on the other side of the sea said to me, 'What in your judgment is Stanley's greatest achievement?' I replied, 'It strikes me as an American it was that a reporter for a New York newspaper should reach a position where he could so stir public opinion against the British Ministry by his simple declaration that England had been overreached in the agreement with Germany, that the Government was compelled to modify it, and that then his statement that the terms were fair restored confidence in the administration.'

"Not satisfied with his adventures, his hair-breadth escapes, his marvelous experiences, Mr. Stanley, finding no more continents to explore, has essayed a journey often tried and by less intrepid men. In wishing him a long life of health, peace, and happiness, we congratulate him that in the state of matrimony he will find that superior to the treasures of Africa are the joys of connubial bliss. [Laughter and warm applause.] Ladies and gentlemen, I introduce to you Mr. Henry M. Stanley."]

MR. CHAIRMAN, LADIES AND GENTLEMEN :—In a future lecture I hope to give you a few incidents of our march across the continent of Africa. In this one I propose to take you through the great forest up to the Mountains of the Moon, around the great lakes and across Africa. Our journey measured over 6,000 miles. The time occupied was 987 days. The first section of about 1,000 miles was along an unknown country by steamer up the Aruwimi River, to a place called Yambuya. The navigation was interrupted by rapids. On foot next for 160 days we went through one unbroken forest. That journey was not through poetic glades, with here and there thrown in a bit of mossy dell, with little or no undergrowth, and free access and an open view into sylvan wilds. You may remember your experiences of last summer when you took an excursion into the woods. There you found a poetic seclusion, a graceful disorder, mossy grounds, trees of familiar kinds, springy turf, bits of picturesque skies, and the sun shedding softened streams of light upon tree and turf.   Ah! the African forest furnishes no such picturesque sights or pleasant glades.

Language is too poor to describe it.   First think of the tropics and a climate of humidity and the heat of perpetual summer.   You feel, as you enter into this unknown region, the robustness of vegetation.   There is a still, warm vapor in suffocating volumes.   First you dispense with your upper garments, and then you want to get rid of the rest.   The gloom is so great that you can only compare it to the twilight of evening.   You see the leafage rising up black and green; impenetrable clumps of trees, some of them reaching a height of two hundred and fifty feet. There is no symmetry, grace or softness, but all is wild, uncouth and awful.   At every step you see masses of bewildering undergrowths, a wonderful variety of plants. There is an absence of any sense of decay; rather the sense of the general healthfulness of the plants, an enduring youth, exhaustless wonders.

There is no longer any energy among us.   We behold everlasting greenness, eternal vitality and fertility.   Above all is a protecting, impenetrable canopy.   Sacred trees, with leafy crowns, tower above us.   African mahogany, the unyielding iron-wood, the butternut-tree, and other varieties too numerous to mention, all united in closest embrace, darken the life below till it is suggestive of mystery and awe.   As we march silently, slowly, and painfully on, the forest changes its aspect, and we note the labors of forgotten tribes and come to swampy grounds. One day our march is very slow through masses of forest wilderness.   On the next day we go through a more open section; on the following day through frowning depths and over ground strewn with dead leaves, worm-eaten trunks or dried branches.   But always and above all tower the primeval woods, the deep shadows unbroken save by the flashes of lightning.

On some days the march has to be prolonged beyond the usual hour for halting that has been fixed upon, because of the difficulty of choosing a ground fit for a camp. For we bear with us tons of perishable goods that have to be protected from the floods of rain.   But at last a suitable spot is found.   The whistle is sounded and the loaded files come up, and one by one they deposit their burdens in due order. Then, when the tents are erected, the camp resounds with the sound of voices. Some men with axes trim the poles of the tents or cut fuel. Some with knives peel the saplings to utilize the bark for bedding. Some dig holes in the ground for the tent-poles.

In a couple of hours a little town will be seen, and a hundred fires will blaze, and a hundred pots will be sending up clouds of savory steam. The camp is animated and resounds with chatter, all the louder because confined by the four sides of our forest home. After the guards are set around the camp we feel safe from the surprises of the cannibals, and those who wish are free to wander away. At such a time I have been sensible of the utter poverty of words to describe my surroundings. It is not a time for poetic brooding, but one after another the senses yield to the charm of seclusion. Then I behold a magnificent forest in listening attitude, a great gloom, trees eloquent of antiquity and of venerable brotherhood. I marvel at the age of these giants. Since the period when the nuts dropped from the trees and took root, what generations have passed! generation after generation, dynasty after dynasty, empire after empire, one national period after another,—and the trees grow taller and taller through the centuries, yearly extending in growth, extending in limb, and rising steadily, invincibly upward, indifferent whether their crested tops are illuminated by sunshine or dripped with rain, or are tossed by the raging tornado of the tropics. [Applause.] That old patriarch yonder, with massive and wrinkled bark, was probably born a thousand years before the siege of Troy. That head you see above you was a shrub in the days of Herod the Great. Even the palm by the river bank, which seems so utterly out of place among the forest kings, probably sprouted first when Columbus started his course across the Atlantic.

They are brimming over with vitality. We feel that their vegetable life is incomparable with our own. They stand and have stood while the centuries rolled by, mute and rigid in the gloaming; they are there to-day in enormous multitudes. The sun shines on their tops with utmost fervor. The mist floods around them with grayish clouds. They will brave the elements in the future with the same peaceful, proud endurance as they have done in the past. The forest there faithfully represents human life in pantomime—that struggle for space,—selfish indifference to others may be found there as with us. When the topmost bough is shattered by lightning, another fed by the air and light springs up triumphantly to usurp its place. You can see with what greed others hasten to occupy the opening made by the uniform height and equal growth.

I found also that they are subject to diseases, as is humanity. Countless parasites are around the stems and strangle their growth. The ants eat into their boles, and great branches are pushed aside by the elephants rubbing their sides against them. You will see among them large tumors on their stems. Others falling into decay with age are bleached white by death. The ground underneath consists of the dust of others which are gone. It is carpeted with their dead leaves and strewn with their broken limbs. Scarcely an hour passes but in your neighborhood a tree falls. There is a sound as of an explosion and a shock that shakes the earth, and a branch comes tumbling down with a startling crash. A twig snaps or a leaf falls every second of time. But with this death there is life, for seeds also fall, and as often as a tree dies, another has sprouted, or with the fall of a leaf another has sprouted.

During a year of wanderings we noted 560 hours of rain, which would be about one hour of rain for every fifteen of dry weather during twelve months. How much sunshine there was we would not say. It seemed to us there was only one hour of sun brightness to every hour of night or fog or gloom. We could only tell from the heat in the forests that the sun was out. We could only feel its dry fervor in the clearings, but the effect of this super-moisture is the exceeding vegetation. The trees from summit to branch are clothed with verdure and wound around by enormous parasites and climbers. The grander trees bear the heaviest and thickest species, which run from fourteen to sixteen inches in diameter. The climber of the greatest diameter reaches 1,400 feet, and they continue their serpentine twisting from one limb to another, and finally hang suspended thirty or forty feet above like immense anacondas, swinging with every gust, or they ascend to the branches of other trees until they are lost in the depth above. There are hundreds of them. They are seen in a great net-work, web-like formations. There is not a sapling or tree, from the infant of one year to the holy patriarch of forty centuries, but is invested with both vegetable and animal parasites. Thin vines and serpent-like creepers all swing solemnly hither and thither under the influence of a strong wind, with countless millions of leaves resting on the great limbs of the trees, embracing the rigid branches, creaking and grinding.

You can hardly realize the scene of desolation that is found in the sepulchral gloom of the forests. But when the storm king is in the air above and every tree seems starting from its sepulchral stillness in a mad dance, and there is a mad massing and warring and rushing through the foliage shades, and the woods bow their heads in agonized grief, try however you may, you cannot help sympathizing with the scene. It is awful and horrible to hear all these sounds in the pitch-black night, when the tornado descends on the forests, and the elements are accompanied with all their terrors, with blinding brands of lightning and the cannonade of the thunder, when the whole camp is a blaze of blinding light. It is far more frightful when the rain pours over the desolate scene in drowning showers. You can understand now what effect such experiences of tempest and rain and darkness had upon the minds of our people, who knew not where this endless march was leading, as the days grew into weeks and the weeks into long months, and not a soul could enlighten them as to the possible limits of this demon world;—all this added to continuous pain from hunger, misery and sickness, and the dull pangs of sorrow as they tossed their dead companions into the dark river, in the absence of all hope in the future. Gaunt famine smote them dead by the scores; their limbs were ravaged by rabid ulcers, the stagnant atmosphere poisoning them with its breath, ants and ticks creeping over their bodies, fierce savages jumping upon them with dagger or spears, while they feebly crawled after the caravan; ruthless pigmies lying behind trees shooting their barbed arrows into their bodies; and cannibals attacking them as they gath-

ered over their evening fire.   Death cut our people off
with revolting treachery, and sudden as lightning stroke.
    Finally, after 160 days of marching, we emerged from
the forest.   Then our eyes danced with rapture, for we
beheld fresh young grass spreading out into flowery fields
and pastures; and then beyond round and picturesquely
molded hills.   Such a sight we hailed with shouts of praise
and loud thanksgivings and murmurs of worship according
to our respective faiths.   The delicious grass, the warbling
of birds, this summer loveliness of the land and the warm
life and beauteous earth reposing in peace were sublime.
Our men had dreams of joy and they called it heaven.
[Applause.]   Its length was 620 English miles from north
to south and from west to east 520 miles.   It comprised
320,000 square miles, the whole equal to 400,000 square
miles.
    In the beginning of 1886 the Arab slave-traders had not
penetrated very far into this region.   The Arabs were
for some time deterred from making any serious effort to
push into this forest, but the increasing price of ivory
and the scarcity of it subsequently inspired them with
greater efforts.   In May, 1887, they had gained a footing
in Etura.   Separating from one another, they built three
stations down the Etura, about a hundred miles apart,
one at the Leda, forming the apex of a triangle, the base
line of which was fifty miles away.   They then began killing the aborigines, and appropriating or looting whatever
property they found.   Within five months they cut a swath
227 miles long, and in width about 180 English miles.
Not one village had been left standing.   Their plantain
groves had become so many jungles.   The aborigines had
either been destroyed, or were hidden in the darkest recesses of the forests.   This is the reason why in 1887 our
expedition suffered so terribly from hunger.   Were you
enabled to take a birdseye view of the forests, the native
clearings would have appeared like so many circular bits
of pale green.
    There were no tracks, and we possessed only one steel
boat for the river, and part of the journey, therefore, had
to be made by forcing a way through the bush.   If that
was too thick we scattered through the underbrush, but
we had bill-hook and cutter in constant exercise.   The first

month in the bush we progressed very slowly. When
finally, after many months' labors, we reached a track, our
pace was increased to one and three-quarter miles an hour.

As the column stretched in file over a considerable
length of ground the pioneers had to slash away a broad
blaze on a tree every few yards. It was most difficult to
distinguish the track. But by the time the whole of the
column had passed over it the trail was pretty clear. Some
days, however, when I would be leading a river party, the
pioneers would lose all trace of it. They would leave the
river and relying too much on their knowledge of wood-
land, try to cut a straight course. Thus they frequently
lost their way, and for hours the caravan would be wandering in the woods while the river party would be
anxiously waiting for them. On one occasion the parties
were separated six days.

As we drew nearer the eastern limits the nature of our
difficulties changed. We followed native paths. Then
the voices of the foremost men would be heard bawling
out the character of their troubles, one by one: "Skewers below," "Ants—red ants on the march," "A tangling
root," "Ware skewers," "Mushy mud, with no bottom,"
"Wasps." These warnings, while they served to prevent
us from falling into pitfalls, retarded the march.

If I were to enumerate the names of the various tribes
whose territories we traversed there would be general
hilarity, I fear, in an American audience. The inhabitants
of the forest are divided into big people and little people.
The taller men are those who own clearings in the forest.
The pigmies are unsettled and restless little nomads, who
slide about through the woods, and whose temporary
camps are generally found two or three miles outside of
the banana plantations. The first are very like other
Africans, but much browner than the dwellers in the
plains, probably from living so much in the shade. Each
tribe has its distinguishing marks, tattooings of some figure or another on the forehead or on the cheeks or chins.
Some shave their heads; some wear their hair long or in
ringlets. There is no elaborate hair-dressing in the forest,
as lower down along the Congo. Their ornaments consist of crocodile, monkey or human teeth, strung in neck-
lets and anklets and bracelets. Their dress is a clout of

dark cloth, a strip four feet long. For head-wear these people have a head-piece of basket work adorned with a parrot's red tail-feathers. Their weapons are spears, bows and arrows, broad knives, and sometimes a battle-axe.

These are they who sometimes make great clearings in the woods, and in the midst of a confusion of fallen trees build compact villages. Outside the villages there is a tangle of brushwood, half hidden by plantain groves. The villages swarm with goats and fowls, which now and again furnish the people with food. The natives are addicted to cannibalism, but it must not be supposed that they feed on their own relatives or tribe. Neither is a human victim always easy to secure. The tribes are too far apart; but if a neighboring community, ten or a dozen miles off, advances, there may possibly be an accident, when a body may be secured. I once witnessed the preparations for a cannibal feast. Our men approached an Irwangas village. I fired a shot to warn the chief that we were friendly, and it happened to frighten a party of natives preparing a victim for their repast. In a few seconds our boats were at the bank of the river, and we saw the body of a woman who had been speared in the throat and then washed. The black pots, the bananas were all there, and in a short time everything would have been ready. We found afterward that the woman had been sick and had been left by the Arabs.

We had also a Manuema boy who slipped into the bush to evade the rear guard, after a caravan had passed. He advanced slowly toward the camp and had almost reached it when he was sighted by natives and slain almost at the same time that a party of companions were proceeding to his assistance. Finding the body in the path, they carried it into the woods, and covered it lightly with leaves, with the intention of returning and burying it. The natives, who had been close observers of what had been done, came up and took it off. In the morning the Manuemas found only a few bones.

During many months of marching in the forest we captured hundreds of large and small natives. They were very useful in their own districts, giving information about the tribes, and showing paths to banana plantations, but once beyond their territory they were of no earthly use.

So they were permitted to return to their homes, though in many instances they did not want to be released. My observation and experience led me to the conclusion that morally, the forest natives are the lowest of the human race. They have no idea of a God, and nothing approaching our soft sensibilities. Their gratitude is so short-lived that it might be compared to that of a fierce bull-dog restrained from throttling you only by devouring a piece of beef just thrown to it. What a number of ghastly death scenes I could describe resulting from the cruel persistency and devilish malice of these savages. At the same time many of our men in the presence of such dangers exhibited great carelessness. White men displayed more caution, but it was almost impossible to get the others to exercise their faculties of sight, hearing, and judgment. Had the savages generally been as artful as the pigmies we should all have been lost. But, fortunately, they were themselves thoughtless, although cruel enough to work any mischief upon us.

Our scouts frequently came across newly-formed pigmy camps, and after a while they learned the art of stalking the vicious little creatures. The first one we thus got hold of was a plump little queen of a pigmy tribe. Around her neck were several polished iron collars with long projecting horns at the end, and down her breast hung curiously made native chains. Around her arms were several rings, and her ankles were protected by scores of rings, so close together that they resembled a compact band. Around her waist was a breech-cloth. She must have been about eighteen years old, but she was as well developed as a white woman of twenty-five or twenty-six. Her feet were beautifully formed, the instep arched, the hands small, the fingers slender, and the nails filbert-shaped. The face was broad and round, the lips full, and the large, black, limpid eyes, like those of a young gazelle. The face was singularly impressive, but the eyes were most expressive and seemed to say: "I am much too pretty to be hurt and I very well know what I am worth." The tender treatment that she received reassured her. She was ultimately consigned to the care of the surgeon, whose gentle manner won her from all thoughts of flight. After a while she became an intelligent cook, and a trust-

worthy servant, and she always bore herself most mod-
estly.

In October, 1888, we suddenly pounced on a family of
dwarfs, peeling bananas, and succeeded in capturing a
full-grown adult and his sister, or wife. Before the pair
could recover their faculties, they were led to the center
of our camp, and hundreds of great, burly men thronged
to see the strangers. We had among us some tall Soudanese, ranging from six feet to six feet four in height.
I observed that the head of the pigmy man reached to
about the waist-belts of these Soudanese. Both the man
and woman were considerably agitated, but while they
doubted, and anxiously wondered, what was to be their
fate, my mind recurred to the described scene that took
place twenty-five centuries ago when the five young Nas-
samonian explorers were captured by a band of dwarfs
and taken through the Nigritian villages. How I wished
that I could extract from the representative of this old
people some of their traditions. Before a Phœnician
bark ever sailed to Britain these little people were ranging
these illimitable forests which stretch westward from the
Moon Mountains. In all old maps you will see "pigmies" printed side by side in bold letters, with the Mountains of the Moon.

But the little man who was now the cynosure of the
camp, with his grotesque dignity of manhood, his cap of
basket-work, his noble amplitude of abdomen and narrow
chest, had no conception of the respect I entertained for
him as the scion of a most ancient ancestry, or surely he
would never have trembled for his fate. But in a short
time we succeeded in relieving him of his fears by gently
chucking him under the chin, and administering a friendly
slap on the back. His companion, observing how he was
treated, also recovered from her fright. Gaining confidence, the little man, as though to repay our kindness,
informed us, by the most voluble of sign-language, that
there was abundance of food two days off; that the river
we were in search of was only four days off; that he knew
where bananas grew as big as logs compared with which
the bananas he had been eating when captured were
simply contemptibly small. Personally, I am of opinion
that this particular pigmy would have made a very good

actor, and that in the art of lying it would be difficult
to give him points.   [Applause.]

A few days after this capture another group of pigmies
were secured.   Among them was a shrewish old woman,
and a lad so shy that he could not be made to speak.   But
the old woman talked enough for a whole tribe and kept
up an incessant scolding from morning till night, and
exhibited a consummate mastery of pigmy cuss-words.
[Laughter.]   Despite her age she was remarkably strong
and nimble, and always carried on her back a hamper.
Into this her captor would stow away his pots and kettles
and other equipments until she became a veritable camel
of the forest.   When I discovered this, I came to her
relief and threw out the contents of her hamper.   I received for my pains a rattling expression of gratitude
which sounded very much like swear-words.   [Laughter.]
As for the shy boy, he got over his shyness and became a
pet of the officer who had surprised him.   His intelligence
and industry made him most valuable, far superior to
the average of white servants.   We came in time to regard
these pigmies as indispensable, and some of them would
certainly have been taken with us back to Europe, but
after they got out of the forest the changed conditions
and the difference in climate proved too much for them.
Their little legs could not stand the long marches, and
one after another they collapsed.

The next most interesting discovery we made was that
of the long-lost Mountains of the Moon.   In my book,
" Darkest Africa," I have illustrated with small maps our
knowledge of Africa derived from the ancients.   In these
is clearly shown that ivory-hunters and slave-traders had
reached that region in times past.   Information as to it
varied.   The last traveler there, as now, was regarded as
the best informed.   This is why the great lakes of the
interior and the Mountains of the Moon shifted every
hundred years or so ten degrees north or south of the
Equator.   It was in December, 1887, that we got a
glimpse of the twin cones of Ruwenzori.   There are many,
doubtless, like myself, who, while gazing upon any ancient
work, be it an Egyptian Pyramid, or Sphynx, be it an
Athenian Parthenon, Palmyrene sun temple, Persepolitan
palace, or even an old English castle, will readily confess

to feeling a peculiar emotion at the sight. The vener-
ableness of it, which time only can give, its associations
with men long gathered to their fathers, the builders and
inhabiters now quite forgotten, appeal to a certain sympathy in the living. For its history there is a vague yearn-
ing; its age awakens something like exultation that we
little mortals can build such time-defying structures. But
more powerful and higher is that emotion which is roused
at the sight of a hoary old mountain like this of Ruwenzori, which we know to be countless thousands of years
old. When we think how long it required the melted
snow to carve out these ravines, hundreds of fathoms
deep, through the rocky cone of the range, or we consider the ages required to spread out the debris from its
sides and bosom to cover the Semliki Valley and the
Nyanza plains, we are struck dumb at the immeasurable-
ness of the interval between that age when Ruwenzori
rose aloft into being and now; we become possessed with
a wholesome awe, and can but feel a cheerful faith that it
was good for us to have seen it.

Another emotion is that inspired by the thought that in
one of the darkest corners of the earth, shrouded by perpetual mist, brooding under the eternal storm-clouds, surrounded by darkness and mystery, there has been hidden
to this day a giant among mountains, the melting snow
of whose tops has been for some fifty centuries most vital
to the peoples of Egypt. Imagine to what a God the
reverently inclined primal nations would have exalted this
mountain, which from such a far-away region as this contributed so copiously to their beneficent and sacred Nile.
And this thought of the beneficent Nile brings on another.
In fancy we look down along that crooked silver vein to
where it disports and spreads out to infuse new life to
Egypt near the Pyramids, some 4,000 miles away, where
we behold populous swarms of men—Arabs, Copts, Fel-
lahs, Negroes, Turks, Greeks, Italians, Frenchmen, English, Germans, and Americans—bustling, jostling or loung-
ing; and we feel a pardonable pride in being able to inform them for the first time that much of the sweet water
they drink and whose virtues they so often exalt, issues
from the deep and extensive snowbeds of Ruwenzori or
Ruwenjura—"the Cloud-King."

These brief—too brief—views of the superb Rain-Cre-
ator or Cloud-King, as the Wakonju fondly termed their
mist-shrouded mountains, fill the gazer with a feeling as
of a glimpse of celestial splendor. While it lasted, I
observed the rapt faces of whites and blacks set fixed and
uplifted in speechless wonder toward that upper region
of cold brightness and perfect peace, so high above mortal
reach, so tranquil and restful, of such immaculate and
stainless purity, that thought and desire of expression
were altogether too deep for utterance. What stranger
contrast could there be than our own nether world of
torrid temperature, eternally green, sappy plants, and
never-fading luxuriance and verdure, with its savagery
and war-alarms, and deep stains of blood-red sin, to that
lofty mountain king, clad in its pure white raiment of
snow, surrounded by myriads of dark mountains, low as
bending worshippers before the throne of a monarch, on
whose cold, white face was inscribed "Infinity and Everlasting." These moments of supreme feeling are mem-
orable for the utter abstraction of the mind from all that is
sordid and ignoble, and its utter absorption in the presence
of unreachable loftiness, indescribable majesty, constrain-
ing it not only reverentially to admire, but to adore in
silence, the image of the Eternal. Never can a man be so
fit for Heaven as during such moments, for however scornful and insolent he may have been at other times, he now
has become as a little child, filled with wonder and reverence before what he has conceived to be sublime and
Divine. [Applause.] We had been strangers for many
months to the indulgence of any thought of this character.
Our senses, between the hours of sleeping and waking,
had been occupied by the imperious and imminent necessities of each hour, which required unrelaxing vigilance
and forethought. It is true we had been touched with the
view from the mount called Pisgah of that universal extent
of forest, spreading out on all sides but one, to many hundreds of miles; we had been elated into hysteria when,
after five months' immurement in the depths of forest
wilds, we once again trod upon green grass and enjoyed
open and unlimited views of our surroundings—luxuriant
vales, varying hill-forms on all sides, rolling plains, over
which the long spring grass seemed to race and leap in

gladness before the cooling gale; we had admired the broad sweep and the silvered face of Lake Albert, and enjoyed a period of intense rejoicing when we knew we had reached, after infinite trials, the bourne and limit of our journeyings; but the desire and involuntary act of worship were never provoked, nor the emotions stirred so deeply, as when we suddenly looked up and beheld the skyey crests and snowy breasts of Ruwenzori uplifted into an inaccessible altitude, so like what our conceptions might be of a celestial castle, with dominating battlement, and leagues upon leagues of unscaleable walls.

Revisiting the Lake Albert region at later periods we found that the snow-capped peaks had an exasperating habit of disappearing from view, and it was only in May of last year (1889) that I finally solved the mystery. Rolling clouds and vapors sometimes blot them out. This is why the natives call them "Ruwenzori," which means "the Cloud-King."

The discovery of the Snow Mountains led to two more discoveries—that of the Albert Edward Nyanza, and the head waters of the Albertine Nile; and the confused information given by the priests of Isis in olden times to Egyptian and Greek geographers, furnished by the ivory traders and slave-raiders of old, has now been made perfectly clear in all its important details.

Day after day we marched, marking the features of this splendid primeval world, revealed for the first time. Now and then we caught glimpses of a multitude of precipitous cliffs which towered some 15,000 feet above. As we approached Albert Edward, we emerged from the forest, and a vast plain stretched before us, covered by immense fields of corn and sugar-cane. The natives, black but amiable, collected about us, and sought our protection from incursive tribes. They volunteered to be our guides, and led us up a vast grassy promontory, where for a day we revelled in pure, cold air, and the next day they took us down to the lake where we tasted the tropics once more.

From the eastern shores of Lake Albert two days climbing brought us to a beautiful region. The people here were divided into two tribes, but they were derived, apparently, from a common origin. They were a fine-featured race and the men grew very tall. They lived mainly upon

milk and sugar-cane, and, unfortunately for their future
civilization, they are massed into nations that are ruled by
despotic kings.

From this country we struck the eastern end of Victoria
Nyanza, and by traveling along the shore we discovered
a new addition to this lake of 26,900 square miles. We
struck the region during its dry season. The grass was
sere; chilly winds blew over the uplands; a cold mist frequently obscured the face of the country, and a heavy,
leaden sky seemed to bear down upon us in a searching
cold. Our half-naked people shivered, and one day five
fell dead in their tracks as though they were shot. They
would all have perished had not the officer commanding
the rear guard bolted, and made great bonfires.

During our march to the sea, it had gradually dawned
upon us that there was intense political rivalry between
England and Germany in Africa. But as our expedition
had been solely to relieve Emin, we flattered ourselves
that we had nothing to do with these dissensions. Emin
was a German, and we accepted German hospitality as a
proof of their good-will. We knew Emin was pliable and
yielding. We supposed his gratitude was not very deep.
But we thought that nothing could rupture the good feeling that had hitherto existed between us. But the accident at Bagamoya, the first evening after reaching the sea,
and being embraced by his countrymen, was wholly unexpected, and it gave the Germans on the East Coast a fair
opportunity. We had abundant proof afterward how
beautifully the Germans understood Emin's character.
Frenchmen and Italians, perhaps, would have performed
their parts far more efficiently without advertising the
means employed.

Emin at the banquet in our honor was joyously grateful to each member of our expedition. He embraced
Stairs and Nelson and Jephson, and flung himself on the
neck of Parke; stood between Wissman and myself uttering gayly his happy feelings, and then went away and fell
over the balcony to the dismay of the company. He was
taken to the hospital in an unconscious state. On his re-
covering consciousness we had a kindly parting, and then
the operations of his countrymen began. First, Dr. Parke,
who had volunteered to attend the sufferer, was made to

feel that his presence was irksome. Servants became careless; the food was stinted. If he went to the officers' mess-table, the German officers continued to show their strong disapproval of his presence. Then Dr. Parke fell ill of a fever and was conveyed to Zanzibar almost dying. Our letters to Emin were unanswered. If we expressed a desire to visit him at Bagamoya, at once a bulletin came out with a story of his relapse. We tried it three times with the same result. The play deepened in interest and the conclusion was darkly hinted.

Having succeeded in relieving himself from obligation to us, our acquaintance was renounced. This incivility was presently fanned by his countrymen into a hot hostility. On coming out of the hospital Emin published broadcast through Zanzibar the fact that he had severed himself from us, and wrote letters to Germany to the same effect, which his delighted friends made use of. He next sought to quarrel with the Egyptian Government. He cabled to Cairo for a small credit at Zanzibar. Sir Evelyn Baring kindly telegraphed back that the British Consul at Zanzibar would honor the credit. Emin construed this as an insult—the idea that he, Governor-General of the Equatorial Province, should receive drafts through an English consul-general! To his old officers and generals, Egyptian and Soudanese, he wrote frankly that he would have nothing to do with them, and declined to pay their accounts, so these soldiers, who had been with him fourteen years, were compelled to wait six months before getting any money. To General Casati, with whom he had lived eight years like a brother, he turned the cold shoulder. For a whole month he seemed to be negotiating with the British East African Company for employment. Then suddenly he turned and took employment with the Germans. The Germans had triumphed, according to their view. They certainly had Emin's nature aright, but I think they would have succeeded better had they managed to leave the victim of their political aspirations with some portion of the common virtues, and without exposing him to the contempt of others not quite so interested in their politics.

Dr. Peters and other Germans had raided a broad track through a territory under the guise of assisting Emin.

He reached Uganda and made treaties there. At the same time the poor Pasha, breathing fury against civilization, was returning to the interior to annex the whole of Central Africa for Germany. Meantime seeing pretty clearly how this was tending, I began that series of speeches in England which ended in stimulating greater attention in Britain to Africa. A friendly agreement was concluded between Great Britain and Germany wherein hard and fast boundaries were fixed between the possessions of the two powers. Both nations expressed themselves as satisfied with the agreement, but I fear that Dr. Peters, homeward bound with his pockets full of treaties, and Emin pressing forward bent on large annexations and the Germans of East Africa whose impetuous policy had been the cause of all this, were but little pleased.

So ends this serio-comic story of Emin's reappearance on the verge of civilization after fourteen years' absence in Africa. But all is well that ends well, and if I have succeeded in pleasing you with my rapid and imperfect sketches of the new regions which have been the subject of this lecture, there is nothing wanting to complete my entire satisfaction. [Loud and prolonged applause.]

THE RESCUE OF EMIN PASHA

[Lecture by Henry M. Stanley, delivered in Brooklyn, New York, November 12, 1890.]

In 1886 Emin Pasha was described by the British press as a second Gordon, and as a model of prudence, firmmindedness and courage, with high administrative abilities, great sagacity, and the qualities befitting a stern leader of men, and as being somewhat of a savant devoted to science—especially to natural history. As no one at that time could criticise such statements they came to be generally believed, and considerable enthusiasm was excited for him.

He was known to have been appointed by General Gor-

don to the post of Governor, and it was argued that, as
Gordon was well qualified to be a judge of men, Emin
must necessarily be a unique character.

Emin's letters also overflowed with such beautiful sentiments of devotion to his work, trust in Heaven, loyalty to
Egypt, of self-abnegation, and love for Africa and its peoples, that the hearts of British philanthropists warmed to
him.   After a little while several Scotchmen and Englishmen, under the influence of Sir William Mackinnon, were
induced to subscribe some thousands of pounds to form
a fund for his relief, and the Egyptian Government undertook to furnish an equal sum.   Out of this relief fund an
expedition was equipped, and the command was entrusted
to me.   My orders from the Relief committee were ver-
bal.   They amounted to simply this: that I was to convey
with all possible speed a certain quantity of ammunition
to him, and lend such other aid as I could, and then to
retire.   As the Egyptian Government subscribed half the
money, Nubar Pasha, the Prime Minister, added that I
was to escort such men as were willing to return home—
even Emin, if he chose; but Emin was to be left to be
guided by his own choice entirely.

Before starting, the British Foreign Office handed to
me printed copies of Emin's letters and reports.   Naturally, not knowing anything of him, I studied them with
the closest attention, and in consequence I soon became
an enthusiastic admirer of him myself.   He appeared to
me to be a kind of amalgamate character, possessing certain characteristics such as distinguished Cromwell, Francia, and Gordon.   His sentiments appeared to be devout
and noble; his loyalty seemed to me very evident, while his
determination and his philanthropy were admirable.   I
was greatly touched by such expressions as, " I shall remain myself at my post with my black troops until the
Egyptian Government inform me as to their wishes."
" We propose to hold out until help may reach us, or until
we perish."

This was so like Gordon at Khartoum.   He wrote,
" Deprived of the most necessary things for a long time,
without any pay, my men fought valiantly.   After nineteen days of incredible privation and sufferings their
strength was exhausted, and when the last torn leather of

their last boot had been eaten they then cut their way
through the midst of their enemies."

There is something of Francia of Paraguay in that.
His frequent allusions to Providence, trust in God, and
the brave front he showed to the Mahdists on all occasions
reminded me of Cromwell's steady perseverance and de-
voutness.

Having informed you what manner of man we believed
him to be, I shall now endeavor to describe to you how
we proceeded to relieve Emin, and to suggest what kind
of a character was developed before us—my officers and
myself.

On the 22d of December [1886, from New York] I
landed at Southampton, and by the 21st of the following
month the expedition was organized and equipped. I
then left London for Zanzibar, accompanied by Major
Barttelot, of the Seventh Fusiliers; Lieutenant Stairs, of
the Royal Engineers; Mr. William Bonny, Medical Assistant; Captain Nelson, of South Africa. There were
also Messrs. Jameson and Jephson, who had each paid
five thousand dollars for the privilege of sharing in our
campaign. In Egypt, Surgeon Parke was enlisted. Mr.
John Rose Troup had been sent to the Congo to engage
carriers, and in West Africa Mr. Herbert Ward joined us.

On arriving at Zanzibar we found that our agent, Mr.
Mackenzie, had prepared the goods, enlisted a battalion
of Zanzibaris, and had embarked them on board a steamer
belonging to the British India Company; and four days
later, or on the 25th of February, 1887, we departed on
our voyage to the Congo River. Aboard the steamer
we numbered 9 white officers, 623 Zanzibaris, 64 Soudanese and Syrians, 13 Somalis, and also Tippu Tib and 96 of
his followers, altogether 797 souls, of whom 700 formed
the expedition proper. Tippu Tib, in consideration of his
promise to lend us 600 native carriers, was to be conveyed
to Stanley Falls free of charge, where he personally was
to remain as governor, under the government of the
Congo Free State.

The mouth of the Congo was reached on the 18th of
March, and the next day we transferred the expedition on
board three river steamers and a gunboat, and steamed
up to Mataddi, which is about 100 miles from the sea. In

less than a month we were all assembled at Stanley Pool, after a land march of 235 miles. From the Pool, we had a magnificent and uninterrupted waterway of 1,000 miles, during which course the Congo spreads from three-quarters of a mile to sixteen miles in width. After the wide oval expansion of the river above Leopoldville, which is called the Pool, the river contracts to three-quarters of a mile, and is flanked by high hills for about 100 miles. The hills then sink to a few feet above the river, and the land maintains a uniformly level appearance, and is deeply wooded along the banks, all the way to Stanley Falls, or to Yambuya on the Aruwimi.

We chose to disembark at Yambuya, which is about 1,400 miles distant from the Atlantic Ocean. We were now at a point which was 326 geographical miles due west from Lake Albert. Once on the shores of the lake a boat might easily sail on its waters to inform Emin Pasha that the relief he had required was at hand. All this distance between Yambuya and the Albert Nyanza was utterly unknown to any one outside of Africa at this time, nor had I met any person, native or Arab, who could give any information respecting it.

Owing to want of sufficient transport we had been obliged to leave 130 men of the expedition about 900 miles below Yambuya, at a place called Bolobo. A steamer was despatched to bring these men up, who were under Messrs. Ward and Bonny. In the meantime Major Barttelot was sent to Stanley Falls with Tippu Tib and his party, according to promise, and we employed ourselves in constructing an intrenched and palisaded camp at Yambuya. On the Major's return to us a garrison of about 130 men was left with him to await the arrival of the Bolobo contingent, and these two parties were then to be formed into a rear column under Messrs. Barttelot and Jameson, assisted by Messrs. Troup, Ward, and Bonny.

The steamer was expected to reach Yambuya camp by the 10th of August. A letter of instructions was drawn up for the guidance of the Major and his fellow officers, all of whom had given me to understand that they were burning to assist us in the relief of Emin Pasha, and would prefer marching after us to waiting at Yambuya for our return.

Thus my instructions became a series of suggestions how they could best assist us under various conditions. If Tippu Tib arrived before the Bolobo contingent joined the garrison, there would then be no difficulty in shouldering the packages and marching quickly after us along a blazed track through the forest. If Tippu Tib did not send his 600 carriers by the time the Bolobo people should reach Yambuya, then such long delay should be taken as proof that the Arab chief had broken his contract, and did not intend to join his force with ours, and the Major was then to do the best he could with his own people, and follow us with the reserve ammunition and baggage.

Having, as I thought, and as was acknowledged at the time, prepared for every contingency, the advance column was led out from Yambuya on the morning of June 28, and after half an hour's march through the manioc fields of the settlement, we entered the great forest.

Before we proceed further it would be well for you to remember that at Cairo I met Dr. Junker who had just returned from Emin, and that he gave me the following notes which I jotted down at the time, for of course I had never seen Emin and knew nothing about him :—

" Junker tells me that Emin is very short-sighted, is a great linguist, devoted to the collection of natural history subjects; he is no great fighter, but is a good administrator, and has about seven years' pay due to him from Egypt.   His people desert frequently.   The garrisons of the four northern stations have mutinied, and decline to obey him.   All letters from the Government are declared by the rebels to be forgeries.   They refuse to believe that Khartoum has fallen, or that Gordon is dead.   The second battalion and irregulars, about 4,000 in number, are still faithful to him.   Emin has sufficient ammunition to last him a year, provided no organized attack is made upon him, when, of course, a few hours' fighting would make him helpless.

" When asked what Emin's own inclinations were, Junker says that Emin loves the life he leads so well that it is doubtful whether he will return to civilization.   If, through attacks from Mahdists, there be a break-up, he will retire to Unyoro, and live with Kabba Rega until our

expedition reaches him. If his people were willing to
retire he has often thought that he would like to retreat
by way of Monbuttu Land, and down the Congo; at other
times he has suggested that it would be preferable for him
to return by Masai Land, or south by way of Tanganika.
Emin is a widower, has been married to an Abyssinian
woman, by whom he has a girl, who is now about five years
old."

Soon after we had left Yambuya it seems that letters
were received in Europe from Emin, wherein he stated:
"If, however, the people of Great Britain think that as
soon as Stanley or Thomson comes I shall return with
them they greatly err. For twelve long years I have
striven and toiled, and sown the seeds for future harvest,
and laid the foundation stones for future buildings. Shall
I now give up the work because a way may soon open to
the coast? Never! no, never!"

But in the copies of letters from Emin furnished to us
by Lord Iddesleigh, the Secretary for Foreign Affairs,
there were such phrases as "Help us quickly, ere we
perish," repeated several times over.

Therefore you will understand that on June 28, the day
we last touched civilization and entered that region of
night and fable which proved to be the grave of so many
scores of our band, we were in profound ignorance of
these brave purposes of Emin, and were filled only with a
belief that there was urgent need for us to press on rapidly
to his relief before it would be—as in the case of Gordon at
Khartoum—too late. Had we not been impressed with
this, we assuredly had not left our baggage and reserve
stores, or our officers and men behind us. Indeed, those
little words, "Too late, too late!" had immense sig-
nificance for us. They seemed to be whispered throughout the day; the echo of them was borne to us in muffled
notes until we were steeped in slumber. Therefore physical and mental powers were on the full strain to effect
speedy relief.

For the first time an African expedition traveled into
the unknown, day after day, for a full month without a
single day's halt. On July 28 we were only 179 miles
from Yambuya. Meantime we had carved a road through

a thick umbrageous forest, cleaved a passage through
trackless copses, tunneled our way under vaults of en-
tangling underwood, treaded gingerly our way past raspy
spikelets of calamus, splashed through black ooze, and
waded through miry depths, or plunged through deep
creeks on whose face the lotus and lily luxuriantly lay.
Behind us was a region dark with its great tall woods,
through which only a flickering dust of sunshine could
penetrate when the winds ruffled the impervious leafage;
and extending on either hand to a distance that could only
be measured by many months of marching, there was
nothing but primeval forest, and before us stretched the
yet untraveled unknown—apparently of the same sombre
character.

Then for the first time we met natives of the forest
region who seemed disposed to exchange with us a few
words, for hitherto they had artfully eluded us.   We had
passed numbers of small villages, but their owners, after
skewering the paths around them, had scurried into the
darkest recesses to hide, leaving us to feed on their plan-
tains or manioc tubers comparatively unmolested.   We
burned to know whether they had heard of grass land to
the east, north, or south of their district.   For such tidings would have been the salvation of many of our
men.   We picked up a grass blade from amongst the
riverside bush, and asked, "Is there any open country
growing anything like this?"   It was difficult to make
them understand, but when they did so it struck them as
being an absurd question, and they pointed to the trees
around us, and waved their hands about to all points of
the compass, to indicate that their world was all alike—
with nothing but trees, a tree world crammed with countless trees, under the thick foliage of which was the darkness of evening and the horror of endless gloom.   No
sooner did our men grasp their meaning than they pictured a future even more forbidding than the past month
of travel.

Though Moslem in faith, our men were purely untutored savages, to whom reading and writing were mysteries known only to white men and Arabs.   The little
religion they knew had been transmitted to them in
legends from simple unlettered parents.   Among these

was one of a land that grew darker and darker as one traveled towards the end of the world, and drew nearer to the utmost limits where a great immeasurable serpent lay supine, and coiled round the earth.

"Ah, then," they muttered, dolefully, "the ancients must have referred to this dismal region where the light is so ghastly, the woods so endless, and solemn, and gray; to these vast voiceless solitudes, the loneliness of which deadens our hearts."

The horror grows darker with their gloomy fancies. They think of the cold of the early morning, the comfortless gray of the dawn, the pallid brooding mist, the ceaseless dripping of the dew, the deluging rains, the fell reek and slush, and the tempest rushing through the tree tops, the dazzling spears of the lightning, the fury of the thunder, and the appalling echoes rolling through the aisles of the woods.   And the picture of the night, with its thick palpable darkness and indescribable terrors, strikes their vivid sensibilities.   As they lie cuddled in their little camp huts, the wild winds roar above them, they come with the sound of overwhelming billows, the trees groan and grind, and fall crashing to the earth with such shocks as make their hearts leap—and the accents of mournful desolation wail shrilly around them, and lost souls seem to whisper their griefs, and the rain falls in torrents, beating down upon them, flooding the camp, and intensifying their wretchedness.   Oh, then, what tongue can relate the horrors these poor people felt?

On the eighty-first day of the march from Yambuya we came across a community of ivory-raiders settled at Ugarrowwa's.   We leave fifty-six of our sick people with them, to be boarded for money.   Seventeen days later we arrive at the confluence of two great rivers, and are obliged to leave Captain Nelson with another company of fifty-two men who are unable to travel unless they get a supply of food.   We select six of the most intelligent men, and despatch them as avant-couriers to another Arab settlement to obtain relief, but they lose their way in the woods, and the expedition passes by them, and arrives, after thirteen days' subsistence on fungi, wild fruit, and wood-beans, at Kilonga-Longa's; but we lose nine days more before we can induce the brutish-minded ivory-raiders to send off relief. Finally, after twenty-five days' starvation at the camp, Mr. Jephson reaches Captain Nelson, to find only five skeletons surviving out of the fifty-two. Many have died, many have deserted, many have been wandering for days in search of food, and have not returned.

Then at Kilonga-Longa's we are obliged to leave Captain Nelson and thirty-eight sick men, and Surgeon Parke to attend to their ailments, and we resume the march again with sadly reduced numbers. Though, when men are sodden with despair, preaching is useless, not a day passes without an effort being made to lift them out of their sullen stupor.

The day came at last, after infinite patience, when we were well-nigh exhausted with our troubles, that we reached Ibwiri, 130 miles from the Lake. Here we rested for thirteen days to recuperate and repair the waste of the wilderness, and the effect was such that most of the men had increased in bodily weight of over a pound per day.

At this place the natives could tell us they had seen a grass land five days' journey further east, and this revived the men; but it was twelve days before we came to the end of the forest, and on the 160th day after leaving Yambuya, we filed out of the gloom into the light of broad day shining over one of the loveliest lands we had seen. We raced gleefully, like little wanton children in spring, over the soft young grass; we stared at the great burning sun; we gazed in wondrous delight at the careering waves of green grass as the wholesome wind swept over it; we went into raptures over the billowy contours of the land, and the thin winding lines of boscage between them; and our surprise was equal to that of the herds of game whose domains we had invaded, and who snorted their alarm. We were 173 persons all told remaining out of 389. Out of the 216 we had left we might pick up fifty of those we had left behind, perhaps less. We had no time, however, to think of anything but the present, and I doubt whether there were anywhere happier people than we were on that day as we swung forward over the grassy downs, leaving the dreadful forest behind us.

The nearer we drew towards the lake, the more warlike the natives seemed to be. It was no longer the lying in wait behind a log, a stump, or a tree, to stab with a spear, or to give a knife-thrust, or to drive the poisoned dart. The natives sprang towards us in fighting mobs, the bravest in the front, uttering their furious war-cries and encouraging one another with frightful noise. On the 11th, 12th, and 13th of December, we had to meet new tribes, or sections of tribes, all clamoring for war. But despite the most frantic efforts of the natives, we finally reached the verge of the table-land, and from an altitude of 5,200 feet above the sea we looked down on Lake Albert, which lay about 2,800 feet below us.

The hope had sustained us during our journey from Zanzibar to Lake Albert, that Emin Pasha, upon receipt of information from the Consul-General and myself, would proceed in his steamer a four days' voyage to the south end of the lake, and warn the natives that he expected some friends; but on arrival at the edge of the lake we were sorely disappointed to find that for ten years no white man or steamer had been seen on it, and yet we had arrived on the 14th of December, which was one day earlier than that on which he expected us.

After staying two days, and perceiving that no expedition could subsist near the lake—as its shores were only occupied by four fishing villages, we turned sharply about and returned to Ibwiri.

Our fort having been completed, and about ten acres of ground cleared and put under corn, beans, and tobacco, we set out a second time to Lake Albert, on the 2d of April, 1888, but on this occasion we conveyed our steel boat. On the 20th of the month we received a letter from Emin Pasha. It was dated the 25th of March. It said that hearing the rumors of our having been on the lake in December, he had just returned to the north end from an unsuccessful quest of us, and he asked us to stay at Kavalli, which is near the southwest end, until he could come to us. We could not help smiling at the idea of our staying five or six weeks at a place in Central Africa until news should drift to him by accident. As such a course would have been suicidal to men while in the full swing of action, and hearts throbbing with the desire to accomplish our mission, our boat was launched on the waters of the lake, and Mr. Jephson and a gallant boat's crew set out to find the object of our quest.

Now, apropos of the date of this letter to us, on our return to Zanzibar, we found that Emin had written the same day to "Petermann's Mitteilungen" a letter which he concluded with the strange words, "If Stanley does not come soon, we are lost."

Possibly some logical mind here may be able to assist us with the solution of the question, why, being in so deplorable a condition, he should not have frankly informed us of the fact who were there to render him immediate assistance. He could not have thought then of any defect of sympathy between us—since we were all strangers to him. We confess that this remains an enigma to us, though we—myself and officers—have frequently tried to explain it.

A few days transpired, and the "Khedive" steamer was seen approaching the shore on which we were camped. In the evening Mr. Jephson entered the camp with a large following of Egyptian officers and soldiers, among whom were Emin Pasha and Captain Casati, the Italian traveler.

Naturally I searched by the light of the torches for a person of heroic size, but in answer to my question about the Pasha, a slight, dapper figure in spotless white and red fez, with spectacles over his eyes, took my hand and replied that he owed me a thousand thanks. Our meeting was very cordial, and we celebrated it with some of Mumm's best, which had been treasured for the occasion.

Until the 24th of May our respective camps were close together. We met daily twice, and exchanged freely and familiarly our opinions upon our experiences. The topic uppermost in my mind after delivering into his hands his despatches was, as might be expected, what was to be the probable result of our mission. Would he return to Egypt, or was he going to be contented with the ammunition to be delivered to him? After giving him several days to consider his position, the question was addressed to him. To my surprise he could not answer me—his intentions, he said, depended on those of his people. If his people stayed, he would stay. If they were willing to return, he would accompany them.

His answer created much wonder within me. While I listened to him and observed his manner, there was something inexplicable about it all. I asked myself, Why does

he not know whether his people intend to return to Egypt
or not? Since September, when he received the British
Consul-General's letter stating that we were advancing
towards him with the relief, why has he not set about to
determine whether he or any one were willing to go or
stay? When pressed for an answer he taps his knee, and
looks up at the roof of the tent. He is hesitating and
dubious. There is a burden on his mind which he will
not, or does not know how to deliver. He drops such
expressions as, "Hum, a fine prospect truly! To return
to Egypt. To be received with sugared phrases! and then
bowed out and shelved, and to waste my days in a Cairene
cafe on a small pension!" The muttered thoughts, as I
read them, are: "While here I am king, with thousands
under me to do my bidding. Dispenser of pardon and
grace. What I will is Fate!" Unwillingness to return,
is writ large in his manner, but he is most reluctant to
explain.

I ventured to say: "Well, Pasha, I see you do not wish
to return to Egypt. My first duty was to the Khedive;
but as I came to serve you I offer you £1,500 per annum,
£12,000 a year subsidy, and the rank of general, on behalf
of King Leopold of Belgium, if you will consent to govern
this province in his name."

This took him by surprise, but in a short time he answered in a grateful manner that he could not change the
flag he had served under for thirty years for one he never
saw.

"Very fairly spoken, Pasha," I said; "but I have another proposition to make, which is that you accompany
me to some place on the Victoria Nyanza, where I shall
establish you comfortably, and then proceed to England
and get some English association to engage you and your
troops for the civilization of that region in British interests."

This evidently pleased him, and he expressed his wil-
lingness to be employed in that manner provided his people were willing to accompany him. It was finally settled
that, as he could not answer definitely for his officers and
troops, the matter should be left in abeyance until I returned from the search after the rear column. Meantime I was to leave Mr. Jephson with him to assist him to

discover the sentiments of the troops, and to explain to them our mission.

Towards the latter part of May we left the Pasha and Mr. Jephson with him, with the understanding that both gentlemen would within two months pay a visit to Fort Bodo. On the 8th of June we were at Fort Bodo, where we found Stairs, Nelson, and Dr. Parke.

After a halt of eight days I proceeded alone with about 200 men loaded with grain from our fields in search of the rear column. The uninhabited forest was traversed safely, and after a march of 560 miles from Lake Albert, and on the eighty-third day since leaving the Pasha, we came to a palisaded village called Banalya. At the gate of the village stood Mr. Bonny, the medical assistant who had been left with the Major's column. From him we learned that Major Barttelot was shot; that Mr. Jameson was at Stanley Falls; that Mr. Troup had been invalided home; that Mr. Ward had been sent down to the sea, and since had been detained at Bangala by orders of Major Barttelot. We also learned that out of 271 members of the rear column there were only 102 left, and only 60 of these were in any fit condition for travel.

It seems that the officers had elected to wait for Tippu Tib's carriers, and had been led to do so by repeated promises of immediate compliance with their wishes. Finally, after ten months from the date they should have started they had departed from Yambuya, but in the meantime 100 faithful fellows had been buried in the fatal camp, 33 men were left dying in it, 26 had deserted, and 10 were missing. They left Yambuya June 11; we found them at Banalya, 90 miles distant from it on August 17. Their rate of travel was thus one mile and a quarter per day. Out of 600 loads of goods there were only 230 remaining, and I personally had nothing left but the rags in which I had come to search for them. The details poured into my ears during the first few days after our meeting by Mr. Bonny and his heart-broken followers will not bear repetition. They were so harrowing in their character that we trembled as we heard them, and such a dismal chapter of disaster, suffering, despair, and anguish has never been written during a century of African travel as these would supply if rightly related.

The column was now reorganized, the sick and weakly were placed in the canoes, and on the 31st of August we moved eastward from Banalya towards Lake Albert for the third time.   On the 20th of December we burst out of the forest on the edge of the plantations of Fort Bodo, and were presently greeted by the gallant garrison, from whom we had been absent 187 days.

But there was another mystery that caused profound anxiety.   There was no news of the Pasha or of Mr. Jephson, and it had been understood that one or both were to have visited Fort Bodo and escorted the garrison to the lake.   The garrison had waited patiently for them until the promised period had arrived, and then had become restless, and almost mutinous; but, thanks to the management of Stairs and his officers, the men had been soothed, and they had borne tolerably well the long interval of 187 days in this isolated station in the forest, cultivating their fields, scaring off the elephants with great fires, and patrolling the neighborhood for the protection of the plantations against raiding bands of pigmies.

We concluded that, though the Pasha might have been detained by the affairs of his province, our comrade, Mr. Jephson, would surely have kept his word had not something serious occurred to prevent him; he probably had met with an accident, was ill, or was dead.

We halted only three days at Fort Bodo.   We then set fire to the buildings and palisades, and resumed the march —the advance column, couriers, garrison and remnant of Barttelot's contingent all united now.   Twenty-five days later we were in the grass land, and only one day's march from the Albert Lake.   A native courier came to our camp from the Chief Kavalli, and placed a packet of letters in my hands.   They were in Jephson's handwriting, and they announced that both he and the Pasha had been made prisoners on August 18, 1888.   It was now January 17, 1889.

When I had read the dreadful intelligence, I felt mentally benumbed for a moment.

You will remember that I was listening to Bonny's tragic story of death and disaster on the 18th of August. We now know that on that date, 500 miles west of me, poor Jameson was being buried at Bangala; and on that same date, 900 miles northeast of me, the Governor of Equatoria and Mr. Jephson became prisoners of a violent and menacing soldiery who had revolted from their allegiance to the Pasha.

All this strenuous striving and 4,000 miles of marching, nineteen months of the most terrible experiences, with the loss of over 500 lives, the countless fevers, agonies of hunger, and a long train of unspeakably sad memories, to end thus! The Pasha a prisoner; our young friend Jephson his fellow-captive; the first instalment of ammunition given to him lost; all authority and government gone; and in the hands of rebels, and the Mahdists advancing to annihilate rebels and captives! If you will conceive yourselves in my position, you will understand what I felt perhaps.

Then other thoughts flashed light across many mysteries. The Pasha knew that his people were unreliable, hence he wished to consult with them first before declaring his resolution. This rebellion explains his hesitation, and that effortless, dreamy, soft state of mind which had been such a wonder and perplexed me so. He knew in his heart of hearts that he had no people to command, and therefore did not know whether any one would go with him or whether he himself would be permitted to depart.

In a postscript, Jephson said he could come to me if he were informed of my arrival. Accordingly an imperative message was sent to him not to debate but to act, and like a faithful and obedient officer he came, and gratified everyone with the sight of his face.

"Well, Jephson, my dear fellow, say, now that you have been eight months with the Pasha, is he resolved what to do by this time? Will he remain a prisoner, or will he depart with us if we can get him out?"

"To tell you the truth, sir, I know no more now what the Pasha intends doing than I did before I saw him."

"What! after eight months' intercourse with him?"

"Quite so; not a bit."

"But Jephson, my dear fellow, it was one of your duties, if you recollect, that you were to find out, and have the vexed question settled whether he intended going or not. I simply want a yea or nay. For, bless my soul, we don't wish to stay here forever."

"I assure you, sir, I have done my best. Every day I have returned to the subject. One day he is wild for going, and talks quite joyfully of the prospect of leaving; the next he says he can't go, and that's the way it is to-day."

"But is there anything to prevent him from leaving now that he is deposed, and has no one to look out for but himself?"

"Nothing but sentiment. He is all sentiment. I like him personally very much; he is a dear, good fellow, and very kind and hospitable, but the worst enemy of the Pasha is this sentiment of his. He is hopeful now that things will mend, and that he will be reinstated, and that it will be all right again; but from what I have seen, the man is lost unless we can save him in spite of himself. He has not a friend in the entire province. The Egyptians fool him; the officers kiss his hand; they call him their father and all that, but behind his back they think he is only fit to collect beetles and birds. I dared not say to him all I heard. Where would be the use? He flatters himself he knows his people better than I do. Well, he is in prison, and, if we do not save him, he will be either murdered or sent to Khartoum as a prize to the Mahdi."

I wrote an appealing letter to the Pasha—the most laboriously polite epistle I ever wrote, for I now heard that he was morbidly sensitive, and shrunk from anything like plain speaking—to ask his intentions, and to suggest what measures I should take to assist him. Did he wish me to advance upon Tunguru and rescue him by force, or could he meet me outside by night, or could he seize a steamer and come himself? Any way and every way, agreeable to him, I was prepared to act and assist him to the uttermost.

But before my letters had reached him at Tunguru his fate was settled in quite a singular fashion. Having heard of our arrival on the lake with a large force, machine-guns, and repeating rifles, and dreading the results, the rebel officers embarked on two steamers, and coming up to Tunguru requested the Pasha's pardon, and an introduction to me. To which the Pasha consented. They arrived at our camp on the 13th of February. The real object of the rebels was to examine how far it would be possible to proceed with a scheme they entertained to disarm us, and make us prisoners for the Mahdi; or making use of us to lead them to some country, not too remote from the Albert, where they could be safe from the Mahdists. They were ready for either project.

The Pasha introduced them as being penitent for their mad conduct, and ready to depart. They requested time to collect their families and troops from the northern stations. As Emin suggested that twenty days would be sufficient for the two steamers to proceed to Wadelai and to return to us. I granted them a month. On their departure one of the officers stole a rifle from our camp, which caused a little suspicion of their intentions. One of the steamers was employed to carry Egyptians and their families from Tunguru and Mswa. Two mails came from Wadelai within the month bringing terrible tales of disorder. The thirty days having expired, Emin requested fourteen days' additional delay. It was granted. Daily he asserted his confident belief that the rebels were sincere and faithful, but five days before our departure there were three several attempts made by the Pasha's people in the camp to steal rifles, and Emin himself informed me at last that only nine of his followers intended to accompany him on the 10th of April, though a page of Emin's assured me that there was only one man who was certain of following his master's fortunes.

Perceiving that any further inaction would be fatal to us all, and that our respect for the Pasha was leading us to destruction, our 570 ill-conditioned guests were mustered in the square, and in very energetic language were told that plotting to murder and the intriguing tricks of Wadelai must cease. Frightened by the demonstrations, they swore they had no evil intentions, and that they were all willing to leave on the 10th of April.

On the appointed day we marched from Kavalli's, about 1,500 in number, but two days later I suffered from an almost fatal illness, and we were obliged to halt another twenty-eight days. Thus seventy-three days' grace had been given to the rebel officers, and not one of them had appeared, though Wadelai was only thirty-six hours' steaming from our camp.

What has become of them since is not known. It is

supposed that the Mahdists have taken possession of the country; and if the rebels have fallen into their hands, their officers must have quickly fallen victims to that rage for slaughter which distinguishes those wild fanatics.

On the 8th of May we resumed the march for the Indian Ocean. The fifth day's march brought us to the edge of highlands, whence we looked down into a deep valley 2,600 feet below us. In width it varied from six to twenty miles. To the north we could see a bit of the south end of Lake Albert. Southward, seventy miles off, was another lake, to which we have given the name of Albert Edward, and the surplus waters of the southernmost lake meandered through this valley down into the northernmost, or Albert Lake.

Opposite to the place whence we looked upon the Semliki Valley, rose an enormous range of mountains whose summits and slopes, for about 3,000 feet were covered with perpetual snow. As the snow-line near the Equator is found at a little over 15,000 feet, we may then safely estimate the height of these mountains to be between 18,000 and 19,000 feet above the level of the sea. The singular thing about these mountains is that so many white travelers—Sir Samuel and Lady Baker, Gessi Pasha, Mason Bey, Emin Pasha, and Captain Casati— should have been within observing distance and never had an opportunity to view them.

There were also a thousand of our expedition who were for seventy-two days or thereabouts within easy visual distance of the phenomenon, but not one man saw it until suddenly it issued out from the obscurity, its great peaks islanded in an atmosphere of beautiful translucence. And for three days in succession the wonderful mountains stood aloft in glorious majesty, with an undefinable depth of opaline sky above, beyond, and around them, the marvel of the curious and delighted multitude.

The natives generally call them the Ruwenzori Mountains. Scheabeddin, an Arab geographer, writing about Anno Domini 1400, says, "In the midst of the Isle of Mogreb, which is Africa, are the deserts of the Negroes, which separate the country of the Negroes from that of the Berbers. In this isle is also the source of that great river which has not its equal upon the earth. It comes

from the Mountains of the Moon, which lie beyond the
Equator. Many sources come from these mountains, and
unite in a great lake. From this lake comes the Nile,
the greatest, and most beautiful of the rivers of all the
earth." This is only one of the many early authorities
which I have quoted in my book "Darkest Africa," to
prove that the Ruwenzori Range forms the long-lost
Mountains of the Moon.

The march around the base of Ruwenzori led us to the
discovery of one of the principal sources of the Nile. The
rivers which enter the Victoria Nyanza, which Speke and
Grant discovered, are the first in rank of the Nile sources,
because they are the remotest, and together form a river
somewhat larger than the Semliki further west. But both
the Semliki river and the Victoria river enter the Albert
Nyanza, out of which issues the White Nile.

Still another discovery was that of the Albert Edward
Nyanza—called in ancient times the Sea of Darkness,
whose waters were said to be sweeter than honey, and
more fragrant than musk. We cannot endorse this Oriental estimation of their excellence; to many the waters
of the muddy Missouri would be preferable.

Quitting the headwaters of the Nile we ascended some
3,000 feet into a higher altitude, and began a journey over
a rich pastoral land, which extends to the south end of the
Victoria Nyanza. In consideration of having driven
Kabba Rega's raiders from the shores of the Albert Edward, and freed the Salt Lakes from their presence, we
received hearty ovations and free rations from the various
kings along a march of 500 miles.

At the south end of Lake Victoria we found reserve
stores, which had been deposited there eighteen months
before, awaiting us. Then, greatly strengthened by good
rest and food, on the 16th of September we left that lake,
having discovered an extension to it of 6,000 square
miles. As we drew near to the coast, we were met by
abundant supplies—from the Germans first—of excellent
quality and selection. Four days from the sea, two
American newspaper correspondents arrived at our camp.
One of them, a representative of the New York "Her-
ald," delivered to us a supply of clothes, and other very
necessary articles, besides a judicious supply of good wine

which cheered us greatly. A little later we met a large caravan sent by Sir William Mackinnon, freighted with provisions and clothes for our people.

On the morning of the 4th of December, Emin Pasha, Captain Casati, and myself were escorted by Major Wissmann to Bagamoyo, the port opposite Zanzibar; and in the afternoon the porters of the expedition filed in to lay their weary burdens of sick and moaning creatures down for the last time. Our journey of 6,032 miles from the western ocean to the Indian Sea was now at an end.

That night the German Imperial Commissary gave a banquet to thirty-four persons, consisting of our travelers, German, British, and Italian civil and military officers, after a style that even New York could scarcely excel. The utmost cordiality prevailed, and laudatory and grateful speeches were delivered, and not the least graceful and finished was that of the Pasha. But within ten minutes afterwards, while the guests were most animated, the Pasha wandered away from the banqueting hall out into the balcony, and presently, in some unaccountable manner, fell over the low wall into the street, some eighteen feet below.

Had not a zinc shed five feet below the balcony—which shaded the sidewalk—broken the fall, the accident would no doubt have been fatal. As it was, he received severe contusions, and a sharp concussion of the base of the brain. A German officer had him conveyed to the hospital, while three doctors hastened to his assistance. You know, of course, that in less than a month he was sufficiently recovered to begin arranging his entomological collections; and that on the 5th of February of this year he entered the German service, and that he is now at this moment at the head of a German expedition in the neighborhood of Unyanyembe.

Of all the strange things that happened on this expedition, one of the strangest is that which followed this unlucky accident. The Pasha had intended to have accompanied us to Cairo, and to have presented his friend Casati and some of the most faithful Egyptians, like Shukri Agha, to his Highness the Khedive. He had purposed then to have proceeded to Naples, if the Khedive would grant him leave, to write his book with some such title as "Twelve Years in Equatoria; or, the Work of a Naturalist in the Far Soudan." He professed to be solicitous for the education of his little daughter, to be equally anxious to present himself before the Emin Relief Committee to express his gratitude for their kindness, and he thought he might read a paper before the Royal Geographical Society. To our officers he was always communicative of his intentions, and he delighted in sketching out an outline of his future work to me.

Up to the moment of his fall it had been a pleasant enough intercourse since leaving Mtsora in the middle of June. There had been no grievance or dispute between him and any of our party. The most kindly messages were interchanged daily; we visited one another frequently; presents and choice dishes were exchanged, in fact our intercourse was thoroughly fraternal. But this fall suddenly put a barrier in some strange way between us. If the British Consul-General expressed a desire to pay a visit to him, some excuse of a relapse was given. If I wished to go over to Bagamoyo his condition became immediately critical. Surgeon Parke, who attended to him for the first three weeks, found that things were not so pleasant for him as formerly. If I sent my black boy Sali with a note to him of condolence, and some suggestion, the boy was told he would be hung if he went to the hospital again. To our officers, Dr. Parke and Mr. Jephson, he freely complained of the German officers. My friendly note, asking him to have some regard to his reputation, was at once shown by him to Major Wissmann. It was curious, too, how the Pasha, who thought at Equatoria that his people were so dear to him that he professed himself ready to sacrifice his future for them, dropped his dear people from his mind, and told them with a brutal frankness that he had nothing further to do with them. The muster and pay-roll of the rescued Egyptians was therefore not sent to Egypt, and the poor fellows waited months for the many years' pay due to them, inasmuch as no one knew anything of the accounts.

Finally, in March, the murder was out—the Pasha had engaged himself to the Germans on the 5th of February; and then it transpired that all these strange and wholly unnecessary acts were with a view to cut himself adrift from all connection with his old friends and employers before committing himself to a new employment. Can there be anything more childish than the manner of his changing the Crescent flag, which he had served for thirty years, for the imperial German flag? He cables from Zanzibar to Cairo for a credit of $2,000. The Government of Egypt requests the British Minister at Cairo to authorize the British Consul-General at Zanzibar to pay him the sum. For some reason Emin affects anger, and cables back, "Since you cannot treat me better than this, I send my resignation." Poor, poor Emin—what a fall was yours!

Thus I have told you as much as I dare of the manner we traveled to the relief of this singular man; how our expedition, through want of a little frankness on his part, lost hundreds of lives, and suffered many months of fatigue and toil; and finally, how this want of frankness and sincerity caused his own deposition and imprisonment. We slowly discovered that he was in no way fitted for the rôle of a governor over such turbulent spirits as Soudanese and Egyptians. To have friends one must be friendly, is an old saying. Man is moved mostly by what relates to man—more especially savage man. Had he shown less attention to bugs and beetles, more sympathy would have existed between him and the people placed under his charge by Gordon.

As a man this dreamy, half-blind savant had many estimable qualities. He was devoted to natural history and botany, and his lips, like his letters, overflowed with kindly sentiment. He was extremely courteous. He was a most agreeable conversationalist, and at certain æsthetic tea-parties he would have been considered a treasure. He was courteous and ceremonious. Out of sympathy with him in his misfortunes, we might have told the pitiful tale of his vacillation with even more delicacy than we have used, had there not been so many witnesses, and had we not suspected that he was too deep for us; or, in other words, had we been impressed that, with other good qualities, he possessed a genuine free and open nature. For, as Cæsar is made to say, "There are no tricks in plain and simple faith."

But I will say no more. He cannot be described truly

until he has finished his career. And you must allow us to remember that every whisper or insinuation derogatory to him cheapens somewhat the man for whom we ventured our lives, and for whom we all endured such torture of bodily suffering in that hungry universe of sunless woods which so nearly blotted us out of existence. Better for us had we been able to have maintained our former fond illusions, and dwelt upon those virtues which, as in the case of Livingstone, we believed Emin possessed.

The unselfish joy which caused each man, black and white, to raise that shout of exultation when we first beheld Lake Albert, and knew that the goal was won, and the long train of sad memories behind, deserved that we should have been able to pay him uttermost honor—but it was simply impossible. For, from the beginning of our acquaintance to the receipt of the last letter from him, he has become to us all more and more inexplicable and perplexing. No act of his has been what we should have conceived it ought to have been, and every word he uttered or wrote only deepens the mystery. We are forced to declare that he is not the character we went out to seek —though the avowal is a grief to us.

We console ourselves, however, that through this mission we have been supplied with a store of remarkable reminiscences; that we have explored the heart of the great primeval forest; that we have had unique experiences with its pigmies and cannibals; that we have discovered the long-lost snowy Mountains of the Moon, the sources of the Albertine Nile, and also Lake Albert Edward, besides an important extension of the Victoria Nyanza; and that, finally, four European Governments (British, French, German, and Portuguese) have been induced to agree what their several spheres of influence shall be in the future in the Dark Continent, with a view to exercise their beneficent powers for its redemption out of the state of Darkness and Woe in which it has too long remained.

THOMAS DEWITT TALMAGE

BIG BLUNDERS

[Lecture by T. DeWitt Talmage, clergyman, editor, pastor of the Central Presbyterian Church, Brooklyn, N. Y., for thirty years (born in Bound Brook, N. J., January 7, 1832; died in Washington, April 13, 1902), delivered in many lyceum courses during Dr. Talmage's long career as a lecturer. This was the most popular of his various platform discourses.]

LADIES AND GENTLEMEN:—The man who never made a blunder has not yet been born. If he had been he would have died right away. The first blunder was born in Paradise, and it has had a large family of children. Agricultural blunders, commercial blunders, literary blunders, mechanical blunders, artistic blunders, ecclesiastical blunders, moral blunders, and blunders of all sorts; but an ordinary blunder will not attract my attention. It must be large at the girth and great in stature. In other words, it must be a big blunder.

Blunder the first: Multiplicity of occupations. I have a friend who is a very good painter, and a very good poet, and a very good speaker, and he can do a half dozen things well, but he is the exception. The general rule is that a man can do only one thing well. Perhaps there are two things to do. First, find your sphere; secondly, keep it. The general rule is, masons, stick to your trowel; carpenters, stick to your plane; lawyers, stick to your brief; ministers, stick to your pulpit, and don't go off lecturing. [Laughter.] Fireman, if you please, one locomotive at a time; navigator, one ship; professor, one department. The mighty men of all professions were men of one occupation. Thorwaldsen at sculpture, Irving at literature,

Rothschild at banking, Forrest at acting, Brunel at engineering, Ross at navigation, " Punch " at joking.

Sometimes a man is prepared by Providence through a variety of occupations for some great mission. Hugh Miller must climb up to his high work through the quarries of Cromarty. And sometimes a man gets prepared for his work through sheer trouble. He goes from misfortune to misfortune, and from disaster to disaster, and from persecution to persecution, until he is ready to graduate from the University of Hard Knocks. I know the old poets used to say that a man got inspiration by sleeping on Mount Parnassus. That is absurd. That is not the way men get inspiration. It is not the man on the mountain, but the mountain on the man, and the effort to throw it off that brings men to the position for which God intended them. But the general rule is that by the time thirty years of age is reached the occupation is thoroughly decided, and there will be success in that direction if it be thoroughly followed. It does not make much difference what you do, so far as the mere item of success is concerned, if you only do it. Brandreth can make a fortune at pills, Adams by expressage, Cooper by manufacturing glue, Genin by selling hats, contractors by manufacturing shoddy, merchants by putting sand in sugar, beet juice in vinegar, chicory in coffee, and lard in butter. One of the costliest dwellings in Philadelphia was built out of eggs. Palaces have been built out of spools, out of toothache drops, out of hides, out of pigs' feet, out of pickles, out of tooth-brushes, out of hose,—h-o-s-e and h-o-e-s,—out of fine-tooth combs, out of water, out of birds, out of bones, out of shells, out of steam, out of thunder and lightning.

The difference between conditions in life is not so much a difference in the fruitfulness of occupations as it is a difference in the endowment of men with that great and magnificent attribute of stick-to-itiveness. Mr. Plod-on was doing a flourishing business at selling banties, but he wanted to do all kinds of huckstering, and his nice little property took wing of ducks and turkeys and shanghais and flew away. Mr. Loomdriver had an excellent factory on the Merrimac, and made beautiful carpets, but he concluded to put up another kind of factory for the making of shawls, and one day there was a nice little quarrel between the two factories, and the carpets ate up the shawls, and the shawls ate up the carpets, and having succeeded so well in swallowing each other, they turned around and gulped down Mr. Loomdriver.

Blackstone Large-Practice was the best lawyer in town. He could make the most plausible argument and had the largest retainers, and some of the young men of the profession were proud to wear their hair as he did, and to have just as big a shirt-collar. But he concluded to go into politics. He entered that paradise which men call a caucus. He was voted up and he was voted down. He got on the Chicago platform, but a plank broke and he slipped through. He got on the St. Louis platform, but it rocked like an earthquake, and a plank broke and he slipped through. Then, as a circus rider with one foot on each horse whirls round the ring, he puts one foot on the Chicago platform and another foot on the St. Louis platform, and he slipped between, and landing in a ditch of political obloquy, he concluded he had enough of politics. And he came back to his law office, and as he entered covered with the mire, all the briefs from the pigeon-hole rustled with gladness, and Kent's Commentaries and Livingstone's Law Register broke forth in the exclamation: "Welcome home, Honorable Blackstone Large-Practice; Jack-of-all-trades is master of none." [Applause.]

Dr. Bone-Setter was a master in the healing profession. No man was more welcome in anybody's house than this same Dr. Bone-Setter, and the people loved to see him pass and thought there was in his old gig a kind of religious rattle. When he entered the drug store all the medicines knew him, and the pills would toss about like a rattle box, and the quinine would shake as though it had the chills, and the great strengthening plasters unroll, and the soda fountain fizz, as much as to say: "Will you take vanilla or strawberry?" Riding along in his gig one day he fell into a thoughtful mood, and concluded to enter the ministry. He mounted the pulpit and the pulpit mounted him, and it was a long while before it was known who was of the most importance. The young people said the preaching was dry, and the merchant could not keep from making financial calculations in the back part of the

psalm-book, and the church thinned out and everything
went wrong. Well, one Monday morning Messrs. Plod-
on, Loomdriver, Blackstone Large-Practice, and Dr.
Bone-Setter met at one corner of the street, and all felt so
low-spirited that one of them proposed to sing a song for
the purpose of getting their spirits up. I have forgotten
all but the chorus, but you would have been amused to
hear how, at the end of all the verses the voices came in,
"Jack-of-all-trades is master of none." [Applause.]

A man from the country districts came to be President
of the United States, and some one asked a farmer from
that region what sort of a President Mr. So-and-So would
make. The reply was: "He's a good deal of a man in
our little town, but I think if you spread him out over all
the United States he will be mighty thin." So there are
men admirable in one occupation or profession, but spread
out their energies over a dozen things to do and they are
dead failures. Young man, concentrate all your energies
in one direction. Be not afraid to be called a man of one
idea. Better have one great idea than five hundred little
bits of ones. Are you merchants? You will find abundant sweep for your intellect in a business which absorbed
the energy of a Lenox, a Stewart, and a Grinnell. Are
you lawyers? You will in your grand profession find
heights and depths of attainment which tasked a Marshall,
and a McLean, and a Story, and a Kent. Are you physicians? You can afford to waste but little time outside
of a profession which was the pride of a Rush, a Hervey,
a Cooper, and a Sydenham.

Every man is made to fit into some occupation or profession, just as a tune is made to fit a metre. Make up
your mind what you ought to be. Get your call straight
from the throne of God. We talk about ministers getting
a call to preach. So they must. But every man gets a
call straight from the throne of God to do some one thing,
—that call written in his physical or mental or spiritual
constitution,—the call saying: "You be a merchant,
you be a manufacturer, you be a mechanic, you be an
artist, you be a reformer, you be this, you be that, you be
the other thing." And all our success and happiness depend upon our being that which God commands us to be.
Remember there is no other person in the world that can

do your work. Out of the sixteen hundred millions of the race, not one can do your work. You do your work, and it is done forever. You neglect your work, and it is neglected forever. The man who has the smallest mission has a magnificent mission. God sends no man on a fool's errand. Getting your call straight from the throne of God, and making up your mind what you ought to do, gather together all your opportunities (and you will be surprised how many there are of them), gather them into companies, into regiments, into brigades, a whole army of them, and then ride along the line and give the word of command, " Forward, march!" and no power on earth or in hell can stand before you. I care not what your education is, elaborate or nothing, what your mental calibre is, great or small, that man who concentrates all his energies of body, mind, and soul in one direction is a tremendous man. [Applause.]

Blunder the next: Indulgence in bad temper. Good humor will sell the most goods, plead the best argument, effect the best cure, preach the best sermon, build the best wall, weave the best carpet. [Applause.] The poorest business firm in town is " Growl, Spitfire & Brothers." They blow their clerks. They insult their customers. They quarrel with the draymen. They write impudent duns. They kick the beggars. The children shy off as they pass the street, and the dogs with wild yelp clear the path as they come. Acrid, waspish, fretful, explosive, saturnine, suddenly the money market will be astounded with the defalcation of Growl, Spitfire & ·Brothers. Merryman & Warmgrasp were poor boys when they came from the country. They brought all their possessions in one little pack slung over their shoulders. Two socks, two collars, one jack-knife, a paper of pins, and a hunk of gingerbread which their mother gave them when she kissed them goodby, and told them to be good boys and mind the boss. They smiled and laughed and bowed and worked themselves up higher and higher in the estimation of their employers. They soon had a store on the corner. They were obliging men, and people from the country left their carpet-bags in that store when they came to town. Henceforth when the farmers wanted hardware or clothing or books they went to buy it at the place where their carpet-bags had been treated so kindly. The firm had a way of holding up a yard of cloth and "shining on" it so that plain cassimere would look almost as well as French broadcloth, and an earthen pitcher would glisten like porcelain. Not by the force of capital, but by having money drawer and counting desk and counter and shelves all full of good temper, they rose in society until to-day Merryman & Warmgrasp have one of the largest stores and the most elegant show windows and the finest carriages and the prettiest wives in all the town of Shuttleford.

A melancholy musician may compose a "Dead March," and make harp weep and organ wail; but he will not master a battle march, or with that grand instrument, the organ, storm the castles of the soul as with the flying artillery of light and love and joy until the organ pipes seem filled with a thousand clapping hosannas. A melancholy poet may write a Dante's "Inferno" until out of his hot brain there come steaming up barking Cerberus and wan sprite, but not the chime of Moore's melodies or the roll of Pope's "Dunciad," or the trumpet-call of Scott's "Don Roderick," or the archangelic blast of Milton's "Paradise Lost." A melancholy painter may with Salvator sketch death and gloom and monstrosity. But he cannot reach the tremor of silvery leaf, or the shining of sun through mountain pine, or the light of morning struck through a foam wreath, or the rising sun leaping on the sapphire battlements with banners of flame, or the gorgeous "Heart of the Andes," as though all the bright colors of earth and heaven had fought a great battle and left their blood on the leaves. [Applause.]

Blunder the next: Excessive amusement. I say nothing against amusement. Persons of your temperament and mine could hardly live without it. I have noticed that a child who has no vivacity of spirit, in after life produces no fruitfulness of moral character. A tree that has no blossoms in the spring will have no apples in the fall. A good game at ball is great sport. The sky is clear. The ground is just right for fast running. The club put off their coats and put on their caps. The ball is round and hard and stuffed with illimitable bounce. Get ready the bats and take your positions. Now, give us the ball.

Too low. Don't strike. Too high. Don't strike. There
it comes like lightning. Strike! Away it soars, higher,
higher. Run! Another base. Faster. Faster. Good!
All around at one stroke. [Applause.] All hail to the
man or the big boy who invented ball playing. After tea,
open the checker-board. Now, look out, or your boy
Bob will beat you. With what masterly skill he moves
up his men. Look out now, or he will jump you. Sure
enough, two of your men gone from the board and a
king for Bob. With what cruel pleasure he sweeps the
board. What! Only two more men left? Be careful
now. Only one more move possible. Cornered sure as
fate! and Bob bends over, and looks you in the face with
a most provoking banter, and says, "Pop, why don't you
move?" [Applause.]

Call up the dogs, Tray, Blanchard, and Sweetheart. A
good day for hunting. Get down, Tray, with your dirty
feet! Put on powder-flask and shoulder the gun. Over
the hill and through the wood. Boys, don't make such
a racket, you'll scare the game. There's a rabbit. Squat.
Take good aim. Bang! Missed him. Yonder he goes.
Sic'em, sic'em! See the fur fly. Got him at last. Here,
Tray; here Tray!

John, get up the bays. All ready. See how the buckles
glisten, and how the horses prance, and the spokes flash
in the sun. Now, open the gate. Away we go. Let the
gravel fly, and the tires rattle over the pavement, and the
horses' hoofs clatter and ring. Good roads, and let them
fly. Crack the whip. G'long! Nimble horses with
smooth roads, in a pleasant day, and no toll-gates—clatter,
clatter, clatter. [Applause.]

I never see a man go out with a fishing-rod to sport
but I silently say: "May you have a good time, and the
right kind of bait, and a basketful of catfish and flound-
ers." I never see a party taking a pleasant ride but I
wish them a joyous round, and say. "May the horse not
cast a shoe, nor the trace break, and may the horse's
thirst not compel them to stop at too many taverns." In
a world where God lets His lambs frisk, and His trees
toss, and His brooks leap, and His stars twinkle, and His
flowers make love to each other, I know He intended men
at times to laugh and sing and sport. The whole world

is full of music if we only had ears acute enough to hear it. Silence itself is only music asleep. Out upon the fashion that lets a man smile, but pronounces him vulgar if he makes great demonstration of hilarity. Out upon a style of Christianity that would make a man's face the counter upon which to measure religion by the yard. "All work and no play makes Jack a dull boy," is as true as preaching, and more true than some preaching. "Better wear out than rust out," is a poor maxim. They are both sins. You have no more right to do the one than the other. Recreation is re-creation. But while all this is so, every thinking man and woman will acknowledge that too much devotion to amusement is ruinous. Many of the clergy of the last century lost their theology in a fox chase. Many a splendid business has had its brains kicked out by fast horses. Many a man has smoked up his prospects in Havanas of the best brand. There are battles in life that cannot be fought with sportsman's gun. There are things to be caught that you cannot draw up with a fishing tackle. Even Christopher North, that magnificent Scotchman, dropped a great deal of usefulness out of his sporting jacket. Through excessive amusement many clergymen, farmers, lawyers, physicians, mechanics, and artists have committed the big blunder of their lives. I offer this as a principle: Those amusements are harmless which do not interfere with home duties and enjoyments. Those are ruinous which give one distaste for domestic pleasure and recreation.

When a man likes any place on earth better than his own home, look out! Yet how many men seem to have no appreciation of what a good home is. It is only a few years ago that the twain stood at the marriage altar and promised fidelity till death did them part. Now, at midnight, he is staggering on his way to the home, and as the door opens I see on the face inside the door the shadow of sorrows that are passed, and the shadow of sorrows that are to come. Or, I see her going along the road at midnight to the place where he was ruined, and opening the door and swinging out from under a faded shawl a shriveled arm, crying out in almost supernatural eloquence: "Give him back to me, him of the noble brow and the great heart. Give him back to me!" And the miserable wretches seated around the table of the restaurant, one of them will come forward, and with bloated hand wiping the intoxicant from the lip, will say, " Put her out!" Then I see her going out on the abutment of the bridge, and looking off upon the river, glassy in the moonlight, and wondering if somewhere under the glassy surface of that river there is not a place of rest for a broken heart. Woe to the man that despoils his home! Better that he had never been born. I offer home as a preventive, as an inspiration, as a restraint. Floating off from that, beware!

Home! Upon that word there drop the sunshine of boyhood and the shadow of tender sorrows and the reflection of ten thousand fond memories. Home! When I see it in book or newspaper, that word seems to rise and sparkle and leap and thrill and whisper and chant and pray and weep. It glitters like a shield. It springs up like a fountain. It trills like a song. It twinkles like a star. It leaps like a flame. It glows like a sunset. It sings like an angel. And if some lexicographer, urged on by a spirit from beneath, should seek to cast forth that word from the language, the children would come forth and hide it under garlands of wild flowers, and the wealthy would come forth to cover it up with their diamonds and pearls; and kings would hide it under their crowns, and after Herod had hunted its life from Bethlehem to Egypt, and utterly given up the search, some bright, warm day it would flash from among the gems, and breathe from among the coronets, and the world would read it bright and fair, and beautiful, and resonant, as before,—Home! Home! Home!

Blunder the next: The formation of unwise domestic relation. And now I must be very careful. It is so with both sexes. Some of the loveliest women have been married to the meanest men. That is not poetry, that is prose. The queerest man in the Bible was Nabal, but he was the husband of beautiful Abigail. We are prodigal with our compassion when a noble woman is joined to a husband of besotted habits, but in thousands of the homes of our country, belonging to men too stingy to be dissipated, you may find female excellencies which have no opportunity for development. If a man be cross and grudgeful and unobliging and censorious in his household, he is more of a pest than if he were dead drunk, for then he could be managed. [Applause.] It is a sober fact which every one has noticed that thousands of men of good business capabilities have been entirely defeated in life because their domestic relations were not of the right kind. This thought has its most practical bearing on the young who yet have the world before them and where to choose. There is probably no one in this house who has been unfortunate in the forming of the relation I have mentioned; but if you should happen to meet with any married man in such an unfortunate predicament as I have mentioned, tell him I have no advice to give him except to tell him to keep his courage up, and whistle most of the time, and put into practice what the old lady said. She said she had had a great deal of trouble in her time, but she had always been consoled by that beautiful passage of Scripture, the thirteenth verse of the fourteenth chapter of the book of Nicodemus: "Grin and bear it." [Laughter and applause.]

Socrates had remarkable philosophy in bearing the ills of an unfortunate alliance. Xantippe, having scolded him without any evident effect, threw upon him a pail of water. All he did was to exclaim: "I thought that after so much thunder we would be apt to have some rain." [Laughter.] It is hardly possible that a business man should be thriftless if he have a companion always ready to encourage and assist him—ready to make sacrifices until his affairs may allow more opportunity for luxuries. If during the day a man has been harassed and disappointed, hard chased by notes and defrauded, and he find in his home that evening a cheerful sympathy, he will go back next day to his place of business with his courage up, fearless of protests, and able from ten to three o'clock to look any bank full in the face. During the financial panic of 1857 there was many a man who went through unabashed because while down in the business marts he knew that although all around him they were thinking only of themselves, there was one sympathetic heart thinking of him all day long, and willing, if the worst should come, to go with him to a humble home on an unfashionable street, without murmuring, on a sewing-machine to play "The Song of the Shirt." [Applause.] Hundreds of fortunes that have been ascribed to the industry of men bear upon them the mark of a wife's hand. Bergham, the artist, was as lazy as he was talented. His studio was over the room where his wife sat. Every few minutes, all day long, to keep her husband from idleness, Mrs. Bergham would take a stick and thump up against the ceiling, and her husband would answer by stamping on the floor, the signal that he was wideawake and busy. One-half of the industry and punctuality that you witness every day in places of business is merely the result of Mrs. Bergham's stick thumping against the ceiling. But woe to the man who has an experience anything like the afflicted man, who said that he had during his life three wives—the first was very rich, the second very handsome, and the third an outrageous temper. "So," says he, "I have had 'the world, the flesh, and the devil.'" [Laughter.]

Want of domestic economy has ruined many a fine business. I have known a delicate woman strong enough to carry off her husband's store on her back and not half try. I have known men running the gauntlet between angry creditors while the wife was declaring large and unprecedented dividends among milliners' and confectioners' shops. I have known men, as the phrase goes, "With their nose to the grindstone," and the wife most vigorously turning the crank. Solomon says: "A good wife is from the Lord," but took it for granted that we might easily guess where the other kind comes from. [Laughter.] There is no excuse for a man's picking up a rough flint like that and placing it so near his heart, when the world is so full of polished jewels. And let me say, there never was a time since the world stood when there were so many good and noble women as there are now. And I have come to estimate a man's character somewhat by his appreciation of womanly character. If a man have a depressed idea of womanly character he is a bad man, and there is no exception to the rule. But there have been men who at the marriage altar thought they were annexing something more valuable than Cuba, who have found out that after all they have got only an album, a fashion plate, and a medicine chest. [Laughter and applause.]

Many a man reeling under the blow of misfortune has

been held up by a wife's arm, a wife's prayer, a wife's
decision, and has blessed God that one was sent from
Heaven thus to strengthen him; while many a man in comfortable circumstances has had his life pestered out of
him by a shrew, who met him at the door at night, with
biscuit that the servant let fall in the fire, and dragging
out the children to whom she had promised a flogging as
soon as the " old man " came home, to the scene of domestic felicity.   And what a case that was, where a husband
and wife sat at the opposite ends of the tea-table, and a
bitter controversy came up between them, and the wife
picked up a teacup and hurled it at her husband's head,
and it glanced past and broke all to pieces a beautiful
motto on the wall entitled " God bless our happy home!"
[Applause.]

There are thousands of women who are the joy and the
adornment of our American homes, combining with elegant tastes in the arts and every accomplishment which
our best seminaries and the highest style of literature can
bestow upon them, an industry and practicality which
always insure domestic happiness and prosperity.   Mark
you, I do not say they will insure a large number of dollars.   A large number of dollars are not necessary for happiness.   I have seen a house with thirty rooms in it and
they were the vestibule of perdition, and I have seen a
home with two rooms in it, and they were the vestibule
of heaven.   You cannot tell by the size of a man's house
the size of his happiness.   As Alexander the Great with
pride showed the Persian princesses garments made by
his own mother, so the women of whom I have been
speaking can show you the triumphs of their adroit
womanly fingers.   They are as expert in the kitchen as
they are graceful in the parlor, if need be they go there.
And let me say that that is my idea of a lady, one who
will accommodate herself to any circumstances in which
she may be placed.   If the wheel of fortune turn in the
right direction, then she will be prepared for that position.
If the wheel of fortune turn in the wrong direction (as it
is almost sure to do at least once in every man's life),
then she is just as happy, and though all the hired help
should that morning make a strike for higher wages, they
will have a good dinner, anyhow.   They know without

asking the housekeeper the difference between a washtub and a filter. They never sew on to a coat a licorice-drop for a black button. [Laughter.] They never mistake a bread-tray for a cradle. They never administer Kellinger's horse liniment for the baby's croup. Their accomplishments are not like honeysuckle at your door, hung onto a light frame easily swayed in the wind, but like unto the flowers planted in the solid earth which have rock under them. These are the women who make happy homes and compel a husband into thriftiness.

Boarding-schools are necessities of society. In very small villages and in regions entirely rural it is sometimes impossible to afford seminaries for the higher branches of learning. Hence, in our larger places we must have these institutions, and they are turning out upon the world tens of thousands of young women splendidly qualified for their positions. But there are, I am sorry to say, exceptional seminaries for young ladies which, instead of sending their students back to their homes with good sense as well as diplomas, despatch them with manners and behavior far from civilized. With the promptness of a police officer they arraign their old-fashioned grandfather for murdering the King's English. Staggering down late to breakfast they excuse themselves in French phrase. The young men who were the girl's friends when she left the farm-house for the city school, come to welcome her home, and they shock her with a hard hand that has been on the plow-handle, or with a broad English which does not properly sound the " r " or mince the " s."

> " Things are so awkward, folks so impolite,
> They're elegantly pained from morn 'till night."

Once she could run at her father's heel in the cool furrow on the summer day, or with bronzed cheek chase through the meadows gathering the wild flowers which fell at the stroke of the harvesters, while the strong men with their sleeves rolled up looked down at her, not knowing which most to admire, the daisies in her hair or the roses in her cheeks, and saying: " Bless me! Isn't that Ruth gleaning after the reapers?" Coming home with health gone, her father paid the tuition bill, but Madame Nature sent in an account something like this:—

Miss Ophelia Angelina, to Madame Nature, Dr.

To one year's neglect of exercise	15 chills
To twenty nights of late retiring . .	75 twitches of the nerves
To several months of improper diet .	A lifetime of dyspepsia

Added up, making in all an exhausted system, chronic neuralgia, and a couple of fits. [Applause.]   Call in Dr. Pillsbury and uncork the camphor bottle; but it is too late. What an adornment such a one will be to the house of some young merchant, or lawyer, or mechanic, or farmer. That man will be a drudge while he lives, and he will be a drudge when he dies.

Blunder the next: Attempting life without a spirit of enthusiasm and enterprise.   Over-caution on one side and reckless speculation on the other side must be avoided; but a determined and enthusiastic progress must always characterize the man of thrift.   I think there is no such man in all the world as he who is descended from a New England Yankee on the one side and a New York Dutchman on the other.   That is royal blood, and will almost invariably give a man prosperity, the Yankee in his nature saying: "Go ahead," and the Dutch in his blood saying: "Be prudent while you do go ahead."   The main characteristics of the Yankee are invention and enterprise.   The main characteristics of the Dutchman are prudence and firmness, for when he says "Yah" he means "Yah," and you cannot change him.   It is sometimes said that Americans are short-lived and they run themselves to pieces. We deny this.   An American lives a great deal in a little while—twenty-four hours in ten minutes.   [Applause.]

In the Revolutionary War American enterprise was discovered by somebody who, describing the capture of Lord Cornwallis, put in his mouth these words:—

"I thought five thousand men or less
Through all these States might safely pass.
My error now I see too late,
Here I'm confined within this State.
Yes, in this little spot of ground,
Enclosed by Yankees all around,

In Europe ne'er let it be known,
Nor publish it in Askelon,
Lest the uncircumcised rejoice,
And distant nations join their voice.
What would my friends in Britain say?
I wrote them I had gained the day.
Some things now strike me with surprise,
First, I believe the Tory lies.
What also brought me to this plight
I thought the Yankees would not fight.
My error now I see too late,
Here I'm confined within this State.
Yes, in this little spot of ground,
Enclosed by Yankees all around,
Where I'm so cramped and hemmed about,
The devil himself could not get out."

From that time American enterprise has continued developing, sometimes toward the right and sometimes toward the wrong. Men walk faster, think faster, drive faster, lie faster, and swear faster. New sciences have sprung up and carried off the hearts of the people. Phrenology, a science which I believe will yet be developed to a thorough consistency, in its incomplete stage puts its hand on your head, as a musician on a piano, and plays out the entire tune of your character, whether it be a grand march or a jig; sometimes by mistake announcing that there are in the head benevolence, music, and sublimity, when there is about the same amount of intellect under the hair of the subject's head as in an ordinary hair trunk; sometimes forgetting that wickedness and crime are chargeable, not so much to bumps on the head as to bumps on the heart. [Applause.] Mesmerism, an old science, has been revived in our day. This system was started from the fact that in ancient times the devotees of Æsculapius were put to sleep in his temple, a mesmeric feat sometimes performed on modern worshipers. Incurable diseases are said to slink away before the dawn of this science like ghosts at cock-crowing, and a man under its influence may have a tooth extracted or his head amputated without discovering the important fact until he comes to his senses. The operator will compel a sick person in clairvoyant state to tell whether his own liver or heart is diseased, when if his subject were awake he would not be wise enough to know a heart from a liver. If you have had property stolen, on the payment of one dollar—mind that —they will tell you where it is, and who stole it, and even if they do not make the matter perfectly plain, they have bettered it; it does not all remain a mystery; you know where the dollar went.

There are aged men and women here who have lived through marvelous changes. The world is a very different place from what it was when you were boys and girls. The world's enterprise has accomplished wonders in your age. The broad-brimmed hat of olden times was an illustration of the broad-bottomed character of the father, and the modern hat, rising high up as the pipe of a steam engine, illustrates the locomotive in modern character. In those days of powdered hair and silver shoe buckles, the coat extended over an immense area and would have been unpardonably long had it not been for the fact that when the old gentleman doffed the garment it furnished the whole family of boys with a Sunday wardrobe. [Laughter.] Grandfather on rainy days shelled corn or broke flax in the barn, and in the evening with grandmother went round to visit a neighbor where the men sat smoking their pipes by the jambs of the broad fire-place, telling of a fox chase, or feats at mowing without once getting bushed, and gazing upon the flames as they sissed and simmered around the great back-log, and leaped up through the light wood to lick off the moss, and shrugging tneir shoulders satisfactorily as the wild night wind screamed round the gable, and clattered the shutters, and clicked the icicles from the eaves; and Tom brought in a blue-edged dish of great "Fall pippins," and "Dairclaushes," and "Henry Sweets," and "Grannywinkles," and the nuts all lost their hearts sooner than if the squirrels were there; and the grandmothers talking and knitting, talking and knitting, until John in tow pants, or Mary in linsey-woolsey, by shaking the old lady's arm for just one more "Grannywinkle," made her most provokingly drop a stitch, and forthwith the youngsters were despatched to bed by the starlight that dripped through the thatched garret chinks. [Applause.]

Where is now the old-fashioned fire-place where the

andirons in a trilling duet sang "Home, Sweet Home,"
while the hook and trammels beat time? In our country
houses great solemn stoves have taken their place, where
dim fires, like pale ghosts, look out of the isinglass, and
from which comes the gassy breath of coal, instead of the
breath of mountain oak and sassafras. One icicle frozen
to each chair and sofa is called a sociable, and the milk
of human kindness is congealed into society—that modern freezer warranted to do it in five minutes.

You have also witnessed a change in matters of religion.
I think there is more religion now in the world than there
ever was, but people sometimes have a queer way of showing it. For instance, in the matter of church music. The
musical octave was once an eight-rung ladder, on which
our old fathers could climb up to heaven from their church
pew. Now, the minstrels are robbed every Sunday.

But, oh, what progress in the right direction. There
goes the old stage-coach hung on leather suspenders.
Swing and bounce. Swing and bounce. Old gray balky,
and sorrel lame. Wheel fast in the rut, "All together, yo
heave!" On the morning air you heard the stroke of the
reaper's rifle on the scythe getting ready to fight its way
through the swaths of thick set meadow grass. Now we
do nearly all these things by machinery. A man went all
the way from New York to Buffalo on an express train,
and went so rapidly that he said in all the distance he saw
but two objects: Two haystacks, and they were going
the other way. The small particles of iron are taken from
their bed and melted into liquid, and run out into bars,
and spread into sheets, and turned into screws, and the
boiler begins to groan, and the valves to open, and the
shafts to fly, and the steamboat going "Tschoo! Tschoo!
Tschoo!" shoots across the Atlantic, making it a ferry,
and all the world one neighborhood. In olden times they
put out a fire by buckets of water or rather did not put it
out. Now, in nearly all our cities we put out a fire by
steam. But where they haven't come to this, there still
has been great improvement. Hark! There is a cry in
the street: "Fire! Fire!" The firemen are coming,
and they front the building, and they hoist the ladders, and
they run up with the hose, and the orders are given, and
the engines begin to work, and beat down the flames that

smote the heavens. And the hook and ladder company
with long arms of wood and fingers of iron begin to feel
on the top of the hot wall and begin to pull. She moves!
She rocks! Stand from under! She falls! flat as the
walls of Jericho at the blast of the ram's horns, and the
excited populace clap their hands, and wave their caps,
shouting "Hurrah, hurrah!" [Applause.]

Now, in an age like this, what will become of a man if
in every nerve and muscle and bone he does not have the
spirit of enthusiasm and enterprise? Why, he will drop
down and be forgotten, as he ought to be. He who cannot swim in this current will drown. Young man, make
up your mind what you ought to be, and then start out.

And let me say, there has never been so good a time to
start as just now. I care not which way you look, the
world seems brightening. Open the map of the world,
close your eyes, swing your finger over the map of the
world, let your finger drop accidentally, and I am almost
sure it will drop on a part of the world that is brightening.
You open the map of the world, close your eyes, swing
your finger over the map, it drops accidentally. Spain!
Quitting her cruelties and coming to a better form of government. What is that light breaking over the top of the
Pyrenees? "The morning cometh!" You open the map
of the world again, close your eyes, and swing your finger
over the map. It drops accidentally. Italy! The truth
going on from conquest to conquest. What is that light
breaking over the top of the Alps? "The morning
cometh!" You open the map of the world again, you
close your eyes, and swing your finger over the map, and
your finger drops accidentally. India! Juggernauts of
cruelty broken to pieces by the chariot of the Gospel.
What is that light breaking over the tops of the Himalayas? "The morning cometh!" The army of Civilization
and Christianity is made up of two wings, the English wing
and the American wing. The American wing of the army
of Civilization and Christianity will march across this continent. On, over the Rocky Mountains, on over the
Sierra Nevada, on to the beach of the Pacific, and then
right through, dry shod, to the Asiatic shore. And on
across Asia, and on, and on, until it comes to the Holy
Land and halts. The English wing of the army of Civili-

zation and Christianity will move across Europe, and on,
until it comes to the Holy Land and halts.   And when these
two wings of the army of Civilization and Christianity
shall confront each other, having encircled the world,
there will go up a shout as the world heard never: "Hal-
lelujah, for the Lord God Omnipotent reigneth!"   [Ap-
plause.]

People who have not seen the tides rise at the beach do
not understand them.   Some man who has never before
visited the seashore comes down as the tide is rising.   The
wave comes to a certain point and then retreats, and he
says: "The tide is going out, the sea is going down."
No, the tide is rising, for the next wave comes to a higher
point, and then recoils.   He says: "Certainly, the tide is
going out, and the sea is going down."   No, the tide is
rising, for the next wave comes to a higher point and then
recoils, and to a higher and higher and higher point until
it is full tide.   So with the advance of civilization and
Christianity in the world.   In one decade the wave comes
to a certain point and then recoils for ten or fifteen years,
and people say the world is getting worse, and the tides
of civilization and Christianity are going down.   No, the
tide is rising, for the next time the wave reaches to a still
higher point and recoils, and to a still higher point and
recoils, and to a higher and a higher and a higher point
until it shall be full tide, and the "Earth shall be full of
the knowledge of God as the waters fill the sea."   At
such a time you start out.   There is some special work
for you to do.

I was very much thrilled, as I suppose you were, with
the story of the old engineer on his locomotive crossing
the Western prairie day after day and month after month.
A little child would come out in front of her father's cabin
and wave to the old engineer and he would wave back
again.   It became one of the joys of the old engineer's
life, this little child coming out and waving to him and he
waving back.   But one day the train was belated and
night came on, and by the flash of the headlight of the
locomotive the old engineer saw the child on the track.
When the engineer saw the child on the track a great
horror froze his soul, and he reversed the engine and
leaped over on the cowcatcher, and though the train was

slowing up, and slowing up, it seemed to the old engineer as if it were gaining in velocity. But, standing there on the cowcatcher, he waited for his opportunity, and with almost supernatural clutch he seized her and fell back upon the cowcatcher. The train halted, the passengers came around to see what was the matter, and there lay the old engineer on the cowcatcher, fainted dead away, the little child in his arms all unhurt.

He saved her. Grand thing, you say, for the old engineer to do. Yes, just as grand a thing for you to do. There are long trains of disaster coming on toward that soul. Yonder are long trains of disaster coming on toward another soul. You go out in the strength of the Eternal God and with supernatural clutch save some one, some man, some woman, some child. You can do it.

> " Courage, brother, do not stumble,
>   Though thy path be dark as night;
>   There's a star to guide the humble;
>   Trust in God and do the right.
>
> " Some will love thee, some will hate thee,
>   Some will flatter, some will slight;
>   Cease from man, and look above thee;
>   Trust in God and do the right."

WILLIAM MAKEPEACE THACKERAY

Photogravure after a photograph from life

WILLIAM MAKEPEACE THACKERAY

SWIFT

[Lecture by W. M. Thackeray (born in Calcutta, July 18, 1811; died in London, December 24, 1863), the first of the series on the English Humorists, delivered at Willis's Rooms, London, beginning May 22, 1851, subsequently repeated in many cities of England and Scotland, and delivered in the United States in 1853. When these lectures were first given in London, Thackeray had among his auditors many of the most famous of the English literary world—Hallam, Kinglake, Rawlinson, the Carlyles, Harriet Martineau, Monckton, Milnes, Dickens, and Charlotte Brontë. Macaulay, who attended all, wrote: "He is full of humor and imagination and I only wish that these lectures may answer both in the way of fame and money." Motley has thus characterized Thackeray on the platform: "This light offhand manner suits well the delicate, hovering rather than superficial style of the composition. He skims lightly over the surface of the long epoch, throwing out a sketch here, exhibiting a characteristic trait there, and sprinkling about a few anecdotes, portraits, and historical allusions, running about from grave to gay, from lively to severe, moving and mocking the sensibilities in a breath, in a way which I should say was the perfection of lecturing to high-bred audiences."]

In treating of the English humorists of the past age, it is of men and of their lives, rather than of their books, that I ask permission to speak to you; and in doing so, you are aware that I cannot hope to entertain you with a merely humorous or facetious story. Harlequin without his mask is known to present a very sober countenance, and was himself, the story goes, the melancholy patient whom the doctor advised to go and see Harlequin—a man full of cares and perplexities like the rest of us, whose self must always be serious to him, under whatever mask or disguise or uniform he presents it to the public.   And as all of you here must needs be grave when you think of your own past and present, you will not look to find, in the histories of those whose lives and feelings I am going to try and describe to you, a story that is otherwise than serious, and often very sad.   If humor only meant laughter, you would scarcely feel more interest about humorous writers than about the private life of poor Harlequin just mentioned, who possesses, in common with these, the power of making you laugh.   But the men regarding whose lives and stories your kind presence here shows that you have curiosity and sympathy, appeal to a great number of our faculties, besides our mere sense of ridicule.   The humorous writer professes to awaken and direct your love, your pity, your kindness—your scorn for untruth, pretension, imposture—your tenderness for the weak, the poor, the oppressed, the unhappy.   To the best of his means and ability he comments on all the ordinary actions and passions of life almost.   He takes upon himself to be the week-day preacher, so to speak.   Accordingly, as he finds, and speaks, and feels the truth best, we regard him, esteem him—sometimes love him.   And, as his business is to mark other people's lives and peculiarities, we moralize upon *his* life when he is gone—and yesterday's preacher becomes the text for to-day's sermon.

Of English parents, and of a good English family of clergymen, Swift was born in Dublin in 1667, seven months after the death of his father, who had come to practice there as a lawyer.   The boy went to school at Kilkenny, and afterward to Trinity College, Dublin, where he got a degree with difficulty, and was wild and witty and poor. In 1683, by the recommendation of his mother, Swift was received into the family of Sir William Temple, who had known Mrs. Swift in Ireland.   He left his patron in 1694, and the next year took orders in Dublin.   But he threw up the small Irish preferment which he got and returned to Temple, in whose family he remained until Sir William's death in 1699.   His hopes of advancement in England failing, Swift returned to Ireland, and took the living of Laracor.   Hither he invited Hester Johnson, Temple's

natural daughter, with whom he had contracted a tender
friendship, while they were both dependants of Temple's.
And with an occasional visit to England, Swift now passed
nine years at home.

In 1709 he came to England, and, with a brief visit to
Ireland, during which he took possession of his deanery
at St. Patrick's, he now passed five years in England,
taking the most distinguished part in the political trans-
actions which terminated with the death of Queen Anne.
After her death, his party disgraced and his hopes of
ambition over, Swift returned to Dublin, where he remained twelve years.   In this time he wrote the famous
"Drapier's Letters" and "Gulliver's Travels."   He married
Hester Johnson—" Stella "—and buried Esther Vanhomrigh—" Vanessa "—who had followed him to Ireland from
London, where she had contracted a violent passion for
him.   In 1726 and 1727 Swift was in England, which he
quitted for the last time on hearing of his wife's illness.
Stella died in January, 1728, and Swift not until 1745,
having passed the last five of the seventy-eight years of
his life with an impaired intellect and keepers to watch
him.

You know, of course, that Swift has had many biographers; his life has been told by the kindest and the most
good-natured of men, Scott, who admires but can't bring
himself to love him; and by stout old Johnson, who,
forced to admit him into the company of poets, receives
the famous Irishman, and takes off his hat to him with a
bow of surly recognition, scans him from head to foot, and
passes over to the other side of the street.   Dr. Wilde
of Dublin, who has written a most interesting volume on
the closing years of Swift's life, calls Johnson "the most
malignant of his biographers": it is not easy for an English critic to please Irishmen—perhaps to try and please
them.   And yet Johnson truly admires Swift; Johnson
does not quarrel with Swift's change of politics, or doubt
his sincerity of religion: about the famous Stella and Vanessa controversy the doctor does not bear very hardly
on Swift.   But he could not give the dean that honest
hand of his; the stout old man puts it into his breast, and
moves off from him.

Would we have liked to live with him?   That is a question which, in dealing with these people's works, and thinking of their lives and peculiarities, every reader of biographies must put to himself. Would you have liked to be a friend of the great dean? I should like to have been Shakespeare's shoeblack—just to have lived in his house, just to have worshipped him—to have run on his errands, and seen that sweet serene face. I should like, as a young man, to have lived on Fielding's staircase in the Temple, and after helping him up to bed perhaps, and opening his door with his latchkey, to have shaken hands with him in the morning, and heard him talk and crack jokes over his breakfast and his mug of small beer. Who would not give something to pass a night at the club with Johnson, and Goldsmith, and James Boswell, Esq., of Auchinleck? The charm of Addison's companionship and conversation has passed to us by fond tradition— but Swift? If you have been his inferior in parts (and that, with a great respect for all persons present, I fear is only very likely), his equal in mere social station, he would have bullied, scorned, and insulted you; if, undeterred by his great reputation, you had met him like a man, he would have quailed before you, and not had the pluck to reply, and gone home, and years after written a foul epigram about you—watched for you in a sewer, and come out to assail you with a coward's blow and a dirty bludgeon. If you had been a lord with a blue ribbon, who flattered his vanity, or could help his ambition, he would have been the most delightful company in the world. He would have been so manly, so sarcastic, so bright, odd, and original, that you might think he had no object in view but the indulgence of his humor, and that he was the most reckless, simple creature in the world. How he would have torn your enemies to pieces for you! and made fun of the Opposition! His servility was so boisterous that it looked like independence; he would have done your errands, but with the air of patronizing you, and after fighting your battles, masked, in the street or the press, would have kept on his hat before your wife and daughters in the drawing-room, content to take that sort of pay for his tremendous services as a bravo.

He says as much himself in one of his letters to Bolingbroke: "All my efforts to distinguish myself were only

for want of a great title and fortune, that I might be used
like a lord by those who have an opinion of my parts;
whether right or wrong is no great matter. And so the
reputation of wit and great learning does the office of a
blue ribbon or a coach and six."

Could there be a greater candor? It is an outlaw,
who says, "These are my brains; with these I'll win titles
and compete with fortune. These are my bullets; these
I'll turn into gold"; and he hears the sound of coaches
and six, takes the road like Macheath, and makes society
stand and deliver. They are all on their knees before him.
Down go my lord bishop's apron, and his Grace's blue
ribbon, and my lady's brocade petticoat in the mud. He
eases the one of a living, the other of a patent place, the
third of a little snug post about the court, and gives them
over to followers of his own. The great prize has not
come yet. The coach with the miter and crozier in it,
which he intends to have for *his* share, has been delayed
on the way from St. James'; and he waits and waits until
nightfall, when his runners come and tell him that the
coach has taken a different route and escaped him. So
he fires his pistols into the air with a curse, and rides away
into his own country.

Swift's seems to me to be as good a name to point a
moral or adorn a tale of ambition, as any hero's that ever
lived and failed. But we must remember that the morality was lax—that other gentlemen besides himself took
the road in his day—that public society was in a strange,
disordered condition, and the state was ravaged by other
condottieri. The Boyne was being fought and won, and
lost—the bells rung in William's victory in the very same
tone with which they would have pealed for James'. Men
were loose upon politics, and had to shift for themselves.
They, as well as old beliefs and institutions, had lost their
moorings and gone adrift in the storm. As in the South
Sea Bubble, almost everybody gambled; as in the railway
mania—not many centuries ago—almost everyone took
his unlucky share; a man of that time, of the vast talents
and ambition of Swift, could scarce do otherwise than
grasp at his prize, and make his spring at his opportunity.
His bitterness, his scorn, his rage, his subsequent misanthropy, are ascribed by some panegyrists to a deliberate

conviction of mankind's unworthiness, and a desire to amend them by castigating. His youth was bitter, as that of a great genius bound down by ignoble ties, and powerless in a mean dependence; his age was bitter, like that of a great genius that had fought the battle and nearly won it, and lost it, and thought of it afterward writhing in a lonely exile. A man may attribute to the gods, if he likes, what is caused by his own fury, or disappointment, or self-will. What public man—what statesman projecting a *coup*—what king determined on an invasion of his neighbor—what satirist meditating an onslaught on society or an individual, can't give a pretext for his move? There was a French general the other day who proposed to march into this country and put it to sack and pillage, in revenge for humanity outraged by our conduct at Copenhagen: there is always some excuse for men of the aggressive turn. They are of their nature warlike, predatory, eager for fight, plunder, dominion.

As fierce a beak and talon as ever struck—as strong a wing as ever beat, belonged to Swift. I am glad, for one, that fate wrested the prey out of his claws, and cut his wings and chained him. One can gaze, and not without awe and pity, at the lonely eagle chained behind the bars.

That Swift was born at No. 7 Hoey's Court, Dublin, on the 30th of November, 1667, is a certain fact, of which nobody will deny the sister island the honor and glory; but, it seems to me, he was no more an Irishman than a man born of English parents at Calcutta is a Hindoo. Goldsmith was an Irishman, and always an Irishman; Steele was an Irishman, and always an Irishman; Swift's heart was English and in England, his habits English, his logic eminently English; his statement is elaborately simple; he shuns tropes and metaphors, and uses his ideas and words with a wise thrift and economy, as he used his money, with which he could be generous and splendid upon great occasions, but which he husbanded when there was no need to spend it. He never indulges in needless extravagance of rhetoric, lavish epithets, profuse imagery. He lays his opinion before you with a grave simplicity and a perfect neatness. Dreading ridicule, too, as a man of his humor—above all an Englishman of his humor—cer-

tainly would, he is afraid to use the poetical power which
he really possessed; one often fancies in reading him that
he dares not be eloquent when he might; that he does not
speak above his voice, as it were, and the tone of society.

His initiation into politics, his knowledge of business,
his knowledge of polite life, his acquaintance with literature even, which he could not have pursued very sedu-
lously during that reckless career at Dublin, Swift got
under the roof of Sir William Temple.   He was fond of
telling in after life what quantities of books he devoured
there, and how King William taught him to cut asparagus
in the Dutch fashion.   It was at Shene and at Moor
Park, with a salary of twenty pounds and a dinner at the
upper servants' table, that this great and lonely Swift
passed a ten years' apprenticeship—wore a cassock that
was only not a livery—bent down a knee as proud as
Lucifer's to supplicate my lady's good graces, or run on his
honor's errands.   It was here, as he was writing at Temple's table, or following his patron's walk, that he saw and
heard the men who had governed the great world—measured himself with them looking up from his silent corner,
gauged their brains, weighed their wits, turned them, and
tried them, and marked them.   Ah! what platitudes he
must have heard! what feeble jokes! what pompous commonplaces! what small men they must have seemed under
those enormous periwigs, to the swarthy, uncouth, silent
Irish secretary.   I wonder whether it ever struck Temple
that that Irishman was his master.   I suppose that dismal conviction did not present itself under the ambrosial
wig, or Temple could never have lived with Swift.   Swift
sickened, rebelled, left the service—ate humble pie and
came back again; and so for ten years went on, gathering,
learning, swallowing scorn, and submitting with a stealthy
rage to his fortune.

Temple's style is the perfection of practical and easy
good-breeding.   If he does not penetrate very deeply
into a subject, he professes a very gentlemanly acquaintance with it; if he makes rather a parade of Latin, it was
the custom of his day, as it was the custom for a gentleman to envelop his head in a periwig and his hands in
lace ruffles.   If he wears buckles and square-toed shoes,
he steps in them with a consummate grace, and you never

hear their creak, or find them treading upon any lady's train or any rival's heels in the court crowd. When that grows too hot or too agitated for him, he politely leaves it. He retires to his retreat of Shene or Moor Park; and lets the King's party and the Prince of Orange's party battle it out among themselves. He reveres the sovereign (and no man perhaps ever testified to his loyalty by so elegant a bow); he admires the Prince of Orange; but there is one person whose ease and comfort he loves more than all the princes in Christendom, and that valuable member of society is himself Gulielmus Temple, Baronettus. One sees him in his retreat; between his study-chair and his tulip-beds, clipping his apricots and pruning his essays—the statesman, the ambassador no more; but the philosopher, the Epicurean, the fine gentleman and courtier at St. James' as at Shene; where in place of kings and fair ladies he pays his court to the Ciceronian majesty; or walks a minuet with the Epic Muse; or dallies by the south wall with the ruddy nymph of gardens.

Temple seems to have received and exacted a prodigious deal of veneration from his household, and to have been coaxed, and warmed, and cuddled by the people round about him, as delicately as any of the plants which he loved. When he fell ill in 1693, the household was aghast at his indisposition; mild Dorothea, his wife, the best companion of the best of men—

"Mild Dorothea, peaceful, wise, and great,
  Trembling beheld the doubtful hand of fate."

As for Dorinda, his sister:—

"Those who would grief describe, might come and trace
  Its watery footsteps in Dorinda's face.
  To see her weep, joy every face forsook,
  And grief flung sables on each menial look.
  The humble tribe mourned for the quickening soul,
  That furnished spirit and motion through the whole."

Isn't that line in which grief is described as putting the menials into a mourning livery, a fine image? One of the menials wrote it who did not like that Temple livery nor those twenty-pound wages. Cannot one fancy the

uncouth young servitor, with downcast eyes, books and
papers in hand, following at his honor's heels in the garden walk, or taking his honor's orders as he stands by the
great chair, where Sir William has the gout, and his feet
all blistered with moxa? When Sir William has the gout
or scolds it must be hard work at the second table; the
Irish secretary owned as much afterward; and, when he
came to dinner, how he must have lashed and growled
and torn the household with his gibes and scorn! What
would the steward say about the pride of them Irish
schollards—and this one had got no great credit even at
his Irish college, if the truth were known—and what a
contempt his excellency's own gentleman must have had
for Parson Teague from Dublin! (The valets and chap-
lains were always at war. It is hard to say which Swift
thought the more contemptible.) And what must have
been the sadness, the sadness and terror, of the housekeeper's little daughter with the curling black ringlets
and the sweet smiling face, when the secretary who teaches
her to read and write, and whom she loves and reverences
above all things—above mother, above mild Dorothea,
above that tremendous Sir William in his square-toes and
periwig—when *Mr. Swift* comes down from his master
with rage in his heart, and has not a kind word even for
little Hester Johnson?

Perhaps, for the Irish secretary, his excellency's condescension was even more cruel than his frowns. Sir William *would* perpetually quote Latin and the ancient classics
apropos of his gardens and his Dutch statues and *plates-
bandes*, and talk about Epicurus and Diogenes Lærtius,
Julius Cæsar, Semiramis, and the gardens of the Hesper-
ides, Mæcenas, Strabo describing Jericho, and the As-
syrian kings. *Apropos* of beans, he would mention Pythag-
oras' precept to abstain from beans, and that this precept
probably meant that wise men should abstain from public
affairs. *He* is a placid Epicurean; *he* is a Pythagorean
philosopher; *he* is a wise man—that is the deduction.
Does not Swift think so? One can imagine the downcast
eyes lifted up for a moment, and the flash of scorn which
they emit. Swift's eyes were as azure as the heavens;
Pope says nobly (as everything Pope said and thought of
his friend was good and noble), " His eyes are as azure as

the heavens, and have a charming archness in them."
And one person in that household, that pompous, stately,
kindly Moor Park, saw heaven nowhere else.

But the Temple amenities and solemnities did not agree
with Swift. He was half killed with a surfeit of Shene
pippins; and in a garden-seat which he devised for himself
at Moor Park, and where he devoured greedily the stock
of books within his reach, he caught a vertigo and deaf-
ness which punished and tormented him through life. He
could not bear the place or the servitude. Even in that
poem of courtly condolence, from which we have quoted a
few lines of mock melancholy, he breaks out of the funeral
procession with a mad shriek, as it were, and rushes away
crying his own grief, cursing his own fate, foreboding
madness, and forsaken by fortune, and even hope.

I don't know anything more melancholy than the letter
to Temple, in which, after having broke from his bondage, the poor wretch crouches piteously toward his cage
again, and deprecates his master's anger. He asks for
testimonials for orders. "The particulars required of me
are what relate to morals and learning; and the reasons
of quitting your honor's family—that is, whether the last
was occasioned by any ill action. They are left entirely
to your honor's mercy, though in the first I think I cannot
reproach myself for anything further than for *infirmities*.
This is all I dare at present beg from your honor,
under circumstances of life not worth your regard; what
is left me to wish (next to the health and prosperity of
your honor and family) is that Heaven would one day allow
me the opportunity of leaving my acknowledgments at
your feet. I beg my most humble duty and service be
presented to my ladies, your honor's lady and sister."
Can prostration fall deeper? could a slave bow lower?

Twenty years afterward Bishop Kennet, describing the
same man, says: "Dr. Swift came into the coffee-house
and had a bow from everybody but me. When I came to
the antechamber [at court] to wait before prayers, Dr.
Swift was the principal man of talk and business. He was
soliciting the Earl of Arran to speak to his brother, the
Duke of Ormond, to get a place for a clergyman. He
was promising Mr. Thorold to undertake, with my Lord
Treasurer, that he should obtain a salary of £200 per

annum as member of the English Church at Rotterdam.
He stopped F. Gwynne, Esq., going in to the Queen with
the red bag, and told him aloud he had something to say
to him from my Lord Treasurer. He took out his gold
watch, and, telling the time of day, complained that it was
very late. A gentleman said he was too fast. 'How can
I help it,' says the doctor, 'if the courtiers give me a
watch that won't go right?' Then he instructed a young
nobleman, that the best poet in England was Mr. Pope
(a papist), who had begun a translation of Homer into
English for which he would have them all subscribe:
'For,' says he, 'he shall not begin to print till I have a
thousand guineas for him.' Lord Treasurer, after leaving
the Queen, came through the room, beckoning Dr. Swift
to follow him—both went off just before prayers."
There's a little malice in the bishop's "just before
prayers."

This picture of the great dean seems a true one, and is
harsh, though not altogether unpleasant. He was doing
good, and to deserving men too, in the midst of these
intrigues and triumphs. His journals and a thousand
anecdotes of him relate his kind acts and rough manners.
His hand was constantly stretched out to relieve an honest man—he was cautious about his money, but ready.
If you were in a strait would you like such a benefactor?
I think I would rather have had a potato and a friendly
word from Goldsmith than have been beholden to the
dean for a guinea and a dinner. He insulted a man as he
served him, made women cry, guests look foolish, bullied
unlucky friends, and flung his benefactions into poor men's
faces. No; the dean was no Irishman—no Irishman ever
gave but with a kind word and a kind heart.

It is told, as if it were to Swift's credit, that the Dean
of St. Patrick's performed his family devotions every
morning regularly, but with such secrecy that the guests
in his house were never in the least aware of the ceremony. There was no need surely why a church dignitary
should assemble his family privily in a crypt, and as if he
was afraid of heathen persecution. But I think the world
was right, and the bishops who advised Queen Anne,
when they counseled her not to appoint the author of the
"Tale of a Tub" to a bishopric, gave perfectly good ad-

vice. The man who wrote the arguments and illustrations in that wild book, could not but be aware what must be the sequel of the propositions which he laid down. The boon companion of Pope and Bolingbroke, who chose these as the friends of his life, and the recipients of his confidence and affection, must have heard many an argument, and joined in many a conversation over Pope's port, or St. John's Burgundy, which would not bear to be repeated at other men's boards.

I know of few things more conclusive as to the sincerity of Swift's religion than his advice to poor John Gay to turn clergyman, and look out for a seat on the Bench. Gay, the author of the "Beggar's Opera"—Gay, the wildest of the wits about town—it was this man that Jonathan Swift advised to take orders—to invest in a cassock and bands—just as he advised him to husband his shillings and put his thousand pounds out at interest. The Queen and the bishops, and the world, were right in mistrusting the religion of that man.

I am not here, of course, to speak of any man's religious views, except in so far as they influence his literary character, his life, his humor. The most notorious sinners of all those fellow-mortals whom it is our business to discuss—Harry Fielding and Dick Steele, were especially loud, and I believe really fervent, in their expressions of belief; they belabored free-thinkers, and stoned imaginary atheists on all sorts of occasions, going out of their way to bawl their own creed, and persecute their neighbor's, and if they sinned and stumbled, as they constantly did with debt, drink, with all sorts of bad behavior, they got upon their knees and cried "Peccavi" with a most sonorous orthodoxy. Yes; poor Harry Fielding and poor Dick Steele were trusty and undoubting Church of England men; they abhorred popery, atheism, and wooden shoes, and idolatries in general; and hiccoughed Church and State with fervor.

But Swift? *His* mind had had a different schooling, and possessed a very different logical power. *He* was not bred up in a tipsy guard-room, and did not learn to reason in a Covent Garden tavern. He could conduct an argument from beginning to end. He could see forward with a fatal clearness. In his old age, looking at the

"Tale of a Tub," when he said, "Good God, what a genius I had when I wrote that book!" I think he was admiring not the genius, but the consequences to which the genius had brought him—a vast genius, a magnificent genius, a genius wonderfully bright, and dazzling, and strong—to seize, to know, to see, to flash upon falsehood and scorch it into perdition, to penetrate into hidden motives, and expose the black thoughts of men—an awful, an evil spirit.

Ah, man! you, educated in Epicurean Temple's library, you whose friends were Pope and St. John—what made you to swear to fatal vows, and bind yourself to a life-long hypocrisy before the Heaven which you adored with such real wonder, humility, and reverence? For Swift was a reverent, was a pious spirit—for Swift could love and could pray. Through the storms and tempests of his furious mind, the stars of religion and love break out in the blue, shining serenely, though hidden by the driving clouds and the maddened hurricane of his life.

It is my belief that he suffered frightfuly from the consciousness of his own skepticism, and that he had bent his pride so far down as to put his apostasy out to hire. The paper left behind him, called "Thoughts on Religion," is merely a set of excuses for not professing disbelief. He says of his sermons that he preached pamphlets; they have scarce a Christian characteristic; they might be preached upon the steps of a synagogue, or the floor of a mosque, or the box of a coffee house almost. There is little or no cant—he is too great and too proud for that; and, in so far as the badness of his sermons goes, he is honest. But having put that cassock on, it poisoned him; he was strangled in his bands. He goes through life, tearing, like a man possessed with a devil. Like Abudah, in the Arabian story, he is always looking out for the Fury, and knows that the night will come and the inevitable hag with it. What a night, my God, it was! what a lonely rage and long agony—what a vulture that tore the heart of that giant! It is awful to think of the great sufferings of this great man. Through life he always seems alone, somehow. Goethe was so. I can't fancy Shakespeare otherwise. The giants live apart. The kings can have no company. But this man suffered so; and deserved to suffer. One hardly reads anywhere of such a pain.

The " sæva indignatio " of which he spoke as lacerating
his heart, and which he dares to inscribe on his tombstone
—as if the wretch who lay under that stone awaiting
God's judgment had a right to be angry—breaks out from
him in a thousand pages of his writing, and tears and rends
him.   Against men in office, he having been overthrown;
against men in England, he having lost his chance of preferment there, the furious exile never fails to rage and
curse.   Is it fair to call the famous " Drapier's Letters "
patriotism?   They are masterpieces of dreadful humor
and invective; they are reasoned logically enough too, but
the proposition is as monstrous and fabulous as the Lilliputian island.   It is not that the grievance is so great,
but there is his enemy—the assault is wonderful for its
activity and terrible rage.   It is Samson, with a bone in his
hand, rushing on his enemies and felling them; one admires not the cause so much as the strength, the anger,
the fury of the champion.   As is the case with madmen,
certain subjects provoke him, and awaken his fits of wrath.
Marriage is one of these; in a hundred passages of his
writings he rages against it; rages against children; an
object of constant satire, even more contemptible in his
eyes than a lord's chaplain, is a poor curate with a large
family.   The idea of this luckless paternity never fails to
bring down from him gibes and foul language.   Could
Dick Steele, or Goldsmith, or Fielding, in his most reckless moment of satire, have written anything like the
dean's famous " modest proposal " for eating children?
Not one of these but melts at the thought of childhood,
fondles and caresses it.   Mr. Dean has no such softness,
and enters the nursery with the tread and gayety of an
ogre.   " I have been assured," says he in the " Modest
Proposal," " by a very knowing American of my acquaintance in London, that a young healthy child, well nursed,
is, at a year old, a most delicious, nourishing, and wholesome food, whether stewed, roasted, baked, or boiled; and
I make no doubt it will equally serve in a *ragout*."   And,
taking up this pretty joke, as his way is, he argues it with
perfect gravity and logic.   He turns and twists this subject
in a score of different ways; he hashes it; and he serves it
up cold; and he garnishes it; and relishes it always.   He
describes the little animal as " dropped from its dam,"

advising that the mother should " let it suck plentifully in
the last month, so as to render it plump and fat for a good
table!" "A child," says his reverence, "will make two
dishes at an entertainment for friends; and when the family dines alone, the fore or hind quarter will make a reasonable dish," and so on; and, the subject being so delightful that he can't leave it, he proceeds to recommend,
in place of venison for squires' tables, "the bodies of
young lads and maidens not exceeding fourteen or under
twelve." Amiable humorist! laughing castigator of
morals! There was a process well known and practiced
in the dean's gay days; when a lout entered the coffee
house, the wags proceeded to what they called "roasting" him. This is roasting a subject with a vengeance.
The dean had a native genius for it. As the "Almanach
des Gourmands" says, *On nait rotisseur.*

And it was not merely by the sarcastic method that
Swift exposed the unreasonableness of loving and having
children. In Gulliver, the folly of love and marriage is
urged by graver arguments and advice. In the famous
Lilliputian kingdom, Swift speaks with approval of the
practice of instantly removing children from their parents
and educating them by the State; and among his favorite
horses, a pair of foals are stated to be the very utmost a
well-regulated equine couple would permit themselves.
In fact, our great satirist was of opinion that conjugal love
was unadvisable, and illustrated the theory by his own
practice and example—God help him—which made him
about the most wretched being in God's world.

The grave and logical conduct of an absurd proposition,
as exemplified in the cannibal proposal just mentioned,
is our author's constant method through all his works of
humor. Given a country of people six inches or sixty feet
high, and by the mere process of the logic, a thousand
wonderful absurdities are evolved, at so many stages of
the calculation. Turning to the first minister, who waited
behind him with a white staff near as tall as the mainmast
of the Royal Sovereign, the King of Brobdingnag observes
how contemptible a thing human grandeur is, as represented by such a contemptible little creature as Gulliver.
"The Emperor of Lilliput's features are strong and masculine" (what a surprising humor there is in this descrip-

tion!)—"The emperor's features," Gulliver says, "are strong and masculine, with an Austrian lip, and arched nose, his complexion olive, his countenance erect, his body and limbs well proportioned, and his deportment majestic. He is taller by the breadth of my nail than any of his court, which alone is enough to strike an awe into beholders."

What a surprising humor there is in these descriptions! How noble the satire is here! how just and honest! How perfect the image! Mr. Macaulay has quoted the charming lines of the poet, where the king of the pygmies is measured by the same standard. We have all read in Milton of the spear that was like "the mast of some tall admiral," but these images are surely likely to come to the comic poet originally. The subject is before him. He is turning it in a thousand ways. He is full of it. The figure suggests itself naturally to him, and comes out of his subject, as in that wonderful passage, when Gulliver's box having been dropped by the eagle into the sea, and Gulliver having been received into the ship's cabin, he calls upon the crew to bring the box into the cabin, and put it on the table, the cabin being only a quarter the size of the box. It is the *veracity* of the blunder which is so admirable. Had a man come from such a country as Brobdingnag he would have blundered so.

But the best stroke of humor, if there be a best in that abounding book, is that where Gulliver, in the unpronounceable country, describes his parting from his master the horse. "I took," he says, "a second leave of my master; but, as I was going to prostrate myself to kiss his hoof, he did me the honor to raise it gently to my mouth. I am not ignorant how much I have been censured for mentioning this last particular. Detractors are pleased to think it improbable that so illustrious a person should descend to give so great a mark of distinction to a creature so inferior as I. Neither have I forgotten how apt some travelers are to boast of extraordinary favors they have received. But if these censurers were better acquainted with the noble and courteous disposition of the Houyhnhnms they would soon change their opinion."

The surprise here, the audacity of circumstantial evi-

dence, the astounding gravity of the speaker, who is not
ignorant how much he has been censured, the nature of
the favor conferred, and the respectful exultation at the
receipt of it, are surely complete; it is truth topsy-turvy,
entirely logical and absurd.

As for the humor and conduct of this famous fable, I
suppose there is no person who reads but must admire;
as for the moral, I think it horrible, shameful, unmanly,
blasphemous; and giant and great as this dean is, I say
we should hoot him. Some of this audience mayn't have
read the last part of Gulliver, and to such I would recall
the advice of the venerable Mr. Punch to persons about to
marry, and say, "Don't." When Gulliver first lands
among the Yahoos, the naked, howling wretches clamber
up trees and assault him, and he describes himself as "almost stifled with the filth which fell about him." The
reader of the fourth part of "Gulliver's Travels" is like
the hero himself in this instance. It is Yahoo language:
a monster gibbering shrieks, and gnashing imprecations
against mankind—tearing down all shreds of modesty,
past all sense of manliness and shame; filthy in word, filthy
in thought, furious, raging, obscene.

And dreadful it is to think that Swift knew the tendency
of his creed—the fatal rocks toward which his logic desperately drifted. That last part of "Gulliver" is only a
consequence of what has gone before; and the worthless-
ness of all mankind; the pettiness, cruelty, pride, imbecility, the general vanity, the foolish pretension, the mock
greatness, the pompous dullness, the mean aims, the base
successes—all these were present to him; it was with the
din of these curses of the world, blasphemies against
Heaven, shrieking in his ears, that he began to write his
dreadful allegory—of which the meaning is that man is
utterly wicked, desperate, and imbecile, and his passions
are so monstrous, and his boasted powers so mean, that
he is and deserves to be the slave of brutes, and ignorance
is better than his vaunted reason. What had this man
done? what secret remorse was rankling at his heart?
what fever was boiling in him, that he should see all the
world bloodshot? We view the world with our own eyes
each of us; and we make from within us the world we
see. A weary heart gets no gladness out of sunshine; a

selfish man is skeptical about friendship, as a man with no
ear doesn't care for music.   A frightful self-consciousness
it must have been, which looked on mankind so darkly
through those keen eyes of Swift.

A remarkable story is told by Scott, of Delany, who
interrupted Archbishop King and Swift in a conversation
which left the prelate in tears, and from which Swift
rushed away with marks of strong terror and agitation in
his countenance, upon which the Archbishop said to Delany, "You have just met the most unhappy man on
earth; but on the subject of his wretchedness you must
never ask a question."

The most unhappy man on earth;—Miserrimus—what
a character of him!   And at this time all the great wits of
England had been at his feet.   All Ireland had shouted
after him, and worshipped him as a liberator, a savior, the
greatest Irish patriot and citizen.   Dean Drapier Bicker-
staff Gulliver—the most famous statesmen, and the greatest poets of his day, had applauded him, and done him
homage; and at this time, writing over to Boling'oroke
from Ireland, he says, "It is time for me to have done
with the world, and so I would if I could get into a better
before I was called into the best, and not die here in a
rage, like a poisoned rat in a hole."

We have spoken about the men and Swift's behavior to
them; and now it behoves us not to forget that there are
certain other persons in the creation who had rather intimate relations with the great dean.   Two women whom
he loved and injured are known by every reader of books
so familiarly that if we had seen them, or if they had been
relatives of our own, we scarcely could have known them
better.   Who hasn't in his mind an image of Stella?   Who
does not love her?   Fair and tender creature: pure and
affectionate heart!   Boots it to you, now that you have
been at rest for a hundred and twenty years, not divided
in death from the cold heart which caused yours, while it
beat, such faithful pangs of love and grief—boots it to
you now, that the whole world loves and deplores you?
Scarce any man, I believe, ever thought of that grave, that
did not cast a flower of pity on it, and write over it a sweet
epitaph.   Gentle lady, so lovely, so loving, so unhappy!
you have had countless champions; millions of manly

hearts mourning for you. From generation to generation we take up the fond tradition of your beauty; we
watch and follow your tragedy, your bright morning love
and purity, your constancy, your grief, your sweet martyr-
dom. We know your legend by heart. You are one of
the saints of English story.

And if Stella's love and innocence are charming to contemplate, I will say that in spite of ill-usage, in spite of
drawbacks, in spite of mysterious separation and union,
of hope delayed and sickened heart—in the teeth of Vanessa and that little episodical aberration which plunged
Swift into such woeful pitfalls and quagmires of amorous
perplexity—in spite of the verdicts of most women, I believe, who, as far as my experience and conversation go,
generally take Vanessa's part in the controversy—in spite
of the tears which Swift caused Stella to shed, and the
rocks and barriers which fate and temper interposed, and
which prevented the pure course of that true love from
running smoothly—the brightest part of Swift's story, the
pure star in that dark and tempestuous life of Swift's, is
his love for Hester Johnson. It has been my business,
professionally of course, to go. through a deal of sentimental reading in my time, and to acquaint myself with
love-making, as it has been described in various languages,
and at various ages of the world; and I know of nothing
more manly, more tender, more exquisitely touching, than
some of these brief notes, written in what Swift calls "his
little language," in his journal to Stella. He writes to her
night and morning often. He never sends away a letter to
her but he begins a new one on the same day. He can't bear
to let go her kind little hand, as it were. He knows that
she is thinking of him, and longing for him far away in
Dublin yonder. He takes her letters from under his pillow and talks to them, familiarly, paternally, with fond
epithets and pretty caresses—as he would to the sweet
and artless creature who loved him. "Stay," he writes
one morning—it is the 14th of December, 1710—"Stay,
I will answer some of your letters this morning in bed.
Let me see. Come and appear, little letter! Here I am,
says he, and what say you to Stella this morning fresh
and fasting? And can Stella read this writing without
hurting her dear eyes?" he goes on, after more kind

prattle and fond whispering.   The dear eyes shine clearly
upon him then—the good angel of his life is with him and
blessing him.   Ah, it was a hard fate that wrung from
them so many tears, and stabbed pitilessly that pure and
tender bosom.   A hard fate; but would she have changed
it?   I have heard a woman say that she would have taken
Swift's cruelty to have had his tenderness.   He had a
sort of worship for her while he wounded her.   He speaks
of her after she is gone; of her wit, of her kindness, of
her grace, of her beauty, with a simple love and reverence
that are indescribably touching; in contemplation of her
goodness his hard heart melts into pathos; his cold rhyme
kindles and glows into poetry, and he falls down on his
knees, so to speak, before the angel whose life he had embittered, confesses his own wretchedness and unworthiness, and adores her with cries of remorse and love:—

When on my sickly couch I lay,
Impatient both of night and day,
And groaning in unmanly strains,
Called every power to ease my pains,
Then Stella ran to my relief,
With cheerful face and inward grief,
And though by Heaven's severe decree
She suffers hourly more than me,
No cruel master could require
From slaves employed for daily hire,
What Stella, by her friendship warmed,
With vigor and delight performed.
Now, with a soft and silent tread,
Unheard she moves about my bed;
My sinking spirit now supplies
With cordials in her hands and eyes.
Best pattern of true friends! beware;
You pay too dearly for your care
If, while your tenderness secures
My life, it must endanger yours;
For such a fool was never found
Who pulled a palace to the ground,
Only to have the ruins made
Materials for a house decayed.

One little triumph Stella had in her life—one dear little
piece of injustice was performed in her favor, for which I

confess, for my part, I can't help thanking fate and the dean. That other person was sacrificed to her—that—that young woman who lived five doors from Dr. Swift's lodgings in Bury street, and who flattered him, and made love to him in such an outrageous manner—Vanessa was thrown over.

Swift did not keep Stella's letters to him in reply to those he wrote to her. He kept Bolingbroke's, and Pope's, and Harley's, and Peterborough's; but Stella, "very carefully," the Lives say, kept Swift's. Of course, that is the way of the world; and so we cannot tell what her style was, or of what sort were the little letters which the doctor placed there at night, and bade to appear from under his pillow of a morning. But in Letter IV of that famous collection he describes his lodging in Bury street, where he has the first floor, a dining-room and bedchamber, at eight shillings a week; and in Letter VI he says "he has visited a lady just come to town," whose name somehow is not mentioned; and in Letter VIII he enters a query of Stella's—"What do you mean 'that boards near me, that I dine with now and then?' What the deuce! You know whom I have dined with every day since I left you, better than I do." Of course she does. Of course, Swift has not the slightest idea of what she means. But in a few letters more it turns out that the doctor has been to dine "gravely" with a Mrs. Vanhomrigh; then that he has been to "his neighbor"; then that he has been unwell, and means to dine for the whole week with his neighbor! Stella was quite right in her previsions. She saw from the very first hint what was going to happen; and scented Vanessa in the air. The rival is at the dean's feet. The pupil and teacher are reading together, and drinking tea together, and going to prayers together, and learning Latin together, and conjugating *amo, amas, amavi* together. The little language is over for poor Stella. By the rule of grammar and the course of conjugation, does not *amavi* come after *amo* and *amas?*

The loves of Cadenus and Vanessa you may peruse in Cadenus' own poem on the subject, and in poor Vanessa's vehement expostulatory verses and letters to him; she adores him, implores him, admires him, thinks him something godlike, and only prays to be admitted to lie at his

feet.   As they are bringing him home from church, those
divine feet of Dr. Swift's are found pretty often in Vanessa's parlor.   He likes to be admired and adored.   He
finds Miss Vanhomrigh to be a woman of great taste and
spirit, and beauty and wit, and a fortune too.   He sees
her every day; he does not tell Stella about the business;
until the impetuous Vanessa becomes too fond of him,
until the doctor is quite frightened by the young woman's
ardor, and confounded by her warmth.   He wanted to
marry neither of them—that I believe was the truth; but
if he had not married Stella, Vanessa would have had him
in spite of himself.   When he went back to Ireland, his
Ariadne, not content to remain in her isle, pursued the
fugitive dean.   In vain he protested, he vowed, he
soothed, and bullied; the news of the dean's marriage with
Stella at last came to her, and it killed her—she died of
that passion.

And when she died, and Stella heard that Swift had
written beautifully regarding her, "That doesn't surprise
me," said Mrs. Stella, "for we all know the dean could
write beautifully about a broomstick."   A woman—a true
woman!   Would you have had one of them forgive the
other?

In a note in his biography, Scott says that his friend
Dr. Tuke, of Dublin, has a lock of Stella's hair, enclosed
in a paper by Swift, on which are written, in the dean's
hand, the words: "*Only a woman's hair.*"   An instance,
says Scott, of the dean's desire to veil his feelings under
the mask of cynical indifference.

See the various notions of critics!   Do those words indicate indifference or an attempt to hide feeling?   Did
you ever hear or read four words more pathetic?   Only a
woman's hair; only love, only fidelity, only purity, innocence, beauty; only the tenderest heart in the world
stricken and wounded, and passed away now out of reach
of pangs of hope deferred, love insulted, and pitiless de-
sertion—only that lock of hair left; and memory and remorse, for the guilty, lonely wretch, shuddering over the
grave of his victim.

And yet to have had much love, he must have given
some.   Treasures of wit and wisdom, and tenderness, too,
must that man have had locked up in the caverns of his

gloomy heart, and shown fitfully to one or two whom he took in there. But it was not good to visit that place. People did not remain there long, and suffered for having been there. He shrank away from all affections sooner or later. Stella and Vanessa both died near him and away from him. He had not heart enough to see them die. He broke from his fastest friend, Sheridan; he slunk away from his fondest admirer, Pope. His laugh jars on one's ear after seven-score years. He was always alone—alone and gnashing in the darkness, except when Stella's sweet smile came and shone upon him. When that went, silence and utter night closed over him. An immense genius; an awful downfall and ruin. So great a man he seems to me, that thinking of him is like thinking of an empire falling. We have other great names to mention—none, I think, however, so great or so gloomy.

ZEBULON BAIRD VANCE

THE SCATTERED NATION

[Lecture by Zebulon B. Vance, lawyer, statesman, United States Senator from North Carolina (born near Asheville, Buncombe County, N. C., May 13, 1830; died in Washington, D. C., April 14, 1894), delivered in 1882 and thereafter in various places and called his greatest platform discourse.]

LADIES AND GENTLEMEN:—Says Professor Maury: "There is a river in the ocean. In the severest droughts it never fails, and in the mightiest floods it never overflows. The Gulf of Mexico is its fountain, and its mouth is in the Arctic seas. It is the Gulf Stream. There is in the world no other such majestic flow of waters. Its current is more rapid than the Mississippi or the Amazon, and its volume more than a thousand times greater. Its waters as far out from the Gulf as the Carolina coasts, are of an indigo blue; they are so distinctly marked that their line of junction with the common sea-water may be traced by the eye. Often one half of a vessel may be perceived floating in the Gulf Stream water, while the other half is in the common water of the sea, so sharp is the line and such the want of affinity between those waters, and such too, the reluctance, so to speak, on the part of those of the Gulf Stream to mingle with the common water of the sea."

This curious phenomenon in the physical world has its counterpart in the moral. There is a lonely river in the midst of the ocean of mankind. The mightiest floods of human temptation have never caused it to overflow, and the fiercest fires of human cruelty, though seven times heated in the furnace of religious bigotry, have never caused it to dry up, although its waves for two thousand years have rolled crimson with the blood of its martyrs. Its fountain is in the gray dawn of the world's history, and its mouth is somewhere in the shadows of eternity. It, too, refuses to mingle with the surrounding waves, and the line which divides its restless billows from the common waters of humanity is also plainly visible to the eye. It is the Jewish race.

The Jew is beyond doubt the most remarkable man of this world, past or present. Of all the stories of the sons of men there is none so wild, so wonderful, so full of extreme mutation, so replete with suffering and horror, so abounding in extraordinary providences, so overflowing with scenic romance. There is no man who approaches him in the extent and character of the influence which he has exercised over the human family. His history is the history of our civilization and progress in this world, and our faith and hope in that which is to come. From him have we derived the form and pattern of all that is excellent on earth or in heaven. If, as De Quincey says, the Roman emperors, as the great accountants for the happiness of more men and men more cultivated than ever before, were entrusted to the motions of a single will, had a special, singular, and mysterious relation to the secret councils of heaven—thrice truly may it be said of the Jew. Palestine, his home, was the central chamber of God's administration. He was at once the grand usher to these glorious courts, the repository of the councils of the Almighty, and the envoy of the divine mandates to the conscience of men. He was the priest and faith-giver to mankind, and as such, in spite of the jibe and jeer, he must ever be considered as occupying a peculiar and sacred relation to all other peoples of this world. Even now, though the Jews have long since ceased to exist as a consolidated nation, inhabiting a common country, and for eighteen hundred years have been scattered far and near over the wide earth, their strange customs, their distinct features, personal peculiarities, and their scattered unity, make them still a wonder and an astonishment.

Though dead as a nation—as we speak of nations— they yet live. Their ideas fill the world and move the wheels of its progress, even as the sun, when he sinks

behind the western hills, yet fills the heavens with the
remnants of his glory. As the destruction of matter in
one form is made necessary to its resurrection in another,
so it would seem that the perishing of the Jewish nation-
ality was in order to the universal acceptance and the
everlasting establishment of Jewish ideas. Never before
was there an instance of such a general rejection of the
person and character, and acceptance of the doctrines and
dogmas of a people.

We admire with unlimited admiration the Greek and
Roman, but reject with contempt their crude and beastly
divinities. We affect to despise the Jew, but accept and
adore the pure conception of a God which he taught us,
and whose real existence the history of the Jew more than
all else establishes. When the court chaplain of Frederick the Great was asked by that bluff monarch for a
brief and concise summary of the argument in support of
the truths of Scripture, he instantly replied, with a force
to which nothing could be added—"The Jews, your Majesty, the Jews."

I propose briefly to glance at their history, origin and
civilization, peculiarities, present condition, and probable
destiny.

"A people of Semitic race," says the encyclopedia,
"whose ancestors appear at the very dawn of the history
of mankind, on the banks of the Euphrates, the Jordan,
and the Nile, their fragments are now to be seen in larger
or smaller numbers in almost all of the cities of the globe,
from Batavia to New Orleans, from Stockholm to Cape
Town. When little more numerous than a family, they
had their language, customs, and peculiar observances,
treated with princes and in every respect acted as a nation.
Though broken as if into atoms, and scattered through all
climes, among the rudest and the most civilized nations,
they have preserved, through thousands of years, common features and observances, a common religion, literature, and sacred language. Without any political union,
without any common head or center, they are generally
regarded, and regard themselves as a nation. They began as nomads, emigrating from country to country; their
law made them agriculturists for fifteen centuries; their
exile transformed them into a mercantile people. They

have struggled for their national existence against the Egyptians, Assyrians, Babylonians, Syrians, and Romans; have been conquered and nearly exterminated by each of these powers, and have survived them all. They have been oppressed and persecuted by Emperors and Republics, by Sultans and by Popes, Moors and Inquisitors; they were proscribed in Catholic Spain, Protestant Norway, and Greek Muscovy, while their persecutors sang the hymns of their psalmody, revered their books, believed in their prophets, and even persecuted them in the name of their God. They have numbered philosophers among the Greeks of Alexandria, and the Saracens of Cordova; have transplanted the wisdom of the East beyond the Pyrenees and the Rhine and have been treated as pariahs among Pagans, Mahomedans and Christians. They have fought for liberty under Kosciusko and Blücher, and popular assemblies among the Sclavi and Germans still withhold from them the right of living in certain towns, villages, and streets."

Whilst no people can claim such an unmixed purity of blood, certainly none can establish such antiquity of origin, such unbroken generations of descent. That splendid passage of Macaulay, so often quoted, in reference to the Roman Pontiffs, loses its force in sight of Hebrew history. "No other institution," says he, "is left standing which carries the mind back to the times when the smoke of sacrifice rose from the Pantheon, and when camels, leopards, and tigers bounded in the Iberian amphitheatre. The proudest royal houses are but of yesterday as compared with the line of the Supreme Pontiffs; that line we trace back in unbroken lines, from the Pope who crowned Napoleon in the Nineteenth century, to the Pope who crowned Pepin in the Eighth, and far beyond Pepin the august dynasty extends until it is lost in the twilight of fable. The Republic of Venice came next in antiquity, but the Republic of Venice is modern compared with the Papacy, and the Republic of Venice is gone and the Papacy remains. The Catholic Church was great and respected before the Saxon had set foot on Britain, before the Frank had passed the Rhine, when Grecian eloquence still flourished at Antioch, when idols were still worshipped in the Temple of Mecca; and she may still exist in undiminished vigor when some traveler from New Zealand, in the midst of a vast solitude, shall take his stand on a broken arch of London Bridge to sketch the ruins of St. **Paul.**" This is justly esteemed one of the most eloquent passages in our literature, but I submit it is not history.

The Jewish people, church, and institutions are still left standing, though the stones of the temple remain no longer one upon the other, though its sacrificial fires are forever extinguished; and though the tribes whose glory it was, wander with weary feet throughout the earth. And what is the line of Roman Pontiffs compared to that splendid dynasty of the successors of Aaron and Levi? "The twilight of fable" in which the line of Pontiffs began was but the noonday brightness of the Jewish priesthood. Their institution carries the mind back to the age when the prophet, in rapt mood, stood over Babylon and uttered God's wrath against that grand and wondrous mistress of the Euphratean plains—when the Memphian chivalry still gave precedence to the chariots and horsemen who each morning poured forth from the brazen gates of the abode of Ammon; when Tyre and Sidon were yet building their palaces by the sea, and Carthage, their greatest daughter, was yet unborn. That dynasty of prophetic priests existed even before Clio's pen had learned to record the deeds of men; and when that splendid, entombed civilization once lighted the shores of the Erythrean Sea, the banks of the Euphrates and the plains of Shinar, with a glory inconceivable, of which there is nought now to tell, except the dumb eloquence of ruined temples and buried cities.

Then, too, it must be remembered that these Pontiffs were but Gentiles in the garb of Jews, imitating their whole routine. All Christian churches are but offshoots from or grafts upon the old Jewish stock. Strike out all of Judaism from the Christian church, and there remains nothing but an unmeaning superstition. The Christian is simply the successor of the Jew. The glory of the one is likewise the glory of the other. The Savior of the world was, after the flesh, a Jew, born of a Jewish maiden; so likewise were all of the apostles and first propagators of

Christianity. The Christian religion is equally Jewish
with that of Moses and the prophets.

I am not unaware of the fact that other people besides
the Semites had a conception of the true God long before
he was revealed to Abraham. The Hebrew Scriptures
themselves testify this, and so likewise do the books of
the very oldest of written records. The fathers of the
great Aryan race, the shepherds of Iran, had so vivid a
conception of the unity of God as to give rise to the opinion that they too had once had a direct revelation. It is
more likely, however, that traditions of this God had descended among them from the Deluge, which ultimately
became adulterated by polytheistic imaginings. It seems
natural that these people of highly sensitive intellects,
dwelling beneath the serene skies that impend over the
plains and mountains of southwestern Asia, thickly
studded with the calm and glorious stars, should mistake
these most majestic emblems of the Creator for the Creator himself. Hence, no doubt, arose the worship of
light and fire by the Iranians and Sabæanism or star-wor-
ship by the Chaldeans. But the better opinion of learned
Orientalists is that while the outward or exoteric doctrine
taught the worship of the symbols, the esoteric or secret
doctrines of Zoroaster, his predecessors and disciples,
taught in fact the worship of the Principle, the First Cause,
the Great Unknown, the Universal Intelligence, Magdam
or God. There can be no doubt that Abraham brought
this monotheistic conception with him from Chaldea; but
notwithstanding this dim traditional light, which was
abroad outside of the race of Shem, perhaps over the entire breadth of that splendid prehistoric civilization of the
Arabian Cushite, yet, for the more perfect light, which
revealed to us God and His attributes, we are unquestionably indebted to the Jew.

We owe to him, if not the conception, at least the preservation of pure monotheism. For whether this knowledge was original with these Eastern people or traditional
merely, it was speedily lost by all of them except the Jews.
Whilst an unintelligent use of symbolism enveloped the
central figure with a cloud of idolatry and led the Magi to
the worship of Light and Fire, the Sabean to the adoration
of the heavenly host, the Egyptian to bowing down before

Isis and Osiris, the Carthaginian to the propitiation of
Baal and Astarte by human sacrifice, and the subtle Greek
to the deification of the varied laws of Nature; the bearded
Prophets of Israel were ever thundering forth: "Know,
O Israel, that the Lord thy God is one God, and Him
only shalt thou serve."

Even his half-brother, Ishmael, after an idolatrous sleep
of centuries, awoke with a sharp and bloody protest
against polytheism, and established the unity of God as
the cornerstone of his faith.   In this respect the influence
which the Jew has exercised over the destinies of mankind places him before all the men of this world.   For in
this idea of God all of the faith and creeds of the dominant
peoples of the earth center.   It divides like a great moun-
tain-range the civilizations of the ancient and modern
worlds.   Many enlightened men of antiquity acknowledged the beauty of this conception, though they did not
embrace it.   Socrates did homage to it, and Josephus de-
clares that he derived his sublime ideal from the Jewish
Scriptures.   The accomplished Tacitus seemed to grasp
it, as the following passages will show.   In speaking of
the Jews, and in contrasting them with the Egyptians, he
says: "With regard to the Deity, their creed is different.   The Egyptians worship various animals and also
certain symbolical representatives which are the work of
man.   The Jews acknowledge one God only, and Him
they see in the mind's eye, and Him they adore in contemplation, condemning as impious idolaters all who with
perishable materials wrought into the human form, attempt to give a representation of the Deity.   The God
of the Jews is the great governing mind that directs and
guides the whole frame of nature—eternal, infinite, and
neither capable of change nor subject to decay."

This matchless and eloquent definition of the Deity has
never been improved upon, but it seems that it made
slight impression upon the philosophical historian's mind.
And yet what a contrast it is with his own coarse material
gods!   Indeed the rejection or ignorance of this pure conception by the acute and refined intellects of the mediæval
ancients strikes us with wonder, and illustrates the truth
that no man by searching can find out God.   I am not
unaware that the Arabian idea of Deity received many

modifications from the conceptions of adjoining and contemporary nations—by cross-fertilization of ideas, as the process has been called. From the Egyptians and Assyrians were received many of these modifications, but the chief impression was from the Greeks. The general effect was to broaden and enlarge the original idea whose tendency was to regard the Supreme Being as a tribal Deity, into the grander universal God, or Father of all. If time permitted it would be a most interesting study to trace the action and reaction of Semitic ideas upon Hellenistic thought. How Hellenistic philosophy produced Pharisaism or the progressive party of the Hebrew Theists; how Pharisaism in turn produced Stoicism, which again prepared the way for Christianity itself.

The whole polity of the Jews was originally favorable to agriculture, and though they adhered to it closely for many centuries, yet the peculiar facilities of their country ultimately forced them largely into commerce. The great caravan routes from the rich countries of the East, Mesopotamia, Shinar, Babylonia, Media, Assyria, and Persia, to the ports of the Mediterranean, lay through Palestine, while Spain, Italy, Gaul, Asia Minor, Northern Africa, Egypt, and all the riches that then clustered around the shores of the Great Sea and upon the islands in its bosom, had easy access to its harbors. In fact, the wealth of the New World, its civilization, refinement, and art lay in concentric circles around Jerusalem as a focal point. The Jewish people grew rich in spite of themselves and gradually forsook their agricultural simplicity.

But more than all things else, their institutions interest mankind. Their laws for the protection of property, the enforcement of industry, and the upholding of the State, were such as afforded the strongest impulse to personal freedom and national vigor. The great principle of their real estate laws was the inalienability of the land. Houses in walled towns might be sold in perpetuity if unredeemed within the year; land only for a limited period. At the year of Jubilee every estate reverted without repurchase to the original owners, and even during this period it might be redeemed by paying the value of the purchase of the year which intervened until the Jubilee. Little as we may now be disposed to value this remarkable agrarian

law, says Dean Milman, it secured the political equality
of the people and anticipated all the mischiefs so fatal to
the early Republics of Greece and Italy, the appropriation
of the whole territory of the State by a rich and powerful
oligarchy, with the consequent convulsing of the community from the deadly struggles between the patrician
and the plebeian orders. In the Hebrew State the im-
provident man might indeed reduce himself and his family
to penury or servitude, but he could not perpetuate a
race of slaves or paupers. Every fifty years God the King
and Lord of the soil, as it were, resumed the whole territory and granted it back in the same portions to the descendants of the original possessors.

It is curious to observe, continues the same author, in
this earliest practical Utopia, the realization of Machia-
velli's great maxim, the constant renovation of a State, according to the first principles of its constitution, a maxim
recognized by our own statesmen, which they designate as
a "frequent recurrence to the first principles." How little we learn that is new. The civil polity of the Jews is so
ultimately blended historically with the ecclesiastical that
the former is not easily comprehended by the ordinary
student. Their Scriptures relate principally to the latter,
and to obtain a knowledge of the other, resort must be
had to the Talmud and the Rabbinical expositions, a task
that few men will lend themselves to, who hope to do anything else in this world. Yet a little study will repay richly
the political student, by showing him the origin of many
excellent seminal principles which we regard as modern.
Their government was in form a theocratic democracy.
God was not only their spiritual but their temporal sovereign also, who promulgated his laws by the mouths of
his inspired prophets. Hence their terrible and un-
flagging denunciations of all forms of idolatry—it was not
only a sin against pure religion, but it was treason also.
In most other particulars there was a democracy far purer
than that of Athens. The very important principle of the
separation of the functions of government was recognized.
The civil and ecclesiastic departments were kept apart, the
civil ruler exercised no ecclesiastic functions, and *vice
versa*. When, as sometimes happened, the two functions
rested in the same man, they were yet exercised differently,

as was not long since our custom in the administration of equity as contradistinguished from law.

Their organic law containing the elements of their polity, though given by God Himself, was yet required to be solemnly ratified by the whole people. This was done on Ebal and Gerizim, and is perhaps the first, as it is certainly the grandest constitutional convention ever held among men. On these two lofty mountains, separated by a deep and narrow ravine, all Israel, comprising three millions of souls, were assembled; elders, prophets, priests, women and children, and 600,000 warriors, led by the spears of Judah and supported by the archers of Benjamin. In this mighty presence, surrounded by the sublime accessories to the grandeur of the same, the law was read by the Levites, line by line, item by item, whilst the tribes on either height signified their acceptance thereof by responsive amens, which pierced the heavens. Of all the great principles established for the happiness and good government of our race, though hallowed by the blood of the bravest and the best, and approved by centuries of trial, no one had a grander origin, or a more glorious exemplification than this one, that all governments derive their just powers from the consent of the governed.

So much for their organic law. Their legislation upon the daily exigencies and development of their society was also provided for on the most radically democratic basis, with the practical elements of representation. The Sanhedrim legislated for all ecclesiastical affairs, and had also original judicial powers and jurisdiction over all offences against the religious law, and appellate jurisdiction of many other offences. It was the principal body of their polity, as religion was the principal object of their constitution. It was thoroughly representative. Local and municipal government was fully recognized. The legislation for a city was done by the elders thereof—the prototypes in name and character of our eldermen or aldermen.

They were the keystone of the whole social fabric, and so directly represented the people that the terms elders and people are often used as synonymous. The legislation for a tribe was done by the princes of that tribe, and the heads of families thereof, whilst the elders of all the cities,

heads of all the families, and princes of all the tribes when
assembled, constituted the National Legislature or Congregation.   The functions of this representative body,
however, were gradually usurped and absorbed by the
Sanhedrim.

So thoroughly recognized was the principle of representation that no man exercised any political rights in his
individual capacity, but only as a member of the house,
which was the basis of the Hebrew polity.   The ascending
scale was the family or collection of houses, the tribe or
collection of families, and the congregation or collection
of tribes.

The kingdom thus composed was in fact a confedera-
tion, and exemplified both its strength and its weakness.
The tribes were equal and sovereign within the sphere of
their individual concerns.   A tribe could convene its own
legislative body at pleasure; so could any number of tribes
convene a joint body whose enactments were binding only
upon the tribes represented therein.   A single tribe or
any number combined could make treaties, form alliances
and wage war, whilst the others remained at peace with
the enemy of their brethren.   They were to all intents
and purposes independent States, joined together for common objects on the principle of federal republics, with a
general government of delegated and limited powers.
Within their tribal boundaries their sovereignty was absolute, minus only the powers granted to the central agent.
They elected their chiefs, generals, and kings.   Next to
the imperative necessity of common defense, their bond of
union was their divine constitution, one religion, and one
blood.   Justice was made simple and was administered
cheaply.   Among no people in this world did the law so
recognize the dignity and sacred nature of man made in
the image of God, and the creature of His especial cove-
nanting care.

The constitution of their criminal courts and their code
of criminal laws was most remarkable.   The researches of
the learned have failed to discover in all antiquity anything
so explicit, so humane, and embracing so many of what
are now considered the essential elements of enlightened
jurisprudence.   Only four offences were punished by
death.   By English law no longer ago than the reign of

George II more than 150 offences were so punishable!
The court for the trial of these capital offenders was the
local Sanhedrim, composed of twenty-three members, who
were both judges and jurors, prosecuting attorneys and
counsel for the accused.

The tests applied both to them and the accusing witnesses as to capacity and impartiality, were more rigid
than those known to exist anywhere else in the world.
The whole procedure was so guarded as to convey the idea
that the first object was to save the criminal.

From the first step of the accusation to the last moment
preceding final execution, no caution was neglected, no
solemnity was omitted, that might aid the prisoner's ac-
quittal. No man in any way interested in the result, no
gamester of any kind, no usurer, no store-dealer, no relative of accused or accuser, no seducer or adulterer, no
man without a fixed trade or business, could sit in this
court. Nor could any aged man whose infirmities might
make him harsh, nor any childless man, or bastard, as
being insensible to the relation of parent and child.

Throughout the whole system of the Jewish government there ran a broad, genuine, and refreshing stream
of democracy such as the world then knew little of, and
has since but little improved. For of course the political
student will not be deceived by names. It matters not
what their chief magistrates and legislators were called
if in fact and in substance their forms were eminently
democratic. Masters of political philosophy tell us—and
tell us with truth—that power in a State must and will
reside with those who own the soil. If the land belongs
to a king, the government is a despotism, though every
man in it voted; if the land belongs to a select few, it is an
aristocracy; but if it belongs to the many, it is a democracy, for here is the division of power. Now, where,
either in the ancient or modern world, will you find such
a democracy as that of Israel? For where was there ever
such a perfect and continuing division of the land among
the people? It was impossible for this power ever to be
concentrated in the hands of one or a select few. The
lands belonged to God as the head of the Jewish nation—
the right of eminent domain, so to speak, was in Him,
and the people were His tenants.

The year of Jubilee, as we have seen, came ever in time to blast the schemes of the ambitious and designing.

Their law provided for no standing army; the common defense was intrusted to the patriotism of the people, who kept and bore arms at will, and believing that their hills and valleys would be best defended by footmen, the use of cavalry was forbidden, lest it should tend to feed the passion for foreign conquest.

The ecclesiastical Sanhedrim, as before observed, was the principal body of their polity; its members were composed of the wisest and most learned of their people, who expounded and enforced the law and supervised all the inferior courts. This exposition upon actual cases arising did not suffice the learned doctors, who made the great mistake which modern courts have learned to avoid, of uttering their dicta in anticipated cases. These decisions and dicta constitute the groundwork of the Talmud, of which there are two collections extant. They constitute the most remarkable aggregation of Oriental wisdom, abstruse learning, piety, blasphemy, and obscenity ever got together in the world; and bear the same relation to the Jewish law which our judiciary decisions do to our statute law. Could they be disentombed from the mass of rubbish by which they are covered, said to be so great as to deter all students who are not willing to devote a lifetime to the task, from entering upon their study, they would no doubt be of inestimable value to theologians by furnishing all the aids which contemporaneous construction must ever import.

Time would not permit me if I had the power, to describe the chief city of the Jews, their religious and political capital—"Jerusalem the Holy"—"the dwelling of peace." In the days of Jewish prosperity it was in all things a fair type of this strange country and people. Enthroned upon the hills of Judah, overflowing with riches, the free-will offerings of a devoted people, decked with the barbaric splendor of Eastern taste, its was the rival in power and wondrous beauty of the most magnificent cities of antiquity. Nearly every one of her great competitors has moldered into dust. The bat and the owl inhabit their towers, and the fox litters her young in the corridors of their palaces, but Jerusalem still sits in solitary grandeur upon the lonely hills, and though faded, feeble, and ruinous, still towers in moral splendor above all the spires and domes and pinnacles ever erected by human hands.   Nor can I dwell, tempting as is the theme, upon the scenery, the glowing landscapes, the cultivated fields, gardens and vineyards, and gurgling fountains of that pleasant land.   Many high summits, and even one of the towers in the walls of the city of Jerusalem, were said to have afforded a perfect view of the whole land from border to border.   I must be content with asking you to imagine what a divine prospect would burst upon the vision from the summit of that stately tower; and picture the burning sands of the desert far beyond the mysterious waters of the Dead Sea on the one hand, and the shining waves of the great sea on the other, flecked with the white sails of the Tyrian ships, whilst hoary Lebanon, crowned with its diadem of perpetual snow, glitters in the morning light like a dome of fire tempered with the emerald of its cedars—a fillet of glory around its brow.

The beauty of that band of God's people, the charm of their songs, the comeliness of their maidens, the celestial peace of their homes, the romance of their national history, and the sublimity of their faith, so entice me, that I would not know when to cease, should I once enter upon their story.   I must leave behind, too, the blood-stained record of their last great siege, illustrated by their splendid but unavailing courage; their fatal dissensions and final destruction, with all its incredible horrors; of their exile and slavery, of their dispersion in all lands and kingdoms, of their persecutions, sufferings, wanderings and despair, for eighteen hundred years.   Indeed, it is a story that puts to shame not only our Christianity, but our common humanity.   It staggers belief to be told, not only that such things could be done at all, by blinded heathen or ferocious pagan, but done by Christian people and in the name of Him, the meek and lowly, who was called the Prince of Peace, and the Harbinger of good will to men. Still it is an instructive story; it seems to mark in colors never to be forgotten both the wickedness and the folly of intolerance.   Truly, it serves to show that the wrath of a religious bigot, is more fearful and ingenious than the cruelest of tortures hatched in the councils of hell.

It is not my purpose to comment upon the religion of the Jews, nor shall I undertake to say that they gave no cause in the earlier ages of Christianity for the hatred of their opponents. Undoubtedly they gave much cause, and themselves exhibited much bitterness and ferocity towards the followers of the Nazarene; which, however it ·may be an excuse, is far from being a justification of the centuries of horror which followed. But if constancy, faithfulness and devotion to principle under the most trying circumstances to which the children of men were ever subjected, be considered virtues, then indeed are the Jews to be admired. They may safely defy the rest of mankind to show such undying adherence to accepted faith, such wholesale sacrifice for conscience sake. For it they have in all ages given up home and country, wives and children, gold and goods, ease and shelter and life; for it they endured all the evils of an infernal wrath for eighteen centuries; for it they have endured, and—say what you will— endured with an inexpressible manhood that which no other portion of the human family ever have, or, in my opinion, ever would have endured. For sixty generations the heritage which the father left the son was misery, suffering, shame, and despair; and that son preserved and handed down to his son that black heritage as a golden heirloom for the sake of God.

A few remarks upon their numbers and present status in the world, their peculiarities and probable destiny, and my task will be done.

Originally, as we have seen, the Jews were an agricultural people, and their civil polity was framed specially for this state of things. Indeed the race of Shem originally seemed not to have been endowed with the great commercial instincts which characterize the descendants of Ham and Japheth. Their cities for the most part were built in the interior, remote from the channels of trade, whilst the race of Ham and Japheth built upon the seashore, and the banks of great rivers. But the exile of the Jews converted them necessarily into merchants. Denied as a general rule citizenship in the land of their refuge, subject at any moment to spoliation and expulsion, their only sure means of living was in traffic, in which they soon became skilled on the principles of a specialty in labor.

They naturally, therefore, followed in their dispersion, as they have ever since done, the great channels of commerce throughout the world, with such deflections here and there as persecution rendered necessary. But notwithstanding the many impulses to which their wanderings have been subjected, they have in the main obeyed the general laws of migration by moving east and west upon nearly the same parallels of latitude. Their numbers, in spite of losses by all causes, including religious defection, which, everything considered, has been remarkably small, have steadily increased, and are now variously estimated at seven to nine millions. They may be divided, says Dr. Pressell, into three great classes, the enumeration of which will show their wonderful dispersion. The first of these inhabit the interior of Africa, Arabia, India, China, Turkestan, and Bokhara. Even the Arabs Mr. Disraeli terms Jews upon horseback. They are, however, the sons of Ishmael, half-brothers to the Jews. These are the lowest of the Jewish people in wealth, intelligence, and religion, though said to be superior to their Gentile neighbors in each. The second and most numerous class is found in Northern Africa, Egypt, Palestine, Syria, Mesopotamia, Persia, Asia Minor, European Turkey, Poland, Russia, and parts of Austria. In these are found the strictly orthodox, Talmudical Jews; the sect Chasidim, who are the representatives of the Zealots of Josephus, and the small but most interesting sect, Karaites, who reject all Rabbinical traditions, and are the only Jews who adhere to the strict letter of the Scriptures. This class is represented as being very ignorant of all except Jewish learning—it being prohibited to study any other. Yet they alone are regarded by scholars as the proper expounders of ancient Talmudical Judaism. As might be inferred from the character of the governments under which they live, their political condition is most unhappy and insecure, and their increase in wealth and their social progress are slow.

The third and last class are those of Central and Western Europe, and the United States. These are by far the most intelligent and civilized of their race, not only keeping pace with the progress of their Gentile neighbors, but contributing to it largely. Their Oriental mysticism seems to have given place to the stronger practical ideas of Western Europe, with which they have come in contact, and they have embraced them fully. They are denominated "reforming" in their tenets, attempting to eliminate the Talmudical traditions which cumber and obscure their creed, and adapt it somewhat to the spirit of the age, though in tearing this away, they have also, say the theologians, dispensed with much of the Old Testament itself. In fact, they have become simply Unitarians or Deists.

Many curious facts concerning them are worthy to be noted. In various cities of the Eastern World they have been for ages, and in some are yet, huddled into crowded and filthy streets or quarters, in a manner violative of all the rules of health, yet it is a notorious fact that they have ever suffered less from pestilential diseases than their Christian neighbors. So often have the black wings of epidemic plagues passed over them, and smitten all around them, that ignorance and malignity frequently accused them of poisoning the wells and fountains and of exercising sorcery.

They have also in a very noticeable degree been exempt from consumption and all diseases of the respiratory functions, which in them are said by physicians to be wonderfully adapted to enduring the vicissitudes of all temperatures and climates. The average duration of Gentile life is computed at twenty-six years—it certainly does not reach thirty; that of the Jew, according to a most interesting table of statistics which I have seen, is full thirty-seven years. The number of infants born to the married couple exceeds that of the Gentile races, and the number dying in infancy is much smaller. In height they are nearly three inches lower than the average of other races; the width of their bodies with outstretched arms is one inch shorter than the height, whilst in other races it is eight inches longer on the average. But on the other hand, the length of the trunk is much greater with the Jew, in proportion to height, than with other races. In the negro the trunk constitutes thirty-two per cent. of the height of the whole body, in the European thirty-four per cent., in the Jew thirty-six per cent. What these physical peculiarities have had to do with their wonderful preservation

and steady increase I leave for the philosophers to explain.

Their social life is, if possible, still more remarkable.
There is neither prostitution nor pauperism, and but little
abject poverty among them. They have some paupers,
it is true, but they trouble neither you nor me. Crime in
the malignant, wilful sense of that word, is exceedingly
rare. I have never known but one Jew convicted of any
offence beyond the grade of a misdemeanor, though, I am
free to say, I have known many a one who would have
been improved by a little hanging. They contribute liber-
ally to all Gentile charities in the communities where they
live; they ask nothing from the Gentiles for their own.
If a Jew is broken down in business, the others set him up
again or give him employment, and his children have
bread. If one is in trouble the others stand by him with
counsel and material aid, remembering the command,
" Thou shalt open thine hand wide unto thine brethren,
and shalt surely lend sufficient for his need in that which
he wanteth." Their average education is far ahead of the
races by whom they are surrounded. I have never seen
an adult Jew who could not read, write, and compute figures—especially the figures. Of the four great human in-
dustries which conduce to the public wealth—agriculture,
manufacturing, mining, and commerce—as a general rule
they engage only in one. They are neither farmers, min-
ers, smiths, carpenters, mechanics or artisans of any kind.
They are merchants only, but as such, own few or no
ships, and they are rarely carriers of any kind. They
wander over the whole earth, but they are never pioneers,
and they found no colonies, because, as I suppose, being
devoted to one business only, they lack the self-sustaining
elements of those who build new States; and whilst they
engage individually in politics where they are not disfran-
chised, and contend for offices and honors like other people, they yet seek nowhere political power or national
aggregation. Dealers in every kind of merchandise, with
rare exceptions they manufacture none. They dwell exclusively in towns, cities, and villages, but as a general rule
do not own the property they live upon. They marry
within themselves entirely, and yet in defiance of well-
known natural laws with regard to breeding " in and in,"

their race does not degenerate. With them family government is perhaps more supreme than with any other people. Divorce, domestic discord, and disobedience to parents are almost unknown among them.

The process by which they have become the leading merchants, bankers, and financiers of the world is explained by their history. In many places their children were not permitted to enter the schools, or even to be enrolled in the guilds of labor. Trade was therefore the only avenue left open to them. In most countries they dared not or could not own the soil. Why a nation of original agriculturists ceased to cultivate the soil altogether is therefore only seemingly inexplicable. All nations must have a certain proportion of the population engaged in tilling the soil; since the Jews have no common country they reside in all; and in all countries they have the shrewdness to see that whilst it is most honorable to plow, yet all men live more comfortably than the plowman. In addition to which, as before intimated, agriculture so fixed them to the soil that it would have been impossible to evade persecution and spoliation. They were constantly on the move, and their wealth must therefore be portable and easily secreted—hence their early celebrity as lapidaries, dealers in diamonds and precious stones, and hence too, the introduction of "bills of exchange." The utility of these great aids to commerce had long been known to the world, perhaps by both Greeks and Romans, but could never be made available by them because confidence in the integrity of each other did not exist between the drawer and the drawee. But this integrity which the lordly merchants of the Christian and the Pagan world could not inspire, was found to exist in the persecuted and despised Jew. So much for the lessons of adversity. These arts diligently applied, at first from necessity, afterwards from choice, in the course of centuries made the Jews skilful above all men in the ways of merchandise and money-changing, and finally developed in them those peculiar faculties and aptitudes for a calling which are brought out as well in man by the special education of successive generations as in the lower animals. The Jew merchant had this advantage, too, that, whereas his Gentile competitor belonged to a consolidated nation, con-

fined to certain geographical limits, speaking a certain
tongue, the aid, sympathy, and influence which he derived
from social and political ties were also confined to the
limits of his nation, while the Jew merchant belonged to a
scattered nation, spread out over the whole earth, speaking many tongues, and welded together, not by social ties
alone, but by the fierce fires of suffering and persecution;
and the aid, sympathy, influence and information which he
derived therefrom came out of the utmost parts of the
earth.

When after many centuries the flames of persecution
had abated so that the Jews were permitted more than
bare life, their industry, energy, and talent soon placed
them among the important motive powers of the world.
They entered the fields of commerce in its grandest and
most colossal operations. They became the friends and
counselors of kings, the prime ministers of empires, the
treasurers of republics, the movers of armies, the arbiters
of public credit, the patrons of art, and the critics of literature. We do not forget the time in the near past when
the peace of Europe—of the world—hung upon the
Jewish Prime Minister of England. No people are so
ready to accommodate themselves to circumstances. It
was but recently that we heard of an English Jew taking
an absolute lease of the ancient Persian Empire. The
single family of Rothschild, the progeny of a poor German Jew, who three generations ago sold curious old
coins under the sign of a red shield, are now the possessors of greater wealth and power than was Solomon, when
he could send 1,300,000 fighting men into the field.

Twenty years ago, when this family was in the height
of its power, perhaps no sovereign in Europe could have
waged a successful war against its united will. Two centuries since, the ancestors of these Jewish money kings
were skulking in the caverns of the earth or hiding in the
squalid outskirts of persecuting cities. Nor let it be supposed that it is in this field alone we see the great effects
of Jewish intellect and energy. The genius which showed
itself capable of controlling the financial affairs of the
world necessarily carried with it other great powers and
capabilities. The Jews, in fact, under most adverse circumstances, made their mark—a high and noble mark—in

every other department of human affairs.   Christian
clergymen have sat at the feet of their rabbis to be taught
the mystic learning of the East; Senates have been en-
raptured by the eloquence of Jewish orators; courts have
been convinced by the acumen and learning of Jewish
lawyers; vast throngs excited to the wildest enthusiasm
by Jewish histrionic and æsthetic art; Jewish science has
helped to number the stars in their courses, to loose the
bands of Orion and to guide Arcturus with his sons.

Jewish literature has delighted and instructed all classes
of mankind, and the world has listened with rapture and
with tears to Jewish melody and song.   For never since
its spirit was evoked under the shadow of the vines on
the hills of Palestine to soothe the melancholy of her
King, has Judah's harp, whether in freedom or captivity,
in sorrow or joy, ceased to wake the witchery of its tuneful
strings.

Time forbids that I should even name the greatest of
those who have distinguished themselves and made good
their claim to rank with the foremost of earth.   No section of the human family can boast a greater list of men
and women entitled to be placed among the true children
of genius—going to make up the primacy of our race—
in every branch of human affairs, in every phase of human
civilization.   Mr. Draper says that for four hundred years
of the Middle Ages—ages more dark and terrible to them
than to any others—they took the most philosophical
and comprehensive view of things of all European people.

On the whole, and after due deliberation, I think it
may be truthfully said, that there is more of average
wealth, intelligence, and morality among the Jewish people than there is among any other nation of equal numbers in the world!   If this be true—if it be half true—
when we consider the circumstances under which it has all
been brought about, it constitutes in the eyes of thinking
men the most remarkable moral phenomenon ever exhibited by any portion of the human family.   For not only
has the world given the Jew no help, but all that he has
ever received, and that but rarely, was to be left alone.
To escape the sword, the rack, the fire, and utter spoiling
of his goods, has indeed, for centuries, been to him a

blessed heritage, as the shadow of a great rock in a weary
land.   .

The physical persecution of the Jews has measurably
ceased among all nations of the highest civilization.
There is no longer any proscription left upon their political rights in any land where the English tongue is
spoken. I am proud of the fact. But there remains
among us an unreasonable prejudice of which I am heartily ashamed. Our toleration will not be complete until we
put it away also, as well as the old implements of physical
torture.

This age, and these United States in particular, so
boastful of toleration, present some curious evidences of
the fact that the old spirit is not dead, evidences tending
much to show that the prejudices of 2,000 years ago are
still with us. In Germany, a land more than all others
indebted to the genius and loyal energy of the Jews, a
vast uprising against them was lately excited, for the sole
reason, so far as one can judge, that they occupy too many
places of learning and honor, and are becoming too rich!

In this, our own free and tolerant land, where wars
have been waged and constitutions violated for the benefit
of the African negro, the descendants of barbarian tribes
who for 4,000 years have contributed nothing to, though
in close contact with, the civilization of mankind, save as
the Helots contributed an example to the Spartan youth,
and where laws and partisan courts alike have been used
to force him into an equality with those whom he could
not equal, we have seen Jews, educated and respectable
men, descendants of those from whom we derive our
civilization, kinsmen after the flesh of Him whom we
esteem as the Son of God and Savior of men, ignominiously ejected from hotels and watering-places as unworthy
the association of men who had grown rich by the sale of
a new brand of soap or an improved rat-trap!

I have never heard of one of these indecent thrusts at
the Jews without thinking of the dying words of Sergeant
Bothwell when he saw his life's current dripping from the
sword of Burleigh: "Base peasant churl, thou hast spilt
the blood of a line of kings."

Let us learn to judge the Jew, as we judge other men,
by his merits. And above all, let us cease the abominable

injustice of holding the class responsible for the sins of the individual. We apply the test to no other people. Our principal excuse for disliking him now is that we have injured him. The true gentleman, Jew or Gentile, will always recognize the true gentleman, Jew or Gentile, and will refuse to consort with an ill-bred impostor, Jew or Gentile, simply because he is an ill-bred impostor. The impudence of the low-bred Jew is not one whit more detestable than the impudence of the low-bred Gentile, children of shoddy, who, by countless thousands, swarm into doors opened for them by our democracy. Let us cry quits on that score. Let us judge each other by our best not our worst samples, and when we find gold, let us recognize it. Let us prove all things and hold fast that which is good.

While it is a matter of just pride to us that there is neither physical persecution nor legal proscription left upon the civil rights of the Jews in any land where the English tongue is spoken, or the English law obtains, yet I consider it a grave reproach, not only to us, but to all Christendom, that such injustice is permitted anywhere. The recent barbarities inflicted upon them in Russia revive the recollection of the darkest cruelties of the Middle Ages. That is one crying outrage, one damned spot that blackens the fair light of the Nineteenth century without the semblance of excuse or the shadow of justification. That glare of burning homes, those shrieks of outraged women, those wailings of orphan children, go up to God, not only as witnesses against the wretched savages who perpetrate them, but as accusations also of those who permit them. How sad it is again to hear that old cry of Jewish sorrow, which we had hoped to hear no more forever! How shameful it is to know that within the shadow of so-called Christian churches there are yet dark places filled with the habitations of cruelty. No considerations of diplomacy or international courtesy should for one moment stand in the way of their stern and instant suppression. The Jews are our spiritual fathers, the authors of our morals, the founders of our civilization with all the power and dominion arising therefrom, and the great peoples professing Christianity and imbued with any of its noble spirit should see to it that justice and protection

are afforded them.   By simply speaking with one voice it
could be done, for no power on earth could resist that
voice.   Every consideration of humanity and international
policy demands it.   Their unspeakable misfortunes, their
inherited woes, their very helplessness, appeal to our
Christian chivalry, trumpet-tongued in behalf of those
wretched victims of a prejudice for which tolerant Christianity is not altogether irresponsible.

There are objections to the Jew as a citizen; many objections, some true, and some false, some serious and some
trivial.   It is said that industrially he produces nothing,
invents nothing, adds nothing to the public wealth; that
he will not own real estate nor take upon himself those
permanent ties which beget patriotism and become the
hostages of good citizenship; that he merely sojourns in
the land and does not dwell in it, but is ever in light
marching order, and is ready to flit when the word comes
to go.   These are true objections in the main, and serious
ones, but I submit the fault is not his, even here.

> Quoth old Mazeppa: " Ill betide,
> The school wherein I learned to ride."

These habits he learned by persecution.   He dwelt
everywhere in fear and trembling and had no assurance
of his life.   He was ever ready to leave, because at any
moment he might be compelled to choose between leaving
and death.   He built no house, because at any moment
he and his little ones might be thrust out of it to perish.
He cherished no love for the land because it cherished
none for him, but was cruel and hard and bitter to him.
And yet history shows that in every land where he has
been protected he has been a faithful and zealous patriot.
Also since his rights have been secured he has begun to
show the same permanent attachments to the soil as other
people, and is rapidly building houses, and in some places
cultivating farms.   These objections he is rapidly removing since we have removed their cause.

So, too, the impression is sought to be made that he is
dishonest in his dealings with the Gentiles, insincere in his
professions, servile to his superiors, and tyrannical to his
inferiors, Oriental in his habit and manner.   That the

Jew—meaning the class—is dishonest I believe to be an atrocious calumny; and, considering that we derive all our notions of rectitude from the Jew who first taught the world that command, "Thou shalt not steal," and "Thou shalt not bear false witness," we pay ourselves a shabby compliment in thus befouling our teachers. Undoubtedly there are Jewish scoundrels in great abundance; undoubtedly also there are Gentile scoundrels in greater abundance. Southern reconstruction put that fact beyond a peradventure. But our own scoundrels are orthodox, Jewish scoundrels are unbelievers—that is the difference. If a man robs me I should thank him that he denies my creed also. He compliments both me and it by the denial. The popular habit is to regard an injury done to one by a man of different creed as a double wrong; to me it seems that the wrong is the greater coming from my own. To hold also, as some do, that the sins of all people are due to their creeds, would leave the sins of the sinner of my creed quite unaccounted for. With some the faith of a scoundrel is all-important; it is not so with me.

All manner of crimes, including perjury, cheating, and overreaching in trade, are unhesitatingly attributed to the Jews, generally by their rivals in trade. Yet somehow they are rarely proven to the satisfaction of even Gentile judges and juries. The gallows clutches but few, nor are they found in the jails and penitentiaries—a species of real estate which I honor them for not investing in. I admit that there was and is perhaps now a remnant of the feeling that it was legal to spoil the Egyptians. Their constant life of persecution would naturally inspire this feeling; their present life of toleration and their business estimate of the value of character will as naturally remove it. Again and again, day by day, we evince our Gentile superiority in the tricks of trade and sharp practice. It is asserted by our proverbial exclamation in regard to a particular piece of villainy "That beats the Jews!" And I call your attention to the further fact that, sharp as they undoubtedly are, they have found it impossible to make a living in New England. Outside of Boston, not fifty perhaps can be found in all that land of unsuspecting integrity and modest righteousness. They have managed to endure with long suffering patience the knout of the Czar and the bowstring of the Turk, but they have fled for life from the presence of the wooden nutmeg and the left-handed gimlets of Jonathan. Is there any man who hears me to-night who, if a Yankee and a Jew were to "lock horns" in a regular encounter of commercial wits, would not give large odds on the Yankee? My own opinion is that the genuine "guessing" Yankee, with a jack-knife and a pine shingle could in two hours time whittle the smartest Jew in New York out of his homestead in the Abrahamic covenant.

I agree with Lord Macaulay that the Jew is what we have made him. If he is a bad job, in all honesty we should contemplate him as the handiwork of our own civilization. If there be indeed guile upon his lips or servility in his manner, we should remember that such are the legitimate fruits of oppression and wrong, and that they have been, since the pride of Judah was broken and his strength scattered, his only means of turning aside the uplifted sword and the poised javelin of him who sought to plunder and slay. Indeed, so long has he schemed and shifted to avoid injustice and cruelty, that we can perceive in him all the restless watchfulness which characterizes the hunted animal.

To this day the cast of the Jew's features in repose is habitually grave and sad, as though the very ploughshare of sorrow had marked its furrows across their faces forever.

> "And where shall Israel lave her bleeding feet?
> And when shall Zion's songs again seem sweet,
> And Judah's melody once more rejoice
> The heart that leaped before its heavenly voice?
> Tribes of the wandering foot and weary heart
> How shall ye flee away and be at rest?
> The wild dove hath her nest—the fox his cave—
> Mankind their country—Israel but the grave."

The hardness of Christian prejudice having dissolved, so will that of the Jew. The hammer of persecution having ceased to beat upon the iron mass of their stubbornness, it will cease to consolidate and harden, and the main strength of their exclusion and preservation will have been lost. They will perhaps learn that one sentence of our Lord's Prayer, which it is said is not to be found in the Talmud, and which is the keynote of the difference between Jew and Gentile, "Forgive us our trespasses as we forgive them who trespass against us."

If so, they will become as other men, and taking their harps down from the willows, no longer refuse to sing the songs of Zion because they are captives in a strange land.

I believe that there is a morning to open yet for the Jews, in Heaven's good time, and if that opening shall be in any way commensurate with the darkness of the night through which they have passed, it will be the brightest that ever dawned upon a faithful people.

I have stood on the summit of the very monarch of our Southern Alleghanies and seen the night flee away before the chariot wheels of the God of day. The stars receded before the pillars of lambent fire that pierced the zenith, a thousand ragged mountain peaks began to peer up from the abysmal darkness, each looking through the vapory seas that filled the gorges like an island whose "jutting and confounded base was swelled by the wild and wasteful ocean." As the curtain was lifted more and more and the eastern brightness grew in radiance and glory, animate nature prepared to receive her Lord; the tiny snowbird from its nest in the turf began chirping to its young; the silver pheasant sounded its morning drumbeat for its mate in the boughs of the fragrant fir; the dun deer rising slowly from his mossy couch and stretching himself in graceful curves, began to crop the tender herbage; whilst the lordly eagle rising straight upward from his home on the crag, with pinions widespread, bared his golden breast to the yellow beams and screamed his welcome to the sun in his coming! Soon the vapors of the night were lifted up on the shafts of fire, rolling and seething in billows of refulgent flame, until when far overhead, they were caught upon the wings of the morning breeze and swept away, perfect day was established, and there was peace. So may it be with this long-suffering and immortal people. So may the real spirit of Christ yet be so triumphantly infused amongst those who profess to obey his teachings, that with one voice and one hand they will stay the persecutions and hush the sorrows of these their wondrous kins-

men, put them forward into the places of honor, and the
homes of love, where all the lands in which they dwell shall
be not home to them alone, but to all the children of
men who, through much tribulation and with heroic manhood have waited for this dawning, with a faith whose constant cry through all the dreary watches of the night has
been, " Though He slay me, yet will I trust in Him."

" Roll golden sun, roll swiftly toward the west,
    Dawn happy day when many woes shall cease;
Come quickly Lord, thy people wait the rest
        Of Thine abiding peace!

" No more, no more to hunger here for love;
No more to thirst for blessings long denied.
Judah! Thy face is foul with weeping, but above
        Thou shalt be satisfied! "

JOHN WATSON

Photogravure after a photograph from life

JOHN WATSON

("IAN MACLAREN")

SCOTTISH TRAITS

[Lecture by John Watson—" Ian Maclaren "—clergyman and author, Presbyterian minister in Liverpool since 1880 (born in Manningtree, Scotland, November 3, 1850; ————), delivered in various places during Mr. Watson's tour of the United States in 1896-97.]

LADIES AND GENTLEMEN:—I shall have the pleasure of speaking to you about certain traits of character of the people of my nation. One of the first traits I shall illustrate is their humor. We are, I hope, a Christian people, but I am certain that our Christianity has been tested a good many times by that often repeated proverb of Sidney Smith's that it takes a surgical operation to get a joke into a Scotchman's head. [Laughter.]

A recent writer, whom I cannot identify, and whose name I do not want to know, denies that there is anything in our humor that is light in touch, delicate and graceful. He asserts instead that there is much that is austere and awkward, tiresome, and unpleasant. Now each nation takes its own humor in its own way, some joyously, some seriously, but none more conscientiously than the Scotch.

When an Englishman sees a joke in the distance, he immediately capitulates and laughs right out. He takes it home for the enjoyment of the family, and perhaps the neighbors hear it through the doors. Then for days afterwards the man who captured it shares it with his fellow passengers in conveyances, possibly impressing it forcibly upon them. In the Scotch mind, when a jest pre-

sents itself, the question arises, "Is it a jest at all?" and
it is given a careful and analytical examination, and if,
after twenty-four hours, it continues to appear to be a jest,
it is accepted and done much honor.   Even then it may
not cause a laugh.   As some grief is too deep for tears, so
some humor is appreciated without demonstration, and,
again, as all soils are not productive of the same fruit, so
each country has its own particular humor.   Understand
the humor of a nation and you have understood its character and its traditions, and even had some sort of an insight into its grief.

If you want the most beautiful flower of humor, wit, you
must go to France for it.   There is no wit so subtle, so
finished, so complete as the French wit, especially the wit
of the Parisian.   There you will find what might be termed
the aristocracy of wit.

What I mean by wit is this: Two men were riding together one day through Paris.   One was exceedingly
bright and clever, while the other was correspondingly
dull.   As is usually the case, the latter monopolized the
conversation.   The talk of the dullard had become almost
unendurable, when his companion saw a man on the street
far ahead yawning.   "Look," he exclaimed, "we are
overheard!"   [Laughter.]

That story divides the sheep from the goats.   I was
telling it once to a Scotch lady, who remarked: "How
could they have been overheard at that distance?"
"Madam," I replied, "that never occurred to me before."
[Renewed laughter.]

The Scotch have no wit.   Life to them has been too
intense and too bitter a struggle for the production of
humor of the French kind.   Neither have they drollery,
which is the result of standing the intellect upon its head,
so that it sees things bottom upwards.   This is the possession of the Irish; not the North Irish, who are only
Scotch people who went over to Ireland to be born; but
the South Irishman, the Milesian, who sees things upside
down habitually.   It is because of drollery that these lovable, kind-hearted people are so irresistible.

An Irishman was once sent to deliver a live hare, which
escaped and started to run for its liberty.   The Irishman
made no attempt at pursuit.   Not he.   He simply shook

his sides with laughter, while he exclaimed: "Ye may run, ye may run and kape on running, but small good it'll do yez. Ye haven't got the address!" [Laughter and applause.]

We Scotch have not the most democratic form of humor, which is called "fun." Fun seems to be the possession of the English race. Fun is John Bull's idea of humor, and there is no intellectual judgment in fun. Everybody understands it because it is practical. More than that, it unites all classes and sweetens even political life. To study the elemental form of English humor, you must look to the schoolboy. It begins with the practical joke, and unless there is something of this nature about it, it is never humor to an Englishman. In an English household, fun is going all the time. The entire house resounds with it. The father comes home and the whole family contribute to the amusement; puns, humorous uses of words, little things that are meaningless nonsense, if you like, fly round, and everyone enjoys them thoroughly for just what they are. The Scotch are devoid of this trait, and the Americans seem to be, too.

If I had the power to give humor to the nations I would not give them drollery, for that is impractical; I would not give them wit, for that is aristocratic and many minds cannot grasp it; but I would be contented to deal out fun, which has no intellectual element, no subtlety, belongs to old and young, educated and uneducated alike, and is the natural form of the humor of the Englishman.

Let me tell you why the Englishman speaks only one language. He believes with the strongest conviction that his own tongue is the one that all people ought to speak and will come in time to speak, so what is the use of learning any other? He believes, too, that he is appointed by Providence to be a governor of all the rest of the human race. From our Scottish standpoint we can never see an Englishman without thinking that there is oozing from every pore of his body the conviction that he belongs to a governing race. It has not been his desire that large portions of the world should be under his care, but as they have been thrust upon him in the proceedings of a wise Providence, he must discharge his duty. This theory hasn't endeared him to others of his kind, but that isn't

a matter that concerns him.   He doesn't learn any other
language because he knows that he could speak it only so
imperfectly that other people would laugh at him, and it
would never do that a person of his importance in the
scheme of the universe should be made the object of ridicule.

An Englishman and a German were once speaking of
this subject, and the latter asked the former why it was
that Englishmen did not speak as good French as the
Germans, to which the Englishman replied: "I'll tell
you why.   If Napoleon Bonaparte had come twice to our
nation to teach us his language, we would speak it as well
as you do."

Here is another sample of the English jest.   The Duke
of Wellington was once introduced by King Louis Phi-
lippe to a marshal whose troops the Duke had whipped in
the Peninsula.   The marshal gruffly refused the Duke's
hand, turned and walked away, while the Duke said:
" Excuse him, your Majesty, I taught him that lesson."
[Applause.]

But English humor consists of fair fighting, hitting
above the belt.   It is healthy fun, that has made family
life happy, taken precociousness out of boys, and enabled
the Englishman to give his neighbor a slap when he
needed a slap, and no hard feelings.

If I may venture to say anything of American humor,
I would say that it has two conspicuous qualities.   The
one is its largeness.   It is humor on a great scale, which
I presume is due to the three thousand miles between San
Francisco and New York.   We live in a small, poor country, and our humor is thrifty; your country is large and
rich, and your humor is extravagant.   The other quality
of your humor is its omissions, which perhaps is due to
the fact that, having so huge a country, you cannot travel
through it in daylight.   So in your humor you give the
first and last chapters of a jest, which is like a railroad
journey across this big country, much of the time spent in
sleep, but with frequent sudden awakenings.   [Applause.]
But did it ever occur to you that you Americans are a
terribly serious people?   Your comic papers, for example, contain almost no genuine fun.   They leave a bitter taste.   The fun is there for a purpose; it is bitter, well-

nigh malignant. The items hit, as well as raise a laugh, and they never lack an ulterior motive. You are too busy; you put out too much nervous energy; your life is too tense to make pure fun for the pleasure of it; such, for example, as is found in our " Punch."

There is one department still left, perhaps the most severely intellectual of all. It is irony. In irony there is a sense of the paradox of things, the unexpectedness of things, the conjunction of joy and sorrow, the sense of the unseen. The Scotch literature and life are exceedingly rich in irony. It has come from the bitter indignation of a people who have seen some amazing absurdity or wrong. Hence, the sair laugh of the Scotchman is a bitter laugh, not on the outside, but on the inside, and deep down. Irony is the most profound form of humor, and in that department of humor the Scotch are unexcelled. The Scotchman has to plow ground that is more stones than earth, he has to harvest his crops out of the teeth of the snow storm, three centuries of the sternest Calvinism are behind him, his life has been a continual struggle and surprise, and all these things have taught him the irony of life.

Let an Englishman and a Scotchman come together for a bit of banter. The Englishman asks the Scot why so many of his people go abroad and never return to their native land. The Scotchman tells the Englishman that it is for the good of the world. Then he retorts by telling the Englishman that just across the border is a city in Scotland composed of 30,000 Englishmen. The Englishman is incredulous, until the Scotchman tells him that the name of the town is Bannockburn, that the same Englishmen have been inhabiting it for several centuries, and that they are among the most peaceful and law-abiding citizens of Scotland. Then the Scotchman wants to be alone for a couple of minutes to enjoy the taste of that in his mouth.

A Scot's humor is always grim because he is always in contact with the tragedy of life. A Scotchman goes out to play golf. He is annoyed by a slow player who is ahead of him on the links, and tells his caddie to gather up the sticks and go back to the club, as he does not want to follow a funeral procession all day. The caddie replies, after thought: " Ah noo! Dinna be hasty. He might drop deid afore he has gone three holes." Is there any nation like this, sensible always of the divinities hanging over them? [Applause.]

Scotch humor is always dry and never sweet; always biting and never consoling. There was a Scotch woman whose husband was sick. Although she attended the church of the Rev. Norman McLeod, she sent for another minister to administer spiritual advice to her husband. The minister came and discovered that the man was suffering from typhus fever. In speaking to the wife he asked her what church she attended. She replied that she went to Norman's church.

"Then why did you not have him come?" was the query.

"Why," answered the woman, " do you think we would risk Normie with the typhus fever?" [Laughter and applause.]

The grimmest example of Scotch humor that I ever heard is this story that was told me of a criminal who was condemned to death. Just before the execution his counsel went to see him for the purpose of cheering him up. He told the Scot that sentence had been pronounced, it was perfectly just, and he must hope for no mercy, but he asked if there were anything he could do for him. The condemned man thanked him, said he was most kind, and there was one request he would make.

"What is that?" asked his visitor.

"I would ask you to go to my chest and fetch my Sabbath blacks?"

"And what do you want with your Sabbath blacks?"

"I wish to wear them as a mark of respect for the deceased," said the condemned man. [Applause.]

I will pass on and claim for the Sotchman what no one has ever denied him, although rarely understood, and that is that he is cautious. I will put the phrase in its commonest form, and say that he is canny. We say, not a cautious Scot, but a " canny " Scot. What is canny? you ask. Well, I will leave that answer to any man who has ever done business with a Scotchman. A Scotchman in business is not a creature of impulses; he makes sound bargains. He is perfectly honorable and will not go back on a bargain once made, but I do not think he is accustomed to be bested in a bargain.   It is said that it takes two Jews to outwit a Greek, and two Greeks to outwit an Armenian, and yet an Armenian went to the town of Aberdeen in Scotland and in two weeks had not a dollar. [Laughter.]   Canniness is merely the attitude of a man's mind who has to watch hard to get a harvest.   The Scotchman has acquired the quality from being plundered by the Highlandmen above, the English below, while the French, overseas, were trying to annex his country, and so he has learned to stand with his back to the wall to prevent anybody from getting behind him.   This has made him watchful and self-controlled.   That is "canny."   So this has come to be the intellectual attitude also of the Scotch people and it makes them watchful, careful, and self-controlled.

I should like to emphasize the fact that there are really two nations in Scotland: there is the Lowland Scot and there is the Celtic Scot—the man of Midlothian and Edinburgh, and the man in the district beyond Inverness.   It is the northern Scot that wears the kilt, plays the bagpipes and speaks in Gaelic.   Now, every single virtue which the Lowland Scot has in abundance, the Celtic Scot largely wants, and every little frailty which the Lowland Scot has—if he has any—is wanting in the character of the Celts.   I have already spoken to you of Scottish cautiousness, but the Highlanders are rash and impulsive.   The Lowlander is a good man of business, the Highlander a good man of war.   The Highlander is a good sportsman and a good soldier.   The humor of the Highlander again is entirely different from that of the Lowlander.

Another characteristic of the Scotchman is that he will admit nothing.   He is so careful in picking out his words that never is there room to get back of one of his statements and push it from its citadel.   It is cruel to try to get an admission or an agreement to any statement from a Scot.   Be satisfied if, when you say to Sandy, "You have a splendid crop," he replies, "It might have been waur."   I have tried to get definite answers from Scotchmen, and I know whereof I speak.   I have striven for weeks to get a Scotchman to admit something—on the weather, on the crops, on anything—but he never would make an admission.

An Englishman meets a Scotchman in a pouring rain and remarks that it is a regular deluge. The Scotchman does not say that it is a deluge, in the first place because there will never be another. The most that you are likely to get him to admit is that "If it were gaun to keep on as it's doing, it might be wet afore evening." And he can retreat from that! [Laughter and applause.]

The vice of the adjective has never been the vice of a Scotch mind, which lacks the effusiveness of more southern nations. The reason why a Scotchman has so much trouble in speaking is because he makes the fitting of a noun with an adjective a matter of conscience. An Englishman puts his hand in a bag and takes out half a dozen adjectives and uses them all. The Scotchman knows every one of the words, but does not use them, because he would have to go over the entire list before persuaded which one to use, and this requires too much time.

Conversation in Scotland is a game at chess, and a game played cautiously, move by move, in prospect of an intellectual checkmate. The idea of conversation in Scotland is argument over subjects political or theological, preferably the latter, because there is such a chance to dispute—and to get hold with your teeth. There is none of the rattling, small talk in which some other nations indulge. A Scotchman will carry on an argument even unto death. He can make religious distinctions that no one else can see. He has sharpness, for his sword has been whetted for centuries with argument. The very power of brain which he has acquired by use in this way serves him well in the business world.

To illustrate the extraordinary argumentativeness of the Scots there is a story of a Scotchman who lay dying in a London hospital. A woman visitor wanted to sing him some hymns, but he told her that he had all his life fought against using hymn tunes in the service of God, but he was willing to argue the question with her as long as his senses remained. I say that when a man in the face of death is willing to stand for the truth as it has been taught to him, it is out of such stuff that heroes are made. [Applause.]

Controversy is Scotland's great national game. Some people say that golf is our national sport. We play golf, but we play it and say nothing about it. Other nations play it a little and talk about it a great deal. [Laughter.] But our real sport, our great national pastime, is heresy hunting—and we hunt a heretic according to huntsman's rules. A heresy case is meat and drink to a Scot. We even keep a choice selection of heretics on hand to use in times of scarcity. [Applause.] Every one reads the newspaper accounts of a heresy case, and no one bears the least ill-will to the heretic. I have heard of a kirk where, when a moderator was to be elected, although there had been dissensions without bitterness during the year, "the whole congregation felt bound to this man by the ties of rebellion." The Scotch nation, to a greater degree than any other, is ecclesiastical or theological, for all Scots are either pillars in the church or buttresses outside. Yes, and for various reasons. One is that the Scotchman regards the fear of God as the deepest thing in human knowledge, and that a man cannot have a religion that has got no reason in it and no principle. Again, the Scotchman takes to theology like a duck to water, because it affords him the best opportunity he can get for discussion and argument. Intellect is like a razor, and it matters not what the grindstone is. But there is no better grindstone for the intellect than the Shorter Catechism. Our whole nation, in fact, rejoices in theology. It is the national enjoyment of the Scottish people.

I have heard of a Scottish farmer who kept up a discussion on the topic of "faith or work" during a ten mile railway journey, dismounted at the end of it, and as the train was moving off called out to his antagonist: "I dinna deny what ye brocht forward from the Romans, but I take my stand here and now (he was holding on to a railway post) on the Epistle of James." [Applause.] Now, if working farmers can conduct a discussion of that kind, and conduct it well, after dinner, what cannot such a nation in its serious moments do before dinner?

The reason a Scotchman takes to theology is because he is determined to reason things out. Theology affords the strongest grip for his teeth, and he can get the biggest mouthful. Leave a Scot to the freedom of his own will

and he makes for theology at once.   Other things he is
obliged to talk about.   Theology he loves to talk about.
Whenever or wherever Scotchmen meet, and there is no
particular business on hand, they go as naturally into
theology as a cow into clover, and if there are not enough
of the heterodox kind present, some will take that side
just to keep things a-going.

Another tendency of the Scotch is to go to law.   For
centuries, when there was no other amusement or diver-
sion for a Scotchman, he could engage in a lawsuit.

The Scottish people have long been noted for their
austerity and for the respect shown to the Sabbath.   I
will leave it to my audience to say whether it has been
the weakest or the strongest nations of the earth which
have kept the Sabbath.   Did not the American forefath-
ers themselves consecrate Sunday as a day of rest and
keep it with the utmost strictness?

Another Scottish trait is "dourness," defined in the dic-
tionary as "obstinacy."   This is hardly adequate to express the truth.   I had rather deal with a dozen obstinate
men than with one dour Scotchman.   Dourness is obstinacy raised to the eighth power.   It is one hundred
obstinate people rolled into one.   It fills me with despair
to try to explain it.   If I could present the picture of a
Highland cow, with her calf by her side, watching the approach of a tourist whom she thinks is coming too near—
could I depict the expression of her face, that, I would say,
would fairly represent what is meant by "dour."   Not
that the cow would take the aggressive, but, if interfered
with, I'll warrant she would not be the one permanently
injured.   Led by this trait a certain Scotchman always
stood up during prayers when others were kneeling, and
sat down when others stood to sing, because, as he expressed it, the ordinary method was the only one used by
the English and he wasn't going to do as they did.

Let the Scotch alone and there are no more civil people
in the world, but let some one come bringing them a new
faith, or let the tyrant try to oppress, and they resist to the
end.   There were Scotch martyrs, but they nearly always
designed it so that when they went to their death some one
who brought it about went along with them.   But if you
take a Scotchman on the right side, flatter him and tell

him that you want to be his friend, he is too soft, you can do anything with him, and herein is the inconsistency of his nature. You trust us and you may use us as you please, but take us on the wrong side, try to make us do what we do not want to do, and we would not yield an inch if you proposed the most reasonable thing in the universe. But unless a nation has a backbone, it deserves no honor. [Applause.]

It would not be well if I did not make a plea for the bright intelligence of the common people of Scotland. It is owing to their intelligence, together with other hardy virtues, that our people have had some measure of success. It is because of his intelligence that the Scotchman may be said to have three yards start over his competitors in the race. There is no other nation where the country people and the laboring classes of the city have such general educational facilities. The result of this education is that when a Scot leaves his country he goes by law of Divine Providence to improve other countries. You will not find him a scavenger or day laborer, but a skilled artisan; not a cheap clerk, but rising in the firm with an eye on a junior partnership.

One man, John Knox, is responsible for this Scotch system of education. Your nation had its leader, whom you reverence as the "Father of His Country." Israel had its Moses; Germany her Martin Luther; and Scotland stands to-day an eternal monument to the foresight and determination of a single man—John Knox. It was he, who, in his capacity as a political and social reformer, laid down the same principle in Scotland which you have recognized here—that if a nation is to succeed, it must be educated. It was he who, in the sixteenth century, devised a system of education in which every parish should have its school and every boy should attend that school. Successful there, he was to have been sent by the state to a higher school and thence to a university. The system failed because three-fifths of the money appropriated for it went to the Scottish noblemen. Although I cannot prove it, I feel certain that Knox's scheme must have been known to the founders of the American system of public schools and must have had some influence upon the creation of the American school system. To the influence of John Knox on the Scottish people is due the fact that they are an intellectual race to-day. John Knox took the educational ladder and put its lowest round at the door-sill of the shepherd's cottage and the highest at the door to the university. [Applause.]

The Scotchman regards only two things with absolute reverence. Money is not one of them. His religion is one, learning is the other. If one had pointed out a millionaire in Drumtochty, nobody would have turned his head, but Jamie Souter would have run up a hill to see the back of a scholar disappearing in the distance. [Applause.]

Come with me where the heather rolls in purple billows. Come with me to a district which some of you know or of which you have heard, any Highland glen you can think of or of which you have read. Here is a shepherd's cottage, on top of which the mosses grow. Stooping, we enter the doorway and are shown into the best room, where, in striking contrast to the rest of the poor furniture, is a shelf of calf-bound books. The shepherd's wife is in reality most anxious to have you examine these books and ask about them, though Scotch manners prevent her from calling them to his attention. It would be a vain display and boasting to speak first of them. But when you have broken the ice, she will take you into the kitchen and explain that these were the university books of her son for whom the whole family has toiled and saved that he might have an education.

To have a scholar in the family is one of the greatest ambitions of the people who live in Drumtochty. To prepare a son for college after he has been duly declared by the minister and other authorities as having in him the making of a scholar, no sacrifice is too great, or labor too hard, or planning too arduous. It is worth all it costs to be able to say once in three generations, at least, that there is a scholar in the family. It would be well if between the cottages and the university an open road were kept, and upon that road the grass were never allowed to grow. For professors the Scotchman in the glen has immense reverence. To him the professor is the incarnation of learning, a heavenly body charged with Greek and

Latin. No students have suffered so much to secure an education as those in Scotch universities.

Among all our qualities, the deepest rooted, apart from the fear of God, is sentiment. And yet we do not receive credit for it because we have not sentimentalism, which is the caricature and ghost of sentiment. The sentiment of the Scotch is of the heart and not of the lips. If I saw a couple of Scotchmen kissing each other good-bye, I wouldn't lend five shillings to either of them. It is not an uncommon thing to see such an exhibition among Italians. I do not blame them. They are as God made them and so they must be. People doubt whether we have any sentiment at all. Some think we are hard-hearted and cold-blooded. Our manner is less than genial and not effusive. Our misfortune is not to be able to express our feelings. This inability is allied to our strength; strong people conceal their feelings. The Scot is endowed with an excess of caution; unnecessary reserve. Recently a train in Scotland came to a junction, where the porter shouted inside each carriage: "Change carriages for Duan, Callendar, and the Trossachs." After he had gone an old Scotchman said: "I'm for Duan misel', but I would not let on to that man." [Laughter.] This story shows the national reserve carried too far; it would perhaps be a good thing if the Scotch people "let on" more than they do.

But notwithstanding the irony that underlies the Scot's nature, and his apparent stolidness, there does lie within his bosom, unseen, a store of sentiment; for where do you find ballads touching home life so beautifully as do those of Scotland—such as "Robin Adair," "Will Ye No Come Back Again?" "Auld Lang Syne"? And if you want to know that which no Scotsman can talk to you about, read the poetry written by one of his own type, Robert Burns. [Applause.] If a Scotchman is forced to leave his home, the roots of his life are being torn up; he is outraged in feeling and ready to become an anarchist. There is no greater sin than to dispossess a Scotsman of his home. If you wish a real nice friend to come and have afternoon tea with you, and tell you how sweet your children are, and that she can't live without seeing them, do not send for Elspeth McFayden, unless she has been living a long time away from Drumtochty; but if one of your children is ill with a contagious disease, she will be the first to proffer care and service. [Applause.]

Forgive us that we have no outward manners. Believe us that we have a warm heart. If you want manners, go to another nation. If you want a warm heart, go to a Scotch woman or man. The songs of Robert Burns are indicative of the character of the Scotch people. Reading them you can hear the beating of the Scotch heart. It is true we do not wear our heart on our sleeve, but where do you find a warmer, truer heart than that which beats beneath the blue bonnet? History has no more generous impulsive rebellion than the Rebellion of '45, when men sent their sons, maidens their sweethearts, to the field in behalf of Prince Charlie. They had nothing to win, they had everything to lose, and they gave their blood freely for a sentimental cause. [Applause.]

But we are told that we are a thrifty people, as if that were a reproach. But does not Scottish thrift mean some of the best and most useful qualities—foresight, self-denial, the conscientious use of money? Does it not mean independence? When I contrast this quality with the recklessness and improvidence of the man who gets thereby a reputation for being "generous," I declare before this audience that I am not ashamed of the thrift of our people by which they have maintained their self-respect, have been enabled to help one another, and to keep their poor from becoming a burden in the great cities [applause]; and I trust in no city are they a burden to the police. It is the nations, like the individuals, that know how to deny themselves, who make their mark in the world.

It follows as a natural consequence for the inhabitants of a country so poor as Scotland to emigrate when there are so many rich lands to go to. But everywhere the Scotsman goes he retains his characteristics. Never revolutionary, he is for culture and everything that is for the welfare of his adopted nation. The problem with Scotsmen going to other countries is: How did they get along until we got here? [Laughter and applause.]

"Lord gi'e us a gude conceit o' oursel's," may be called the national prayer, and there is perhaps no prayer that has been so remarkably answered. Once a Scotsman, cornered with Shakespeare, said: "Shakespeare micht a been arn Englishman—we hae nae evidence to the contrary—but he was able enough tae ha'e been a Scotsman." [Laughter.]

The Scotch have one illusion, too. It is that nobody notices their accent. If a Scotsman is asked what part of Scotland he came from, his first remark after answering the question is apt to be: "Now that is curious. How did ye ken I came from Scotland at all?"

There exists between all natives of Scotland a bond of sympathy. Where do you find persons who love their country as do the Scotch? Let three Scotchmen meet in a foreign city and they form a St. Andrew's Society to assist their countrymen.

Scotland has been a stern mother to her children, never over-feeding them, and using the stick when it was necessary; and when they have departed from their native country, they always look back and bless her. Ours is a little country and that is perhaps one reason that we love it so well. Yours is a great and good country, and I wish it peace and prosperity; but there is advantage in a little country—you can carry it more easily in your heart. [Loud applause.]

HENRY WATTERSON

ABRAHAM LINCOLN

[Lecture by Henry Watterson, journalist and orator, editor of the Louisville, Ky., "Courier-Journal" since 1868 (born in Washington, D. C., February 16, 1840; ———), delivered as an oration before the Lincoln Club of Chicago, February 12, 1895, and subsequently repeated on many platforms as a lecture. It has been heard in all parts of the country, but nowhere, as has been stated, with livelier demonstrations of approval than in the cities of the South "from Richmond and Charleston to New Orleans and Galveston." The text here given includes a passage added to the matter as originally spoken, relating to the Hampton Roads Conference. This presents Mr. Watterson's proof for the assertion as to what had actually passed between Mr. Lincoln and Mr. Stephens on that occasion, which had been questioned.]

The statesmen in knee-breeches and powdered wigs who signed the Declaration of Independence and framed the Constitution—the soldiers in blue-and-buff, top-boots and epaulets who led the armies of the Revolution—were what we are wont to describe as gentlemen. They were English gentlemen. They were not all, nor even generally, scions of the British aristocracy; but they came, for the most part, of good Anglo-Saxon and Scotch-Irish stock.

The shoe-buckle and the ruffled shirt worked a spell peculiarly their own. They carried with them an air of polish and authority. Hamilton, though of obscure birth and small stature, is represented by those who knew him to have been dignity and grace personified; and old Ben Franklin, even in woolen hose, and none too courtier-like, was the delight of the great nobles and fine ladies, in

whose company he made himself as much at home as
though he had been born a marquis.

When we revert to that epoch the beauty of the scene
which history unfolds is marred by little that is uncouth,
by nothing that is grotesque.   The long procession passes,
and we see in each group, in every figure, something of
heroic proportion.   John Adams and John Hancock,
Samuel Warren and Samuel Adams, the Livingstons in
New York, the Carrolls in Maryland, the Masons, the
Randolphs and the Pendletons in Virginia, the Rutledges
in South Carolina—what pride of caste, what elegance of
manner, what dignity and dominancy of character!   And
the   soldiers!   Israel   Putnam   and   Nathaniel   Greene,
Ethan Allen and John Stark, Mad Anthony Wayne and
Light Horse Harry Lee, and Morgan and Marion and
Sumter, gathered about the immortal Washington—Puritan and Cavalier so mixed and blended as to be indistin-
guishable the one from the other—where shall we go to
seek a more resplendent galaxy of field marshals?   Surely
not to Blenheim, drinking beakers to Marlborough after
the famous victory; nor yet to the silken marquet of the
great Conde on the Rhine, bedizened with gold lace and
radiant with the flower of the nobility of France!   Ah,
me! there were gentlemen in those days; and they made
their influence felt upon life and thought long after the
echoes of Bunker Hill and Yorktown had faded away,
long after the bell over Independence Hall had ceased to
ring.

The first half of the Republic's first half century of existence the public men of America, distinguished for many
things, were chiefly and almost universally distinguished
for repose of bearing and sobriety of behavior.   It was
not until the institution of African slavery had got into
politics as a vital force that Congress became a bear-gar-
den, and that our law-makers, laying aside their manners with their small-clothes, fell into the loose-fitting
habiliments of modern fashion and the slovenly jargon of
partisan controversy.   The gentlemen who signed the
Declaration and framed the Constitution were succeeded
by gentlemen—much like themselves—but these were
succeeded by a race of party leaders much less decorous
and much more self-confident; rugged, puissant; deeply

moved in all that they said and did, and sometimes turbulent; so that finally, when the volcano burst forth flames that reached the heavens, great human boulders appeared amid the glare on every side; none of them much to speak of according to rules regnant at St. James and Versailles; but vigorous, able men, full of their mission and of themselves, and pulling for dear life in opposite directions.

There were Seward and Sumner and Chase, Corwin and Ben Wade, Trumbull and Fessenden, Hale and Collamer and Grimes, and Wendell Phillips, and Horace Greeley, our latter-day Franklin. There were Toombs and Hammond, and Slidell and Wigfall, and the two little giants, Douglas and Stephens, and Yancey and Mason, and Jefferson Davis. With them soft words buttered no parsnips, and they cared little how many pitchers might be broken by rude ones. The issue between them did not require a diagram to explain it. It was so simple a child might understand. It read, human slavery against human freedom, slave labor against free labor, and involved a conflict as inevitable as it was irrepressible.

Long before the guns of Beauregard opened fire upon Fort Sumter, and, fulfilling the programme of extremism, " blood was sprinkled in the faces of the people," the hustings in America had become a battle-ground, and every rod of debatable territory a ring for controversial mills, always tumultuous, and sometimes sanguinary. No sooner had the camp-fires of the Revolution—which warmed so many noble hearts and lighted so many patriotic lamps —no sooner had the camp-fires of the Revolution died out, than there began to burn, at first fitfully, then to blaze alarmingly in every direction, a succession of forest fires, baffling the energies and resources of the good and brave men who sought to put them out. Mr. Webster, at once a learned jurist and a prose poet, might thunder expositions of the written law, to quiet the fears of the slave-owner and to lull the waves of agitation. Mr. Clay, by his resistless eloquence and overmastering personality, might compromise first one and then another of the irreconcilable conditions that obstructed the pathway of conservative statesmanship. To no purpose, except to delay the fatal hour.

There were moving to the foreground moral forces
which would down at no man's bidding.   The still, small
voice of emancipation, stifled for a moment by self-interest
playing upon the fears of the timid, recovered its breath
and broke into a cry for abolition.   The cry for abolition
rose in volume to a roar.   Slowly, step by step, the forces
of freedom advanced to meet the forces of slavery.   Gradually, these mighty, discordant elements approached the
predestined line of battle; the gains for a while seeming
to be in doubt, but in reality all on one side.   There was
less and less of middle ground.   The middle men who
ventured to get in the way were either struck down or
absorbed by the one party or the other.   The Senate had
its Gettysburg; and many and many a Shiloh was fought
on the floor of the House.   Actual war raged in Kansas.
The mysterious descent upon Harper's Ferry, like a fire-
bell in the night, might have warned all men of the coming
conflagration; might have revealed to all men a prophecy
in the lines that, quoted to describe the scene, foretold
the event—

"The rock-ribbed ledges drip with a silent horror of blood,
    And Echo there, whatever is asked her, answers: 'Death.'"

Greek was meeting Greek at last; and the field of politics
became almost as sulphurous and murky as an actual field
of battle.

Amid the noise and confusion, the clashing of intellects
like sabers bright, and the booming of the big oratorical
guns of the North and the South, now definitely arrayed,
there came one day into the Northern camp one of the
oddest figures imaginable; the figure of a man who, in
spite of an appearance somewhat at outs with Hogarth's
line of beauty, wore a serious aspect, if not an air of command, and, pausing to utter a single sentence that might
be heard above the din, passed on and for a moment disappeared.   The sentence was pregnant with meaning.
The man bore a commission from God on high!   He said:
"A house divided against itself cannot stand.   I believe
this Government cannot endure permanently half free and
half slave.   I do not expect the Union to be dissolved; I
do not expect the house to fall; but I do expect it will

cease to be divided." He was Abraham Lincoln. [Applause.]

How shall I describe him to you? Shall I do so as he appeared to me, when I first saw him immediately on his arrival in the national capital, the chosen President of the United States, his appearance quite as strange as the story of his life, which was then but half known and half told, or shall I use the words of another and a more graphic word-painter?

In January, 1861, Colonel A. K. McClure, of Pennsylvania, journeyed to Springfield, Illinois, to meet and confer with the man he had done so much to elect, but whom he had never personally known. "I went directly from the depot to Lincoln's house," says Colonel McClure, "and rang the bell, which was answered by Lincoln, himself, opening the door. I doubt whether I wholly concealed my disappointment at meeting him. Tall, gaunt, ungainly, ill-clad, with a homeliness of manner that was unique in itself, I confess that my heart sank within me as I remembered that this was the man chosen by a great nation to become its ruler in the gravest period of its history. I remember his dress as if it were but yesterday—snuff-colored and slouchy pantaloons; open black vest, held by a few brass buttons; straight or evening dress-coat, with tightly fitting sleeves to exaggerate his long, bony arms, all supplemented by an awkwardness that was uncommon among men of intelligence. Such was the picture I met in the person of Abraham Lincoln. We sat down in his plainly furnished parlor and were uninterrupted during the nearly four hours I remained with him, and little by little, as his earnestness, sincerity, and candor were developed in conversation, I forgot all the grotesque qualities which so confounded me when I first greeted him. Before half an hour had passed I learned not only to respect, but, indeed, to reverence the man."

A graphic portrait, truly, and not unlike. I recall him, two months later, a little less uncouth, a little better dressed, but in singularity and in angularity much the same. All the world now takes an interest in every detail that concerned him, or that relates to the weird tragedy of his life and death.

And who was this peculiar being, destined in his moth-

er's arms—for cradle he had none—so profoundly to affect the future of human-kind? He has told us, himself,
in words so simple and unaffected, so idiomatic and direct,
that we can neither misread them, nor improve upon
them. Writing, in 1859, to one who had asked him for
some biographic particulars, Abraham Lincoln said:—

"I was born February 12, 1809, in Hardin county, Kentucky. My
parents were both born in Virginia, of undistinguished families—
second families, perhaps I should say. My mother, who died in my
tenth year, was of a family of the name of Hanks. . . . My
paternal grandfather, Abraham Lincoln, emigrated from Rockingham
county, Virginia, to Kentucky about 1781 or 1782, where, a year or two
later, he was killed by the Indians, not in battle, but by stealth, when
he was laboring to open a farm in the forest.

"My father (Thomas Lincoln) at the death of his father was but
six years of age. By the early death of his father, and the very narrow
circumstances of his mother, he was, even in childhood, a wandering,
laboring boy, and grew up literally without education. He never did
more in the way of writing than bunglingly to write his own name.
. . . He removed from Kentucky to what is now Spencer county,
Indiana, in my eighth year. . . . It was a wild region, with many
bears and other animals still in the woods. . . . There were some
schools, so-called, but no qualification was ever required of a teacher
beyond 'readin', writin', and cipherin' to the rule of three.' If a
straggler supposed to understand Latin happened to sojourn in the
neighborhood he was looked upon as a wizard. . . . Of course,
when I came of age I did not know much. Still, somehow, I could
read, write, and cipher to the rule of three. But that was all. . . .
The little advance I now have upon this store of education I have
picked up from time to time under the pressure of necessity.

"I was raised to farm work . . . till I was twenty-two. At
twenty-one I came to Illinois,—Macon county. Then I got to New
Salem, . . . where I remained a year as a sort of clerk in a store.
Then came the Black Hawk war; and I was elected captain of a
volunteer company, a success that gave me more pleasure than any
I have had since. I went into the campaign—was elated—ran for the
Legislature the same year (1832), and was beaten—the only time I
ever have been beaten by the people. The next, and three succeeding
biennial elections, I was elected to the Legislature. I was not a candidate afterward. During the legislative period I had studied law and
removed to Springfield to practice it. In 1846 I was elected to the
lower house of Congress. Was not a candidate for re-election. From
1849 to 1854, inclusive, practised law more assiduously than ever
before. Always a Whig in politics, and generally on the Whig elec-

toral tickets, making active canvasses. I was losing interest in politics when the repeal of the Missouri Compromise aroused me again.

"If any personal description of me is thought desirable, it may be said that I am in height six feet four inches, nearly; lean in flesh, weighing on an average one hundred and eighty pounds; dark complexion, with coarse black hair and gray eyes. No other marks or brands recollected."

There is the whole story, told by himself, and brought down to the point where he became a figure of national importance.

His political philosophy was expounded in four elaborate speeches; one delivered at Peoria, Illinois, the 16th of October, 1854; one at Springfield, Illinois, the 16th of June, 1858; one at Columbus, Ohio, the 16th of September, 1859, and one the 27th of February, 1860, at Cooper Institute, in the city of New York. Of course Mr. Lincoln made many speeches and very good speeches. But these four, progressive in character, contain the sum total of his creed touching the organic character of the Government and at the same time his party view of contemporary issues. They show him to have been an old-line Whig of the school of Henry Clay, with strong emancipation leanings; a thorough anti-slavery man, but never an extremist or an abolitionist. To the last he hewed to the line thus laid down.

Two or three years ago I referred to Abraham Lincoln —in a casual way—as one "inspired of God." I was taken to task for this and thrown upon my defense. Knowing less then than I know now of Mr. Lincoln, I confined myself to the superficial aspects of the case; to the career of a man who seemed to have lacked the opportunity to prepare himself for the great estate to which he had come, plucked as it were from obscurity by a caprice of fortune.

Accepting the doctrine of inspiration as a law of the universe, I still stand to this belief; but I must qualify it as far as it conveys the idea that Mr. Lincoln was not as well equipped in actual knowledge of men and affairs as any of his contemporaries. Mr. Webster once said that he had been preparing to make his reply to Hayne for thirty years. Mr. Lincoln had been in unconscious train-

ing for the Presidency for thirty years. His maiden address as a candidate for the Legislature, issued at the ripe
old age of twenty-three, closes with these words, " But if
the good people in their wisdom shall see fit to keep me in
the background, I have been too familiar with disappointment to be very much chagrined." The man who wrote
that sentence, thirty years later wrote this sentence: " The
mystic chords of memory, stretching from every battlefield and patriot-grave to every living heart and hearth-
stone all over this broad land, will yet swell the chorus of
the Union, when again touched, as surely they will be, by
the angels of our better nature." Between those two sentences, joined by a kindred, somber thought, flowed a life-
current—

> " Strong, without rage, without o'erflowing, full,"

pausing never for an instant; deepening whilst it ran, but
nowise changing its course or its tones; always the same;
calm; patient; affectionate; like one born to a destiny,
and, as in a dream, feeling its resistless force.

It is needful to a complete understanding of Mr. Lincoln's relation to the time and to his place in the political
history of the country, that the student peruse closely the
four speeches to which I have called attention; they underlie all that passed in the famous debate with Douglas; all
that their author said and did after he succeeded to the
Presidency. They stand to-day as masterpieces of popular oratory. But for our present purpose the debate with
Douglas will suffice—the most extraordinary intellectual
spectacular the annals of our party warfare afford. Lincoln entered the canvass unknown outside the State of
Illinois. He closed it renowned from one end of the land
to the other.

Judge Douglas was himself unsurpassed as a stump-
speaker and ready debater. But in that campaign, from
first to last, Judge Douglas was at a serious disadvantage.
His bark rode upon an ebbing tide; Lincoln's bark rode
upon a flowing tide. African slavery was the issue now;
and the whole trend of modern thought was set against
slavery. The Democrats seemed hopelessly divided. The
Little Giant had to face a triangular opposition embracing the Republicans, the Administration, or Buchanan

Democrats, and a little remnant of the old Whigs, who fancied that their party was still alive and thought to hold some kind of balance of power. Judge Douglas called the combination the "allied army," and declared that he would deal with it "just as the Russians dealt with the allies at Sebastopol—that is, the Russians did not stop to inquire, when they fired a broadside, whether it hit an Englishman, a Frenchman, or a Turk." It was something more than a witticism when Mr. Lincoln rejoined, " In that case, I beg he will indulge us whilst we suggest to him that those allies took Sebastopol." [Applause.]

He followed this center-shot with volley after volley of exposition so clear, of reasoning so close, of illustration so pointed, and, at times, of humor so incisive, that, though he lost his election—though the allies did not then take Sebastopol—his defeat counted for more than Douglas' victory, for it made him the logical and successful candidate for President of the United States two years later.

What could be more captivating to an out-door audience than Lincoln's description " of the two persons who stand before the people of the State as candidates for the Senate," to quote his prefatory words? " Judge Douglas," he said, " is of world-wide renown. All the anxious politicians of his party . . . have been looking upon him as certainly . . . to be President of the United States. They have seen in his round, jolly, fruitful face, post-offices, land-offices, marshalships, and cabinet appointments, chargeships and foreign missions, bursting and spreading out in wonderful exuberance, ready to be laid hold of by their greedy hands. And as they have been gazing upon this attractive picture so long, they can not, in the little distraction that has taken place in the party, bring themselves to give up the charming hope; but with greedier anxiety they rush about him, sustain him and give him marches, triumphal entries and receptions, beyond what in the days of his highest prosperity they could have brought about in his favor. On the contrary, nobody has ever expected me to be President. In my poor, lean, lank face nobody has ever seen that any cabbages were sprouting."

As the debate advanced, these cheery tones deepened into harsher notes; crimination and recrimination fol-

lowed; the two gladiators were strung to their utmost tension. They became dreadfully in earnest. Personal collision was narrowly avoided. I have recently gone over
the entire debate, and with a feeling I can only describe
as most contemplative, most melancholy.

I knew Judge Douglas well; I admired, respected, loved
him. I shall never forget the day he quitted Washington
to go to his home in Illinois to return no more. Tears
were in his eyes and his voice trembled like a woman's.
He was then a dying man. He had burned the candle at
both ends from his boyhood; an eager, ardent, hardworking, pleasure-loving man; and though not yet fifty,
the candle was burned out. His infirmities were no
greater than those of Mr. Clay; not to be mentioned with
those of Mr. Webster. But he lived in more exacting
times. The old-style party organ, with its mock heroics and
its dull respectability, its beggarly array of empty news
columns and cheap advertising, had been succeeded by
that unsparing, tell-tale scandal-monger, Modern Journalism, with its myriad of hands and eyes, its vast retinue of
detectives, and its quick transit over flashing wires, an-
nihilating time and space. Too fierce a light beat upon
the private life of public men, and Douglas suffered from
this as Clay and Webster, Silas Wright, and Franklin
Pierce had not suffered.

The presidential bee was in his bonnet, certainly; but its
buzzing there was not noisier than in the bonnets of other
great Americans, who have been dazzled by that wretched
bauble. His plans and schemes came to naught. He
died at the moment when the death of those plans and
schemes was made more palpable and impressive by the
roar of cannon proclaiming the reality of that irrepressible conflict he had refused to foresee and had struggled
to avert. His life-long rival was at the head of affairs.
No one has found occasion to come to the rescue of his
fame. No party interest has been identified with his memory. But when the truth of history is written, it will be told
that, not less than Webster and Clay, he, too, was a
patriotic man, who loved his country and tried to save the
Union. He tried to save the Union, even as Webster
and Clay had tried to save it, by compromises and expe-
dients. It was too late. The string was played out.

Where they had succeeded he failed; but, for the nobility of his intention, the amplitude of his resources, the splendor of his combat, he merits all that any leader of losing cause ever gained in the report of posterity; and posterity will not deny him the title of statesman. [Applause.]

In that great debate it was Titan against Titan; and, perusing it after the lapse of forty years, the philosophic and impartial critic will conclude which got the better of it, Lincoln or Douglas, much according to his sympathy with the one or the other. Douglas, as I have said, had the disadvantage of riding an ebb-tide. But Lincoln encountered a disadvantage in riding a flood-tide, which was flowing too fast for a man so conservative and so honest as he was. Thus there was not a little equivocation on both sides foreign to the nature of the two. Both wanted to be frank. Both thought they were being frank. But each was a little afraid of his own logic; each was a little afraid of his own following; and hence there was considerable hair-splitting, involving accusations that did not accuse and denials that did not deny. They were politicians, these two, as well as statesmen; they were politicians, and what they did not know about political campaigning was hardly worth knowing. Reverently, I take off my hat to both of them; and I turn down the page; I close the book and lay it on its shelf, with the inward ejaculation, "there were giants in those days." [Applause.]

I am not undertaking to deliver an oral biography of Abraham Lincoln, and shall pass over the events which quickly led up to his nomination and election to the Presidency in 1860.

I met the newly elected President the afternoon of the day in the early morning of which he had arrived in Washington. It was a Saturday, I think. He came to the Capitol under Mr. Seward's escort, and, among the rest, I was presented to him. His appearance did not impress me as fantastically as it had impressed Colonel McClure. I was more familiar with the Western type than Colonel McClure, and, whilst Mr. Lincoln was certainly not an Adonis, even after prairie ideals, there was about him a dignity that commanded respect.

I met him again the forenoon of the 4th of March in his apartment at Willard's Hotel as he was preparing to

start to his inauguration, and was touched by his unaffected kindness; for I came with a matter requiring his
immediate attention.   He was entirely self-possessed; no
trace of nervousness; and very obliging.   I accompanied
the cortege that passed from the Senate chamber to the
east portico of the Capitol, and, as Mr. Lincoln removed
his hat to face the vast multitude in front and below, I
extended my hand to receive it, but Judge Douglas, just
beside me, reached over my outstretched arm and took the
hat, holding it throughout the delivery of the inaugural
address.   I stood near enough to the speaker's elbow not
to obstruct any gestures he might make, though he made
but few; and then it was that I began to comprehend something of the power of the man.

He delivered that inaugural address as if he had been
delivering inaugural addresses all his life.   Firm, resonant, earnest, it announced the coming of a man; of a
leader of men; and in its ringing tones and elevated style,
the gentlemen he had invited to become members of his
political family—each of whom thought himself a bigger
man than his master—might have heard the voice and
seen the hand of a man born to command.   Whether they
did or not, they very soon ascertained the fact.   From the
hour Abraham Lincoln crossed the threshold of the White
House to the hour he went thence to his death, there was
not a moment when he did not dominate the political and
military situation and all his official surbordinates.   [Ap-
plause.]

Mr. Seward was the first to fall a victim to his own
temerity.   One of the most extraordinary incidents that
ever passed between a chief and his lieutenant came about
before the first month of the new administration had
closed.   The 1st of April Mr. Seward submitted to Mr.
Lincoln a memorandum, entitled " Some Thoughts for the
President's Consideration."   He began this by saying:
" We are at the end of a month's administration, and yet
without a policy, either foreign or domestic."   Then follows a series of suggestions hardly less remarkable for
their character than for their emanation.   There are quite
a baker's dozen of them, for the most part flimsy and
irrelevant; but two of them are so conspicuous for a lack
of sagacity and comprehension that I shall quote them as

a sample of the whole: "We must change the question before the public," says Mr. Seward, "from one upon slavery, or about slavery, to one upon Union or disunion," —as if it had not been thus changed already,—and, "I would demand explanations from Spain and France, energetically, at once, . . . and if satisfactory explanations are not received from Spain and France, I would convene Congress and declare war against them. . . . I would seek explanations from Great Britain and Russia, and send agents into Canada, Mexico, and Central America to arouse a vigorous spirit of Continental independence on this continent against European intervention."

Think of it! At the moment this advice was seriously given the head of the Government by the head of the Cabinet—supposed to be the most accomplished statesman and astute diplomatist of his time—a Southern Confederacy had been actually established, and Europe was only too eager for some pretext to put in its oar, and effectually, finally, to compel a dissolution of the Union and to compass the defeat of the Republican experiment in America. The Government of the United States had but to make a grimace at France and Spain; to bat its eye at England and Russia, to raise up a quadruple alliance, Monarchy against Democracy, bringing down upon itself the navies of the world, and double assuring, double confirming the Government of Jefferson Davis.

In concluding these astounding counsels, Mr. Seward says: "But whatever policy we adopt, there must be an energetic prosecution of it. For this purpose it must be somebody's business to pursue and direct it incessantly. Either the President must do it himself and be all the while active in it, or devolve it on some member of his Cabinet. Once adopted, all debates on it must end and all agree and abide. It is not in my especial province; but I neither seek to evade nor assume responsibility."

Before hearing Mr. Lincoln's answer to all this, consider what it really implied. If Mr. Seward had simply said: "Mr. Lincoln, you are a failure as President, but turn over the direction of affairs exclusively to me, and all shall be well and all be forgiven," he could not have spoken more explicitly and hardly more offensively.

Now mark how a great man carries himself at a critical moment under extreme provocation.   Here is the answer Mr. Lincoln sent Mr. Seward that very night:—

"EXECUTIVE MANSION, April 1, 1861.—Hon. W. H. Seward—My Dear Sir: Since parting with you I have been considering your paper dated this day and entitled 'Some Thoughts for the President's Consideration.'   The first proposition in it is, 'We are at the end of a month's administration and yet without a policy, either domestic or foreign.'

"At the beginning of that month in the inaugural I said: 'The power confided to me will be used to hold, occupy and possess the property and places belonging to the Government, and to collect the duties and imports.'   This had your distinct approval at the time; and taken in connection with the order I immediately gave General Scott, directing him to employ every means in his power to strengthen and hold the forts, comprises the exact domestic policy you urge, with the single exception that it does not propose to abandon Fort Sumter.

. . . .

"The news received yesterday in regard to Santo Domingo certainly brings a new item within the range of our foreign policy, but up to that time we have been preparing circulars and instructions to ministers and the like, all in perfect harmony, without even a suggestion that we had no foreign policy.

"Upon your closing proposition—that 'Whatever policy we adopt, there must be an energetic prosecution of it.   For this purpose it must be somebody's business to pursue and direct it incessantly. Either the President must do it himself, and be all the while active in it, or devolve it upon some member of his Cabinet.   Once adopted, debates must end, and all agree and abide.'   I remark that if this be done, I must do it.   When a general line of policy is adopted, I apprehend there is no danger of its being changed without good reason, or continuing to be a subject of unnecessary debate; still, upon points arising in its progress, I wish, and suppose I am entitled to have, the advice of all the Cabinet.   Your obedient servant,

"A. LINCOLN."

I agree with Lincoln's biographers that in this letter not a word was omitted that was necessary, and not a hint or allusion is contained that could be dispensed with.   It was conclusive.   It ended the argument.   Mr. Seward dropped into his place.   Mr. Lincoln never referred to it. From that time forward the understanding between them was mutual and perfect.   So much so that when, the 21st of the following May, Mr. Seward submitted to the President the draft of a letter of instruction to Charles Francis Adams, then Minister to England, Mr. Lincoln did not hesitate to change much of its character and purpose by his alterations of its text. The original copy of this despatch, in Mr. Seward's handwriting, with Mr. Lincoln's interlineations, is still to be seen on file in the Department of State. It is safe to say that, if that letter had gone as Mr. Seward wrote it, a war with England would have been inevitable. Mr. Lincoln's additions, hardly less than his suppressions, present a curious contrast between the seer in affairs and the scholar in affairs. Even in the substitution of one word for another, Mr. Lincoln shows a comprehension both of the situation and the language which seems to have been wholly wanting in Mr. Seward, with all his experience and learning. It is said that, pondering over this document, weighing in his mind its meaning and import, his head bowed and pencil in hand, Mr. Lincoln was overheard murmuring to himself: "One war at a time—one war at a time." [Applause.]

Whilst I am on this matter of who was really President whilst Abraham Lincoln occupied the office, I may as well settle it. We all remember that, in setting up for a bigger man than his chief, Mr. Chase fared no better than Mr. Seward. But it is sometimes said that Mr. Stanton was more successful in this line. Many amusing stories are told of how Stanton lorded it over Lincoln. On a certain occasion it is related that the President was informed by an irate friend that the Secretary of War had not only refused to execute an order of his, but had called him a fool into the bargain. "Did Stanton say I was a fool?" said Lincoln. "Yes," replied his friend, "he said you were a blank, blank fool!" Lincoln looked first good-humoredly at his friend and then furtively out of the window in the direction of the War Department, and carelessly observed: "If Stanton said that I was a blank fool, it must be true, for he is nearly always right and generally says what he means. I will just step over and see Stanton."

On another occasion Mr. Lincoln is quoted as saying: "I have very little influence with this Administration, but I hope to have more with the next."

Complacent humor such as this simply denotes assured position. It is merely the graciousness of conscious power. But there happens to be on record a story of a different kind. This is related by General James B. Fry, Provost Marshal General of the United States, on duty in the War Department. As General Fry tells it, Mr. Stanton seems to have had the right of it. The President had given an order which the Secretary of War refused to issue. The President thereupon came into the War Department and this is what happened. In answer to Mr. Lincoln's inquiry as to the cause of the trouble, Mr. Stanton went over the record and the grounds for his action, and concluded with: "Now, Mr. President, these are the facts, and you must see that your order cannot be executed."

Lincoln sat upon a sofa with his legs crossed—I am quoting General Fry—and did not say a word until the Secretary's last remark. Then he said in a somewhat positive tone: "Mr. Secretary, I reckon you'll have to execute the order."

Stanton replied with asperity—"Mr. President, I cannot do it. The order is an improper one and I cannot execute it."

Lincoln fixed his eye upon Stanton, and in a firm voice, and with an accent that clearly showed his determination, he said:—

"Mr. Secretary, it will have to be done."

"Stanton then realized"—I am still quoting General Fry—"that he was overmatched. He had made a square issue with the President and been defeated, notwithstanding the fact that he was in the right. Upon an intimation from him I withdrew and did not witness his surrender. A few minutes after I reached my office I received instructions from the Secretary to carry out the President's order. Stanton never mentioned the subject to me afterward, nor did I ever ascertain the special, and no doubt sufficient reason, which the President had for his action in the case."

Once General Halleck got on a high horse, and demanded that, if Mr. Lincoln approved some ill-natured remarks alleged to have been made of certain military men about Washington, by Montgomery Blair, the Postmaster-General, he should dismiss the officers from the service, but, if he did not approve, he should dismiss the Postmaster-General from the Cabinet. Mr. Lincoln's reply is very characteristic. He declined to do either of the things demanded. He said: "Whether the remarks were really made I do not know, nor do I suppose such knowledge necessary to a correct response. If they were made, I do not approve them; and yet, under the circumstances, I would not dismiss a member of the Cabinet therefor. I do not consider what may have been hastily said in a moment of vexation . . . sufficient ground for so grave a step. Besides this, truth is generally the best vindication against slander. I propose continuing to be myself the judge as to when a member of the Cabinet shall be dismissed." [Applause.]

Next day, however, he issued a warning to the members of his political family, which, in the form of a memorandum, he read to them. There is nothing equivocal about this. In language and in tone it is the utterance of a master. I will read it to you, as it is very brief and to the purpose. The President said: "I must myself be the judge how long to retain and when to remove any of you from his position. It would greatly pain me to discover any of you endeavoring to procure another's removal, or in any way to prejudice him before the public. Such endeavor would be a wrong to me, and much worse, a wrong to the country. My wish is, that on this subject no remark be made, nor any question be asked by any of you, here or elsewhere, now or hereafter."

Always courteous, always tolerant, always making allowance, yet always explicit, his was the master-spirit, his the guiding hand; committing to each of the members of his Cabinet the details of the work of his own department; caring nothing for petty sovereignty; but reserving to himself all that related to great policies, the starting of moral forces and the moving of organized ideas.

I want to say just here a few words about Mr. Lincoln's relation to the South and the people of the South.

He was, himself, a Southern man. He and all his tribe were Southerners. Although he left Kentucky when but a child, he was an old child; he never was very young; and he grew to manhood in a Kentucky colony; for what

was Illinois in those days but a Kentucky colony, grown
since somewhat out of proportion? He was in no sense
what we in the South used to call "a poor white." Awkward, perhaps; ungainly, perhaps, but aspiring; the spirit
of a hero beneath that rugged exterior; the soul of a
prose-poet behind those heavy brows; the courage of a
lion back of those patient, kindly aspects; and, long before
he was of legal age, a leader. His first love was a Rut-
ledge; his wife was a Todd. Let the romancist tell the
story of his romance. I dare not. No sadder idyl can
be found in all the short and simple annals of the poor.

We know that he was a prose-poet; for have we not
that immortal prose-poem recited at Gettysburg? We
know that he was a statesman; for has not time vindicated
his conclusions? But the South does not know, except
as a kind of hearsay, that he was a friend; the one friend
who had the power and the will to save it from itself. He
was the one man in public life who could have come to the
head of affairs in 1861 bringing with him none of the
embittered resentments growing out of the anti-slavery
battle. Whilst Seward, Chase, Sumner and the rest had
been engaged in hand-to-hand combat with the Southern
leaders at Washington, Lincoln, a philosopher and a
statesman, had been observing the course of events from
afar, and like a philosopher and a statesman. The direst
blow that could have been laid upon the prostrate South
was delivered by the assassin's bullet that struck him
down.

But I digress. Throughout the contention that preceded the war, amid the passions that attended the war
itself, not one bitter, proscriptive word escaped the lips
of Abraham Lincoln, whilst there was hardly a day that
he was not projecting his great personality between some
Southern man or woman and danger. [Applause.]

Under date of February 2, 1848, and from the hall of
the House of Representatives at Washington, whilst he
was serving as a member of Congress, I find this short
note to his law partner at Springfield:—

" DEAR WILLIAM: I take up my pen to tell you that Mr. Stephens,
of Georgia, a little, slim, pale-faced, consumptive man, with a voice
like Logan's [that was Stephen T., not John A.], has just concluded

the very best speech of an hour's length I ever heard. My old, withered, dry eyes [he was then not quite thirty-seven years of age] are full of tears yet."

From that time forward he never ceased to love Stephens, of Georgia.

After that famous Hampton Roads conference, when the Confederate Commissioners, Stephens, Campbell, and Hunter, had traversed the field of official routine with Mr. Lincoln, the President, and Mr. Seward, the Secretary of State, Lincoln, the friend, still the old Whig colleague, though one was now President of the United States and the other Vice-President of the Southern Confederacy, took the " slim, pale-faced, consumptive man " aside, and, pointing to a sheet of paper he held in his hand, said: " Stephens, let me write ' Union ' at the top of that page, and you may write below it whatever else you please." [Applause.]

In the preceding conversation Mr. Lincoln had intimated that payment for the slaves was not outside a possible agreement for reunion and peace. He based that statement upon a plan he already had in hand, to appropriate four hundred millions of dollars to this purpose.

There are those who have put themselves to the pains of challenging this statement of mine. It admits of no possible equivocation. Mr. Lincoln carried with him to Fortress Monroe two documents that still stand in his own handwriting; one of them a joint resolution to be passed by the two Houses of Congress appropriating the four hundred millions, the other a proclamation to be issued by himself, as President, when the joint resolution had been passed. These formed no part of the discussion at Hampton Roads, because Mr. Stephens told Mr. Lincoln they were limited to treating upon the basis of the recognition of the Confederacy, and to all intents and purposes the conference died before it was actually born. But Mr. Lincoln was so filled with the idea that next day, when he had returned to Washington, he submitted the two documents to the members of his Cabinet. Excepting Mr. Seward, they were all against him. He said: "Why, gentlemen, how long is the war going to last? It is not going to end this side of a hundred days, is it? It is costing us four millions a day. There are the four hundred millions, not counting the loss of life and property in the meantime. But you are all against me, and I will not press the matter upon you." I have not cited this fact of history to attack, or even to criticise, the policy of the Confederate Government, but simply to illustrate the wise magnanimity and justice of the character of Abraham Lincoln. For my part I rejoice that the war did not end at Fortress Monroe —or any other conference—but that it was fought out to its bitter and logical conclusion at Appomattox.

It was the will of God that there should be, as God's own prophet had promised, "a new birth of freedom," and this could only be reached by the obliteration of the very idea of slavery. God struck Lincoln down in the moment of his triumph, to attain it; He blighted the South to attain it. But He did attain it. And here we are this night to attest it. God's will be done on earth as it is done in Heaven. But let no Southern man point finger at me because I canonize Abraham Lincoln, for he was the one friend we had at Court when friends were most in need; he was the one man in power who wanted to preserve us intact, to save us from the wolves of passion and plunder that stood at our door; and as that God, of whom it has been said that "whom He loveth He chasteneth," meant that the South should be chastened, Lincoln was put out of the way by the bullet of an assassin, having neither lot nor parcel, North or South, but a winged emissary of fate, flown from the shadows of the mystic world, which Æschylus and Shakespeare created and consecrated to tragedy!

I sometimes wonder shall we ever attain a journalism sufficiently upright in its treatment of current events to publish fully and fairly the utterances of our public men, and, except in cases of provable dishonor, to leave their motives and their personalities alone?

Reading just what Abraham Lincoln did say and did do, it is inconceivable how such a man could have aroused antagonism so bitter and abuse so savage, to fall at last by the hand of an assassin.

We boast our superior civilization and our enlightened freedom of speech; and yet, how few of us—when a strange voice begins to utter unfamiliar or unpalatable things—how few of us stop and ask ourselves, may not this man be speaking the truth after all? It is so easy to call names. It is so easy to impugn motives. It is so easy to misrepresent opinions we cannot answer. From the least to the greatest what creatures we are of party spirit, and yet, for the most part, how small its aims, how imperfect its instruments, how disappointing its conclusions!

One thinks now that the world in which Abraham Lincoln lived might have dealt more gently by such a man. He was himself so gentle—so upright in nature and so broad of mind—so sunny and so tolerant in temper—so simple and so unaffected in bearing—a rude exterior covering an undaunted spirit, proving by his every act and word that—

> " The bravest are the tenderest,
> The loving are the daring."

Though he was a party leader, he was a typical and patriotic American, in whom even his enemies might have found something to respect and admire. But it could not be so. He committed one grievous offense; he dared to think and he was not afraid to speak; he was far in advance of his party and his time; and men are slow to forgive what they do not readily understand.

Yet, all the while that the waves of passion were dashing over his sturdy figure, reared above the dead-level, as a lone oak upon a sandy beach, not one harsh word rankled in his heart to sour the milk of human kindness that, like a perennial spring from the gnarled roots of some majestic tree, flowed within him. He would smooth over a rough place in his official intercourse with a funny story fitting the case in point, and they called him a trifler. He would round off a logical argument with a familiar example, hitting the nail squarely on the head and driving it home, and they called him a buffoon. Big wigs and little wigs were agreed that he lowered the dignity of debate; as if debates were intended to mystify, and not to clarify truth. Yet he went on and on, and never backward, until his time was come, when his genius, fully developed, rose to the great exigencies intrusted to his hands. Where did he get

his style?   Ask Shakespeare and Burns where they got
their style.   Where did he get his grasp upon affairs and
his knowledge of men?   Ask the Lord God who created
miracles in Luther and Bonaparte!   [Applause.]

Here, under date of November 21, 1864, amid the excitement attendant upon his re-election to the Presidency,
Mr. Lincoln found time to write the following letter to
Mrs. Bixby, of Boston, a poor widow who had lost five
sons killed in battle:—

"MY DEAR MADAM: I have been shown in the files of the War
Department a statement of the Adjutant-General of Massachusetts
that you are the mother of five sons who have died gloriously on the
field of battle. I feel how weak and fruitless must be any words of
mine which should attempt to beguile you from a loss so overwhelming. But I cannot refrain from tendering you the consolation
that may be found in the thanks of the Republic they died to save. I
pray that our Heavenly Father may assuage the anguish of your
bereavement and leave you only the cherished memory of the loved
and lost, and the solemn pride that must be yours to have laid so
costly a sacrifice upon the altar of freedom.

"Yours very sincerely and respectfully,

"A. LINCOLN."

Contrast this exquisite prose-poem with the answer he
made to General Grant, who asked him whether he should
make an effort to capture Jefferson Davis. "I told
Grant," said Lincoln, relating the incident, "the story of
an Irishman who had taken Father Matthew's pledge.
Soon thereafter, becoming very thirsty, he slipped into a
saloon and applied for a lemonade, and whilst it was being
mixed he whispered to the bartender: 'Av ye could drap
a bit o' brandy in it, all unbeknown to myself, I'd make no
fuss about it.' My notion was that if Grant could let Jeff
Davis escape all unbeknown to himself, he was to let him
go. I didn't want him."

When we recall all that did happen when Jefferson
Davis was captured, and what a white elephant he became
in the hands of the Government, it will be seen that there
was sagacity as well as humor in Lincoln's illustration.

A goodly volume, embracing passages from the various
speeches and writings of Abraham Lincoln, might be com-
piled to show that he was a master of English prose.   The

Gettysburg address has innumerable counterparts, as far as mere style goes. But there needs to be no further proof that the man who could scribble such a composition as that with a lead pencil on a pad in a railway carriage was the equal of any man who ever wrote his mother tongue. As conclusive example—as short as it is sublime—let me read it to you. Like a chapter of Holy Writ, it can never grow old or stale :—

" Fourscore and seven years ago our fathers brought forth upon this continent a new nation, conceived in liberty, and dedicated to the proposition that all men are created equal.

"Now we are engaged in a great civil war, testing whether that nation, or any nation so conceived and so dedicated, can long endure. We are met on a great battlefield of that war. We have come to dedicate a portion of that field as a final resting-place for those who here gave their lives that that nation might live. It is altogether fitting and proper that we should do this.

"But in a larger sense we cannot dedicate, we cannot consecrate, we cannot hallow this ground. The brave men, living and dead, who struggled here, have consecrated it far above our poor power to add or detract. The world will little note nor long remember what we say here, but it can never forget what they did here. It is for us, the living, rather, to be dedicated here to the unfinished work which they who fought here have thus far so nobly advanced. It is rather for us to be here dedicated to the great task remaining before us: that from these honored dead we take increased devotion to that cause for which they gave the last full measure of devotion; that we here highly resolve that these dead shall not have died in vain; that this nation, under God, shall have a new birth of freedom; and that government of the people, by the people, and for the people, shall not perish from the earth."

I have said that Abraham Lincoln was an old-line Whig of the school of Henry Clay, with strong free-soil opinions, but never an extremist or an abolitionist. He was what they used to call in those old days "a Conscience Whig." He stood in actual awe of the Constitution and his oath of office. Hating slavery, he recognized its constitutional existence and rights. He wanted gradually to extinguish it, not to despoil those who held it as a property interest. He was so faithful to these principles that he approached emancipation, not only with great deliberation, but with many misgivings. He issued his final proclamation as a military necessity; as a war measure; and even then, so just was his nature that he was meditating some kind of just restitution.

I gather that he was not a Civil Service Reformer of the School of Grover Cleveland, because I find among his papers a short, peremptory note to Stanton, in which he says: "I personally wish Jacob Freese, of New Jersey, appointed colonel of a colored regiment, and this regardless of whether he can tell the exact color of Julius Cæsar's hair." [Laughter.]

His unconventionalism was only equaled by his humanity. No custodian of absolute power ever exercised it so benignly. His interposition in behalf of men sentenced to death by courts-martial became so demoralizing that his generals in the field united in a round-robin protest. Both Grant and Sherman cut the wires between their headquarters and Washington to escape his interference with the iron rule of military discipline.

A characteristic story is told by John B. Ally, of Boston, who, going to the White House three days in succession, found each day in the outer halls a gray-haired old man, silently weeping. The third day, touched by this not uncommon spectacle, he went up to the old man and ascertained that he had a son under sentence of death and was trying to reach the President.

"Come along," said Ally, "I'll take you to the President."

Mr. Lincoln listened to the old man's pitiful story, and sadly replied that he had just received a telegram from the general in command, imploring him not to interfere. The old man cast one last heart-broken look at the President, and started shuffling toward the door. Before he reached it Mr. Lincoln called him back. "Come back, old man," he said, "come back! the generals may telegraph and telegraph, but I am going to pardon that young man."

Thereupon he sent a despatch directing sentence to be suspended until execution should be ordered by himself. Then the old man burst out crying again, exclaiming: "Mr. President, that is not a pardon, you only hold up the sentence of my boy until you can order him to be shot!"

Lincoln turned quickly and, half smiles, half tears, said:

"Go along, old man, go along in peace; if your son lives until I order him to be shot, he'll grow to be as old as Methuselah!" [Applause and laughter.]

I could keep you here all night relating such incidents. They were common occurrences at the White House. There was not a day of Lincoln's life that he was not doing some act of charity; not like a sentimentalist, overcome by his emotions, but like a brave, sensible man, who knew where to draw the line and who made few, if any, mistakes.

I find no better examples of the peculiar cast of his mind than are interspersed throughout the record of his intercourse with his own relations. His domestic correspondence is full of canny wisdom and unconscious humor. In particular, he had a ne'er-do-well step-brother, by the name of Johnston, a son of his father's second wife, of whom he was very fond. There are many letters to this Johnston. One of these I am going to read you, because it will require neither apology nor explanation. It is illustrative of both the canny wisdom and unconscious humor. Thus:—

"SPRINGFIELD, January 2, 1851.—Dear Brother: Your request for eighty dollars I do not think it best to comply with now. At the various times I have helped you a little you have said: 'We can get along very well now,' but in a short time I find you in the same difficulty again. Now this can only happen through some defect in you. What that defect is I think I know. You are not lazy, and still you are an idler. I doubt whether since I saw you you have done a good, whole day's work in any one day. You do not very much dislike to work, and still you do not work much, merely because it does not seem to you you get enough for it. This habit of uselessly wasting time is the whole difficulty. It is vastly important to you, and still more to your children, that you break the habit. . . .

"You are now in need of some money, and what I propose is that you shall go to work, 'tooth and nail,' for somebody who will give you money for it. Let father and your boys take charge of your things at home, prepare for a crop and make the crop, and you go to work for the best money wages you can get, or in discharge of any debt you owe, and, to secure you a fair reward for your labor, I promise you that for every dollar you will get for your labor between this and the 1st of May, either in money, or in your indebtedness, I will then give you one other dollar. By this, if you hire yourself for ten dollars a month, from me you will get ten dollars more, making twenty dollars, , , ,

"In this I do not mean that you shall go off to St. Louis or the lead mines in Missouri, or the gold mines in California, but I mean for you to go at it for the best wages you can get close to home in Coles county. If you will do this you will soon be out of debt, and, what is better, you will have acquired a habit which will keep you from getting in debt again. But if I should now clear you out of debt, next year you would be just as deep in debt as ever.

"You say you would almost give your place in Heaven for seventy or eighty dollars? Then you value your place in Heaven very cheap, for I am sure you can, with the offer I make, get the seventy or eighty dollars for four or five months' work.

"You say if I will lend you the money, you will deed me the land, and, if you don't pay the money back, you will deliver possession. Nonsense! If you cannot now live with the land, how will you then live without it?

"You have always been kind to me, and I do not mean to be unkind to you. On the contrary, if you but follow my advice, you will find it worth eighty times eighty dollars to you.

"Affectionately your brother,

"A. LINCOLN."

Could anything be wiser, sweeter, or delivered in terms more specific yet more fraternal? And that was Abraham Lincoln from the crown of his head to the soles of his feet.

I am going to spare you and myself, and the dear ones of his own blood who are here to-night, the story of the awful tragedy that closed the life of this great man, this good man, this typical American. Beside that tragedy, most other tragedies, epic and real, become insignificant. "Within the narrow compass of that stage-box that night were five human beings; the most illustrious of modern heroes, crowned with the most stupendous victory of modern times; his beloved wife, proud and happy; two betrothed lovers with all the promise of felicity that youth, social position and wealth could give them; and a young actor, handsome as Endymion upon Latmus, the idol of his little world. The glitter of fame, happiness and ease was upon the entire group; but in an instant everything was to be changed with the blinding swiftness of enchantment. Quick death was to come on the central figure of that company. . . . Over all the rest the blackest fates hovered menacingly; fates from which a mother might pray that kindly death would save her children in

their infancy.   One was to wander with the stain of murder on his soul, with the curses of a world upon his name,
with a price set upon his head, in frightful physical pain,
till he died a dog's death in a burning barn.   The stricken
wife was to pass the rest of her days in melancholy and
madness; of those two young lovers, one was to slay the
other, and then end his life a raving maniac!"   No book
of tragedy contains a single chapter quite so dark as that.
   What was the mysterious power of this mysterious man,
and whence?

   His was the genius of common sense; of common sense
in action; of common sense in thought; of common sense
enriched by experience and unhindered by fear.   "He
was a common man," says his friend Joshua Speed, "ex-
panded into giant proportions; well acquainted with the
people, he placed his hand on the beating pulse of the
nation, judged of its disease, and was ready with a remedy."   Inspired he was truly, as Shakespeare was inspired;
as Mozart was inspired; as Burns was inspired; each, like
him, sprung directly from the people.   [Applause.]

   I look into the crystal globe that, slowly turning, tells
the story of his life, and I see a little heart-broken boy,
weeping by the outstretched form of a dead mother, then
bravely, nobly trudging a hundred miles to obtain her
Christian burial.   I see this motherless lad growing to
manhood amid the scenes that seem to lead to nothing but
abasement; no teachers; no books; no chart, except his
own untutored mind; no compass, except his own undis-
ciplined will; no light, save light from Heaven; yet, like
the caravel of Columbus, struggling on and on through
the trough of the sea, always toward the destined land.
I see the full-grown man, stalwart and brave, an athlete in
activity of movement and strength of limb, yet vexed by
weird dreams and visions; of life, of love, of religion, sometimes verging on despair.   I see the mind, grown as
robust as the body, throw off these phantoms of the imagination and give itself wholly to the work-a-day uses of
the world; the rearing of children; the earning of bread;
the multiplied duties of life.   I see the party leader, self-
confident in conscious rectitude; original, because it was
not his nature to follow; potent, because he was fearless,
pursuing his convictions with earnest zeal, and urging

them upon his fellows with the resources of an oratory
which was hardly more impressive than it was many-sided.
I see him, the preferred among his fellows, ascend the
eminence reserved for him, and him alone of all the statesmen of the time, amid the derision of opponents and the
distrust of supporters, yet unawed and unmoved, because
thoroughly equipped to meet the emergency.   The same
being, from first to last; the poor child weeping over a
dead mother; the great chief sobbing amid the cruel horrors of war; flinching not from duty, nor changing his life-
long ways of dealing with the stern realities which pressed
upon him and hurried him onward.   And, last scene of all,
that ends this strange, eventful history, I see him lying
dead there in the capitol of the nation, to which he had
rendered " the last, full measure of his devotion," the flag
of his country around him, the world in mourning, and,
asking myself how could any man have hated that man,
I ask you, how can any man refuse his homage to his
memory?   Surely, he was one of God's elect; not in any
sense a creature of circumstance, or accident.   Recurring
to the doctrine of inspiration, I say again and again, he
was inspired of God, and I cannot see how any one who
believes in that doctrine can regard him as anything else.
[Applause.]

From Cæsar to Bismarck and Gladstone the world has
had its statesmen and its soldiers—men who rose to
eminence and power step by step, through a series of
geometric progression as it were, each advancement following in regular order one after the other, the whole
obedient to well-established and well-understood laws of
cause and effect.   They were not what we call " men of
destiny."   They were " men of the time."   They were
men whose careers had a beginning, a middle and an end,
rounding off lives with histories, full it may be of interesting and exciting event, but comprehensive and compre-
hensible; simple, clear, complete.

The inspired ones are fewer.   Whence their emanation,
where and how they got their power, by what rule they
lived, moved and had their being, we know not.   There is
no explication to their lives.   They rose from shadow and
they went in mist.   We see them, feel them, but we know
them not.   They came, God's word upon their lips; they

did their office, God's mantle about them; and they vanished, God's holy light between the world and them, leaving behind a memory, half mortal and half myth. From first to last they were the creations of some special Providence, baffling the wit of man to fathom, defeating the machinations of the world, the flesh and the devil, until their work was done, then passing from the scene as mysteriously as they had come upon it.

Tried by this standard, where shall we find an example so impressive as Abraham Lincoln, whose career might be chanted by a Greek chorus as at once the prelude and the epilogue of the most imperial theme of modern times?

Born as lowly as the Son of God, in a hovel; reared in penury, squalor, with no gleam of light or fair surrounding; without graces, actual or acquired; without name or fame or official training; it was reserved for this strange being, late in life, to be snatched from obscurity, raised to supreme command at a supreme moment, and intrusted with the destiny of a nation.

The great leaders of his party, the most experienced and accomplished public men of the day, were made to stand aside; were sent to the rear, whilst this fantastic figure was led by unseen hands to the front and given the reins of power. It is immaterial whether we were for him, or against him; wholly immaterial. That, during four years, carrying with them such a weight of responsibility as the world never witnessed before, he filled the vast space allotted him in the eyes and actions of mankind, is to say that he was inspired of God, for nowhere else could he have acquired the wisdom and the virtue.

Where did Shakespeare get his genius? Where did Mozart get his music? Whose hand smote the lyre of the Scottish plowman, and stayed the life of the German priest? God, God, and God alone; and as surely as these were raised up by God, inspired by God, was Abraham Lincoln; and a thousand years hence, no drama, no tragedy, no epic poem will be filled with greater wonder, or be followed by mankind with deeper feeling than that which tells the story of his life and death. [Loud applause.]

EDWIN PERCY WHIPPLE

WIT AND HUMOR

[Lecture by Edwin P. Whipple, critic and essayist (born in Gloucester, Mass., March 18, 1819; died in Boston, Mass., June 16, 1886), delivered first before the Boston Mercantile Library Association, in the Odeon, Boston, December 24, 1845, and becoming a favorite with lyceum audiences in many places and through many seasons.]

LADIES AND GENTLEMEN:—It has been justly objected to New England society, that it is too serious and prosaic. It cannot take a joke. It demands the reason of all things, or their value in the current coin of the land. It is nervous, fidgety, unreposing, full of trouble. Striving hard to make even religion a torment, it clothes in purple and fine linen its apostles of despair. Business is followed with such a devouring intensity of purpose that it results as often in dyspepsia as in wealth. We are so overcome with the serious side of things that our souls rarely come out in irrepressible streams of merriment. The venerable King Cole would find few subjects here to acknowledge his monarchy of mirth. In the foppery of our utilitarianism we would frown down all recreations which have not a logical connection with mental improvement or purse improvement. For those necessary accompaniments of all life out of the Insane Asylum—qualities which the most serious and sublime of Christian poets has described with the utmost witchery of his fancy,—

> " Quips, and cranks, and wanton wiles,
> Nods, and becks, and wreathed smiles,
> Sport that wrinkled Care derides,
> And Laughter holding both his sides,"—

for these we have the suspicious glance, the icy speech, the self-involved and mysterious look.   We are gulled by all those pretences which require a vivid sense of the ludicrous to be detected; and with all our boasted intelligence, there is hardly a form of quackery and fanaticism which does not thrive better by the side of our schools and colleges than anywhere else.   And the reason is, we lack generally the faculty or feeling of ridicule,—the counterfeit detector all over the world.   We have, perhaps, sufficient respect for the great, the majestic, and the benevolent, but we are deficient in the humorous insight to detect roguery and pretence under their external garbs.   As we cannot laugh at our own follies, so we cannot endure being laughed at.   A Grub-street scribbler, tossing at us from a London garret a few lightning-bugs of jocularity, can set our whole population in a flame.   Public indignation is the cheapest article of domestic manufacture.   There is no need of a tariff to protect that.   We thus give altogether too much importance to unimportant things,— breaking butterflies on the wheel, and cannonading grasshoppers; and our dignity continually exhales in our spasmodic efforts to preserve it.

Now it is an undoubted fact that the principle of Mirth is as innate in the mind as any other original faculty. The absence of it in individuals or communities is a defect; for there are various forms of error and imposture which wit, and wit alone, can expose and punish.   Without a well-trained capacity to perceive the ludicrous, the health suffers, both of the body and the mind; seriousness dwindles into asceticism, sobriety degenerates into bigotry, and the natural order of things gives way to the vagaries of distempered imaginations.   " He who laughs," said the mother of Goethe, " can commit no deadly sin."   The Emperor Titus thought he had lost a day if he had passed it without laughing.   Sterne contends that every laugh lengthens the term of our lives.   Wisdom, which represents the marriage of Truth and Virtue, is by no means synonymous with gravity.   She is L'Allegro as well as Il Penseroso, and jests as well as preaches.   The wise men of old have sent most of their morality down the stream of time in the light skiff of apothegm or epigram; and the proverbs of nations, which embody the common sense of nations, have the brisk concussion of the most sparkling wit. Almost every sensible remark on a folly is a witty remark. Wit is thus often but the natural language of wisdom, viewing life with a piercing and passionless eye. Indeed, nature and society are so replete with startling contrasts, that wit often consists in the mere statement and comparison of facts; as when Hume says, that the ancient Muscovites wedded their wives with a whip instead of a ring; as when Voltaire remarks, that Penn's treaty with the Indians was the only one ever made between civilized men and savages not sanctioned by an oath, and the only one that was ever kept. In the same vein of wise sarcasm is the observation that France under the Ancient Regime was an absolute monarchy moderated by songs, and that Russia is a despotism tempered by assassination; or the old English proverb, that he who preaches war is the devil's chaplain.

In view of this ludicrous side of things perceived by Wit and Humor, I propose, in this lecture to discourse of Mirth,—its philosophy, its literature, its influence. The breadth of the theme forbids a complete treatment of it, for to Wit and Humor belong much that is important in history and most agreeable in letters. The mere mention of a few of the great wits and humorists of the world will show the extent of the subject, viewed simply in its literary aspect; for to Mirth belong the exhaustless fancy and sky-piercing buffooneries of Aristophanes; the matchless irony of Lucian; the stern and terrible satire of Juvenal; the fun-drunken extravagance of Rabelais; the self-pleased chuckle of Montaigne; the farcical caricature of Scarron; the glowing and sparkling verse of Dryden; the genial fun of Addison; the scoffing subtilities of Butler; the ærial merriment of Sterne; the hard brilliancy and stinging emphasis of Pope; the patient glitter of Congreve; the teasing mockery of Voltaire; the polished sharpness of Sheridan; the wise drolleries of Sydney Smith; the sly, shy, elusive, ethereal humor of Lamb; the short, sharp, flashing scorn of Macaulay; the careless gaiety of Béranger; the humorous sadness of Hood; and the comic creations, various almost as human nature, which have peopled the imaginations of Europe with everlasting forms of the ludicrous, from the time of Shakespeare and Cervantes to that of Scott and Dickens. Now all these writers either represented or influenced their age. Their works are as valuable to the historian as to the lover of the comic; for they show us what people in different ages laughed at, and thus indicate the periods at which forms of faith and government, and social follies and vices, passed from objects of reverence or respect into subjects of ridicule and contempt. And only in Dr. Barrow's celebrated description of facetiousness, "the greatest proof of mastery over language," says Mackintosh, "ever given by an English writer," can be represented the manifold forms and almost infinite range of their mirth. "Sometimes it lieth in pat allusion to a known story, or in seasonable application of a trivial saying, or in forging an apposite tale; sometimes it playeth in words and phrases, taking advantage from the ambiguity of their sense or the affinity of their sound; sometimes it is wrapped up in a dress of humorous expression; sometimes it lurketh under an odd similitude; sometimes it is lodged in a sly question, in a smart answer, in a quirkish reason, in a shrewd intimation, in cunningly diverting or cleverly retorting an objection; sometimes it is couched in a bold scheme of speech, in a tart irony, in a lusty hyperbole, in a startling metaphor, in a plausible reconciling of contradictions, or in acute nonsense; sometimes a scenical representation of persons or things, a counterfeit speech, a mimical look or gesture, passeth for it; sometimes an affected simplicity, sometimes a presumptuous bluntness, giveth it being; sometimes it riseth only from a lucky hitting upon what is strange; sometimes from a crafty wresting obvious matter to the purpose. Often it consisteth in one hardly knows what, and springeth up one can hardly tell how, being answerable to the numberless rovings of fancy and windings of language."

To this description, at once so subtle and so comprehensive, little can be added. It remains, however, to indicate some characteristics which separate wit from humor. Neither seems a distinct faculty of the mind, but rather a sportive exercise of intellect and fancy, directed by the sentiment of Mirth, and changing its character with the variations of individual passions and peculiarities. The essence of the ludicrous consists in surprise,—in unexpected turns of feeling and explosions of thought,—often by bringing dissimilar things together with a shock;—as when some wit called Boyle, the celebrated philosopher, the father of chemistry and brother of the Earl of Cork; or as when the witty editor of a penny paper took for the motto of his journal—" The price of liberty is eternal vigilance, the price of the ' Star ' is only one cent." When Northcote, the sculptor, was asked what he thought of George IV he answered that he did not know him. " But," persisted his querist, " His Majesty says he knows you." " Know me," said Northcote, " pooh! pooh! that's all his brag!" Again, Phillips, while traveling in this country, said that he once met a Republican so furious against monarchs that he would not even wear a crown to his hat. The expression of uncontrolled self-will is often witty as well as wicked, from this element of unexpectedness. Peter the Great, observing the number of lawyers in Westminster Hall, remarked that he had but two lawyers in his whole dominions, and that he intended to hang one of them as soon as he got home.

Wit was originally a general name for all the intellectual powers, meaning the faculty which kens, perceives, knows, understands; it was gradually narrowed in its signification to express merely the resemblance between ideas; and lastly, to note that resemblance when it occasioned ludicrous surprise. It marries ideas, lying wide apart, by a sudden jerk of the understanding. Humor originally meant moisture, a signification it metaphorically retains, for it is the very juice of the mind, oozing from the brain, and enriching and fertilizing wherever it falls. Wit exists by antipathy; humor by sympathy. Wit laughs at things; humor laughs with them. Wit lashes exterial appearances, or cunningly exaggerates single foibles into character; humor glides into the heart of its object, looks lovingly on the infirmities it detects, and represents the whole man. Wit is abrupt, darting, scornful, and tosses its analogies in your face; humor is slow and shy, insinuating its fun into your heart. Wit is negative, analytical, destructive; humor is creative. The couplets of Pope are witty, but Sancho Panza is a humorous creation. Wit, when earnest, has the earnestness of passion seeking to destroy; humor has the earnestness of affection, and would lift up what is seemingly low into our charity and love. Wit, bright, rapid and blasting as the lightning, flashes, strikes and vanishes, in an instant; humor, warm and all-embracing as the sunshine, bathes its objects in a genial and abiding light. Wit implies hatred or contempt of folly and crime, produces its effects by brisk shocks of surprise, uses the whip of scorpions and the branding-iron, stabs, stings, pinches, tortures, goads, teases, corrodes, undermines; humor implies a sure conception of the beautiful, the majestic and the true, by whose light it surveys and shapes their opposites. It is a humane influence, softening with mirth the ragged inequalities of existence, promoting tolerant views of life, bridging over the spaces which separate the lofty from the lowly, the great from the humble. Old Dr. Fuller's remark, that a negro is "the image of God cut in ebony," is humorous; Horace Smith's inversion of it that the taskmaster is "the image of the devil cut in ivory," is witty. Wit can coexist with fierce and malignant passions; but humor demands good-feeling and fellow-feeling, feeling not merely for what is above us, but for what is around and beneath us. When wit and humor are commingled, the result is a genial sharpness, dealing with its object somewhat as old Izaak Walton dealt with the frog he used for bait,—running the hook neatly through his mouth and out at his gills, and in so doing" using him as though he loved him!" Sydney Smith and Shakespeare's Touchstone are examples.

Wit, then, being strictly an assailing and destructive faculty, remorselessly shooting at things from an antagonistic point of view, it not infrequently blends with great passions; and you ever find it gleaming in the van of all radical and revolutionary movements against established opinions and institutions. In this practical, executive form, it is commonly called satire; and in this form it has exercised vast influence on human affairs. Its character has varied with the character of individual satirists; in some taking the beak and talons of the eagle or the hawk, in others putting on the wasp and the dragon-fly. Too often it has but given a brighter and sharper edge to hatred and malignity. In a classification of satirical compositions, they may be included in two great divisions, namely, satire on human nature, and satire on the perversions and corruptions of human nature. The first and most terrible of these, satire on human nature, dipping its pen in " Scorn's fiery poison," represents man as a bundle of vices and weaknesses, considers his aspirations merely as provocatives of malignant scoffing, and debases whatever is most beautiful and majestic in life, by associating it with whatever is vilest and most detestable. This is not satire on men, but on Man. The laughter which it creates is impish and devilish, the very mirth of fiends, and its wit the gleam and glare of infernal light. Two great dramatists, Shakespeare and Goethe, have represented this phase of satire artistically, in the characters of Iago and Mephistopheles; and Dean Swift and Lord Byron have done it personally in Gulliver and Don Juan; —Swift, from following the instincts of a diseased heart, and the analogies of an impure fancy; Byron, from recklessness and capricious misanthropy. Only, however, in Iago and Mephistopheles do we find the perfection of this kind of wit,—keen, nimble, quick-sighted, feelingless, undermining all virtue and all beauty with foul suspicions and fiendish mockeries. The subtle mind of Iago glides to its object with the soft celerity of a panther's tread; that of Mephistopheles darts with the velocity of a tiger's spring. Both are malignant intelligences, infinitely ingenious in evil, infinitely merciless in purpose; and whereever their scorching sarcasm falls, it blights and blackens all the humanities of life.

Now for this indiscriminate jibing and scoffing at human nature there can be no excuse. There is no surer sign of a bad heart than for a writer to find delight in degrading his species. But still there are legitimate objects for the most terrible and destructive weapons of satire; and these are the corruptions and crimes of the world, whether embodied in persons or institutions. Here wit has achieved great victories, victories for humanity and truth. Brazen impudence and guilt have been discrowned and blasted by its bolts. It has overthrown establishments where selfishness, profligacy, and meanness, had hived for ages. It has felt its way in flame along every nerve and artery of social oppressors, whose tough hearts had proved invulnerable to wail and malediction. It has torn aside the masks which have given temporary ascendancy to every persecutor calling himself priest, and every robber calling himself king. It has scourged the bigot and the hypocrite, and held up to " grinning infamy " the knaveries and villainies of corrupt governments. It has made many a pretension of despotism, once unquestioned, a hissing and a by-word all over the earth. Tyrannies, whose iron pressure had nearly crushed out the life of a people,—tyrannies, which have feared neither man nor God, and withstood prayers and curses which might almost have brought down Heaven's answering lightnings,—these, in the very bravery of their guilt, in the full hallo of their whole pack of unbridled passions, have been smitten by the shaft of the satirist, and passed from objects of hatred and terror into targets of ridicule and scorn. As men neither fear nor respect what has been made contemptible, all honor to him who makes oppression laughable as well as detestable. Armies cannot protect it then; and walls which have remained impenetrable to cannon have fallen before a roar of laughter or a hiss of contempt.

Satirists generally appear in the dotage of opinions and institutions, when the state has become an embodied falsehood, and the church a name; when society has dwindled into a smooth lie, and routine has become religion; when appearance has taken the place of reality, and wickedness has settled down into weakness. If we take the great comic writers who represent their age, we shall find that satire, with them, is the expression of their contempt for the dead forms of a once living faith. Faith in paganism at the time of Homer as contrasted with the time of Aristophanes,—faith in Catholicism in Dante's age as contrasted with the age of Voltaire,—faith in the creations of the imagination at the time of Spenser as contrasted with the age of Pope,—in some degree measure the difference between these writers, and explain why the ridicule of the one should be pitched at what awakened the reverence of the other. Great satirists, appearing in the decay of an old order of civilization, descend on their time as ministers of vengeance, intellectual Alarics, " planetary plagues,"

> " When Jove
> Shall o'er some high-viced city hang his poison
> In the sick air."

They prepare the way for better things by denouncing
what has become worn, and wasted, and corrupt,—that
from the terrible wreck of old falsehoods may spring
"truths that wake to perish never."   With invincible courage they do their work, and wherever they see accredited
hypocrisy or shameless guilt, they will speak to it,

> "Though Hell itself should gape,
> And bid them hold their peace."

Thus we shall find that many satirists have been radical
legislators, and that many jests have become history. The
annals of the eighteenth century would be very imperfect
that did not give a large space to Voltaire, who was as
much a monarch as Charles XII or Louis XIV.   Satirical
compositions, floating about among a people, have more
than once produced revolutions.   They are sown as
dragons' teeth; they spring up armed men.   The author
of the ballad of Lillibulero boasted that he had rhymed
King James II out of his dominions.   England, under
Charles II, was governed pretty equally by roues and wit-
snappers.   A joke hazarded by royal lips on a regal object has sometimes plunged kingdoms into war; for dull
monarchs generally make their repartees through the cannon's mouth.   The biting jests of Frederick the Great on
the Empress Elizabeth and Madame de Pompadour were
instrumental in bringing down upon his dominions the
armies of Russia and France.   The downfall of the French
monarchy was occasioned primarily by its becoming contemptible through its vices.   No government, whether
evil or good, can long exist after it has ceased to excite
respect and begun to excite hilarity.   Ministers of state
have been repeatedly laughed out of office.   Where scorn
points its scoffing finger, servility itself may well be
ashamed to fawn.   In this connection I trust no one will
consider me capable of making a political allusion, or to
be wanting in respect for the dead, if I refer in illustration
to a late administration of our own government,—I mean
that which retired on March 4, 1845.   Now, during that
administration measures of the utmost importance were
commenced or consummated; the country was more generally prosperous than it had been for years; there were

no spectacles of gentlemen taking passage for France or Texas, with bags of the public gold in their valises; the executive power was felt in every part of the land; and yet the whole thing was hailed with a shout of laughter, ringing to the remotest villages of the East and the West. Everybody laughed, and the only difference between its nominal supporters and its adversaries was, that whereas one party laughed outright, the other laughed in their sleeves. Nothing could have saved such an administration from downfall, for whatever may have been its intrinsic merits, it was still considered not so much a government as a gigantic joke.

And now, in further illustration of the political importance of satirists, and their appearance in periods of national degradation, allow me to present a few leaves from literary history. The great satirical age of English literature, as you are all aware, dates from the restoration of Charles II in 1660, and runs to the reign of George II, a period of about seventy years. During this period flourished Dryden, Pope, Swift, Young, Gay, and Arbuthnot, and during this period the national morality was at its lowest ebb. It was an age peculiarly calculated to develop an assailing spirit in men of talent, for there were numberless vices which deserved to be assailed. Authors moved in, or very near, the circle of high life, and political life, in the full view of the follies and crimes of both. They were accustomed to see Man in his artificial state,—busy in intrigue, pursuing selfish ends by unscrupulous means, counting virtue and honor as ornamental non-existences, looking on religion as a very good thing for the poor, conceiving of poetry as lying far back in tradition or out somewhere in the country, hiding his hate in a smile, pocketing his infamy with a bow. They saw that the star of the earl, the ermine of the judge, and the surplice of the prelate, instead of representing nobility, justice, and piety, were often but the mere badge of apostasy, the mere livery of liberticide. They saw that every person seemed to have his price, and that if a man ascertained that he himself was not worth buying, he was perfectly willing to sell his sister or his wife, and strutted about after the sale, bedizened with infamy, as happy and as pleasant a gentleman as one would wish to meet on a summer's

day. It was from the depth of such infamy as this last that
the Duke of Marlborough emerged, the first general of
his time.   In such a mass of dissimulation, effrontery, pec-
ulation, fraud,—in such a dearth of high thoughts and
great passions,—in such a spectacle of moral nonchalance,
dignified imbecility, and elegant shamelessness,—the
satirical poet could find numberless targets for the scorn-
winged arrows of his ridicule; could sometimes feel that
he, too, had his part in the government of the country; and
with honest delight could often exclaim with Pope:—

> " I own I'm proud—I must be proud, to see
> Men not afraid of God afraid of me."

Among these satirists, Pope, of the age of Queen Anne,
was by far the most independent, unflinching, and merciless.   Inferior to Dryden, perhaps in genius, he was still
placed in a position which rendered him more independent
of courts and parties, and his invective, unlike that of
Dryden, was shot directly at crime and folly, without respect to persons.   Although he was terribly bitter when
galled and goaded by personal opponents, and, in his
satire, too often spent his strength against mere imbecility
and wretchedness; yet, take him as he is, the great representative writer of his time; the uncompromising smiter
of powerful guilt, the sturdy defender of humble virtue;
the satirist of dukes, but the eulogist of the Man of Ross;
his works the most perfect specimens of brilliant good
sense, his life free from the servility which hitherto had
disgraced authorship; and though charity may find much
in him that needs to be forgiven, though justice may even
sometimes class him with those moral assassins who wear,
like Cloten, their daggers in their mouths, yet still great
merit cannot be denied to the poet and the man who
scourged hypocrisy and baseness, at a time when baseness paved the way to power, and hypocrisy distributed
the spoils of fraud.   The courage exercised by such a
satirist was by no means insignificant.   The enmities which
Pope provoked were almost as numerous as knaves and
fools.   After the publication of the Dunciad, he was generally accompanied in the street by a huge Irishman,
armed with a club, so that if any lean-witted rhymer or

fat-fisted member of Parliament, whom he had gibbeted
with his sarcasm, desired to be revenged on his person,
the brawny Hibernian had full commission to conduct that
controversy, according to the most approved logic of the
shillalah.

The other great satirist of the age of Queen Anne was
Dean Swift, a "darker and a fiercer spirit" than Pope,
and one who has been stigmatized as "the apostate politician, the perjured lover, and the ribald priest,—a heart
burning with hatred against the whole human race, a mind
richly laden with images from the gutter and the lazar-
house." Swift has been justly called the greatest of libel-
ers,—a libeler of persons, a libeler of human nature, and
we may add, a libeler of himself. He delighted to drag all
the graces and sanctities of life through the pools and
puddles of his own mind, and after such a baptism of mud,
to hold them up as specimens of what dreamers called the
inborn beauty of the human soul. He was a bad man,
depraved in the very center of his nature; but he was still
one of the greatest wits, and, after a fashion, one of the
greatest humorists, that ever existed. His most effective
weapon was irony, a kind of saturnine, sardonic wit, having the self-possession, complexity, and continuity of humor, without its geniality; and, in the case of Swift,
steeped rather in the vitriol of human bitterness than the
milk of human kindness. Irony is an insult conveyed in
the form of a compliment; insinuating the most galling
satire under the phraseology of panegyric; placing its victim naked on a bed of briars' and thistles, thinly covered
with rose-leaves; adorning his brow with a crown of gold,
which burns into his brain; teasing and fretting, and
riddling him through and through, with incessant dis-
charges of hot shot from a masked battery; laying bare
the most sensitive and shrinking nerves of his mind, and
then blandly touching them with ice, or smilingly prick-
ing them with needles. Wit, in this form cannot be withstood even by the hardest of heart and the emptiest of
head. It eats and rusts into its victim. Swift used it
with incomparable skill, sometimes against better men
than himself, sometimes against the public plunderer and
the titled knave, the frauds of quackery and the abuses of
government. His morose, mocking, and cynical spirit,

combined with his sharp insight into practical life, enabled him to preserve an inimitable coolness of manner, while he stated the most nonsensical or atrocious paradoxes as if they were self-evident truisms. He generally destroyed his antagonists by ironically twisting their opinions into a form of hideous caricature, and then setting forth grave mockeries of argument in their defence, imputing, by inference, the most diabolical doctrines to his opponents, and then soberly attempting to show that they were the purest offspring of justice and benevolence. Nothing can be more perfect of its kind, nothing more vividly suggests the shallowness of moral and religious principle which characterized his age, nothing subjects practical infidelity to an ordeal of more tormenting and wasting ridicule, than his ironical tract, giving a statement of reasons why, on the whole, it would be impolitic to abolish the Christian religion in England. This is considered by Mackintosh the finest piece of irony in the English language.

Swift's most laughable specimen of "acute nonsense" was his prophecy that a certain quack almanac-maker, by the name of Partridge, would die on a certain day. Partridge, who was but little disposed to die in order to give validity to the prediction of a rival astrologer, came out exultingly denying the truth of the prophecy, after the period fixed for his decease, and not he, had expired. Swift, nothing daunted, retorted in another tract, in which he set forth a large array of quirkish reasons to prove that Partridge was dead, and ingeniously argued that the quack's own testimony to the contrary could not be received, as he was too notorious a liar to be entitled to belief on so important a point.

But perhaps the most exquisite piece of irony in modern literature, and, at the same time, the most terrible satire on the misgovernment of Ireland, is Swift's pamphlet entitled, "A Modest Proposal to the Public, for Preventing the Children of Poor People in Ireland from Being a Burden to Their Country, and for Making Them Beneficial to the Public";—which modest proposal consisted in advising that the said children be used for food. He commences with stating that the immense number of children in the arms, or on the backs, or at the heels, of their starving mothers, has become a public grievance, and that

he would be a public benefactor who should contrive some
method of making them useful to the commonwealth.
After showing that it is impossible to expect that they
should be able to pick up a livelihood by stealing much
before they are six years old, and saying that he had been
assured by merchants that a child under twelve years was
no salable commodity,—that it would not bring on
'change more than three pounds, while its rags and nutri-
ments would cost four times that amount,—he proceeds
to advise their use as food for their more fortunate fellow-
creatures; and as this food, from its delicacy, would be
somewhat dear, he considers it all the more proper for
landlords, who, as they have already devoured the parents,
seem to have the best right to the children.   He answers
all objections to his proposal by mock arguments, and
closes with solemnly protesting his own disinterestedness
in making it; and proves that he has no personal interest
in the matter, as he has not himself a child by whom he
can expect to get a penny, the youngest being nine years
old!   So admirably was the irony sustained, that the
pamphlet was quoted by a French writer of the time, as
evidencing the hopeless barbarity of the English nation.

It would be easy to trace the influence of satirical compositions further down the course of English history; but
enough has already been said to indicate the check which
social and political criminals have received, from the presence of men capable of holding them up to the world's
laughter and contempt.   This satire, in all free common-
wealths, has a share in the legislation and policy of the
government; and bad institutions and pernicious opinions
rarely fall, until they have been pierced by its keen-edged
mockeries, or smitten by its scathing invectives.

The lighter follies and infirmities of human nature, as
seen in everyday life, have afforded numberless objects for
light-hearted or vinegar-hearted raillery, jibe, satire, banter, and caricature.   Among the foibles of men, Wit plays
and glances, a tricksy Ariel of the intellect, full of mirth
and mischief, laughing at all, and inspiring all to laugh at
each other.   Egotism and vanity are prominent provoca-
tions of this dunce-demolishing fun; for a man, it has been
truly said, is ridiculous "not so much for what he is, as
for pretending to be what he is not."   It is very rare to

see a frank knave or a blockhead who knows himself. The life of most men is passed in an attempt to misrepresent themselves, everybody being bitten by an ambition to appear instead of to be. Thus few can visit sublime scenery without preparing beforehand the emotions of wonder and awe they ought to feel, and contriving the raptures into which they intended to fall. We mourn, make love, console, sentimentalize, in cant phrases. We guard with religious scrupulousness against the temptation of being betrayed into a natural expression of ourselves. A perception of the ludicrous would make us ashamed of this self-exaggerating foible, and save us from the cuffs and pats by which Wit occasionally reminds us of it. "Dr. Parr," said a young student once to the old linguist,—"Let's you and I write a book."—"Very well," replied the doctor, "put in all that I know, and all that you don't know, and we'd make a big one." The doctor himself was not free from the conceit he delighted to punish in others; for satire is apt to be a glass, "in which we see every face but our own." He once said in a miscellaneous company, "England has produced three great classical scholars; the first was Bentley, the second was Porson, and the third modesty forbids me to mention." Occasionally egotists will strike rather hard against each other, as in the case of the strutting captain of a militia company, who once, in a fit of temporary condescension, invited a ragged negro to drink negus with him. "Oh! certainly," rejoined the negro; "I'm not proud; I'd just as lieve drink with a militia captain as anybody else." Dr. Johnson was famous for smashing the thin egg-shells of conceit which partly concealed the mental impotence of some of his auditors. One of them once shook his head gravely, and said he could not see the force and application of one of the doctor's remarks. He was crushed instantly by the gruff retort—"It is my business, sir, to give you arguments, not to give you brains."

Sometimes the ridiculousness of a remark springs from the intense superficiality of its conventional conceit, as in the case of the young lady, who, on being once asked what she thought of Niagara, answered that she had never beheld the falls, but had always heard them highly spoken of. Ignorance which deems itself profoundly wise is also exquisitely ludicrous. A German prince once gave his subjects a free constitution; at which they murmured continually, saying that heretofore they had paid taxes and been saved the trouble of government, but that now they were not only taxed but had to govern themselves. Wit easily unmasks the hypocrisy and selfishness which underlie loyal and patriotic catch words. Parr said that the toast "Church and King" usually meant a "church without a gospel and a king above the law," and Sydney Smith, while lashing some Tory placemen, ebullient with loyalty, observed that "God save the King" meant too often, "God save my pension and my place, God give my sisters an allowance out of the privy-purse,—make me clerk of the irons, let me survey the meltings, let me live upon the fruits of other men's industry, and fatten upon the plunder of the public."

Again, all sniveling hypocrisy in speculation, such as that which, when discoursing of the world's evils, delights to call Man's sin God's providence,—all boisterous noodleism in reform, whose champions would take society on their knee, as a Yankee takes a stick, and whittle it into shape;—to these satire gravitates by a natural law. The story told by Horace Smith of the city miss is a good instance of a shock given to affected and mincing elegance. She had read much of pastoral life, and once made a visit into the country for the purpose of communing with a real shepherd. She at last discovered one, with the crook in his hand, the dog by his side, and the sheep disposed romantically around him; but he was without the indispensable musical accompaniment of all poetic shepherds, the pastoral reed. "Ah! gentle shepherd," softly inquired she, "tell me where's your pipe." The bumpkin scratched his head, and murmured brokenly, "I left it at home, miss, 'cause I haint got no baccy!"

Wit is infinitely ingenious in what Barrow calls "the quirkish reason," and often pinches hard when it seems most seriously urbane. Thus a gentleman once warmly eulogized the constancy of an absent husband in the presence of his loving wife. "Yes, yes!" assented she; "he writes me letters full of the agony of affection, but he never remits me any money." "I can conceive of that," replied the other, "for I know his love to be unremitting."

Byron's defense of the selfish member of **Parliament is** another pertinent instance :—

> " —— has no heart, you say, but I deny it;
> He has a heart—he gets his speeches by it."

Satire is famous for these quiet side cuts and sympathetic impertinences. An officer of Louis XIV was continually pestering him for promotion, and at last drew from him the peevish exclamation—"You are the most troublesome man in my army." "That, please your Majesty, is what your enemies are continually saying," was the reply. When George Wither, the Puritan poet, was taken prisoner by the Cavaliers, there was a general disposition displayed to hang him at once; but Sir John Denham saved his life by saying to Charles I—"I hope your Majesty will not hang poor George Wither, for as long as he lives, it can't be said that I am the worst poet in England." Sheridan, it is well known, was never free from pecuniary embarrassments. As he was one day hacking his face with a dull razor, he turned to his eldest son and said, "Tom, if you open any more oysters with my razor, I'll cut you off with a shilling."—"Very well, father," retorted Tom, " but where will the shilling come from?"

Thus into every avenue of life and character Wit darts its porcupine quills,—pinching the pompous, abasing the proud, branding the shameless, knocking out the teeth of Pretension. The foibles and crimes of men, indeed, afford perpetual occasions for wit. As soon as the human being becomes a moral agent, as soon as he has put off the vesture of infancy and been fairly deposited in trousers, his life becomes a kind of tragi-comical caricature of himself. Tetchy, capricious, wayward, inconsistent,—his ideas sparks of gunpowder which explode at the first touch of fire,—running the gantlet of experience, and getting cornered at every step,—making love to a Fanny Squeers, thinking her an Imogen, and finding her a Mrs. Caudle,—buffeting and battling his way through countless disappointments and ludicrous surprises,—it is well for him if his misfortune of one year can constitute his mirth of the next. One thing is certain, that if he cannot laugh as well as rail,—if he cannot grow occasionally jubilant over his own verdancy,—if he persists pragmatically in referring his failures to the world's injustice instead of his own folly, —he will end in moroseness and egotism, in cant that snivels and misanthropy that mouths. Even genius and philanthropy are incomplete, without they are accompanied by some sense of the ludicrous; for an extreme sensitiveness to the evil and misery of society becomes a maddening torture if not modified by a feeling of the humorous, and urges its subjects into morbid exaggerations of life's dark side. Thus many, who, in our day, leap headlong into benevolent reforms, merely caricature philanthropy. Blinded by one idea, they miss their mark, dash themselves insanely against immovable rocks, and break up the whole stream of their life into mere sputter and foam. A man of genius, intolerant of the world's prose, or incompetent to perceive the humor which underlies it, cannot represent life without distortion and exaggeration. Had Shelley possessed humor, his might have been the third name in English poetry. The everlasting delight we take in Shakespeare, and Scott, comes from the vivid perception they had of both aspects of life, and their felicitous presentment of them, as they jog against each other in the world.

As Wit in its practical executive form usually runs into some of the modifications of satire, so Humor, which includes Wit, generally blends with sympathetic feeling. Humor takes no delight in the mere infliction of pain; it has no connection with the aggressive or destructive passions. In the creation and delineation of comic character it is most delightedly employed, and here "Jonathan Wild is not too low for it, nor Lord Shaftesbury too high;" it deals with the nicest refinements of the ludicrous, and also with what Sterling calls "the trivial and the bombastic, the driveling, squinting, sprawling clowneries of nature, with her worn-out stage-properties and rag-fair emblazonments." The man of humor, seeing at one glance, the majestic and the mean, the serious and the laughable; indeed, interpreting what is little or ridiculous by light derived from its opposite idea; delineates character as he finds it in life, without any impertinent intrusion of his own indignation or approval. He sees deeply into human nature; lays open the hidden structure and most complex machinery of the mind, and understands not merely the motives which guide actions, but the processes by which they are concealed from the actors. For instance, life is filled with what is called hypocrisy,—with the assignment of false motives to actions. This is a constant source of the laughable in conduct. Wit, judging simply from the act, treats it as a vice, and holds it up to derision or execration; but Humor commonly considers it as a weakness, deluding none so much as the actor, and in that self-delusion finds food for its mirth. The character of old John Willett, in "Barnaby Rudge," so delicious as a piece of humor, would be but a barren butt in the hands of Wit. Wit cannot create character. It might, for instance, cluster innumerable satirical associations around the abstract idea of gluttony, but it could not picture to the eye such a person as Don Quixote's squire. It cannot create even a purely witty character, such as Thersites, Benedict, or Beatrice. In Congreve's plays, the characters are not so much men and women as epigrammatic machines, whose wit, incessant as a shower of fiery rain, still throws no light into their heads or hearts. Now, Humor will have nothing to do with abstractions. It dwells snugly in concrete personal substances, having no toleration either for the unnaturally low or the factitiously sublime. It remorselessly brings down Britannia to John Bull, Caledonia to Sawney, Hibernia to Paddy, Columbia to Jonathan. It hates all generalities. A benevolent lady, in a work written to carry on a benevolent enterprise, commended the project to the humanity, the enlightened liberality, the enlarged Christian feeling, of the British nation. The roguish and twinkling eye of Sydney Smith lighted on this paragraph, and he cried out to her to leave all that, and support her cause with ascertained facts. "The English," said he, with inimitable humor, "are a calm, reflecting nation; they will give time and money when they are convinced; but they love dates, names, and certificates. In the midst of the most heart-rending narratives, Bull inquires the day of the month, the year of our Lord, the name of the parish, and the countersign of three or four respectable householders. After these affecting circumstances have been given, he

can no longer hold out; but gives way to the kindness of
his nature, puffs, blubbers, and subscribes!"

There is probably no literature equal to the English in
the number and variety of its humorous characters, as we
find them in Shakespeare, Jonson, Fletcher, Fielding,
Goldsmith, Addison, Scott, and Dickens. There is nothing so well calculated to make us cheerful and charitable,
nothing which sinks so liquidly into the mind, and floods
it with such a rich sense of mirth and delight as these
comic creations. How they flash upon our inward world
of thought, peopling it with forms and faces whose beautiful facetiousness sheds light and warmth over our whole
being! How their eyes twinkle and wink with the very
unction of mirth! How they roll and tumble about in a
sea of delicious Fun, unwearied in rogueries, and drolleries, and gamesome absurdities, and wheedling jibes, and
loud-ringing extravagant laughter,—reveling and rioting
in hilarity,—with countless jests and waggeries running
and raining from them in a sunlit stream of jubilant merriment! How they flood life with mirth! How they roll
up pomposity and pretence into great balls of caricature
and set them sluggishly in motion before our eyes, to tear
the laughter from our lungs! How Sir Toby Belch, and
Sir Andrew Aguecheek, and Ancient Pistol, and Captain
Bobadil, and old Tony Weller, tumble into our sympa-
thies! What a sneaking kindness we have for Richard
Swiveller, and how deeply we speculate on the potential
existence of Mrs. Gamp's Mrs. Harris! How we stow
away, in some nook or cranny of our brain, some Master
Silence, or Starveling the tailor, or Autolychus the rogue,
whom it would not be genteel to exhibit to our Reason
or Conscience! How we take some Dogberry or Verges,
or Snug the joiner, tattooed and carbanadoed by the
world's wit, and lay him on the soft couch of our esteem!
How we cuff that imp of mischief, Mr. Bailey, as though
we loved him! How Peter Peebles, and Baillie Nicol
Jarvie, and Dominie Sampson, and old Andrew Fairserv-
ice, push themselves into our imaginations, and imperti-
nently abide there, whether we will or no! How Beatrice
and Benedict shoot wit at us from their eyes, as the sun
darts beams! There is Touchstone, "swift and senten-
tious," bragging that he has "undone three tailors, had

four quarrels, and like to have fought one." There is
Sancho Panza, with his shrewd folly and selfish chivalry,—
his passion for food an argument against the dogma of the
soul's residing in the head,—a pestilent fine knave and
unrighteous good fellow,—tossed about from generation
to generation, an object of perpetual merriment. "That
man," said King Philip, pointing to one of his courtiers,
rolling on the floor in convulsions of laughter, "that
man must either be mad or reading ' Don Quixote.'"

But what shall we say of Falstaff?—filling up the whole
sense of mirth,—his fat body, "larding the lean earth," as
he walks along,—coward, bully, thief, glutton, all fused
and molten in good humor,—his talk one incessant storm
of "fiery and delectable shapes," from his forgetive brain!
There, too, is Mercutio, the perfection of intellectual
spirits, the very soul of gaiety,—whose wit seems to go
on runners,—the threads of his brain light as gossamer,
and subtle as steel,—his mirthful sallies tingling and glan-
cing and crinking, like heat-lightning, on all around him!
How his flashing badinage plays with Romeo's love-for-
lorness! "Romeo is dead! stabbed,—with a white wench's
black eye! Shot through the heart with a love-song!
The very pin of his heart cleft with the blind bow-boy's
butt shaft!" Look, too, at Thersites:—his lithe jests
piercing, sharper than Trojan javelins, the brawny Ajax,
and Agamemnon, and his hard "hits" battering their
thick skulls worse than Trojan battle-axes!

If ye like not the sardonic Grecian, then cross from
Shakespeare to Scott, and shake hands with that bundle
of amiable weaknesses, Baillie Nicol Jarvie. Who can resist the cogent logic by which he defends his freebooter
kinsman, Rob Roy, from the taunts of his brother magistrates? "I tauld them," said he, "that I would vindicate
nae man's faults; but set apart what Rob had done agin
the law, and the misfortune o' some folk losing life by
him, and he was an honester man than stude on any o'
their shanks!"

Look ye now, for one moment, at the deep and delicate
humor of Goldsmith. How at his touch the venial infirmities and simple vanity of the good Vicar of Wake-
field lived lovingly before the mind's eye! How we sympathize with poor Moses in that deep trade of his for the

green spectacles! How all our good wishes for aspiring rusticity thrill for the showman, who would let his bear dance only to the genteelest tunes! There, too, is Fielding. Who can forget the disputes of Square and Thwackem; the raging, galvanized imbecility of old Squire Western; the good, simple Parson Adams, who thought schoolmasters the greatest of men, and himself the greatest of schoolmasters!

But why proceed in an enumeration of characters whose name is legion—who spring up, at the slightest call, like Roderick Dhu's men, from every bush and brake of memory, and come thronging and crowding into the brain! There they are, nature's own capricious offspring—with the unfading rose in their puffed cheeks, with the unfailing glee in their twinkling eyes:—

> " Age cannot wither, nor custom stale
>   Their infinite variety!"

If "time and the hour" would admit, it would not be out of place to refer to Wit as an auxiliary power in contests of the intellect; to its influence in detecting sophisms which elude serious reasoning, such as the substitution, so common among the prejudiced and the ignorant, of false causes for striking effects. In Mirth, too, are often expressed thoughts of the utmost seriousness, feelings of the greatest depth. Many men are too sensitive to give voice to their most profound or enthusiastic emotions, except through the language of caricature, or the grotesque forms of drollery. Tom Hood is an instance. We often meet men whose jests convey truths plucked from the bitterest personal experience, and whose very laughter tells of the "secret wounds which bleed beneath their cloaks." Whenever you find Humor, you find Pathos close by its side.

Every student of English theological literature knows that much of its best portions gleams with wit. Five of the greatest humorists that ever made the world ring with laughter were priests,—Rabelais, Scarron, Swift, Sterne, and Sydney Smith. The prose works of Milton are radiant with satire of the sharpest kind. Sydney Smith, one of the most benevolent, intelligent, and influential Englishmen of the Nineteenth century, a man of the most accurate insight, and extensive information, embodied the large stores of his practical wisdom in almost every form of the ludicrous. Many of the most important reforms in England are directly traceable to him. He really laughed his countrymen out of some of their most cherished stupidities of legislation.

And now let us be just to Mirth. Let us be thankful that we have in Wit a power before which the pride of wealth and the insolence of office are abased; which can transfix bigotry and tyranny with arrows of lightning; which can strike its object over thousands of miles of space, across thousands of years of time; and which, through its sway over an universal weakness of man, is an everlasting instrument to make the bad tremble and the foolish wince. Let us be grateful for the social and humanizing influences of Mirth. Amid the sorrow, disappointment, agony, and anguish of the world,—over dark thoughts and tempestuous passions, the gloomy exaggerations of self-will, the enfeebling illusions of melancholy,— Wit and Humor, light and lightning, shed their soft radiance, or dart their electric flash. See how life is warmed and illumined by Mirth! See how the beings of the mind, with which it has peopled our imaginations, wrestle with the ills of existence,—feeling their way into the harshest or saddest meditations, with looks that defy calamity; relaxing muscles made rigid with pain; hovering o'er the couch of sickness, with sunshine and laughter in their beneficent faces; softening the austerity of thoughts whose awful shadows dim and darken the brain,—loosening the gripe of Misery as it tugs at the heart-string! Let us court the society of these gamesome, and genial, and sportive, and sparkling beings, whom Genius has left to us as a priceless bequest; push them not from the daily walks of the world's life; let them scatter some humanities in the sullen marts of business; let them glide in through the open doors of the heart, let their glee lighten up the feast, and gladden the fireside of home:—

> "That the night may be filled with music,
>   And the cares that infest the day
> May fold their tents, like the Arabs,
>   And as silently steal away."

HOMER T. WILSON

AMERICA'S UNCROWNED QUEEN

[Lecture by Homer T. Wilson, popular Southern lecturer, delivered at national conventions of Traveling Men in Nashville, Tenn.,
Omaha, Neb., and at various other places before assemblies of commercial travelers.]

MY FRIENDS:—With tender recollections of a mother's
love, and the memory of a precious home, I come to offer
the tribute of a grateful heart. If I could gather the
most beautiful adjectives from the languages of the
world, and with the skill of an orator fashion them into
beautiful garlands of rhetoric, and place them upon the
brow of woman, I should fail in my greatest effort to do
justice to her grandeur and glory.

I once heard an agnostic pay a beautiful tribute to
woman. He placed her upon the throne of exalted affection, and crowned her with liberty and love. The eloquence of his glowing tribute touched a responsive chord
in every heart; but alas! with one fatal stroke the picture
was marred, hope was crushed, and love lay bleeding at
the point of his cruel dagger.

The triumphant march of woman began when she held
in her arms the infant King in the star-lit manger of
Bethlehem. The age preceding the coming of the Christ,
a period of five hundred years, noted in literature as the
golden age of thought, was the most brilliant of all the
ages of antiquity. Philosophic thought had almost
reached its zenith. It was an age of statesmen, philosophers, poets, and artists. An age that gave to the world
Plato; that heard the thundering eloquence of Demos-
thenes, and saw the Olympian Jupiter fresh from the

1213

hands of the immortal Phidias.   But with all its glory and
its gifted men, woman was but a slave, groping her way in
darkness, until the Star of Bethlehem arose and the
pathetic voice of a world's Redeemer broke the silence,
and His word of love unchained the captive soul when He
said, "Son, behold your mother."

Had I the power of an artist I would place on canvas
my conception of the most marvelous event in the life of
the Compassionate One.   I have gazed with rapture upon
the greatest paintings of the world's gifted artists.   The
scene of the crucifixion, by the great master, is so real, so
perfect, that it seems as if the world's chief tragedy were
being enacted again.   The very earth on which we stand
seems to tremble; the rocks of the everlasting hills break
from their places and roll to the valley beneath; while the
mantle of darkness veils the sun's fair face as he refuses
to look upon a scene so cruel.   So vivid was the rich
delineation, that listening love could hear the expressed
agony of the Savior when the last dark billow rolled over
his soul and he said, "My God, why hast thou forsaken
me?"

But the picture I would paint is that of Christ in the
temple.   A wicked, motley group of men approach him,
and in the midst of them is a poor, defenseless woman.
One of the wicked group points the finger of scorn at the
wounded soul and says, "Master, this woman is guilty."
Another voice exclaims, "Yes, Master, I know she is
guilty"; and another, speaking with authority, says,
"Master, she ought to be stoned according to the law."
The calm, clear voice of the Savior is heard above the
clamoring throng as he replies, "You that are without
sin may throw the first stone"; and turning from them,
he writes a sentence upon the ground, while the wicked
wretches hang their heads and skulk like demons away.
What a picture! The world's Redeemer in tenderest
compassion looking into the face of a broken-hearted
woman! Were I an artist I would paint the picture of
that helpless victim in Satan's snare.   My brush would
paint her with colorless cheeks; eyes with the luster of
hope and beauty faded; a sunken breast, beneath which
you could almost hear the throbs of her broken heart.
The Master speaks, and the very fountains of his sym-

pathetic nature flood her benighted soul with light and liberty, when he says, " Go and sin no more." The artists who have painted the "baptismal scene" and "the ascending Christ" placed above His brow a halo of glory; but could I paint the picture just described, I would place above his brow a halo of exceeding glory as He breaks the fetters of woman's bondage and proclaims her free.

From the time woman bathed the feet of the Compassionate One with her tears and wiped them with the tresses of her hair, her march has been onward and upward. Wherever she has entered our institutions of learning, she has divided honors with man.

In the realms of literature, science, and the arts, she has measured swords with man. If man can tell the course of the stars, and measure with accuracy their relative distance from the sun, woman can look through the same instrument, contemplate with mathematical precision the movement of the heavenly bodies, the star-dust of the milky way, the great gulf stream of worlds, and sweeping on through limitless space, at last, with the hand of faith, touch the golden circle of the Infinite. Then like an angel of light she will soar onward and upward until her feet press the summit of moral beauty where man has never gone. As we look upon her, a creature almost divine, let us view her in a practical light. An old philosopher once sat for an artist to paint his portrait. The artist, out of the goodness of his heart, was painting a lock of hair on the forehead, when the philosopher abruptly said, "What are you doing?" The artist replied, "I am painting a lock of hair on the forehead to hide a scar"; and the matter-of-fact philosopher at once replied, "Paint me as I am." In like manner, it is my purpose, ladies, to paint you (those of you who are not painted) as you are.

Some writer has said that a young man reaches the zenith of his detestability between the ages of eighteen and twenty-three. I have never seen a detestable boy. They may be down in the gutter, but there lingers in each breast a spark of manhood responsive to the touch of the helping hand. Young ladies never become detestable, of course. They are all sweet (as the boys inform me). They pass through a difficult period however, from sixteen

to nineteen.   I never saw a young lady over nineteen—
they either marry or their birthdays mysteriously stop!

Let us consider for a time the girl of sixteen summers.
She is a great study—an unsolved problem.   Few shadows flit across her pathway.   For her, each zephyr is
freighted with perfume of flowers, and thoughts of love.
In the novel she leaves this world and soars to realms of
poetic beauty and fairy dreams of unrealities.   She sees
in all this the ideal man, and at last marries the one of
whom she has dreamed, when lo! she wakes to find he is
only a—man.   She grows tired of the problems of school-
girl life, heaves a sigh, and from her heart breaks forth
the piteous wail, "I would rather die than be an old
maid."   Let me assure you, young ladies, this thought
should not be so terrible.   Old maids are always noble
in life and character.   Better be an old maid than a neglected wife, taking care of a worthless husband.   Old
maids sometimes marry.   I heard of one recently who was
preparing for the grand march to Hymen's altar, and on
being asked what she desired the choir to sing, she replied,
"Well, I believe you may sing, 'This is the way I long
have sought, and mourned because I found it not.'"

The influence of young women in shaping the destiny of
young men cannot be measured by mathematical rules.
They can erect a standard of intellectual and moral excellence, and the young men of our country will struggle to
attain to it.   Young ladies, your power is great, and the
field of your influence is limitless.   Joan of Arc, a maid of
sixteen summers, without education, hailing from a
humble home, appeared before the Court of France, and
in childish ardor plead for the privilege of raising the siege
of Orleans.   She was driven away as mad; but the soul
of purity and the determined will of the child gained for
her another opportunity to plead her cause.   As she approaches the ruler, her step is that of a queen; her eyes
flash the fire of inspiration, through falling tears of patriotic sympathy and love; her plea is piteous and earnest in
the extreme.   "Only give me the commission," she cried,
"and I will raise the siege of Orleans and place again the
crown upon the brow of the deposed monarch."   The
commission was finally given, and we see her clad in male
attire and mounted upon a white horse.   As she enters

the camp of the disheartened soldiers, her girlish voice in clarion tones shouts the signal to advance. Her saber leaps from its scabbard and the army is inspired by the angelic leader. One desperate charge of the whole line, and the banner of France floats in triumph on the fortifications of the enemy. All honor to the Maid of Orleans! The young women of to-day are ready to ask, "What can we do?" There is no siege of Orleans to raise, but the opportunities of to-day are greater than ever before for the hand and brain of the heroine. One stroke of your matchless powers will raise the siege of sin around the heart of young manhood, and break the chains of its bondage.

A little girl, only eight years of age, returning from school one afternoon, saw her drunken father in the gutter. She sat down beside him and waited patiently until he awoke. Stooping low, she kissed the bloated face, and said, "Papa, won't you come home with your little girl? Mama cried all night, and prayed again and again that you would come. Please come with me, Papa!" and the tears fell from her rosy cheeks upon his face. For a moment he looked into the face of his child. The spirit of God through those falling tears sent the arrow of conviction into his unregenerate soul. He struggled to his feet, held the child close to his heart, raised his hand towards heaven and said, "By the grace of God I'll drink no more." The child in triumph led him home. As his step was heard on the threshold, the wife sprang to him, true to woman's love, threw her arms about his neck, and said, "Husband, I am so glad you have at last come home!" He tenderly drew her to his bosom and said, "Wife, I have broken my marriage vow. I have torn the rose of maiden beauty from your cheek, I have broken your heart. But, wife, forgive me now, and by the grace of God I swear I'll drink no more." That man became one of the greatest temperance reformers America ever produced, and he was saved by the hand of a little girl.

We stand at last at Hymen's altar and see the maiden assume the responsibilities of the wife. The happy pair sail for a time on the unruffled waters of the matrimonial sea, with no thought of danger, when lo! on the horizon appears the faint glare of the lightning upon the brow of

an approaching storm.   The deep-toned muttering of distant thunder sounds the signal of danger.   One blast of
the howling winds, and the ocean billows leap mountain
high.   The gods of storm and sea, the allied forces of destruction, play well their part.   The husband standing at
the wheel relaxes his hold; alarm seizes his brain; he reels
and is about to fall, when, " quick as imagination or the
thoughts of love," his wife stands beside him, lays her
hand upon his arm, while her voice quivers with emotion
and fear.   In plaintive tones she says, " Husband, stand
firm at the wheel; our vessel is strong; it will outweather
the storm and we shall cast anchor in the harbor.   Only
be true to yourself and to your wife.   We will face the
storm together; beyond the raging elements there is a
peaceful, unruffled sea."

Under the inspiration of that voice he grasps the wheel,
stands erect, and with heroic hand drives the proud vessel
into wind and wave.   Raging billows, like charging battalions, burst upon her, but she heeds them not.   The husband knows no danger now.   The noble wife stands fearless upon the deck and boldly faces the warring elements.
She speaks peace to the storm, and to the waves she says,
" Be still "; and under her magic touch the winds cease
to blow, and the turbulent waves fold themselves in each
other's arms and like little children fall asleep.

But why does the storm in cyclonic power wreck and
ruin so many homes?   Why are there so many divorce
cases in the courts of our own fair land; and why is the
number constantly increasing?   The answer is not difficult; the problem is easily solved.   Neglect—saddest of
all words—neglect is the rock on which so many vessels
have been wrecked.   Love is but a tender flower, and like
the rose that unfolds its bosom in the morning of spring,
it must have the light of the sun, or it will soon wither and
die.   The love that blooms on the altar of a woman's
heart must have the sunlight of a husband's devotion; if
that is withheld the tint of maiden beauty will fade from
her cheeks, she will go to her grave with a broken heart,
and the world will never know the secret of her sorrow.

The only panacea for this terrible evil is—courting.   I
believe in courting early and late—not late at night, boys,
but—late in life.   Courting after marriage is better than

before and decidedly more profitable. From the culinary department to the parlor, everything has a tinge of cheerfulness and beauty when courting after marriage is properly done. A beautiful motto, not to hang on the walls, but to speak from the heart, is this: "Well done!" It should be spoken to the servants and to the children. If the biscuits are brought to the table burnt top and bottom, repeat the motto to the wife; tell her they are "well done."

When you, my elderly friend, were a young man, you were very kind and attentive to the girl you loved. You waited patiently for her to prepare to accompany you to an entertainment. How is it now? You walk about restlessly and scream with all your might, "Wife, why in the name of common sense don't you come on?" Walking down the street, you are about ten feet ahead of her, complaining because she cannot keep up. Don't you imagine she is delighted with her company? You used to walk close beside her, whispering words of tenderest devotion, but oh, what a change! I think it would be well for every young lady to have a phonograph to catch these tender expressions, so that twenty years after marriage, when sitting alone waiting for him who comes not, she may turn the machine and listen to the wooings of the love of other days. In those days you often sent her flowers and let them tell their own sweet story. How long since you sent your wife a rose? If you should send her a flower tomorrow, she would think you were going to die. You once told her she was beautiful. My friend, when you go home, tell your wife she is pretty. It may be the biggest lie you ever told, but I believe the Lord will forgive you for it.

It is not the wealth of the world that makes home happy and lightens the burdens of the wife. It is the tender acts of kindness lovingly bestowed; the precious words of love spoken with each passing day. These are the jewels in a woman's crown that make the halo of unfading glory about her blessed life. Husbands too often spend their evenings at the lodge or club and neglect the home. A man came home from a club one evening very late. His wife had retired but was not asleep. He entered the room very cautiously, sat in front of the fire and raised his um-

brella. Upon sight of his peculiar position his wife rose
up in bed and in an excited voice exclaimed, "What on
earth do you mean?" "I am just waiting for the storm
to pass over," replied the wayward husband. The next
morning at breakfast the wife said, "Husband, I had a
dream last night." "Did you?" he replied. "Oh, yes;
I dreamed I was at a sale where they were selling men.
I saw one man sold for ten thousand dollars, and I think
he was worth every cent of it." "Wife, did you (hic) see
any of my sort (hic) in the market?" "Yes, indeed,
plenty of them." "What were they (hic) fetching?"
"Why, they were tied up in bundles like asparagus and
priced ten cents a bunch, but there were no buyers." But
is it not possible that husbands sometimes seek the lodge
and club, and even the gamblers' resort, because of the
neglect which they suffer at home? It is well to remember that men have hearts that can feel. When the sunlight of a woman's love is withheld from the flower that
blooms upon the altar of a man's heart, it too will wither
and die. Therefore the philosophy of a beautiful home
requires each to dispense the genial rays of tenderest affection; then the flower will perpetually bloom and the home
will be a type of heaven. Let us now consider the influence of the wife, as she sways the scepter of her power,
in shaping the destiny of her husband.

Shakespeare has portrayed with graphic power the
trials, struggles, and ultimate fall of Macbeth, and the part
Lady Macbeth played in the awful tragedy. Waiving all
controversy as to which of the two was most responsible,
we see the plot worked out, and how, when Macbeth
faltered, his wife wrought upon him and made him
"screw" his "courage to the sticking-place" of foulest
murder, no sooner done that bitterly, though vainly re-
pented. Thus we see the fatal power of the wife's hand
in shaping her husband's destiny.

On the other hand, not only in literature, but in real
life everywhere is seen the noble wife leading to the altar
of redeeming love a husband who has fallen so low in the
scale of moral being that it seemed as though nothing
could restore him. It is largely due to the compassionate
influence of woman that the door of mercy is anywhere
in this world open to the returning penitent wanderer;

that the church itself—the only institution among men
that extends the hand of pity and love to the sin-cursed
soul—bids him welcome home. Of one such redeemed
man we are told, who, after giving up alcohol, lingered
upon the brink between life and death. Strong drink had
done its awful work. Periodically he had spells of unut-
terable suffering. While passing through one of these
paroxysms, the doctor said, "My friend, you will have to
take liquor, or you will die." The poor sufferer looked
up in the face of his wife, who bathed with loving hands
his fevered brow. Inspired by the courage she had given
him, he fervently said, "Then, doctor, let me die. I'll
die without the odor of liquor on my breath." For many
years he has lived, and still lives, a noble Christian; saved
by the hands of his faithful wife.

A man in New York, while intoxicated, struck his wife
with a club, and from the effect of the blow she died the
next day. Before her death, an officer brought the mur-
derer into her presence, and asked, "Madam, is this the
man that struck you the fatal blow?" The dying woman
with trembling hands raised the bandage from her eyes,
and with pathetic emotion replied, "No, that is not the
man that struck me; that is my husband," placed her arms
about his neck, and gave him the kiss of forgiving love.

Shakespeare has said, "Frailty, thy name is woman."
Let me change it, in token of my love for my old mother,
who rocked me in the cradle of childhood, who sang the
sweet lullaby of a mother's love in my infant ears. Let
me change it in token of my love for my wife, the queen
of my home, who with me shares the joys of life and bears
its disappointments and sorrows. Let me change it in
token of my love for my little girls, the bright jewels of
my home, the glittering stars, the angels that accompany
us on life's voyage. Yes, let me change it in token of
my regard for the exalted character of woman. "Frailty,
thy name is no longer woman; but Love, Fidelity, and
Truth, *ye* are woman's other names!"

Let us now with feelings of deepest devotion approach
the altar of home and look upon her who sways the scepter
of love, and reigns as queen in the hearts of the civilized
world. The immortal Grady said, "The home is the
strength of the American republic." Let us enter this

paradise of the soul, and for a time contemplate its beauty. The mother is seated beside a table at eventide. A little boy and girl are quietly preparing their evening lesson. The little boy says, " Mama what is the meaning of this word?" The mother replies, " The word is duty. Robert E. Lee called it the sublimest word in the English language. Observe it, my boy, and your friends will approve you as a child; observe it, and as a young man you will be honored and loved; observe it and, as a husband and father, a crown of glory will rest upon your brow; and when life's eventful pilgrimage shall have closed, you will enter the haven of eternal rest." The little girl says, " Mama, what is the meaning of this word?" She replies, " The word is chastity, and stands for the crowning glory of woman. Observe it, my child, and the world will ever respect you. It is woman's robe of unfading beauty. Observe it, and when life's pilgrimage is over, its battles fought and victories won, in the robe of celestial beauty you should walk through the pearly gates, and forever live in the city of light." I hear the cry of the babe at the mother's side. With loving hand she rocks the cradle and sings that sweet old song, " Be it ever so humble, there's no place like home." How grand the picture! There the hand that rocks the cradle is indeed the strength of the American republic.

I once looked upon England's queen, as she passed through the beautiful park in front of Buckingham palace. I bared my head and in silence contemplated that noble woman. On her brow there was a crown brighter and more dazzling than the crown of state. On her person there was a robe ornamented with the flowers of **unfading** beauty. All hail to England's Christian Queen! After the grand procession passed by, I stood beneath an ancient English oak, and my mind crossed the sea to my old Kentucky home so far away. It was eventime. The evening lessons were finished. The wife and mother read a chapter from the story of redeeming love. The little ones bowed with her at the same altar. I heard her pray, " Father in Heaven, watch over us while we slumber, and keep us from all harm." I heard her when she said, " Oh! God, protect the absent one and bring him safely across the sea." The tears unbidden started down my cheek, and I said, " All hail to the queen of my own precious home! On your brow there is a crown of unfading beauty, on your person there is a robe ornamented with the flowers of unfading beauty. All hail to the queen of my home!"

If I could walk through the floral gardens of the world and pluck the flowers of rarest beauty and sweetest perfume, and then select from the crowns of kings and queens the rarest jewels that glisten there, I would fashion them into a more beauteous crown, and with the hand of love, I would place that crown upon the brow of the Mother —America's Uncrowned Queen. [Applause.]

WU TING-FANG

Photogravure after a photograph from life

WU TING-FANG

THE TEACHINGS OF CONFUCIUS

[Lecture by Wu Ting-fang, Envoy Extraordinary and Minister Plenipotentiary from China to the United States (born in the District of Hsin-hui, in the Province of Kwangtung, about half a day's journey from the city of Canton), delivered before the Society for Ethical Culture of New York, in Carnegie Hall, New York City, December 9, 1900. His Excellency was introduced to the very large audience assembled, by Professor Felix Adler, the president of the Society, with a few words in compliment of his official services, the speaker remarking that " at a time when the diplomatic knots were tangled, the tact, shrewd common sense, and responsibility of the Chinese Minister had done much to strengthen the Administration at Washington in its wise and humane. course towards the Chinese."]

There is a general impression that China has three systems of religious belief: Confucianism, Taoism, and Buddhism. True it is that the government of .China recognizes these three systems in its constitution and laws; but it is a mistake to suppose that each has an equally strong hold upon the esteem and affection of the people. It is true that each of these three attempted to become supreme. This struggle for supremacy was decided long ago, and the nation declared for Confucianism. Confucianism has ever since remained master of the field. Taoism and Buddhism take only what Confucianism has left untouched. Confucianism has appropriated to itself the realm of the living; so there is nothing else for Taoism and Buddhism to do but to take possession of the realm of the dead. On this account, tempted by the allurement of future reward, after death, many women as well as a great many men of the uneducated class profess to be

Buddhists or Taoists.   On the death of a well-to-do Chinese it frequently happens that they employ Buddhist and Taoist priests to chant requiems for the departed soul; and in funeral processions you will see the Taoist priests and the Buddhist priests, joining and taking part in the ceremonies for the dead.   You see, we are a practical people, and we are not sure what is to take place after death; hence the idea of having these priests—Taoist, Buddhist, etc., join in the funeral rites—so as to make sure that if one religion will not bring everlasting happiness to the dead soul, the other may do so.   But you must not understand that the people belong to either the Taoist or the Buddhist faith.   Such services as I have been enumerating are looked upon as more or less professional, and are invariably paid for.

Superstition and ignorance are the chief supports of Taoism and Buddhism.   For this reason their influence grows weaker and weaker as the people become more intelligent.   Not so with Confucianism.   It is dominant in the national life of the Chinese.   In schools we read the classics of Confucius.   All students have to be examined in those classics; and when the examination is held, every year, in every province, the theme is taken from these classics, and any Chinese who wants to enter into official life has to study them; so you will see that Confucianism lies at the foundation of the social and political and national life of China.   It binds the diverse elements of the empire into a homogeneous whole; it exercises an influence upon the character, thought, and language of the people which grows with the lapse of time.   It is not hard to find in China a man who frequently goes to a Taoist or Buddhist temple to offer sacrifices, and who can recite page after page of Taoist or Buddhist writings from memory, but who does not call himself a Taoist or Buddhist on this account.   He regards such acts as having no effect upon the conduct of his life. You ask him what he is, and he will undoubtedly say that he is a follower of Confucius.   Throughout the length and breadth of the country, the statesman, the peasant, the merchant, and the school-boy, would be ashamed to range themselves among the believers of any other system of doctrines than that of Confucius.   If America is called a

Christian nation (as it is called) because the members of the Christian faith constitute a large portion of the inhabitants of this country, with equal propriety I maintain that China may be called a Confucian land.

Now, what is Confucianism? It may be well, perhaps, to mention in a few words, what it is not, before stating what it is. It is not a religion, in the strictest sense of the word. What I understand by religion, is a system of doctrines and of worship; as such, it recognizes the existence of a divine Supreme Being, and of spirits having control of human destiny; it attempts to win man back from the error of his ways, by holding up constantly before his eyes eternal punishment for the wicked, and everlasting happiness for the righteous. One of its cardinal doctrines is that there is such a thing as life after death. I must confess that the immortality of the soul is a pleasant thing to contemplate. I wish it were true, and I hope it is true; but all the subtle reasonings of Plato cannot make it amount to anything more than a strong probability. I am not aware that, with the light of modern science, we have advanced a step further towards certainty than Plato did.

Confucianism has nothing to do with all these questions about the spiritual world and a future life. It must not be supposed, on the other hand, that Confucianism denies their existence altogether. Confucius only holds that we do not know anything about them, and he regards all speculation upon them as useless and unprofitable. He would be called an agnostic nowadays. It is said there are four topics upon which he would not speak: Extraordinary things, feats of strength, disorder, and spiritual beings. One of his disciples one day asked him, "What have I to do to render acceptable service to spirits and divinities?" "While you are not able to serve men yet," says Confucius; "how can you serve spirits?" "What is death?" asked another. "You do not yet know life," answered the sage; "how can you know about death?" Such are the words of Confucius unto his disciples. Life itself is full of mystery, and is too deep for the human mind to fathom. There is no use laying rude hands upon the veil that enshrouds death, and trying to tear it apart, to take a peep into the darkness. No operation of the mind, no flight of fancy, no straining of the soul, has ever been able to add one tittle to the knowledge which the world has always possessed concerning the future existence of man after death and of a world of spirits. Confucius was, therefore, right in not discussing these subjects—in not giving a direct answer.   Horace Greeley once said, "Those who discharge promptly and faithfully all their duties to those who live in the flesh, can have but little time for peering into the life beyond the grave. Better to attend to each world in its proper order." This is not an unfair statement of the aim of Confucianism. Confucius undertakes to guide men through this world. His system is, accordingly, intensely human and practical. He did not speculate on what would be after death.

Let us now proceed to state what Confucianism is in its positive aspect.   Man is regarded as an animal endowed with social instincts.   He does not live by himself, he seeks his fellows.   Out of this fellowship of man with man, Confucius deduces the five relations, viz.: Sovereign and subject; parent and child; elder and younger; husband and wife; friend and friend.

In connection with these five relations, I would illustrate, from actual observation the relation between elder and younger.   That means the relations that exist between superior and inferior in age.   Some years ago I was in Tien Tsin with Earl Li Hung-Chang.   Tien Tsin, as you know, is a treaty port, where the consuls of the different nations are stationed, to look after the interests of their respective countries.   On one occasion, the American consul came to the official residence of Viceroy Li Hung-Chang to see the Viceroy, with a view of requesting him to do him a favor.   The favor he requested was this: he had heard that some of the American missionaries got into trouble in a neighboring province.   Missionaries in China somehow or other get into trouble.   I do not blame them; you know, the situation they are placed in is a very difficult and peculiar one; and the consequence is that unless they are very discreet and behave themselves with great tact, they are inevitably led into some disturbance or trouble.   Now this consul asked Viceroy Li Hung-Chang to telegraph to the governor of that province to take active steps to protect these missionaries, and, in fact, to do everything he could for them. This was out of the jurisdiction of Li Hung-Chang, because he was only Viceroy of Chih-li province; and to telegraph to another province was beyond his jurisdiction. So Viceroy Li properly said he did not feel himself justified in interfering with the affairs of his colleague in another province; but this American consul was very persistent. He remained there, chatting with the Viceroy, and then said, " Now just do this favor for me." But the Viceroy did not see his way clear to please him. Then the conversation drifted into other matters, and somehow or other the Viceroy asked him, " What is your age?" Mind you, this consul was very old—older than the Viceroy. I forget the age exactly, he was over seventy. Now at that time the Viceroy was under seventy. So the consul said, " I am seventy-four." The Viceroy was struck with the answer. " Oh! you are so old! Well, Mr. Consul, I will do the favor for you. I will do it for you, not because you are entitled to it, but to show respect to you on account of your age. You are my superior in age." And this was done, and the thing was settled to the satisfaction of the consul. You see this illustrates strongly the doctrine of Confucianism, and the fact that, in carrying out this doctrine, we are being guided by the rules laid down by Confucius.

Now these five relations I am speaking of comprise all conceivable positions in which a man may find himself in society. To each position are attached specific duties. The fulfilment of these duties makes one a desirable member of society. Of the five relations, Confucius lays special stress upon that of parent and child. Filial piety may be said to be the pivotal point of his system. It is said that a dutiful son cannot but be a loyal subject, a good brother, a faithful husband, a trusty friend. I cannot forbear, in this connection, to give you the story of Confucius' mother as an illustration. Confucius' mother, at the time of her marriage, was still in her teens, while (Shuh-liang Hoh) his father was over sixty years old. The union came about this way: Shuh-liang Hoh had already married twice before. By his first wife he had nine children—all daughters. His second wife bore him a son that was a cripple; so, though advanced in years, he was anxious to take to himself a third wife, and became a suitor for the hand of any of the three daughters of the Yen family. Now Yen did not by any means look upon the old man's suit with disfavor. He accordingly called together his three daughters, and told them the situation. He said to them, "Shuh-liang Hoh is indeed an old man, but he is strong and vigorous for his years. He came of a noble family, and holds a high position in the government. Which of you daughters shall I give him to be his wife?" The two eldest remained silent. Finally the younger one said to the father. "Father, it is for you to command, and for us to obey." "Very well," answered the father, "You will do." Thus she married Shuh-liang, and became the mother of Confucius. Now this, perhaps, may be considered a somewhat extreme case of filial duty; and I am afraid not many people in this country would have obeyed that injunction of the father; but, you see, the advice of parents is always good, and if you obey it, you will find it works well, and brings you happiness, as in this case it had its reward in the son who turned out to be the greatest sage in China.

The aim, then, of Confucius' teaching is to make men desirable members of society. In order to be such, they have to do good to others, by performing the duties of their position; and, at the same time, be good themselves by practising the five virtues, viz.: Benevolence, righteousness, propriety, understanding, and truthfulness.

The general character of Confucius' teachings can best be understood, it seems to me, by instituting a comparison with those of the founder of the Christian religion. Christ says, "Resist not him that is evil, but whosoever smitest thee on thy right cheek, turn to him the other also. And if any man would go to law with thee, and take away thy coat, let him take thy cloak also. And whosoever shall compel thee to go one mile, go thou with him twain." This, it seems to me, is meekness carried too far. I am told, however, that this is the Christian teaching of "nonresistance," that is, if you show no animosity or "spirit of fight" towards your fellow men, even though he would impose on you, it may lead him to gentler, kinder ways. This may be true in some cases, but such teaching seems to me inapplicable to the present state of human society. Whoever smites another without cause on the right cheek, is a dangerous person, and does not need any invitation to repeat the blow on the other cheek.   As for the man who has taken another man's coat, he is a thief and a robber. If he had the chance, he would take away his victim's cloak also, without saying as much as " By your leave." Persons of this character ought not to be left at large, much less allowed to have their own way.   I perceive that there is no disposition on the part of Christian men and women in this country to take these words of Christ in their literal sense.   I think, however, the teaching of Confucius on this head is more in accord with reason. This is what the great sage inculcates: " Do not quarrel with those who offend you."   This is all that good sense requires.

Christ says, " Love your enemy.   Bless them that curse you.   Be good to them that hate you, and pray for them which despitefully use you and persecute you, that ye may be the children of your Father which is in heaven ; for he maketh the sun to rise on the evil and the good, and sendeth his rain on the just and the unjust.   For if ye love them that love you, what reward have you ?   Do not the publicans the same ?   And if ye salute your brethren only, what do ye more than others ?   Do not even the Gentiles the same ? "   These, I must confess, are noble and grand sentiments ; but such a standard of moral excellence seems to me too high for frail humanity.   There is no likelihood, I fear, that men of this world would ever be able to attain it.   The conduct of Christian people, or Christian nations, falls far short of it.   " Love your enemy " is Christ's command ; but at this very moment some Christian missionaries are crying out for vengeance and bloodshed, and Christian armies are devastating fields, burning towns, villages and houses, sparing neither age nor sex in their indiscriminate slaughter, and carrying away everything they can lay hands on.   What a vast gulf is there between those professions and these actions.   But, in any case, I think what is required is difficult of performance.   Ask yourself whether you can love any one who has killed your father or mother, or ruined your house.   I have never yet met one who has acted up to that injunction.

Confucius, however, does not demand so much of man. The question was once presented to him by one of his fol-

lowers, who asked, "Would you requite an injury with
kindness?" And he replied, "How do you requite a
kindness, then?" and he quietly added, "Requite kindness with kindness, and an injury with justice." By saying that an injury shall be requited with justice, be it
noted, he meant that the requital should be just, fair, and
right; but he did not sanction retaliation, much less revenge carried out in a spiteful and vindictive spirit, as it
is sometimes done, I regret to say, by people professing to
follow the tenets of Christianity. Christ says, "Judge not
and ye shall be not judged, for with what judgment ye
judge, ye shall be judged: and with what measure ye mete,
it shall be measured again. And why beholdest thou the
mote that is in thy brother's eye, but considerest not the
beam that is in thine own eye? Or how wilt thou say
to thy brother, Let me pull out the mote out of thine eye;
and behold, a beam is in thine own eye. Thou hypocrite,
first cast out the beam out of thine own eye; and then
shalt thou see clearly to cast the mote out of thy brother's
eye." The above quoted passage has a parallel in these
words of Confucius: "You must be possessed of good
qualities, and then you can require them from other people. You must have no fault yourself, before you can
blame others."

It must not be supposed that there is any intention on
my part to belittle the doctrines of Christ, for, so far as I
know, I believe Christianity is the highest form of religion
that has ever been founded in this world. I am only pointing out the great and almost insurmountable difficulty of
literally following the grand teachings of Christ.

The most striking instance in which the minds of Christ
and Confucius meet, is to be found in the enunciation of
the Golden Rule. Christ says, "As ye would that men
should do unto you, even so do ye also unto them." Confucius says, "Do not do to others what you do not want
them to do to yourself." This was enunciated five hundred years before Christ; and though it is in a negative
form, yet if we come to examine the meaning there is not
much difference. If any one does not do anything that he
does not want done to himself, naturally he will not do
anything displeasing to another; therefore he will do
whatever is pleasing to that other; and in effect, it comes

to the same thing as that proverb of Christ. But some hair-splitters try to make out that these two forms do not express exactly the same idea. I, however, consider the difference in wording merely nominal. At any rate, the spirit of the Golden Rule is plain enough. Any one who acts up to it, whether he be a professed Christian, or a professed Confucian, is a truly good man.

So far as this world is concerned, it is evident that Christ and Confucius lead men in the same direction, and practically in the same path. A good Christian is a good man, and a good Confucian is also a good man, therefore from a moral standpoint a good Christian is a good Confucian; and a good Confucian is a good Christian. As far as I can see, a man who follows the precepts of Confucius, though by so doing he does not consider himself as making preparations for the life to come, is certainly entitled to the enjoyment of whatever happiness there may be in the great Hereafter. I do not believe that heaven is an exclusive place, though Mohammedanism, Buddhism, Taoism, and many other " isms," all try to appropriate the ground and make a private park of it for their respective adherents. I believe that if heaven is the place for the good, there are many ladders which lead to it, and any one who has done good in life, will be able to go up by one of these ladders, and enjoy the happiness he is entitled to. It is the place for all good men, I take it, irrespective of their doctrines and creeds. A true Confucian, who has lived an upright and useful life, will, I venture to assert, get there as quickly as any of them.

The hold which Confucianism has upon the Chinese people is due to its absolute practicability. The Chinese are an eminently practical race, and the teachings of Confucius suit exactly the views of the people. Confucius himself set an example of what he considered a man should try to be in the world. He entered into public life, and did his duties well; and when he found that the time was against him, he resigned and retired into private life, and devoted his time to teaching his disciples. In that he was a model man. He did not withdraw from the business and turmoil of life, and retire to some sequestered field, where he could sit in profound meditation and commune with nature itself; but he took an active part in public affairs, and conscientiously discharged his duties, both as a private citizen, and as a public official. When he found that his exhortations fell only on deaf ears, he could not help offering this despairing cry: "Alas, the birds of the air, and the beasts of the field are not companionable. If I were not to associate with my fellow men, with what should I associate?" Thus he practised what he preached.

The crowning glory of Confucianism, it seems to me, is that it teaches men to do good for the sake of goodness. It promises no reward, and threatens no punishment. Confucius simply says to every man, "Do good, because it is good." Naturally happiness comes to a man for doing good as a matter of course, but it is not regarded as the motive for doing good. In other words, happiness is the effect of goodness, and not the reward for goodness. This is the essential difference between Confucianism and other systems of doctrine and belief; for all other systems hold up constantly before the eyes of the believer a glorious reward for being good and severe punishment for being bad. Confucius alone teaches that goodness is a reward sufficient in itself. I will admit that the teaching of Confucius is not so taking or so fascinating as the other teachings, because it does not hold up a reward to those who practise its doctrine; but let me ask you, when seeing a beggar you give him charity, do you expect a return or reward from him? If you give money as charity, do you expect something to be returned to you, for the charity given? I tell you that Confucianism is one of the highest forms of civilization and morality, although it is not so taking and fascinating as the others.

The world is gradually coming around to the teachings of Confucius. One of the signs is the growing agnosticism of the age. The advancement of science has compelled the abandonment of many strongholds which religion once occupied. The harmonizing tendencies of the time have necessitated a modification of the "fire and brimstone" theology of by-gone days. I do not know whether people are getting more callous in proportion as they become more civilized; but the fact remains that they no longer tremble with fear when all the terrors of the infernal world are pictured to them by fervid preachers from the pulpit.   This is due to the spirit of agnosticism fostered by science.   Thus the world, at the present day, is drifting slowly and unconsciously towards Confucianism.

Another sign of the world's coming around to the teachings of Confucius, is the progress which the cause of universal peace is making among the nations of the world. Five hundred years before Christ came into the world Confucius had already begun to preach the gospel of peace.   Under the influence of his teachings, the Chinese people have turned from the horrors of war to the arts of peace.   They have thus been able to learn by experience that peace has its victories as well as war.   The day may now seem distant when "nation shall not lift up sword against nation, neither shall they make war any more," but we have already witnessed, even in our day, the first steps towards that consummation devoutly to be wished. The Peace Conference at The Hague has given us an earnest of what may be accomplished in the near future. I regard the growing desire on the part of the nations of the earth for universal peace as an unconscious tribute to the teachings of Confucius.   Confucianism is not confined to China alone.   It has taken root in Japan and Korea also.   Its spread is not the result of armed conquest or of aggressive propaganda.   Neither the sword nor the missionary has ever been employed to gain for it a single adherent.   No trail of blood marks its progress; and it has not sent missionaries to other climes and nations, urging people to embrace Confucianism, and, if any trouble should occur, to commence war, in order to compel men to embrace its religion; but Confucianism appeals to human sympathy, human interest, and human aspiration.   Its power is exercised, not through force, but through voluntary submission of the heart.